SCIENTIFIC ROMANCE IN BRITAIN 1890 – 1950

Scientific Romance in Britain 1890 – 1950

BRIAN STABLEFORD

For Charlie Brown
with best wishes

Brian Stableford

FOURTH ESTATE · LONDON

© Brian Stableford 1985

First published 1985
Fourth Estate Limited
100 Westbourne Grove
London W2 5RU

Produced by Charmian Allwright

British Library Cataloguing in Publication Data
Stableford, Brian
    Scientific romance in Britain 1890-1950.
    1. Science fiction, English——History and criticism 2. English fiction——
    19th century——History and criticism 3. English fiction——20th
    century——History and criticism
    I. Title
    823'.0876'09   PR888.S35

ISBN 0–947795–85–5

Typeset in 10/11½ Palatino by
Falcon Graphic Art Limited
Wallington, Surrey
Printed and bound by
Billings & Sons Ltd, Worcester

Contents

Acknowledgements

I am indebted to the bibliographers and biographers who did a great deal of groundwork in mapping the field that this book covers: Sam Moskowitz, I.F. Clarke, Darko Suvin and George Locke. I am also indebted to the specialist bookdealers who helped me to obtain many of the books I have studied: George Locke, John Eggeling, Dave Gibson and Ted Ball.

I am grateful for the considerable assistance rendered by Chris Morgan, during my search for relevant materials, and for the loan of several books. I should also like to thank various people who have taken an interest in my research while it was in progress, and have offered encouragement and advice: Andy Tudor, Bill Russell, Peter Nicholls, Neil Barron and Chip Delany.

Several members of S. Fowler Wright's family were most kind and helpful in assisting my research into the life and works of the author, and I am very grateful to them: Nigel and Margaret Fowler Wright, Patricia Fowler Wright, Valerie Deeson and Lady Blair-Kerr. Only one of the authors whose works I have dealt with in some detail was available for direct questioning, and I am most grateful to John Gloag for the assistance which he was able to give me before his death in 1981.

PART ONE
The Origins Of Scientific Romance

1
THE IDEA OF
SCIENTIFIC ROMANCE

'Scientific Romance' and 'Science Fiction'

THIS BOOK is an examination of the history of a particular tradition in English literature. The text will follow the tradition from its point of origin to its dissolution although there is a certain artificiality in identifying these two 'events'. Although the numbers have been rounded for aesthetic convenience, the dates 1890 to 1950 will do well enough to indicate the span of time within which we can speak of 'scientific romance' having been a distinctive species of English fiction.

The novels and stories to be discussed in this book are elsewhere subsumed under the heading 'science fiction', and the ground to be covered herein is partially explored in a number of histories of science fiction. By coincidence, the present work picks up more or less where another recent work – Darko Suvin's *Victorian Science Fiction in the UK: the Discourses of Knowledge and Power* – leaves off, and although this book and Professor Suvin's are very different in style and character they can nevertheless be juxtaposed to provide a reasonably comprehensive account of the development in Britain of the literature of the scientific imagination. In view of this, the decision to use the old-fashioned and rather quaint term 'scientific romance' as a description may seem odd, but the reason for doing so is to make the point that the British tradition of speculative fiction developed during the period under consideration quite separately from the American tradition of science fiction, and can be contrasted with it in certain important ways.

When he speaks of 'Victorian science fiction' Suvin is not, of course, using a term which was current at the time. He follows the procedure of defining exactly what it is that qualifies a text

3

to be described in that way, then scrupulously gathers together all the texts which fit his definition, and ruthlessly excludes all those which do not. (He conscientiously includes in his survey 'An Annotated Checklist of Books Not to Be Regarded as SF, with an Introductory Essay on the Reasonable Reasons Thereof'.) In trying to outline the history of British scientific romance, this book follows a rather different *modus operandi*. No strict definition of the term can or will be offered, on the grounds that – like Wittgenstein's famous example of the word 'game' – 'scientific romance' identifies members of a class that have only 'family resemblances' between them. What entitles us to think of scientific romances as a kind is not a set of classificatory characteristics which demarcate them as members of a set, but loose bonds of kinship which are only partly inherent in the imaginative exercises themselves and partly in the minds of authors and readers who recognise in them some degree of common cause. What binds together the authors and books to be discussed here is mainly that they were perceived by the contemporary audience as similar to one another and different from others. There is a vagueness about the term, but it reflects a vagueness about these perceptions.

Perhaps the most important thread which bound British scientific romances together from the viewpoints of their producers and consumers was the example and inspiration of H.G. Wells. Wells's unique position in the world of English letters helped to create the niche that was colonised by the other writers to be discussed here. Some of them were personally acquainted with him, all of them knew his work, and almost all were well enough aware of the fact that in their own speculative fictions they were to some extent following in his footsteps. Wells was widely read in America too, and his works were reprinted as exemplars in the early science fiction magazines, but his status in America was not the same (partly because he was taken less seriously, and partly because his works appeared in a different social and literary context) and instead of creating a new literary niche he was instead absorbed into one that was indigenously formulated. Although several historians of speculative fiction, most notably Sam Moskowitz and Brian Aldiss, have made British writers of scientific romance and American science fiction writers characters in the same unfolding story, the points of contact and similarity between them are less than is sometimes implied. In addition, the fact that most such historians have been more interested in fiction that was actually labelled 'science fiction' than in unlabelled speculative fiction has helped to de-emphasise British material published between the wars. This book will hopefully serve to redress the balance.

The term 'scientific romance' appears to have been used first in a book title by Charles Howard Hinton, who published a collection of short pieces as *Scientific Romances* in 1886. He issued a second collection under the same title (subtitled 'Second Series') in 1898. Both volumes were reprinted several times, helping to maintain the currency of the term. Taken together, the two volumes contain three stories and six articles. The subject matter of these items will be discussed in a later chapter, but it must be noted here that there is a certain propriety in the juxtaposition of speculative fiction and speculative non-fiction in these collections. The term 'scientific romance' was generally used to refer to fiction, and it refers to fiction in the title of this book, but there has always been a close relationship between British scientific romance and a typically British species of speculative essays.

Several British scientists of the late nineteenth and early twentieth century show a poetic streak in their writing which led them to rhapsodise about the wonderful implications of their discoveries. To some extent this arose from a desire to dramatise their findings for the layman, communicating something of the excitement of enlightenment, but it was also connected with an ongoing war of ideas whereby men of science were trying to displace the dogmas of religion. In this war, it was often considered strategic folly simply to argue that certain beliefs encouraged by religion had been found to be false, and that the actual truth of some of these matters had now been ascertained. It was primarily not a battle about individual items of belief, but a struggle of world-views, to which aesthetic and moral considerations were far from irrelevant, and many popularisers of science who went in search of converts were very sensitive to the aesthetic considerations in their work.

Running parallel to the tradition of British scientific romance, therefore, is a tradition of essay-writing which is itself Romantic: always speculative, often futuristic, frequently blessed with an elegance of style and a delicate irony. One can see this trait in Darwin's *Descent of Man* and Thomas Henry Huxley's

Evolution and Ethics, but the finest examples are perhaps to be found in Julian Huxley's collection *Essays of a Biologist* (1923) and J.B.S. Haldane's *Possible Worlds* (1927). Wells began his literary career with the writing of speculative essays and journalistic pieces, and many later scientific romancers were essayists as well as novelists.

Howard Hinton's essays in *Scientific Romances* deal with abstract issues in physical science – specifically, with the possibility of there being a fourth spatial dimension – and with the psychology of perception. The other writers so far named, though, were all primarily interested in biological science, and especially in the implications of evolutionary theory. The impact of evolutionary theory on traditional views of man's place in nature, and on moral and metaphysical philosophies, is one of the central themes of scientific romance. In dealing with this theme the best writers of scientific romance exhibited a philosophical ambition which was quite remarkable, and it is in scientific romance that we find the most significant modern examples of the Voltairean *conte philosophique*. American writers after the turn of the century were much less disposed to adopt premises from evolutionary theory, and early American speculative fiction was mostly content to steer clear of this particular war of ideas. This is one of the main distinguishing features separating American science fiction from British scientific romance, and has to do with the different religious cultures of the two nations, and the different influences of religious culture on publishing policy.

The relationship between speculative fiction and non-fiction in Britain continued throughout the history of scientific romance. It was particularly close in the period between the wars, when the London publisher Kegan Paul, Trench & Trubner followed their successful issue of J.B.S. Haldane's *Daedalus; or, Science and the Future* (1923) with a whole series of speculative essays under the general title *Today and Tomorrow*. The series will be discussed in detail later, but it is worth noting now that many contributors to the series were writers of scientific romance or subsequently became writers of scientific romance. Hinton's example of putting essays and stories together in the same collection was not copied to any great extent, but Haldane was not averse to including the occasional scientific romance in his essay collections, and Bertrand Russell's final collection includes both fiction and non-fiction.

In Hinton's time the term 'scientific romance' actually featured very rarely as a category description used in the titles or subtitles of books. Many of the works to be discussed under this heading were simply subtitled 'A Romance', and some 'A Romance of the Future', but 'scientific romance' itself seems to have been used far more frequently by reviewers. Wells's early novels – the archetypes of the genre – were initially described in the classified lists of previous works given in his books as 'fantastic and imaginative romances', and it was not until 1933 that Victor Gollancz issued an omnibus edition of eight novels as *The Scientific Romances of H.G. Wells*, thus giving the phrase its authoritative status. Few authors followed Wells in separating their works into categories for the benefit of lists given in their later books, but one who did – Neil Bell – also chose the term 'scientific romances' to demarcate his imaginative works from his 'novels'. Some other writers obviously thought of this kind of discrimination as inconvenient or slightly insulting to the scientific romances, and Aldous Huxley's two early scientific romances stand on their dignity in bearing the subtitle 'A Novel'.

Despite its late elevation to quasi-definitive status, though, the term 'scientific romance' was in common use early in Wells's career. In an interview with Arthur H. Lawrence published in *The Young Man* in 1897[1] Wells notes that he is thinking of starting 'another scientific romance', and Lawrence uses the term as a generic description. St Loe Strachey, reviewing *The War of the Worlds* in the *Spectator* in January 1898,[2] refers to Wells as 'a writer of scientific romances', while R.A. Gregory, reviewing the same work in *Nature* the following month,[3] speaks of Wells's 'contributions to scientific romance'. It is probable that the reason Wells did not adopt the term in his own classification of his works is that reviewers using the term habitually did so in order to assimilate him into the same category as Jules Verne and Edgar Allan Poe. Wells wanted to be his own man, and certainly did not want to be accounted a follower of earlier writers of dubious similarity and (in Verne's case) dubious reputation. In a letter to Arnold Bennett he once exclaimed in horror at the thought of being classed together with George Griffith. In all these cases, though, the kinship recognised by reviewers was real enough to some degree, as was the kinship suggested by some critics between Wells and the French astronomer Camille Flammarion, perhaps the most poetic of all scientific essayists and the most imaginative populariser of science in his day.

The characteristics of scientific romance have become the focal points of many attempted 'definitions of science fiction', although such definitions have failed to draw convincing lines of demarcation.[4] Suvin, in *Victorian Science Fiction in the UK*, refers back to an earlier definition of his own, whereby the distinguishing feature which separates science fiction from narratives of other kinds is 'a fictional novelty' which, despite its failure to refer to anything in the experiential world of writer and reader, is nevertheless 'valid' because of its continuity with the aspects of that experience and with beliefs about what *could* exist. The account of the novelty given in the story thus becomes a kind of thought experiment.[5] This is not entirely satisfactory as a definition, largely because of problems in passing judgment on what Suvin calls the 'validity' of the innovations in the story, but it does call attention to the important features of scientific romance. A scientific romance is a story which is built around something glimpsed through a window of possibility from which scientific discovery has drawn back the curtain.

It cannot be claimed that the things which happen in scientific romances really *are* possibilities, or *were* possibilities in terms of the scientific knowledge of their day. They often include 'plausible impossibilities' supported by an apologetic jargon borrowed from science. H.G. Wells realised well enough that his invisible man would not be able to see with invisible eyes, and knew that the Cavorite which provided his characters with a means of flying to the moon was an arbitrary invention for the sake of convenience. Bernard Bergonzi insists that because of this we should think of Wells's early novels as 'romances' and not as 'scientific romances', but this is setting too high a standard of qualification.[6] The point of identifying some romances as *scientific* is not to make them into a species of scientific speculation to be judged by scientific standards, but rather to separate them from other kinds of imaginative fiction, variously describable as supernatural fiction or fantasy. The distinguishing characteristic is not that scientific romances *are* scientific, but that they pretend to be, and that they pretend to be in order to serve some rhetorical purpose.

Karl Popper has pointed out the logical impossibility of

attempting to anticipate the future growth of scientific knowledge. Scientific romance cannot be and is not 'prophetic' in this sense. Whenever a writer of scientific romance imagines future technology or alien technology he must fudge the scientific principles which he supposes to lie behind that technology – a jargon of apology is all that he can possibly provide. The means by which Wells's invisible man renders himself invisible are actually no more responsible to the limits of scientific possibility than the means employed by Perseus in Greek mythology, but the jargon used to excuse them is not mere empty bluster – it serves to establish within the story a particular world-view which is decisively different from the world-view of stories where people are rendered invisible by magical means. Scientific romance is the romance of the disenchanted universe: a universe in which new things can and must appear by virtue of the discoveries of scientists and the ingenuity of inventors, and a universe where alien places are populated according to the logic of the theory of evolution.

Once we abandon the notion of a strict definition for scientific romance it becomes easy to appreciate the fact that there are matters of degree involved in characterising stories thus. Some of Wells's stories are 'pure' scientific romance – *The Time Machine* and *The War of the Worlds* are cardinal examples – but in the rich spectrum of his works there are stories which are much more difficult to categorise, including many of his later works; *Star-Begotten* and *The Croquet Player* may stand as examples. Some of his contemporary novels have elements of scientific romance in them – *Tono-Bungay*, for instance – while some of his imaginative works lie in the borderlands between scientific romance and fantasy. If the difference between scientific romance and supernatural fiction is to be seen in terms of the world-view of the stories, then there is a particular class of fictions which becomes problematically ambiguous: stories which deal explicitly with the clash of world-views in partially allegorical fashion, like *The Undying Fire* or *All Aboard for Ararat*.

Scientific romance has its own internal spectrum, ranging from the heavily didactic and passionately earnest (exemplified by Wells's careful Utopian novels and Olaf Stapledon's 'essays in myth-creation') to the deliberately frivolous and farcical (exemplified by the more extravagant works of Fred T. Jane and J. Storer Clouston). The existence of this spectrum should not be allowed to obscure the fact that scientific romance is always inherently playful and is never without at least a hint of seriousness. Both these things are inherent in the nature of the exercise and we should not fall into the trap of considering playfulness and seriousness to be contradictory; Johann Huizinga points out emphatically in *Homo ludens* that this is not the case. Scientific romances play with scientific notions in different ways, sometimes painstakingly and sometimes exuberantly, but the outcome of their play always reflects back into everyday experience. The lessons of scientific romance always have the power to change our minds by modifying our world-views, and they always have that intention, no matter how thickly coated they are with the sugar of mere amusement.

This combination of playfulness and seriousness makes scientific romance inherently iconoclastic. The better writers of scientific romance have shared with Francis Bacon a heightened awareness of the extent to which our ideas about the world are confused by 'idols' – false beliefs entangled with our true ones. There is a crusading fervour about much scientific romance, because many writers consciously used it as a way of taking arms against the idols of the tribe and the idols of the theatre: false beliefs handed down by tradition, and popular follies of the day. The weapons adopted to this purpose are varied, including melodrama and satire as well as reasoned argument, but in every scientific romance the noise of the battle can be heard.

The foregoing description of scientific romance is not only loose, but at present rather abstract. It is to be hoped, though, that it will be gradually clarified by the discussion of concrete examples which will fill out the chapters of this book. The process of clarification will begin with the account, contained in the next chapter, of how several different kinds of story, which enjoyed distinct histories before 1890, came to be intermingled and seen as part of a common enterprise. Before undertaking such a detailed study of the co-mingling of these literary subspecies, though, there are some more general matters of historical context to be discussed.

Scientific Romance and the Literary Marketplace

The advent of an identifiable genre of scientific romance in the 1890s can be explained partly in terms of the stimulus of new scientific ideas. Darwin's theory of evolution was a hot topic of debate, a boom in new inventions was under way in connection with the exploitation of electricity, and theoretical developments in physics were beginning to open up the wonders of the subatomic microcosm. Scientific romance was not just a logical consequence of the emergence of these ideas, though, and if we are to understand its origins more fully we will need to look at certain aspects of the economics of the British literary marketplace.

Before 1890 the fiction market in Britain was sharply divided, with a wide gap of price and prestige separating the respectable three-decker novel from the popular fiction of the penny dreadfuls and twopenny novelettes. The width and depth of this gap was something unique to Britain – while fiction in America and France likewise spanned a wide spectrum from 'highbrow' to 'lowbrow' the spectrum in those nations was much better filled in its middle regions. In America and in France literary products were more various, and it was not unusual for prestigious fiction to be produced in a relatively cheap format. In Britain, highbrow fiction was imprisoned by a curious publishing pattern which resulted from the enormous influence on publishers of the circulating libraries.

Early in the nineteenth century the price of books had stablised at 10s 6d per volume, and it became conventional for novels to be three volumes in length. 31s 6d was a huge price to pay for a novel, which might justifiably be regarded as a disposable item of only transient interest. There grew up in consequence circulating libraries which, for an annual fee of one guinea, would allow a subscriber to borrow one volume at a time, exchanging it as often as he or she desired. By mid-century the largest of the circulating libraries, Mudie's, was taking such a high proportion of the print runs of new novels that Mudie had a powerful influence over literary production. When technological innovations made books cheaper to produce, the price of new non-fiction was allowed to fall, but Mudie and the publishers conspired to maintain the form and the price of new fiction in order to preserve and protect their market interests.

11

Many Victorian novels were issued prior to book publication in cheaper formats, as part-works or as serials in literary periodicals, and payment for serialisation was an important aspect of the income of novelists, but even this kind of publication was more restricted in the opportunities which it offered to British writers than the parallel opportunities presented in France or America. In France and America newspapers provided important economic opportunities to writers of fiction, but in the years before 1890 British newspapers used very little fiction – there were no British *feuilletonistes*. The British literary periodicals like *The Cornhill* and *Belgravia* were mostly produced by the book publishers, as much for the purpose of advertising their wares as for their own sake, and there was not the same complex array of markets presented to the British writer as American writers like Hawthorne and Poe had available. Thus, British writers of prestigious aspirations tended to write very little short fiction, and were constrained to make their longer works very long indeed.

British writers before 1890 did occasionally try to bridge the 'middlebrow gap' which separated the literary world of Thackeray and George Eliot from the *demi-monde* of G.M.W. Reynolds and Edward Lloyd's 'Salisbury Square fiction'.[7] Dickens tried to do it, both as a writer and as publisher of *Household Words*, but he failed to achieve the synthesis and was forced to abandon his more populist ambitions – the later periodical *All the Year Round* was cast much more in the mould of the major literary journals of the day. As Disraeli observed, Britain was really 'two nations' rather than one, divided by unusually rigid class barriers, and this was reflected in its literary culture as elsewhere.

The relevance of all this to the development of scientific romance is subtle but significant. It has considerable bearing on the fact that relatively little speculative fiction was produced in Britain before the 1880s. (Suvin's bibliography lists 56 titles published before 1880, some of which were reprints and translations of foreign works. Nearly double that number were produced between 1881 and 1890, and the figure doubled again in the next decade.) This was not the case in either America or France, where the middle range of the literary spectrum easily accommodated writers like Poe and Verne.

The three-decker novel was a form dominated by tradition in its every aspect. Price-fixing and moral censorship went hand in hand with a much more sweeping conservatism of theme and method than is seen in the literary traditions of the other nations cited for comparison. Following the decline of Gothic horror stories Victorian novelists tended to steer clear of the *outré* and the speculative. In any case, the sheer mass of detail required to flesh out a novel to three-volume length tied it down very firmly to the careful reproduction and analysis of known situations (present and past). To create a hypothetical world with the same density as the customary worlds of three-decker fiction was an imaginatively appalling task. It was also, to some degree, a self-defeating exercise, because part of the appeal of scientific romance is its openness and flexibility. There are some long novels with elements of scientific romance in them, but in most of the successful ones the elements of scientific romance are peripheral. It is noticeable even today, as novel series and trilogies are promiscuously produced under the banner of science fiction, that such series usually proceed by a method of ever more intense recapitulation, losing imaginative impetus as they gain in historical detail. John Sutherland, contributing a brief comment to Suvin's book, notes that Victorian speculative fiction lay almost entirely outside the literary mainstream of the day because so little of it adopted the three-decker form.[8] The difficulties of adapting speculative material to that form are amply displayed by the few examples of three-decker speculative fiction that were produced. The two most significant are perhaps Edward Maitland's *By and By: An Historical Romance of the Future* (1873) and Andrew Blair's anonymously published *Annals of the Twenty-Ninth Century* (1874). Both are very awkward in their attempts to describe hypothetical situations, and both perpetually lapse into semi-documentary form. Blair offers a good deal of fake history and autobiographical introspection, while Maitland makes exemplary characters carry on moral and political arguments in their conversations.

Ironically, the penny-dreadful market was just as hidebound by its own traditions. The crudity of such fiction – which makes it virtually impossible to read today – was not simply a matter of the incompetence or inelegance of its writers, but rather a reflection of the conditions of production and the demands of its audience. Penny-dreadful fiction was written in standardised lumps for part-work publication, each element having its quota of melodrama. It was heavily padded, especially with irrelevant dialogue and elaborate description of the emotional upheavals of the characters, to avoid putting too much strain on the imagination of writers who were forced to make up their plots as they went along because the length of a work would be entirely determined by the longevity of popular demand. Successful works had to be strung out almost interminably, into millions of words if need be; this militated strongly against structure and encouraged internal repetitiveness. In addition, of course, penny-dreadful fiction was relentlessly imitative, adapting successful highbrow works for the vulgar taste, and recklessly plagiarising its own triumphs. Penny-dreadful fiction was never ambitious enough to be serious, but it was never relaxed enough to be playful either; it could accommodate crude horror stories of the *grand guignol* variety, but it could not accommodate speculative fiction.

Scientific romance is particularly well adapted to presentation in the form of short stories and relatively short novels. In many short stories the focal point of the tale is the irony of a particular event or the juxtaposition of circumstances; they do not rely on the intricate development of character or the extensive description of background. This very sketchiness makes the short story easily able to contain the half-formed and half-finished speculations which were to become the staple crop of scientific romance. In Britain before 1890, though, economic incentives for British writers to explore the uses of the short story format were virtually non-existent. Similarly, there were few economic opportunities in the production of single-volume novels. Cheap fiction was produced in abundance in the form of 'railway novels' or 'yellowbacks', but this was almost all reprinted, and such volumes were regarded with scorn despite the difference they made to the popularity and economic fortunes of such writers as Lord Lytton. Foreign writers who filled the middlebrow gap in their native lands – mostly with single-volume novels – were often reprinted in Britain, but in formats which carried a built-in lack of prestige. Jules Verne became a popular author in Britain, but his works were marketed in Britain as 'boys' books', fit for the consumption of adolescents but alien to the horizons of the mature British reader. This is not to say that Verne's books were read in Britain only by adolescents, but the fact that they were seen to belong there meant that any British fiction inspired by the example of Verne had to be aimed at that category and confined by its conventions.

For these reasons, the few important speculative fictions produced in Britain before 1890 are literary mavericks, isolated from the mainstreams of literary production. Mary Shelley's classic *Frankenstein* (1818) was partially assimilated to the Gothic boom of the time, and her subsequent three-decker speculative novel *The Last Man* (1826) was a failure. Lord Lytton's *The Coming Race* (1871) was originally published anonymously, and stands quite apart from the bulk of the author's fiction. Edwin Abbott's *Flatland: A Romance of Many Dimensions* (1884) is a consciously eccentric piece, originally published in soft covers under the pseudonym 'A Square'. Richard Jefferies' *After London; or, Wild England* (1885) is a deeply personal and reflective work. None of these works was really a commercial venture.

After 1890 the market situation changed dramatically for British writers. The three-decker novel was in rapid decline (Mudie finally pronounced his sentence of death upon it in 1894). More importantly, the middlebrow gap was finally and firmly blocked up by a host of new periodicals, ranging from tabloid weeklies to plush illustrated monthlies, which frequently mingled fiction and non-fiction, using short stories and short serial novels in abundance. Some of these new periodicals, which aimed simultaneously for a degree of respectability and wide popularity, were spectacularly success-ful in hitting their mark: *The Strand Magazine* provided the cardinal example, and was much imitated.

The British reading public, which had earlier in the century been composed of distinct sectors, was much more diffuse by 1890, and presented a much more various constituency to publishers eager to create and serve its demands. The 1890s was an era of experimentation by publishers as they explored the new opportunities presented to them, and it is hardly surpris-ing that it became an era of experimentation for authors too. Most of the new periodicals were produced by an up-and-coming generation of publishing entrepreneurs, including George Newnes, C. Arthur Pearson and Alfred Harmsworth. Their interests tended to extend across a wide publishing spectrum, from popular newspapers to handsome illustrated magazines, though they usually only dabbled in the production of books. *The Strand* and its imitators secured large circulations by carefully bridging the middlebrow gap from the upper side, retailing at 6d but offering value for money in terms of quality of production. Simultaneously, lightweight weeklies like *Tit-Bits* and *Pearson's Weekly* extended themselves into the gap from the lower end, often boosting circulation with gimmicks like correspondence columns and competitions.

The impact of these new periodicals on the development of speculative fiction has been extensively explored by Sam Moskowitz, especially in his critical anthology *Science Fiction by Gaslight* and in his long introduction to a collection of stories by George Griffith, *The Raid of Le Vengeur*. It will suffice here to make the point that it was the new marketplace constituted by these magazines that permitted the early writers of scientific romance to begin and to build their careers. All six of the writers identified in Chapter 3 as the major contributors to the early scientific romance initially found their niche in these magazines, and so did minor writers like Cutcliffe Hyne, Louis Tracy and Fred T. Jane.

The closing of the middlebrow gap at this point in time was not, of course, an arbitrary accident of history. It reflected organic changes in British society, particularly the development of near-universal literacy. Many contemporary commentators, including H.G. Wells,[9] attributed the timing of this upheaval to the influence of the 1870 Education Act, whose legacy came to fruition in the late 1880s when the children taught to read in the new state schools became economically independent. Some modern commentators, though – notably Raymond Williams[10] – consider the importance of the act to have been exaggerated, and argue that the growth of literacy was gradual and relatively undisturbed by legislative interference. It does seem evident, however, that some kind of critical threshold was reached in the late 1880s, so that the history of British publishing exhibits a marked qualitative change unlike anything that happened in America or France. This sudden qualitative change has much to do with the unique features of the history of speculative fiction in Britain.

After 1890, it became much easier for would-be writers to think in terms of a career. It became much easier for writers to serve a kind of 'apprenticeship', producing short pieces for periodicals before moving on to a more ambitious scale of production. As the number of professional writers increased, so the manner of their professionalism changed. The new generation of writers delighted in an exceptional versatility. Traditions could no longer confine them, and they found in their audiences a new hunger for originality and novelty. They were encouraged to work in different forms in order to exploit the range of opportunities presented by the marketplace, and they were encouraged too into a competition to capture the attention of readers who had plenty of material to choose from. Natural selection was not merely an issue of debate in intellectual circles – it was a force at work in the literary marketplace. The magazines which adapted best to the eccentric patterns of demand with which they were confronted thrived; those which did not went under. It was the same with writers, and this became an era of literary vogues: Conan Doyle's detective stories; Marie Corelli's feverish occult romances and historical extravaganzas; Rider Haggard's African adventure stories. Scientific romance was, in its inception, one such vogue, and it was the search for such new fashions which encouraged readers and publishers to seize upon the *idea* of scientific romance as a kind of fiction which had some measure of economic mileage in it. In a different economic climate, the chain of influences which spread like wildfire from the early successes of Wells and Griffith would have been much less powerful. As we shall see in due course, it was another set of changes in the literary marketplace which sent the idea of scientific romance into its terminal decay, to be superseded even in Britain by the idea of science fiction.

2

SCIENTIFIC ROMANCE
AND ITS LITERARY ANCESTORS

Imaginary Voyages

THE IMAGINARY voyage is one of the oldest forms of story – presumably as old as storytelling itself. It is the primal form of fantastic fiction: the hypothetical 'elsewhere' is a vacant space waiting to be filled by the creative imagination. Myth and folklore abound with accounts of such voyages, and the role which such stories play in oral tradition provides an excellent example of playful seriousness. As Philip Babcock Gove points out in *The Imaginary Voyage in Prose Fiction*, literary examples of the imaginary voyage are unified not so much by virtue of the mere fact that they all involve journeys, but by the fact that they provide 'evidence of the activity of the human mind'.[1] Like the thought-experiment in science, the imaginary voyage in literature plays a more fundamental and important role than is apparent at first glance; it is an authentic form of exploration.

Historians in search of a noble ancestry for the modern genre of science fiction have co-opted ancient tales of imaginary journeys to strange lands in a wholesale manner, but they have always had a special affection for voyages to the moon. The tradition of fanciful lunar voyages can be connected readily enough with what was (until overtaken by reality) one of the 'classical' themes of science fiction. The history of such voyages, as discussed in Marjorie Hope Nicolson's *Voyages to the Moon*, Russell Freedman's *2000 Years of Space Travel* and elsewhere, makes a reasonably coherent story, and the way that imagined lunar landscapes and populations have changed along with actual scientific theories and speculations reveals a fascinating pattern.

There is no space here to track the history of lunar voyages from Lucian of Samosata to the series of excellent seventeenth-century fantasies which were written in the wake of the revelation that the moon was, in fact, a world in its own right. In any case, Nicolson has done that job admirably well already. What is relevant to the emergence of scientific romance in the nineteenth century is really the question of the 'verisimilitude' of lunar voyages, emphatically raised by Edgar Allan Poe in the note which he appended to his story 'The Unparalleled Adventure of one Hans Pfaall' (1835) when it was reprinted in book form. Poe – aggrieved by what he considered to be the promiscuous borrowing of his idea in a newspaper hoax – laid claim in this epilogue to the originality of being the first writer to produce an account of a lunar voyage that was plausible in the context of the scientific knowledge of the day. The claim was, of course, over-inflated, but Poe called attention to the fact that there really was scope for a more rigorous approach to the business of concocting a traveller's tale which would take the hypothetical traveller outside the earth. Awareness of this new scope coincided, happily enough, with the imminent exhaustion of the scope inherent in earthbound travellers' tales; it was becoming increasingly difficult to locate alien worlds in unexplored corners of the globe. Thus, the possibility of writing a genuinely plausible story of a journey to another planet came into being at a useful point in time – all the more useful because new possibilities in the imaginative construction of alien worlds were also opening up in response to the stimulus of evolutionary philosophy.

Imaginary voyage stories received a considerable boost in the mid-nineteenth century when the everyday world of the European middle class was invaded by impressive new means of locomotion. The advent of railways and steamships meant that the world was opened up to tourism, and the real tourists who embarked upon Mr Thomas Cook's famous excursions were preceded (but only just) by the imaginary tourists of Jules Verne's novels. Verne had one advantage over Cook: he could invent a host of new vehicles to take his characters into parts of the world unreachable by conventional means, and he could even devise ways of taking them beyond the earth's atmosphere.

In 1863 Verne spent an imaginary *Five Weeks in a Balloon*. In 1864 he ventured forth on *A Journey to the Centre of the Earth* (though he did not get quite that far). In 1865 he planned but did not execute a trip *From the Earth to the Moon*. In 1866 he described *The Adventures of Captain Hatteras* around the north pole (which was in those days unexplored). In 1868 he sent *The Children of Captain Grant* on a trip around the world. By 1870 he was ready to take the ambitious journey planned five years earlier, and went *Round the Moon*. In the same year he published his famous account of Captain Nemo's submarine *Nautilus* and its journey of *Twenty Thousand Leagues Under the Sea*. There followed in 1871 a fictionalised memoir of his real voyage on the early steamship *Great Eastern* called *A Floating City*. In 1870 he dispatched three Englishmen and three Russians to southern Africa in a novel known by various titles, including *Meridiana*. In 1873 he produced what retains its status as the ultimate story of imaginative tourism when he sent Phileas Fogg *Around the World in Eighty Days*, although Cook had already produced an itinerary for such a trip, albeit one that would be conducted at a more leisurely pace.

After his first hectic decade as an imaginary tourist Verne slowed down a little. He continued to produce books at a fast pace, but his characters took their time. In 1875 he becalmed himself for nearly a quarter of a million words on *The Mysterious Island*, where even the restless Nemo had taken his retirement, and his exploratory drive was never as strong thereafter. He attempted a more ambitious space journey in *Hector Servadac* (1877), but could not make it convincing. The only significant fantastic vehicles which he invented in the later part of his career were the aëronef in *The Clipper of the Clouds* (1886) and the free-floating city in *Propeller Island* (1895).

Verne imported a new kind of realism into the imaginary voyage. He not only paid scrupulous attention to the means by which his characters travelled, but was equally earnest in constructing the sensations attendant on their hypothetical experience. He was, however, a rather one-dimensional writer, because in concentrating so earnestly on the *means* by which his voyagers proceeded, he tended to lose sight of their possible *ends*. Often, his characters are carried away in spite of themselves, often they are travelling for the sake of it. Unlike the chicken in the time-honoured joke, they rarely cross the road because they want to get to the other side. In his space journeys, the characters never make an alien landfall – partly because he could not think of a way to get them started on a homeward journey, but partly because he really was not particularly interested in the imaginative construction of alien worlds.

H.G. Wells was later to deny any real literary kinship with Verne,[2] and Verne was to deny any kinship with Wells,[3] but each writer was probably being a little too jealous in guarding his originality. In fact, the influence of Verne's work on British scientific romance was considerable, and many writers learned a lesson from his method. The authors of Vernian boys' books, who manufactured airships and submarines with gay abandon, were simply imitators (they include Herbert Strang, Harry Collingwood and Gordon Stables), but the more subtle influence which Verne had on George Griffith and Arthur Conan Doyle was more productive, because they used what they took from him in a much broader context.

The earliest British writer to use the Vernian method to import a degree of realism into an interplanetary voyage was Percy Greg, author of the early Martian fantasy *Across the Zodiac* (1880). Painstaking attention is paid here to the description of the journey between worlds – even though the force of propulsion used is entirely imaginary – and this helps to lend credence to the adventures which the hero subsequently has. Greg is far from being an imaginary tourist for tourism's sake, though; the hero's experiences serve to dramatise some of the debates on social and moral issues raised in his earlier non-fiction work *The Devil's Advocate* (1878).[4] A less didactic work which also appears to owe something to the example of Verne is *Mr Stranger's Sealed Packet* (1889) by Hugh MacColl. This uses the interplanetary voyage as the *entrée* to an exotic adventure story of the kind which later became a favourite province of American pulp science fiction writers, but there are some reflections on the implications of Darwin's theory of evolution for life on other worlds.

The fact that the surface of the earth was by now thoroughly explored did not administer a death-blow to terrestrial imaginary voyages of a fantastic nature. What it did do was to reduce the scale of the strange lands that were visited, so that they became remote valleys or tiny islands instead of whole nations. These geographical microcosms had a fascination in their own right, which was sufficient to generate a whole sub-genre of fantastic fiction: the 'lost race story'. As popularised by Henry Rider Haggard and others this kind of story had little scientific romance in it, although some important scientific romances did borrow the format.

The potential utility of the lost race story for writers of scientific romance was that it opened up space for exercises in speculative anthropology and speculative biology. In particular, it offered the possibility of bringing modern observers into confrontation with survivals from the very distant past: proto-humans and dinosaurs, barely glimpsed in Verne's *Journey to the Centre of the Earth*, were to play more dramatic roles in later scientific romances. The best early work of this kind is James de Mille's anonymously published *A Strange Manuscript Found in a Copper Cylinder* (1888), which describes a society existing in permanent twilight, whose values are very different from ours; the people revere darkness, celebrate death and embrace a cruelly nihilistic religion.

The imaginary voyage framework – both the interplanetary version and the 'secret enclave' variant – was frequently used in the nineteenth century to contain satirical and Utopian fantasies. In an earlier era, of course, it had been the standard framework for such exercises, but an increasing tendency to set Utopian states in the future had reduced its importance in this regard. Traditionally, the voyage element in such stories had been treated as a mere convenience, and only in some satirical works (most notably Cyrano de Bergerac's interplanetary stories) was there much attention paid to the means of travel. For the most part, this remained the case, but in some stories attempts to develop verisimilitude began to intrude into the Utopian aspects of such stories, helping to bring about a subtle transformation of their content. One can see this in a very interesting early work: *The History of a Voyage to the Moon* (1864) 'edited' by Chrysostom Trueman (a pseudonym). Here there is a remarkable balance between the attempt to describe an ideal state and the attempt to present a coherent and plausible account of life adapted to lunar circumstances (albeit circumstances which do not much resemble the actual conditions on the moon, even as estimated at the time). This kind of syncresis – a fertile mixing of motives – is something very much in keeping with the spirit of scientific romance. H.G. Wells was the writer who mixed his motives most cleverly and with great effect: *The Time Machine* immediately established itself as a classic imaginary voyage, and *The First Men in the Moon* found an ideal combination of imaginative liveliness and Darwinian allegory.

Scientific romance absorbed the imaginary voyage almost

completely – the more mystical variants of lost race fantasy dwindled away after the turn of the century. In being absorbed, though, the imaginary voyage was also rejuvenated – enlivened by the strategies used to cultivate an appearance of verisimilitude, and endowed with more versatility of purpose. It was the writers of scientific romance who were to produce the best rounded of all imaginary voyages, transcending the unidimensionality of the Vernian novel of imaginary tourism and the narrow didacticism of traditional Utopias and satires.

Utopian Fantasies

The construction of hypothetical ideal societies has not such a long history as the imaginary voyage (which often provides a framework for it) but it nevertheless dates back to Classical times – most notably to Plato's *Republic*. The tradition of such exercises in imaginary social engineering has always been complicated by a satirical element, such as is seen in More's *Utopia* itself, and many descriptions of imaginary societies are a little more ambivalent than they may seem at first glance. Very earnest attempts to present images of ideal societies often become parodic in spite of themselves, reflecting an ironic consciousness that men are ill-fitted for life in Heaven, and a cynical suspicion that all attempts to build the New Jerusalem might inevitably be frustrated. The road to Utopia is always paved with good intentions, but few writers have ever been convinced that it would be a comfortable route to follow.

Frank Manuel has noted that in the history of Utopian speculation there are two crucial shifts, which are of some relevance to the origin and nature of scientific romance. He notes that near to the end of the eighteenth century static descriptions of other places – which he calls 'utopias of calm felicity' – gave way to dynamic images of the progressive state of the future. These 'euchronias' remained closely connected with the mythology of progress and with socialist political movements throughout the nineteenth century, but gradually gave way thereafter to 'psychological and philosophical utopias' for which he borrows Abraham Maslow's term 'eupsychia'.[5]

The shifting of Utopian fantasies into the euchronian mode is correlated with a growing consciousness of the connection between a society's technological resources and its social organisation. With the Industrial Revolution well under way it became easy to believe that further developments in mechanical technology would create greater wealth, and the potential for a better life for all. The redistribution of wealth remained a major preoccupation with euchronian writers, but they commonly regarded future political change as something that would go hand in glove with the further development of mechanical production and the transformation of the labour process.

Although this general principle was widely accepted, most Utopian writers in the early part of the nineteenth century actually had a very limited view of the possibilities inherent in future technological advancement. This is not surprising: it would have taken a tremendous leap of the imagination for a writer in the 1870s to foresee the marvellous applications of electricity, or even the potential of the internal combustion engine. The first important Utopian fantasy which imagines the prolific use of a new source of energy, Lytton's *The Coming Race* (1871), actually draws its inspiration from the same source as the author's earlier occult romances, *Zanoni* (1842) and *A Strange Story* (1861). *Vril* is really a kind of magic power rather than a new technology. Edward Maitland's *By and By* (1873) does feature imaginative applications of electromagnetic energy, but on a relatively modest scale. By the time the decade was coming to a close, though, the horizon of expectation had shifted quite considerably, as can be seen in H.C.M. Watson's anonymously published *Erchomenon: or, The Republic of Materialism* (1879), which features a wider range of mechanical gadgets in a world dominated by social Darwinist philosophy. Significantly, this is not a Utopian novel, but one of the earliest images of an evil future: a 'dystopia'.

Watson's work serves to remind us that the period which saw the emergence of scientific romance witnessed *two* important breaks in the tradition of Utopian fantasy. As speculative writers began to catch glimpses of the wealth of possibilities opened up by scientific progress they were forced to pay far more attention to the likely impact of highly versatile new technologies on everyday life and social relations. At the same time, many writers began to wonder whether the idea of progress was really worth very much, and whether in fact the world might just as easily get worse as better. It was not entirely coincidence that these two breaks came together, because many people thought as Watson did that it was the dominance of materialist philosophy which would simultaneously lead to a proliferation of mechanical wonders and a desolation of human experience. There were, of course, optimists who saw things very differently, the most conspicuous being the American socialist Edward Bellamy, whose euchronian novel *Looking Backward, 2000–1887* (1888) rapidly overhauled *Uncle Tom's Cabin* in its native land to become the second best-selling book of all time. (It was second, of course, to the Bible.) Bellamy offered to his readers the naive but comforting message that technological progress would inevitably deliver them into a promised land of harmony, equality and contentment.

It is interesting to note that in Suvin's bibliography of Victorian science fiction anxious futuristic speculations already outnumber euchronian fantasies in the 1880s. This anxiety seems to have come earlier to Britain than to other nations – certainly earlier than it came to America. Perhaps England, the first industrialised nation, was even then undergoing its metamorphosis into the first post-industrial society. At any rate, there was after 1890 a massive displacement of Utopian images of the future by dystopian ones, and it is British speculative fiction which has provided the leading edge of this new pessimism. The first wholeheartedly dystopian novel of the future – Ignatius Donnelly's *Caesar's Column* (1891) – was produced in America, and one of the finest such fictions – Egevny Zamyatin's *We* (1924) – was produced in Russia, but it was Britain which built up the tradition of cynical thought that was ultimately to produce *Brave New World* and *Nineteen Eighty-Four*.

Scientific romance has a very curious relationship with Utopian fantasy. It did not absorb Utopian fantasy in the way that it absorbed the imaginary voyage; instead it took up where Utopian fantasy left off. There is a good deal of Utopianism in early scientific romance – Wells was the last of the great Utopian writers, mass-producing Utopian schemes and endlessly debating their merits and their feasibility, and there is a powerful Utopian element in some of the novels of George Griffith and M.P. Shiel – but this Utopian thought enjoys a much more precarious existence in scientific romance than it ever had in classical Utopian fantasy. The kind of complacency which characterises euchronian writers from Mercier to Bellamy has no place in British scientific romance. If Utopia is to be won,

then it will be with difficulty, and the struggle will be desperate. The philosophy of progress in its naive form was dead
before scientific romance was born, and it is no coincidence
that Wells began the series of his great scientific romances with
a novel presenting a devastating denial of that mythology. As
his later career was to demonstrate, *The Time Machine* was not
simply a counsel of despair, but it emphasised very strongly the
complexity and uncertainty of man's relationship with his
evolving technology.

For the writers of scientific romance, the question of how
future developments in technology would affect the organisation of society and the quality of human life was wide open. It
was there to be explored, and it *needed* to be explored, because it
was highly problematic. In this respect the attitude of British
writers was characteristically different from the attitude of
American writers of speculative fiction. American writers of
futuristic fiction – most especially those who became associated
with the emergent genre of science fiction – did not appear to
feel this problem with the same intensity. Many refused to see
the development of powerful and versatile technologies as
problematic at all; those who did, saw the problem as something that could be corrected by a relatively minor adjustment
of attitude. There were anxious science fiction writers and
pessimistic science fiction writers, but neither the anxiety nor
the pessimism cut as deep as the parallel feelings in Britain.
Because the intensity of the suspicion was missing, so too in the
main was the fervid determination which the likes of Wells and
Shiel could infuse into their hypothetical solutions of the
problem.

Just as the imaginary voyage in scientific romance becomes
complicated by a mixture of motives, so the element of Utopianism in scientific romance becomes entangled with other themes
and other projects. Writers of scientific romance found it very
difficult simply to sketch out their idea of the ideal state,
because they could not help but be aware of all the doubts and
difficulties besieging such ideals. Again, this syncretic confusion of Utopian and other themes was entirely in keeping with
the spirit of scientific romance.

Evolutionary Fantasies

The theory of evolution had an impact on the imagination of scientists and laymen alike that is quite without parallel. It presented a dramatic challenge to cherished beliefs, and called into question the nature of man. Disraeli summed up the emotive issue when he told an Oxford Diocesan Conference that he had come to debate the question of 'whether man is an ape or an angel'. This was hardly a scientific way of posing the question, but it was an apt expression of the doubt that was clouding the minds of ordinary people. Disraeli remained on the side of the angels, but all the reasoned argument pointed the other way.

Evolutionist ideas became quite widely dispersed in Victorian literature. Charles Darwin's grandfather Erasmus always fancied himself a poet as well as an evolutionary philosopher, and frequently put his biological ideas into poetic form. More significant, perhaps, is the vein of evolutionist thought in Tennyson's poetry, particularly in *In Memoriam* (written 1833-50). Here Tennyson shows an appreciation of the cruel side of the evolutionary process – as in the famous reference to 'Nature, red in tooth and claw' – as well as a conviction as to the inherently progressive pattern of evolution by means of which God is guiding His Creation towards perfection. Similar ideas can be found in Robert Browning's verse play *Paracelsus* (1835), where evolution is also an essentially creative and progressive process. Matthew Arnold, by contrast, found it hard to maintain such a faith in the ultimate beneficence of nature, and thus, in a fashion, anticipated the shock that was to be generated by Darwin's theory of natural selection: a theory which removed the notion of progress towards perfection from evolutionary philosophy.

A good example of the impact which this idea could have is provided by George Meredith, who had shown no particular interest in evolutionism before the publication in 1859 of the *Origin of Species*, but who afterwards became so impressed with it that, in the words of D.R. Oldroyd in *Darwinian Impacts*, it 'took a dominant grip on the poet's whole philosophy of nature'.[6] Meredith was content to have God displaced from his role in human affairs by natural selection, and tried to deduce a new code of ethics from the logic of evolution. He was not at all downhearted by this change in his outlook, but others found the new philosophy of nature terribly bleak. Thomas Hardy became fascinated by the notion, and it served to accentuate the pessimism that was already ingrained in him. J.O. Bailey co-opts Hardy's novel *Two on a Tower* (1882) into the bibliography of 'Scientific Romances' which he offers at the end of his pioneering study of speculative fiction, *Pilgrims Through Space and Time*, but it is not a speculative work.

In fact, Darwin's new theory of evolution did not generate any considerable number of speculative fictions in the 1860s or the 1870s. The one major exception to this is the section in Samuel Butler's *Erewhon* (1872) called 'The Book of the Machines', in which the author satirically applies the theory of natural selection to machines, suggesting that machines must ultimately become fitter than men, and hence condemn mankind to extinction, unless we follow the example of the Erewhonians and abandon them. The argument is not serious, but Butler's interest in evolutionary theory was. He had already written articles debating the merits of Darwin's theory, and he was later to become one of the most vociferous 'heretics', abandoning Darwinian orthodoxy in favour of his own version of neo-Lamarckism, popularised in his book *Luck or Cunning?* (1887).

A handful of Darwin-influenced speculative fictions were produced in the 1880s, but none was particularly impressive in the quality of its extrapolations from the theory. The first speculative stories about man's distant ancestors appeared in this decade, but Andrew Lang's *Romance of the First Radical* (1886) is simply a satirical mockery of taboos and Henry Curwen's *Zit and Xoe: Their Early Experience* (1887) is deliberately silly in its presentation of an Adam and Eve putting aside the traditions of their apelike forebears and rushing through millennia of cultural evolution in the space of a generation. H.B.M. Watson – son of the author of *Erchomenon* – dealt with Darwinian ideas in his curious lost race story *Marahuna* (1888), but in a quasi-allegorical fashion that did them no justice. There was at this time one disciple of Darwin already active as a writer of short stories which (he claimed) always had a seed of scientific speculation in them, but Grant Allen's first collection of such stories, *Strange Stories* (1884), has no evolutionary fantasy in it, though there is a story championing the cause of eugenics: 'The Child of the Phalanstery'.

This peculiar absence of any prose fiction making serious and constructive use of Darwinian ideas can probably be accounted for in terms of the nature of the literary marketplace, though it is worth noting that the rather different American marketplace also afforded little space for evolutionist speculations. (In France, by contrast, Camille Flammarion made abundant use of evolutionary theory in devising life-systems for hypothetical alien worlds in his *Récits de l'Infini* (1872; subsequently revised as *Lumen* and translated under that title for publication in Britain in 1887) and the ambitious speculative writer J.H. Rosny the elder made prolific use of evolutionary theory in his work from 1887 onwards.[7]) In any case, the situation in Britain was to change very dramatically with the advent on the literary scene of H.G. Wells, whose imagination had been fired in no uncertain terms by the lectures in evolutionary science which he had attended at the Normal School of Science in 1884, given by Thomas Henry Huxley – Darwin's champion in the great tournament of ideas.

Wells adopted the Darwinian faith with the fervour of a religious convert, and it permeated everything that he wrote. Wells took up the task that had been left frustratingly undone, and began to work out the logical consequences of Darwinian theory in a series of literary thought-experiments. His stories carried great conviction, and were constructed with an imaginative power that was hitherto unparalleled. Indeed, he filled the vacant space so brilliantly that he left little scope for others to do anything but echo his themes. Such scope as *was* left was rapidly taken up by two of the other early writers of scientific romance: M.P. Shiel and William Hope Hodgson. Neither of these writers, though, had either the competence or the commitment to deal with evolutionary ideas as Wells did. It is one thing to be carried away with the aesthetic appeal of the idea of evolution – as Shiel was, or as John Davidson was in his comic tale of *Earl Lavender* (1895)[8] – and quite another to have the intellectual and imaginative resources to extrapolate from the theory. In this regard, Wells was unique in his day, and the fact that evolutionary fantasies came to play such an important role in British scientific romance was largely due to the enormity of his influence.

Despite the extensive influence on literary men of evolutionist ideas, therefore, there really was no tradition of evolutionary fantasy for scientific romance to absorb; instead, scientific romance quickly came to compensate for a remarkable absence.

Future Wars

The May 1871 issue of *Blackwood's Magazine* featured an un-signed story called 'The Battle of Dorking: Reminiscences of a Volunteer'. It tells the story of an invasion of the British mainland by Prussian troops. The British armed forces, even with their ranks swelled by volunteers, have no chance of repelling the invasion because their equipment is obsolete and their tactics are ineffective. Britain is defeated just as France had been defeated a few months earlier in the Franco–Prussian War.

The Battle of Dorking was quickly released as a pamphlet, and enjoyed a spectacular success. It was translated into several other languages, including German, and provoked a good deal of interest abroad. It proved, in fact, to be a remarkably effective item of propaganda in the call for the reform of the Army and the rearmament of Britain's defence forces. The fuss which it stirred up was sufficient to spur Gladstone into an angry reference to it in a speech against 'alarmism'. A full account of this remarkable episode, and an elaborate commentary on the genre of future war stories spawned by *The Battle of Dorking* can be found in I.F. Clarke's excellent study of *Voices Prophesying War, 1763–1984*. Clarke's bibliography of the *Tale of the Future* lists more than a dozen other pamphlets produced in the same year, replying in kind with their own accounts of what would happen if England were to be suddenly invaded.

The author of *The Battle of Dorking*, George T. Chesney, achieved the almost unique feat of starting off a literary tradition single-handed. Even after the initial panic had died down fictitious accounts of near-future wars continued to be produced in Britain in some profusion. Similar stories were produced in other European nations, but it was Britain which was most obsessed by them. It is not difficult to understand why. Britain had been a great military power, but had grown – according to some vociferous critics in and out of parliament – complacent. The men controlling the armed forces were living in the past, trading on an assumption of invulnerability which could no longer stand up to inspection. On the horizon, dangers were lurking: the newly consolidated German Empire was hungry to become a colonial power and to assert its military might, and this was not the only conflict that threatened. There was trouble in various far-flung parts of the globe where British influence, though powerful, was a trifle unsteady: India, South

Africa, China, and – of course – Ireland. No other nation enjoyed a political situation which justified the intensity of paranoia that was manifest in British tales of imaginary uprisings and invasions.

Even before Chesney began the fashion, some stories of future wars had shown an awareness of the fact that technological change might potentially make a big difference to the manner in which wars would be fought. As early as 1859 a British writer signing himself Herrmann Lang had offered an account of *The Air Battle*, but this was safely set five thousand years in the future. In the 1870s and 1880s most imaginary future wars were fought with conventional weapons, although a brigade of winged troops fought for Irish liberty in Tom Greer's *A Modern Daedalus* (1885), and the French occasionally used the, as yet, unconstructed Channel Tunnel as a means of invading Britain. The most radical transformation of warfare was, interestingly enough, envisaged by George Chesney himself, in *The New Ordeal* (1879), which looks forward to a day when bombs have become so very powerful that they can obliterate whole nations. Chesney proposes that this will make war impossible, and that disputes between nations will have to be settled by limited pseudo-gladiatorial contests.

By the 1890s, the popularity of this kind of fiction was sufficient to encourage many military men to think in terms of the possibilities of future conflict, and close attention was being paid to the possibilities associated with each new item of military hardware. The popular magazines which proliferated in the early 1890s naturally took the opportunity to cash in on the potential of this kind of story. In 1892 *Black and White* serialised 'The Great War of 1892', a mock-journalistic account by P.H. Colomb and several collaborators of a conflict involving several European nations. The story gave careful and fairly scrupulous attention to the manner in which modern battles might be fought on land and on sea. The story was reprinted in book form as *The Great War of 189–*. Also in 1892 *The Engineer* serialised 'The Captain of the *Mary Rose*' by W. Laird Clowes, who had collaborated with A.H. Burgoyne five years earlier to produce a Chesneyesque propaganda pamphlet, *The Great Naval War of 1887*. Clowes's story was also quickly reprinted in book form. Another book published in the same year, A.N. Seaforth's *The Last Great Naval War*, is similar in spirit. All these works took their imaginative task fairly seriously, and were

31

careful to stick closely to the kinds of weaponry which were already in existence and ready for use.

One of the crucial events in the history of scientific romance, however, was the decision by C. Arthur Pearson to use a future war story in the attempt to boost circulation of his tabloid *Pearson's Weekly*, which was in 1892 an imitation of *Tit-Bits*, carrying no fiction. The job of writing this future war serial was handed over to one of the journalists working for the paper, on the strength of an outline which he produced. The journalist was George Griffith, and his novel, *The Angel of the Revolution*, transformed the future war story at a stroke. Griffith was impatient with careful extrapolation dealing with known weaponry; in his view the pace of technological change was adequate to permit an overnight transformation of the whole business of warfare. His future war is fought with airships and with submarines, as well as more powerful explosives. It is no mere squabble between neighbouring nations, but a *world war*, in which the side of right is not represented by Britain but by an international brotherhood of socialists who are happy to call themselves Terrorists. When they smash the armed forces of the imperial powers of Europe they are not merely winning a war but putting an end to war, for this is the climax of the story of mankind: a virtual day of judgment.

With the publication of this story, which proved enormously successful and widely influential, the future war story was gobbled up by scientific romance. Accounts of future wars published after 1893, when *The Angel of the Revolution* appeared, carried an imaginative *carte blanche* which they had not had before. There was a massive injection of imaginative scope and daring which took the future war story out of its own narrow groove, connecting it up to romances of invention via the marvellous vehicles which Vernian writers had devised for the purposes of extravagant imaginary tourism. By the time Griffith had provided his pioneering work with a sequel, *Olga Romanoff; or, The Syren of the Skies*, another connecting link had been forged and the future war story expanded into eschatological fantasy – a linkage which was to become very much more important as the history of scientific romance progressed.

The great significance of future war stories in British scientific romance is one of the principal features distinguishing it from American science fiction. There were, of course, future war stories written in America, including *The Great War Syndicate* (1889) by Frank R. Stockton and the misleadingly titled *Armageddon* (1898) by Stanley Waterloo. These novels showed an awareness of the ways in which technological advancement might alter the business of war, but the idea never had the power over the minds of the American public that it had in Britain. The geography of the two nations was so very different, and so were their political situations. The possibility that America might be invaded seemed very much more remote than the possibility of an invasion of Britain, and while Europe was a seething mass of conflicts America could assume a posture of lofty isolation, hardly prejudiced by such minor affairs as the Spanish–American war. As we shall see in later chapters, this initial difference was massively compounded by the very different experiences of the two nations in World War I. The effects of that war on the British people, and on the British imagination, were immeasurably greater than its effects on American consciousness. It makes perfect sense to speak of the development of scientific romance after 1918 under the heading of 'the imaginative legacy of the Great War', but in the history of American science fiction one can see hardly a trace of any such legacy. The distinction remains evident even in the years following 1945, when the revelation of the power of the atom bomb took place in two very different imaginative contexts on either side of the Atlantic.

It is in the realm of the future war story that the early writers of scientific romance scored their most conspicuous predictive successes. Most can be credited to the account of H.G. Wells, who was rather late coming into the action but then performed better than anyone. He offered more convincing aerial combats than anyone else, anticipated the value of tanks, and invented atomic bombs on the eve of the Great War. Ironically, though, these successes were due not so much to prophetic cleverness as to the restless quest for novelty which was an essential aspect of scientific romance. Because the writers were always looking for something new, trying to go one better than they had before, they were forced to make their instruments of destruction ever more powerful. George Griffith started fighting the next war with airships and submarines, but he wound up fighting it with disintegrator rays and atomic cannons, in the desperate attempt to keep up melodramatic momentum. The fact that the real history of twentieth-century armaments has kept comfort-

33

ably abreast of the imagination of the scientific romancers is not their triumph, but rather their tragedy.

Eschatological Fantasies

In his book *The Image of the Future* Fred Polak points out that there are two different species of futuristic imagery: one consisting of images of the historical future (which he calls Utopian) and one consisting of images of the ultimate future, of the world *beyond* this one (which he calls Eschatological). Polak argues that just as Utopian fiction underwent a crucial transformation at about the time of the origin of genre scientific romance, so too was eschatological thought transformed by a virtual reversal. Thus, he discusses 'de-utopianising' and 'de-eschatologising' together in his chapter on 'Devastation of the Image of the Future'.[9]

It is more difficult to speak of a 'tradition' of eschatological fiction than of Utopian fiction, because much eschatological thought has remained confined within academic theology, but there have been brief phases in literary history when eschatological influences have come very much into vogue. There was one such phase in the 1740s, when Edward Young, James Hervey and others produced quantities of 'graveyard poetry', and there was another in the 1820s when Thomas Campbell wrote a poem, Mary Shelley a novel and Thomas Hood a skit, all under the title *The Last Man*, which they might have borrowed from a French novel by Jean-Baptiste Cousin de Grainville that was translated into English in 1806. Ryszard Dubanski associates with this second vogue the apocalyptic paintings of John Martin and other gloomy themes in Romantic poetry.[10]

Eschatological imagery is not nearly so evident in British fiction between 1830 and the end of the 1870s, but it began to recur more frequently in the 1880s, after a rather different fashion. In its earlier phases, of course, eschatological speculation in literature is firmly rooted in religious thought. Even when the world is depopulated by a great plague, as in Mary Shelley's *The Last Man* (1826), the plague is – like the plagues of Egypt – an instrument of the Divine Will. Even at this stage the ideas entertained by cosmologists about the development and ultimate fate of the solar system were becoming influential, but they had not yet come to constitute a mythology of 'secular eschatology' – an 'eschatology without an *eschaton*', as Polak has it.[11] By the last decades of the century, though, the advancement of scientific thinking about the ultimate fate of the earth, and the erosion of Christian faith by rationalism, had created a very different intellectual climate.

The first response to this new intellectual climate which took the form of eschatological fantasy was a defensive reaction against the inroads of scepticism. Thus, in the elder Watson's *Erchomenon* (1879) the dream vision of the 'republic of materialism' culminates with the fugitive Christians who have kept the faith rewarded by the Day of Judgment. In *The Doom of the Great City* (1880) by William Delisle Hay, London is punished for the wickedness of its inhabitants by a divinely dispatched lethal fog. Similar stories were produced in a trickle through the next few decades. A similar hostility to modern materialistic civilisation underlies Richard Jefferies' *After London* (1886), although here the story is not loaded with religious cant, and after the unspecified catastrophe which has obliterated the great cities life goes on in a saner and more innocent fashion.

There were, however, two sides to the coin of religious faith. Hand in hand with the belief that God could and would one day put an end to the world went the faith that in the meantime He would look after it. Along with the belief that there was unlikely to be a divinely ordained Apocalypse, therefore, came the notion that the earth *could* be destroyed by some random accident of cosmic happenstance, such as being hit by a comet. There grew up a certain amount of literary interest not simply in the melodramatic idea of such a comet strike, but in the question of how people might react to the knowledge that such an end was imminent. We find, therefore, not only stories of actual cosmic disaster, but a peculiar sub-genre of 'frustrated apocalypse stories' whose authors are interested in the psychology of imminent doom and are content to allow a *deus ex machina* to save the day. An early example of this kind of story is a three-decker novel, *The Crack of Doom* (1886) by William Minto.

The writer who took this whole business much more seriously than anyone else was both an astronomer of an unusually speculative bent and a committed, if slightly unorthodox, Christian. This was the Frenchman Camille Flammarion, whose early *Récits de L'Infini* (1872) combined cosmological speculation and evolutionary theory to construct an ideative apparatus of support for a theory of personal immortality which imagines the soul being serially reincarnated on different worlds and free in between times to explore the wonders of the cosmos in disembodied form. For Flammarion, the *eschaton* was identical with the vast and wonderful world revealed by his telescopes, and he was able to fuse secular and religious ideas about the fate of the world into a coherent whole. The *Récits* were eventually published in a specially revised translation in Britain in 1887, as *Lumen* (they had appeared earlier in a collection called *Stories of Infinity*, but this had been published only in the USA). The British edition of *Lumen* was followed within a few years by the most celebrated of all Flammarion's speculative works, *La Fin du Monde* (1893), translated into English in 1894 as *Omega; the Last Days of the World*. Part romance and part essay, this novel has an early sequence in which the earth is threatened by a comet strike, and follows the likely social consequences of such a realisation. It goes on to discuss several contemporary theories about how the world might end, and concludes with a description of social life in a far-future earth nearing that point in time when it will no longer support life.

This dramatic combination of theories and images does not appear to have been a commercial success in Britain, but it was influential in the early days of scientific romance. George Griffith certainly read it and plundered its ideas, and the probability seems strong that Wells knew it too. With or without the aid of Flammarion, though, all the early writers of scientific romance drew upon the new secular mythology of the end of the world, often embedding it in their most memorable works. Griffith climaxed his sequel to *The Angel of the Revolution* with a cometary disaster. Wells eventually wrote an exceptionally elegant and compact disaster story in 'The Star', but not before he had explored the ultimate fate of mankind in his speculative essay 'The Man of the Year Million' and *The Time Machine*. M.P. Shiel built his literary reputation on the success of his last man story *The Purple Cloud*, and William Hope Hodgson inserted a startling vision of the end of the solar system into his hallucinatory account of *The House on the Borderland*. Conan Doyle wrote a cosmic disaster story as a sequel to *his* most famous scientific romance, *The Lost World*. The ultimate 'anti-scientific romance' following the example set by *Erchomenon* was ultimately provided by Robert Hugh Ben-

36

son, son of an Anglican archbishop and convert to Roman Catholicism, who brought the Last Judgment triumphantly into a scientifically developed world of the future in *The Lord of the World* (1907). Only a year later, though, James Elroy Flecker proposed in *The Last Generation* that men might be almost ready to bring the story of mankind to a close by choice, supporting ennui with legislation against childbirth.

It is hardly surprising that writers of scientific romance should have taken so enthusiastically to stories of the end of the world. The melodramatic potential of such stories could not possibly be overlooked. What is interesting, though, is the philosophical bent that such stories always have. Even an undistinguished magazine story like 'The Last Days of Earth' (1901) by George C. Wallis is weighed down by sonorous pronouncements about 'the unconscious enmity of the whole Universe of Matter' and 'the end of Humanity's troubled dream'.[12] Contemplation of 'last things' always brings out a curiously pompous humility – a seriousness within playfulness which has the grip of the proverbial iron hand within the velvet glove. This particular aspect of scientific romance has remained important throughout its history, though there are marked changes of attitude involved in the imaginative confrontation with the end. It is significant that one of the last writers of scientific romance, publishing one of the first apologias for science fiction, chose to single out this eschatological thread as something worthy of special praise:

> Work of this kind gives expression to thoughts and emotions which I think it good that we should sometimes entertain. It is sobering and cathartic to remember, now and then, our collective smallness, our apparent isolation, the apparent indifference of nature, the slow biological, geological and astronomical processes which may, in the long run, make many of our hopes (possibly some of our fears) ridiculous.[13]

As with the other genres that were absorbed into scientific romance, eschatological fantasy was transformed in being taken over. Partly this transformation was a 'natural' historical process resulting from the secularisation of the imagination, but it was also partly a result of the connection of such fantasies to ideas drawn from other sources. As was noted in the last chapter, British scientific romance in the later phases of its development introduced a strong dose of apocalyptic imagery and sentiment into its future war stories, but it was also in the medium of scientific romance that the connection was explored – by Wells and others – between the theory of evolution and the ultimate fate of mankind. This combination of ideas, too, was to become an important element in scientific romance.

Scientific Romance and Metaphysical Fantasy

If we are to talk about the 'literary ancestors' of scientific romance we must consider not only those pre-existent genres which it absorbed or borrowed from, but also those genres from which it separated itself by emphasising contrasts. The origin of scientific romance was not merely a consolidation of quasi-realistic imaginary voyages, futuristic Utopian fantasies, evolutionary fantasies and future war stories, with a delicate spice of secular eschatology; it was also a process of discrimination which isolated the speculative fiction which owed its inspiration to the scientific imagination from that which employed a 'supernatural' framework. It also needs to be emphasised that despite a certain amount of protestation to the contrary, this separation was only partially achieved.

It has been suggested in previous sections of this chapter that the transformation of the genres which combined to form scientific romance near the end of the nineteenth century had much to do with the rise of the rationalist and materialist world-view, and with the competition between that world-view and the world-view of religious metaphysics which it was gradually replacing. The positivist philosopher and social scientist Auguste Comte had declared early in the century that the intellectual progress of mankind was a three-stage movement, from naive theology through mystified metaphysics to hard science. To embrace the new and superior world-view of science was therefore a matter of casting out old idols, of repudiating 'superstition'. Thus, while the emergent genre of scientific romance gathered in the kinds of story which could properly belong to it, it cast out ghost stories and tales of magic, accounts of demonic possession and tales of vampires, were-wolves and witches. Such, at least, was the theory.

It may seem ironic, and perhaps puzzling, that the boom in scientific romance coincided with a boom in supernatural fiction. Fantastic fiction showed no sign of passing through Comte's three stages; as belief in the supernatural waned, fiction based on its premisses thrived. In the previous section it was suggested that the renewed production of Christian eschatological fantasies in the late nineteenth century was actually a product of positivist opposition – it was a kind of reactionary backlash. No such case can be made out, though, with respect to the new flourishing of the Victorian ghost story or the spectacular career of Count Dracula and his kindred. This is not the place to attempt a full explanation of the flourishing of supernatural fiction and heroic fantasy in parallel with scientific romance and science fiction, but one aspect of this curious situation does require closer inspection and analysis, and that is the way in which the two thriving halves of the tradition of fanatastic fiction failed to disentangle themselves completely from one another. The writers of scientific romance never did manage to exclude the old imaginative apparatus from their *oeuvres*; indeed, they often remained fascinated by it, seemingly unable to leave it alone. Thus, for instance, we find Wells writing stories about ghosts as well as tanks, angels as well as aliens, mermaids as well as Morlocks, debating with God in his fiction just as he debated with Hilaire Belloc in real life.

We must remember, when we characterise the intellectual turmoil of the nineteenth century partly as a conflict between opposing world-views, that there is more than one way to resolve a conflict. There is victory, and there is reconciliation. People involved in conflicts are often ambivalent in their hopes and desires regarding ultimate resolution, and it is not surprising that we find a similar ambivalence in the attitudes of many people caught up in the conflict between world-views. In the nineteenth century, as in previous ones, many pious men were drawn to science as a way of gaining a better understanding of God through the study of His Creation. They did not anticipate that their faith could or would be contradicted by what they found. There is a good deal of speculative fiction, therefore, which deliberately aims at the reconciliation of traditional religious beliefs with scientific discovery.

The work of Camille Flammarion has already been mentioned as a daring attempt of this kind: *Lumen* has a greater imaginative sweep than any other speculative fiction produced in the nineteenth century, and the breadth of its concern is generated by the ambition of its mission. Flammarion was following in the steps (whether he knew it or not) of the founder of the New Jerusalem Church, Emmanuel Swedenborg, whose early scientific training was used copiously to furnish the revelations presented in his visionary *Arcana*. Swedenborg journeyed in these visions to other planets within the solar system and to the worlds of other suns, visiting the people and the spirits that dwelt there. He took the trouble to imagine different ecologies for worlds whose circumstances were different from earth's, and different ways of life for people who had different material resources – all this in works first published in 1758. Flammarion was by no means the last to follow this particular trail, in philosophy or in fiction.

The late nineteenth century saw the flourishing of numerous religious cults which tried to recombine science and religion into a new dogma. Founders of such cults were usually ignorant of science, and often succeeded in doing no more than importing a little fashionable jargon into an idiosyncratic set of heretical beliefs, but the followers they attracted were equally confused and hungry for a new enlightenment which could provide the illusion of explaining everything. Helena Blavatsky, one of the most successful of these new mystics, was most active in the 1870s, during which time she popularised her version of 'Theosophy'. Mary Baker Eddy's Christian Science movement started in the same period. This climate of thought inevitably generated the Society for Psychical Research, which was founded in 1882 with the purpose of bringing the scientific method to the investigation of occult phenomena, so that the limits of possibility could be clarified and explanations could be found for all the happenings which narrow-minded scientists would not accept as real.

Cultists of this kind often borrowed from imaginative fiction. Madame Blavatsky obtained some of her 'revelations' from the pages of Lord Lytton's Rosicrucian novels *Zanoni* and *A Strange Story* – stories which Conan Doyle once categorised facetiously as belonging to the 'animal-magnetico-electro-hysterical-biological-mysterious sort'. The most successful British writer of the period which saw the emergence of scientific romance, Marie Corelli, also wrote stories of this sort, beginning with *A Romance of Two Worlds* (1886), whose charismatic hero reveals to the narratrix the secrets of the Electric Creed. At one point, like Swedenborg, she is carried off by an angel on a cosmic journey which reveals to her that the earth is the unhappiest world in the universe, because only there have people failed so completely to embrace the true faith.[14]

Many cosmic voyage stories which have a good deal of scientific romance in them also contain a good deal of religious mysticism. W.S. Lach-Szyrma's *Aleriel; or, A Voyage to Other Worlds* (1883) is an account of life on the other worlds of the solar system, which reflect different stages in an evolutionary progress which is moral and religious as well as organic and social. This book enjoyed considerable success and several other variations of its basic schema were provided by other writers. In J.J. Astor's *A Journey in Other Worlds* (1894) the characters use an imaginary technology borrowed from Greg's *Across the Zodiac* to visit several other worlds, where they find the agents responsible for all the supernatural incidents recorded in the scriptures. (This is, of course, an early version of the kind of mythology enthusiastically promoted in more recent times by Immanuel Velikovsky and Erich von Däniken.) George Griffith's cosmic voyage story *A Honeymoon in Space* (1901) also owes something to this kind of syncretic theorising. The eponymous hero of Lach-Szyrma's *Aleriel*, who offers his account of life on other worlds, is a quasi-angelic visitor from Venus, and this aspect of the story was also echoed in other works, most famously in *The Martian* (1897) by George du Maurier.

The other late-nineteenth-century movement which frequently attempted to borrow a jargon of apology from science was the spiritualist movement, whose followers often complicated their accounts of life after death with talk of 'other dimensions' in space, after the fashion of Johann Zöllner's bizarre book on *Transcendental Physics* (1880). The idea that there might be other spatial dimensions had been popularised by the remarkable Edwin Abbott, a Shakespearian scholar whose hobby was higher mathematics, in his unique work *Flatland* (1884). *Flatland* reconstructs hypothetically the way that a two-dimensional being would perceive things, adds some satirical commentary on the organisation of two-dimensional society, and then presents a flatlander's imaginative discovery of the third dimension, encouraging the reader to use his or her own imagination to come to terms with the possibility of there being a fourth dimension, and perhaps even a fifth and sixth. One reader who was inspired by Abbott was C.H. Hinton, whose essays in his two books of *Scientific Romances* take up Abbott's propagandist thread. Hinton suggests, *en passant*, that ghosts might be explicable as four-dimensional entities briefly intersecting our three-dimensional world, and observes that a being in 'higher space' would be able to observe us intimately without there being any possibility of our perceiving him. The proposal that God might reside in the fourth dimension is left delicately unspoken, but the long story in the first book of the pair, 'The Persian King', is an exercise in hypothetical metaphysics which has obvious allegorical parallels with Christian doctrine.

It is with some embarrassment that today's historians of science note that some of the most prestigious physicists of the day were seduced by the spiritualists and the Society of Psychical Research. William Crookes and Oliver Lodge are the cardinal examples. Historians of speculative fiction are often just as embarrassed when they observe the similar corruption of Sir Arthur Conan Doyle, who created that master of ratiocination Sherlock Holmes, and yet ended up being hoaxed by the Cottingley fairies. Fans of the robust hero Professor Challenger were desperately dismayed by his dreadful collapse between *The Poison Belt* and *The Land of Mist.* What happened to these men, however, serves to remind us of something very important about the intellectual climate of the period under discussion. The conflict between the world-view of religion and the world-view of science was not a battle between equals, nor was it a matter of like replacing like. It is perhaps too easy to see what was happening in Comtean terms, as an obsolete system of false beliefs being carefully devastated by the true belief of justified knowledge. There was more involved than truth; there was pride, and feeling, and morality. If the rationalists were to win the war of ideas, the losers would have to sacrifice far more than a few illusions: they would be thrust into an existential and psychological situation far more precarious and far less comfortable than the one they had previously enjoyed. It is small wonder that at the level of belief and at the level of speculation people tried to save what they could from the destructive effects of ideative *blitzkrieg*.

All the early scientific romancers were on the side of reason against superstition. When they went forth on their journeys within the imagination, they followed the signposts that the rationalists had planted, but they often tried to find along their new routes some of those places which had hitherto been thought to lie in the other direction. Even when they were content to leave those other places far behind them, they often found it convenient to describe the new places that they discovered in terms which compared them to the old. They were always keen to spot parallels, and enthusiastic to find products in the new realms which could stand in place of ones whose supply had dried up when the old were forsaken. Thus, Wells tried to discover in his imagination not merely a new morality, but also a new theology and a new sense of existential security and purpose. M.P. Shiel did the same. It is arguable that they could not possibly have succeeded, and that all they ended up doing was what William Hope Hodgson did more explicitly: demonstrating and dramatising the anxiety – the Sartrean *nausea* – that came with the loss of the old sense of security and purpose. In any case, this is why scientific romance never finally detached itself from metaphysical fantasy, and why scientific romance seems so frequently to be 'looking over its shoulder' at the apparatus of an older imagination. There is no paradox in the fact that the last of the scientific romancers identified by this book – C.S. Lewis and Gerald Heard – were both synthesists who tried in their own way to recombine the scientific and religious world-views.

3

THE MAJOR WRITERS
OF THE PRE-WAR PERIOD

George Griffith

GEORGE GRIFFITH was the form of his name used for writing by
George Chetwynd Griffith-Jones, who was born on 20 August
1857 in Plymouth. His father had been a colonel in the Indian
Army, but had recently become a clergyman when George – his
second son – was born. Thus, most of Griffith's youth was spent
in poor parishes near Manchester, and he attended school only
briefly, after his father's death in 1872. He then went to sea as
an apprentice, but found the cruel conditions unbearable and
jumped ship in Australia. There he was a casual labourer for a
while, but eventually went to sea again, shipping in happier
circumstances and ultimately finding his way home again by
the time he was twenty. He then became a teacher in a
preparatory school, educating himself in the meantime and
accumulating the qualifications which would allow him to
build a career in the teaching profession. During this period he
wrote for a local paper in Brighton and apparently did some
writing for the freemasons. He published some poetry in the
1880s and contributed to *The Secular Review*, where he acquired
something of a reputation as an outspoken freethinker.[1]

There is much in this personal background which is echoed
in the histories of other writers of scientific romance. In
particular, it is significantly common for writers of scientific
romance to be sons of clergymen converted to freethought; we
shall be meeting several others in these pages.[2] The number of
such individuals who became associated with the genre is too
large for the matter to be dismissed as mere coincidence, and it
is not too difficult to see the logic of it. In this era of declining
faith and warring world-views there were many sons abandon-

ing the faith of devout fathers, and many combined the customary zeal of the convert with a desire to justify their abandonment of one set of ideas for another. It has already been pointed out that scientific romance is inherently iconoclastic, and this is reflected in the temperament of many of its leading practitioners, who were determinedly independent of thought, sometimes to the point of dogged perversity, and often possessed of an awesome intellectual conceit. The perverse streak in Griffith's character is amply demonstrated by the fact that when he had finally obtained the last of his teaching diplomas in 1887 he promptly quit the profession and went to London to become a journalist crusading for secularism and socialism.

Griffith's activities in the line of idealistic freelance journalism could not support him, and he eventually went to work for C. Arthur Pearson, initially addressing envelopes connected with the competitions with which Pearson was trying to boost the circulation of *Pearson's Weekly*. He was soon entrusted with a column in the paper, and wrote feature articles for it. He was thus in exactly the right place when Pearson decided to experiment with a future war story as a further aid to sales. *The Angel of the Revolution* ran as a serial there between January and October of 1893, and was published in book form by the Tower Publishing Company, which was also attempting to cash in on the vogue for future war stories by producing a whole line of them in a fairly lavish format.

The Angel of the Revolution, as has been noted, transformed the shape of future war stories with its spectacular accounts of aerial battles and submarine attacks. It did so, though, simply by combining materials borrowed from other sources. For all his importance as a writer of scientific romances, Griffith actually appears to have had little imagination of his own. We cannot be sure, of course, exactly how many of his ideas he stole, or where from, but he was frequently sufficiently unselfconscious in his adaptations to mention his sources in his texts. There is obviously a strong Vernian influence in *The Angel of the Revolution*: the airships are similar to the one in *The Clipper of the Clouds* and one of the chief characters – Natas, leader of the Terrorists – is strikingly reminiscent of Captain Nemo and Robur (the builder of the airship in *The Clipper of the Clouds*). Verne had reserved his fighting-machines to the private purposes of lonely social outsiders, but Griffith made his into great fleets that could serve as agents of Armageddon – his airships bear the names of the Heavenly Host which cast Satan's legions into Hell. (Natas is a reversed Satan in more than one sense!)

Chesney had already pointed out in *The New Ordeal* the possibility that new technology might make available powers of destruction that would facilitate bloodshed on an unprecedented scale. Chesney, though, had concluded that if this were to happen men would refuse to fight wars. The American writer Stanley Waterloo came to the same conclusion at the end of his novel *Armageddon* in 1898. Griffith had no such naive reasonableness to guide him. He accepted that the next war would probably be 'the most frightful carnival of destruction the world has ever seen', but he did not imagine that this would prevent it being fought, and he was quite prepared to look forward to it with enthusiasm and excitement. Partly, this enthusiasm derived from the fact that he subscribed to the myth of a 'war to end war' – a climactic conflict which would set the world to rights and establish a regime which would use its might to outlaw further conflict. Partly, though, it was a simple reflection of the fact that at this stage in his career he loved describing massive conflicts and vast destruction, and could do so with amazing fervour and relish.

The novel is the story of Richard Arnold, a young inventor who has solved the problem of flight but lacks the capital to put his knowledge into practice. He briefly contemplates a prize of one million pounds offered for this achievement by the Tsar of Russia, but puts this temptation vehemently behind him, swearing aloud that he will use his power to destroy tyrants rather than to support them. He is fortunately overheard by a member of the inner circle of the secret Brotherhood of Freedom, which controls the actions of nihilists, anarchists and socialists throughout the world. The Brotherhood finances the building of the airship Ariel on a remote Scottish island. It is first employed on a couple of rescue missions, and to secure a base in an otherwise inaccessible African valley, Aeria, where a fleet of similar ships is built.

In the meantime, Europe has plunged into war. Though Arnold's airships remain unique (winged ships with hulls and decks, three masts, giant propellers and cannons) the Tsar's prize has been claimed by the inventors of a dirigible balloon, and the Tsar is trying to use this advantage to secure dominion over the Western World. Natas, leader of the Brotherhood, plans to let the European powers exhaust themselves in fighting, then take control when they are spent, welding the forces of Europe together ready to meet an 'impending flood of yellow barbarians' which he assumes to be gathering in the East. Natas claims that it is the destiny of the Anglo-Saxon race to rule the world (though he is himself a Hungarian Jew) and that the Terror will be the means to secure this end, as well as to establish socialism and abolish war.

Matters are complicated by the theft of one of Arnold's airships and by dissent within the Brotherhood's ranks, but the tide is turned by a revolution in America (*The Angel of the Revolution* was not reprinted in America for some considerable time, and most of Griffith's books never appeared there). Britain initially refuses to join the Anglo-Saxon Federation founded in America, but capitulates after a Russian invasion. Then the power of the Terrorists is finally unleashed. Victory in Europe is followed by a confrontation with the forces of Islam, who have recently defeated the Buddhists in a Holy War. Once they see the forces arrayed against them, though, the Moslems capitulate and the whole world is pacified (the invasion from the Far East never does materialise). National boundaries are redrawn, private property in land is abolished, and private wealth is assaulted by what Griffith obviously considered a mercilessly punitive tax, though its predatory power is less than present-day British income tax. Richard Arnold is free then to return to his wife Natasha (daughter of Natas) and his baby son, secure in the knowledge that peace is scheduled to reign on earth for ever.

Actually, peace reigned only as long as it took Griffith to realise that a sequel was commercially necessary. 'The Syren of the Skies' was announced as a successor in the pages of *Pearson's Weekly* before the end of 1893.

Olga Romanoff, as 'The Syren of the Skies' was retitled in book form, is set 125 years after the end of *The Angel of the Revolution*, in the year 2030. Throughout this period the descendants of the Brotherhood of Freedom, the Aerians, have kept the peace by means of their exclusive command of the air. They have at their disposal an awesome destructive force borrowed (with acknowledgement) from Lord Lytton's *The Coming Race*. The eponymous villainess of the story is a descendant of the defeated Tsar who has sworn to exact revenge; she steals an airship, uses drugs to obtain all the secrets of Aeria from a descendant of Richard Arnold, and then joins forces with the

47

ruler of Islam, who is also nursing a long-held grievance. War returns to earth, promising an even greater carnival of destruction than before. Even war, though, cannot compete with the Flammarionesque cosmic disaster which is now discovered to be imminent: the earth will be hit by a cloud of incandescent gas which will set the whole world aflame. The Aerians take refuge in caverns far below the surface, but in a world crazed by the knowledge of its impending destruction must still fight to secure themselves. Olga Romanoff, like the Aerians, survives the world's purgation, but falls victim to the ambition of her own scheme to be a new Eve, and dies; it is the pure in heart who inherit the world.

Having concluded this serial, though, Griffith found himself in a situation which many other writers of extravagant fiction were subsequently to encounter. One can cap a story of all-out world war with a tale of cosmic disaster, but once the world has been destroyed, what is there left for an encore? Griffith, having pushed on to the limit, could only revert to lesser matters, and from then on he was a lesser writer, with much of the fervour gone out of his work.

Pearson had made an exclusive contract with Griffith after the success of *The Angel of the Revolution*, and he now put the author to work to boost the fortunes of another of his periodicals, *Short Stories*, for which he wrote *The Outlaws of the Air*, a lacklustre reprise of his first novel, on a much smaller scale. Here the Brotherhood of the Better Life has established an island Utopia where they are building a fast-moving ship and an aircraft. An English aristocrat who arrives on the island by chance tells them of the depredations of a fast pirate ship, *Destroyer*, and they hurry to finish their own *Nautilus* in order to provide effective opposition to it. Unfortunately, the Brotherhood has been infiltrated by an anarchist who is a member of the same organisation as the *Destroyer's* master, and he eventually makes off with the new airship, naming it *Vengeur* and embarking upon a reign of terror. By the time the Utopians, with help from Hiram Maxim, have built more airships, the anarchists also have a fleet of them. The ultimate defeat of the anarchists is, however, made easier by dissent in their own ranks.

The Outlaws of the Air is a disjointed work, which moves uneasily through a series of sub-climaxes manufactured for serial purposes without ever reaching a proper climax. The reduction of scale involved weakens it considerably, though an oblique reference in the plot to Max Pemberton's *The Iron Pirate* (1893) – a work whose charismatic villain is a much exaggerated version of Verne's Captain Nemo – reveals whose success Griffith was now trying to follow. It is very noticeable, too, that Griffith here softens his political line; the reckless radicalism of *The Angel of the Revolution* has given way to a more careful discrimination between idealistic peace-loving Utopian socialists and dangerous fanatically evil anarchists. Ironically, this reflects the sentiments of one of the first works to copy *The Angel of the Revolution* – Edward Douglas Fawcett's *Hartmann the Anarchist* (1893) – and may well be a case of Griffith imitating his own imitator. It is very noticeable that as his work progressed Griffith drifted a long way to the right of his initial political position. Even in *The Angel of the Revolution* an English aristocrat plays a leading role in the Brotherhood of Freedom and Griffith was consistent in choosing heroes from that class, but in later novels they ally themselves with capitalists rather than socialists and exercise a benevolent paternalism when they become masters of the world.

Griffith was never to recapture the narrative force which he handled with conviction in his first two novels. Although the structure of almost all his books is cursed by the fact that he made them up as he went along, dictating to a secretary, with the requirements of serialisation very much in mind, this was probably not the sole reason for their decay. The fact that he ultimately died of cirrhosis of the liver suggests that he was already drinking heavily in the mid-1890s, and there is a seemingly alcoholic quality about the garrulous fluency of his later works.

Valdar the Oft-Born, which was serialised in *Pearson's Weekly* in 1895, is an obvious copy of a novel by Edwin Lester Arnold, *The Wonderful Adventures of Phra the Phoenician*, which had been serialised in *The Illustrated London News* in 1890. Both stories feature the adventures in different time periods of a swashbuckling hero, who enjoys sporadic immortality so that he can make his contribution to the great conflicts of human history. Valdar outdoes Phra slightly, beginning his career in Asgard, witnessing the destruction of Babel, the fall of Cleopatra and the death of Christ before getting involved with such conventional matters as the Spanish Armada and the Napoleonic war. Griffith's novel also has a sub-theme involving

Valdar's constantly interrupted love affair; this may reflect a debt which he – and perhaps Arnold too – owed to an even earlier story of serial revivification, Edgar Lee's *Pharaoh's Daughter* (1889). The probability that Griffith had read Lee's book is increased by the substance of another novel serialised in *Short Stories* in 1895, 'Golden Star' (reprinted in abridged form as the book *The Romance of Golden Star).* Although set in Peru instead of Egypt this story of a revivified mummy who attempts to win a similar revivification for his sister strongly echoes *Pharaoh's Daughter,* though it also has a future war element concerning the unification of South America into a new Incan empire.

In 1896 Arthur Pearson moved upmarket when he created *Pearson's Magazine,* an imitator of *The Strand,* but Griffith's serial stories were not in keeping with the image of the new periodical, and Griffith's contributions were limited to articles, poems and the occasional short story. He continued to write, though, for both *Pearson's Weekly* and *Short Stories.* For the former he wrote *Briton or Boer?,* a journalistic future war story relying heavily on firsthand research in South Africa. The book version appeared shortly after the serial ended, in 1897 – the real Boer War began, of course, in 1899. For *Short Stories* he then wrote 'The Gold Magnet', retitled *The Gold Finder* in book form because the title of the serial too closely resembled that of George Manville Fenn's adventure story *The Golden Magnet.* This is one of many stories involving a mechanical device for locating earthly treasures. Griffith's version is unexceptional.

Perhaps all too conscious that his work was becoming dull, Griffith returned to Flammarion for inspiration. For the Christmas 1897 issue of *Pearson's Weekly* he wrote 'The Great Crellin Comet', in which it is discovered that a comet will soon strike the earth. Here, though, giant cannons are built to fire projectiles which will destroy the comet's head. Most of the story was later incorporated into the otherwise routine future war story *The World Peril of 1910,* published posthumously in 1907. Another of Griffith 's last novels, *The Mummy and Miss Nitocris* (1906) similarly cannibalises two shorter pieces – 'The Vengeance of Nitocris' (1896) and 'The Conversion of the Professor' (1899). This is an interesting prefiguration of a strategy frequently employed in a later era by pulp science fiction writers; A.E. van Vogt was a prolific producer of such 'fix-up' novels.

By 1898 Griffith's serials had lost their impetus and their commercial significance. His last future war serial was *The Great Pirate Syndicate*, written for the penny weekly *Pick-Me-Up*, a sea story in which a secret conspiracy of plutocrats become masters of the world, defeating the forces of greedy enemy nations with the aid of 'aerial torpedoes' (primitive guided missiles) and a radiation device that makes metal brittle and ignites explosives at a distance. It is a pale shadow of *The Outlaws of the Air*, just as that novel was a pale shadow of *The Angel of the Revolution*

Griffith must have concluded at this point that a change of direction was called for if he was to rescue his dwindling fortunes. His other serial of 1898 was a historical novel set in Biblical times, *The Rose of Judah*, but he also tried a much more ambitious historical novel, *The Virgin of the Sun*, about the conquest of Peru. Written with some seriousness of purpose, and without the demands of serialisation in mind, this is the most substantial and coherent of his later novels, but it cannot be described as an artistic success. He only did one more serial for Pearson thereafter – one which demonstrated clearly that he was not the same radical secularist he once had been; this was a pseudonymous moralistic story of prostitution for the religious magazine *The Sunday Reader*.

Griffith was still writing some scientific romance in 1898, though most of the short fiction which he did in that year was non-fantastic, including a series of detective stories for *Pearson's Magazine*. The most significant speculative story was 'Hellville, USA', about the creation in Arizona of a colony of criminals. The colony decays into anarchy and the story peters out with the exhaustion of its initial inspiration, until a meteor shower is invoked as a *deus ex machina*. In 1899 he put up a more interesting performance in a fourth dimension fantasy, 'The Conversion of the Professor' (one of the stories absorbed into *The Mummy and Miss Nitocris*), which is also a *doppelgänger* story. 'The Searcher of Souls', published the same year, is similar in using pseudo-scientific jargon to support a theme borrowed from supernatural fiction. It was later built up into the novel *A Mayfair Magician* (1905).

After the turn of the century Griffith lost contact with the magazine markets which had sustained him through seven reasonably good years, and his later publications were obscure and unsuccessful books of various kinds. In the very last year of the nineteenth century, though, he produced his last important scientific romance. Excerpts from it appeared in *Pearson's Magazine* as a series of 'Stories of Other Worlds', and it eventually appeared in book form as *A Honeymoon in Space*. It is clearly based on Lach-Szyrma's *Aleriel*, which had generated a similar series of magazine pieces in *Cassell's Magazine*, collectively titled 'Letters from the Planets'. The speculations in the story are also supported occasionally by references to Flammarion's works, and there are conspicuous Vernian elements in the plot.

The most interesting aspect of *A Honeymoon in Space* is the manner in which the accounts of life in the other worlds of the solar system are used to display phases in a quasi-Spencerian evolutionary scheme. The moon is a dead world whose giant inhabitants are long gone, leaving the ruins of their ancient civilisation to testify to their achievements and to offer visitors a worldly *memento mori*. (It serves the same purpose in Lach-Szyrma, and also in Edgar Fawcett's pioneering American cosmic voyage story *The Ghost of Guy Thyrle*.) Mars, too, is further along its evolutionary path, and has become decadent; the Martians have given themselves over to an extreme and ruthless rationalism, eliminating emotion and physical differences between individuals (this seems to owe more to Wells than to Lach-Szyrma).

Like Lach-Szyrma's Venus – and somewhat at odds with his Spencerian schema – Griffith's Venus is without sin, and his honeymooners must leave it quickly for fear that the taint of original sin might somehow pass from them to its innocent angelic inhabitants. On Ganymede, where advanced super-scientists live in domed 'Crystal Cities', the characters catch a glimpse of a more opulent future awaiting mankind, but here too there is a reminder that despite their sophistication these people can only expect the same ultimate fate as the Martians and the giants of the moon. For Saturn Griffith attempts to construct an alien life-system adapted to life in its 'semi-gaseous ocean', after which the tour is cut short by two near-fatal accidents, one involving an encounter with the gravitational pull of a dead sun whose regeneration the characters are privileged to witness.

The materials in *A Honeymoon in Space* are almost entirely secondhand, and paradoxically it is because of this that it qualifies as an archetypal scientific romance. It builds items of

Vernian detail into a matrix of casually daring Wellsian invention, is perfectly willing to offer earnest comments on various grand philosophical matters, and is content to juxtapose all this with a quaintly conventional love story. It is an absurd conglomerate of a book, whose silliness is accentuated by a lack of literary skill, but it has an undeniable panache. It is a celebration of the conviction that the twentieth century would be an era when adventures as extravagant as any to be found in *The Thousand-and-One Nights* could be related with a new plausibility, maintaining a pose of respect for the horizons of scientific and social possibility.

Griffith continued to write prolifically after the turn of the century, though he did little for Pearson save for a few short pieces. More than half of his books were fantastic novels, but in many of them the elements of scientific romance were largely displaced by occult ideas. *Denver's Double* (1901) is a story about hypnotism and personality displacement – themes common in contemporary fiction and recently featured in Robert Hichens's lurid novel *Flames* (1897). *Captain Ishmael* (1901) is the story of a piratical immortal who occasionally bumps into the Wandering Jew. *The White Witch of Mayfair* (1902) has much the same plot as Conan Doyle's early occult romance *The Parasite* (1895). *The World Masters* (1903) and *The Lake of Gold* (1903) are both pale imitations of Griffith's earlier future war stories. *The Stolen Submarine* (1904) is another future war story, which has the advantage of topicality in dealing with the Russo–Japanese war, but the corresponding disadvantage of imaginative modesty. Slightly more adventurous is *A Criminal Croesus* (1904), where the gold financing a war to unify South America is provided by a subterranean lost race, while *The Great Weather Syndicate* (1906) is one of the earlier stories in which control of the weather is used to blackmail the world into peace. There is a little more imaginative daring in Griffith's one significant short scientific romance of this period, 'From Pole to Pole' (1904), but this account of a journey through a tunnel connecting the world's poles is apologetically humorous in tone, and the idea may have been borrowed from an American novelette about a similar tunnel, 'Through the Earth' (1898) by Clement Fezandie.

Throughout these years Griffith's health was in decline, but he did try to gather his resources together for one last substantial effort: a final future war story, *The Lord of Labour*. This story starts much more determinedly than its immediate predecessors, though it borrows some ideas Griffith had already used – notably the ray for making steel brittle, which featured in *The Great Pirate Syndicate* and *The World Masters*. The story's heroes, however, are armed with nuclear missiles fired from bazooka-like rifles. Griffith managed to dictate the complete text despite the fact that he was dying by degrees, but failed to retain control over the shape of the plot; the characters introduced as protagonists are largely forgotten in the later chapters, which become a mechanical account of military manoeuvres and the negotiations of kings and generals. The story was the last of Griffith's posthumous works to appear, in 1911. He died on 4 June 1906.

The story of Griffith's career gives the impression that whatever literary and imaginative talents he had were quickly squandered, and he settled for producing hurried and superficial work in as much quantity as he could manage. He probably tried to stretch himself only once, in *The Virgin of the Sun*, and appears to have accepted the failure of that experiment. He is now a forgotten writer, although *The Angel of the Revolution* and its sequel have lately been reprinted for the benefit of students of the history of speculative fiction. It is difficult for the modern reader to appreciate the influence that this rather inept writer actually had in the brief years of his early fame. He helped Arthur Pearson to open up an important space in the literary marketplace, which was quickly colonised by several other writers. It was for Pearson, in the wake of *The Angel of the Revolution*, that Wells wrote *The War of the Worlds* and *The Invisible Man*, Louis Tracy wrote *The Final War* and M.P. Shiel *The Yellow Danger*. There would have been scientific romance even if Griffith had never set pen to paper, and no doubt Pearson would have found someone else to write a future war serial for *Pearson's Weekly* if Griffith had not been on the spot. Griffith, though, was the man who drew together at this propitious moment a whole set of speculative ideas, intertwining them into a complex pattern. Wells was to weave a much more complicated and more elegant pattern, without having to borrow his materials from other writers, but Griffith did help to set a stage for him.

There is a certain propriety in the fact, recorded with some pride in Sam Moskowitz's biography of Griffith, that his son Alan Arnold (named for two characters in *The Angel of the Revolution* and born while it was being serialised) was later honoured for practical and theoretical contributions to the development of aviation.[3]

H.G. Wells

Herbert George Wells was born on 21 September 1866. His father was Joseph Wells, at that time a shopkeeper, although he tried his hand at several things; he had been a first-class cricketer but failed consistently in his attempts to earn a reasonable living. It was Wells's mother, Sarah, who provided for him, and he lived for much of his early life at Uppark, where she was housekeeper. After an unsuccessful apprenticeship in a draper's shop he became a pupil-teacher at Midhurst Grammar School, and his studies there ultimately won him a scholarship to the Normal School of Science in South Kensington. In his first year there he studied biology under Thomas Henry Huxley, an experience which made an impression on him so deep that it can only be compared to a religious conversion. The teachers who took over in his second and third years, when he took physics and geology, made no such impression and he failed both those years, returning to Uppark in 1890 in poor health and without a degree (he compensated for this failure a few years later, when he took a degree externally). He attempted to take up his teaching career again, despite his health problems, and he was also experimenting with journalistic essays in the popularisation of science. His first significant success was in selling 'The Rediscovery of the Unique' to the *Fortnightly Review*, where it appeared in 1891, but he had already published in the *Science Schools Journal* a series of fanciful essays called 'The Chronic Argonauts', which was later to form the basis of *The Time Machine*.

Wells began to write speculative essays in some profusion. A second piece for the *Fortnightly Review*, 'The Universe Rigid', was rejected by editor Frank Harris, who found it incomprehensible, but in 1893 he began writing regularly for the *Pall Mall Gazette*, a newspaper made famous by the crusading journalist W.T. Stead. Another early essay from the 1880s was rewritten as 'The Man of the Year Million', offering an image of man remade by evolution as a being with huge head and eyes, delicate hands and much reduced limbs. Wells suggested that our ultimate descendants might outlive the sun, permanently immersed in nutrient baths, living a purely mental life. The success of this flight of fancy encouraged him to do more in the same vein, including 'The Advent of the Flying Man' (1893), which concludes by suggesting that bat-like winged people might one day congregate in suburban rookeries. Wells was adept at finding aspects of contemporary scientific theory which lent themselves to poetic rhapsody, including in 'An Excursion to the Sun' (1894) a vision of solar storms and electromagnetic tides. He could also be argumentative, taking to task the authors of books he reviewed, whether they be astronomers (Henry Pratt in 'Decadent Science', 1894) or social theorists (Benjamin Kidd in 'The New Optimism', 1894).

In 1894 Wells began to produce stories to supplement his articles and reviews, and his fascination for oddments of scientific information provided many of his early plots. Most of the early stories are slight, featuring meetings between men and strange creatures: 'The Flowering of the Strange Orchid', 'In the Avu Observatory' and 'Aepyornis Island' are all of this type. The extravagance of the more adventurous essays did not initially spill over into his stories, but in the most effective of the pieces collected in *The Stolen Bacillus and Other Incidents* (1895), the non-speculative 'The Lord of the Dynamos', he did provide an elegant parable of contrasting human attitudes to technology. He was persuaded to undertake something much more ambitious, though, when he rewrote 'The Chronic Argonauts' into a series of stories for the *National Observer* in 1894. These stories were rewritten again at the behest of W.E. Henley into a serial novel, 'The Time Traveller's Story', which was reprinted with some further minor revisions as *The Time Machine*. Thus Wells arrived, by degrees, at a new synthesis of adventurous speculation and literary form.

Robert Philmus and David Hughes, in their anthology *H.G. Wells: Early Writings in Science and Science Fiction*, point out that there is an important duality in the world-view of these early essays and fictions.[4] On the one hand, Wells embraced a 'cosmic perspective' which appreciated the true size and time-scale of the universe. This was a deterministic perspective, in which the entire future might be calculated by deduction if one only had a full enough knowledge of the present; the theory of natural selection provided the law which controlled the evolution of life wherever it might be found. On the other hand, though, he could look at things from a purely human point of view, where human choice and human purpose are the important causal factors. From the former viewpoint the human species is of little significance, and might easily be subject to casual extinction – a possibility raised explicitly in his essay 'The Extinction of Man' (1894) – but from the latter man is indeed the measure of all things and the question of how men ought to live is *the* question. Philmus and Hughes argue that there is no inconsistency; these two positions represent complementary aspects of a coherent pattern of thought. In one sense they are right – the world looks different from different standpoints, but it can still be the same world – but we must be careful not to gloss over the difficulty that Wells had in trying to reconcile them. The contrast between these perspectives is clearly problematic as far as Wells is concerned, and the intellectual unease which makes him explore their ramifications and apparent paradoxes is an important motive force in his work.

It is clear that there is no unified theory behind Wells's early writings – he often seems to be trying ideas out for size, looking at several sides of a question without feeling any pressing need to come to a conclusion. Indeed, there is often to be found in his early essays a delight in contradiction and dissent; Philmus and Hughes gather several essays together in a section entitled 'The Opposite Idea'.[5] This fascination is more than a mere enthusiasm for attacking commonly held beliefs, it is an ironic sensibility perhaps best represented by 'The Rediscovery of the Unique', which points out that the measuring devices which have given us the data on which the triumphant generalisations of modern science are based should also make us realise that all the entities in any class are only more or less alike, and that each in some way is unique. This sensibility is evident in the beautiful last paragraph of the essay, which celebrates the perverseness of the fact that the more we discover, the more we realise how ignorant we are:

> Science is a match that man has just got alight. He thought he was in a room – in moments of devotion, a temple – and that his light would be reflected from and display walls inscribed with wonderful secrets and pillars carved with philosophical systems wrought into harmony. It is a curious sensation, now that the preliminary sputter is over and the flame burns up clear, to see his hands lit and just a glimpse of himself and the patch he stands on visible, and around him, in place of all that human comfort and beauty he anticipated – darkness still.[6]

In his early days, Wells was essentially a *sceptical* speculator, and his scepticism had its own particular flavour. This is an important element in the distinctiveness of his great scientific romances. In *The Time Machine* and its successors he laid down a deliberate challenge to cherished ideas and ideals – including some of his own – and embraced with all due seriousness a pessimism which he actually wanted to resist. This was a kind of experiment in thought which had not often been carried out, and never with such imaginative verve and flair.

The Time Machine (1895) was the first story of the future which dealt neither with history nor with destiny but with evolutionary possibility. Its story deals with the physical re-making of man by adaptation to new circumstances of life, though Wells recognises that for human beings – unlike non-sentient animals – the circumstances of life to which human nature will adapt itself are partly a matter of choice.

The time traveller's first stop is in the world of 802,701 AD, and it is here that he becomes involved in what is going on – elsewhere he is merely an observer. In this world there are two human races: the frail, beautiful and fearless Eloi; and the subterranean predators, the Morlocks. Many commentators see in this division an ironic reflection of social class divisions in Victorian Britain – Disraeli's 'two nations' – but it can better be seen as a reflection of opinions about basic human nature – Disraeli's 'apes and angels'. The Eloi might be seen as the end-product of the kind of progress envisioned by the philosophers of the Enlightenment: sociable, comfortable, morally above suspicion, living a life of innocent ease. The Morlocks are a Huxleyan nightmare: man the predator, master of nature red in tooth and claw.

The question posed by this section of the story is whether the kind of idealistic thought that might approve of the Eloi can possibly be sustained in a post-Darwinian world. The conclusion is that it cannot: the Morlocks emerge from their dark hiding places by night to devour their ethereal cousins. The world cannot be inherited by the meek, because the meek cannot guard their inheritance:

> It is a law of nature that we overlook, that intellectual versatility is the compensation for change, danger and trouble. An animal perfectly in harmony with its environment is a perfect mechanism. Nature never appeals to intelligence unless habit and instinct are

useless. There is no intelligence where there is no change and no
need of change.[7]

In further futures the time traveller finds worlds that are even
more alien. In one brief stop he sees life-forms resembling a
huge white butterfly and a giant crab, but his final observations, made in a world more than thirty million years hence,
show him a sky dominated by a bloated red sun and a world
almost devoid of life. Apart from lichens and liverworts he
catches only an enigmatic glimpse of a thing like a tentacled
football. In the end, the earth proves to be no legacy at all.

Wells was to remain fascinated for a good many years by the
dialectical opposition of ape and angel, Eloi and Morlock, and
his investigations of it were all the more striking while he was
content to dramatise the thesis and antithesis without attempting a synthesis, and without even conceding that a synthesis
might be possible. In his second novel of 1895, *The Wonderful
Visit*, Wells took as his starting point a remark made by Ruskin
that if an angel were to appear in contemporary England some
intrepid sportsman would be sure to shoot him. There are no
Morlocks here; it is only the bestiality in civilised man that is a
point at issue.

The angel of *The Wonderful Visit*, as Wells takes pains to make
clear, is not the angel of religious feeling or popular belief, but
the angel of Art. He falls to earth not from the Christian Heaven
but from the Land of Dreams, a world which complements ours
in being populated exclusively by the products of the imagination. Ironically, the sportsman who brings the angel down is a
man of the cloth whose hobby is ornithology. He is no villain,
though, and the story takes a relatively charitable view of the
animality of man, which is characterised as ignorance, ugliness,
meanness, and most of all an incapacity to live up to the ideals
that are represented by the Land of Dreams. The story ends on a
conventionally hopeful note (albeit confused by a careful ambiguity) which suggests that it is through love that men might
eventually transcend their cruel limitations. But Wells was later
to become impatient with such sentimentality.

A much more melodramatic display of the opposition between the ape and the angel in human nature is offered by *The
Island of Dr Moreau* (1896). *The Time Machine* had been greeted
with great enthusiasm by critics and public alike, but *The Island
of Dr Moreau* called forth many expressions of horror and

disgust. Arthur Lawrence, who interviewed Wells in 1897, was astonished when Wells chose it as his own favourite among his early works.[8] Although many readers saw it as a lurid tale similar to the 'shilling shockers' of the day, it is actually a complex work with more ideative depth than any of the other scientific romances. Its literary antecedents include both *Gulliver's Travels* and *Frankenstein*, and it provides a unique blending of very different perspectives.

The seed of the story can be found in one of Wells's journalistic essays, 'The Limits of Individual Plasticity' (1895), in which he marvelled at the successes achieved by surgeons in grafting, and looked forward to a day when it might be possible to transplant tissues and alter their physiology. In the conclusion of the essay he observed that the moulding of an individual might take in mental as well as physical attributes:

> The thing does not stop at a mere physical metamorphosis. In our growing science of hypnotism we find the promise of a possibility of replacing old inherent instincts by new suggestions, grafting upon or replacing the inherited fixed ideas. Very much indeed of what we call moral education is such an artifical modification and perversion of instinct; pugnacity is trained into courageous self-sacrifice, and suppressed sexuality into pseudo-religious emotion.[9]

The Island of Dr Moreau is a sceptical extension of this argument. Moreau, aspiring to a godlike power of creation, attempts to mould men out of the 'clay' of animal flesh, using surgery to give them humanoid form and psychological techniques to give them humanoid morality: souls with the potential to redeem themselves from the legacy of their origin. Moreau's achievements are displayed to the protagonist, Prendick, as an enigma to be solved. The story begins with Prendick's harrowing experiences while cast away in an open boat – experiences which serve not only to display the beast in human nature, but also to shock him into an unusual state of open-minded innocence by obliterating his civilised expectations. The suspense in the story is sustained by Prendick's various hypotheses concerning the nature of the beast-folk, and no sooner does he realise the entire truth than the situation begins to break down. Moreau's attempts to create a civilised society of beasts fails – the 'perversion of instinct' which he has achieved will not stick and he is killed by one of his creations. This mirrors, ironically, the 'death' of the idea of God the creator in the wake of Darwin. Prendick is saved, but like Gulliver returned from the land of the Houyhnhnms he finds that his new innocence allows him to perceive the world from which he came as a transfiguration of Moreau's island. The men of the church, in particular, come to seem like the Ape Man who gabbled nonsense under the impression that he was doing 'Big Thinks'. Prendick begins to feel as uncomfortable in our world as the angel did in *The Wonderful Visit*, and he becomes a recluse, able to take comfort in reading, in scientific experiments and in the contemplation of the majesty of the night sky. Here the cold vistas of the cosmic perspective become a merciful relief from the assaults of human intimacy. It is hardly surprising that the story called forth such a fierce reaction from many who read it.

Wells undoubtedly took a delight in startling his readers with *The Island of Dr Moreau*. There is a savage Swiftian glee about the way he attacks their self-esteem and comfortable assumptions. Like Swift, though, Wells was also capable of feeling the distress he was inflicting on others, and feeling it very acutely. Unlike the angel in *The Wonderful Visit* Prendick does not come from a world where pain is unknown, and does not have to learn about it from scratch, but he learns to feel a new kind of pain in his realisation of the way the world really works: the pain of being denuded of comforting illusions. It is significant that Moreau, in the story, advances a thesis which Wells toyed with in another of his essays, 'The Province of Pain' (1894), to the effect that a truly rational being would have no more need of pain than a plant or a lower animal. Pain, in this view, is functional only within the limits of a particular evolutionary phase; but transcendence of that phase is not to be attained as cheaply as Moreau believes and hopes, and perhaps ought not to be. Wells did not react like Prendick to the revelation of the post-Darwinian view of human existence; for him, pain was a spur which encouraged him to search for a solution to the Sphinx's riddle of how men might be saved from their animal selves.

The Invisible Man (1897) – the first novel which Wells wrote for Arthur Pearson – has not the imaginative scope of its predecessors. It is basically an attempt to bring a new rigour to the development of a familiar premiss. Recently published fantasies of invisibility included *The Eavesdropper* (1888) by James Payn and 'Stella' (1895) by C.H. Hinton, but even the importation of some scientific jargon into Hinton's scientific romance had not sufficed to make the story credible. The attractions of the basic idea were ready-made – everyone can get a thrill from imagining what one might do if one were invisible – but Wells provided a robust plot framework to rejuvenate it completely. Griffin, the scientist who learns the secret of invisibility, is a slightly Vernian figure: an alienated anti-hero with a grudge against the world, who relishes the chance to pay back his fellow men for the miseries of his early life. (Wells, who had experienced a good measure of poverty, wretchedness and ill-health, must have been familiar with the aesthetics of revenge-fantasy.) As with daydreams of this general type, Griffin's self-assertion is ultimately frustrated: pride, as the book of Proverbs reminds us, goeth before destruction, and haughty manner before a fall. Griffin dies and is re-materialised, and his secret passes into the uneasy custody of the tramp with delusions of opportunity, Thomas Marvel.

The moral of *The Invisible Man* is apparently quite straightforward, and not out of step with the prevailing morality of the time. It resembles a stereotyped format that was to be copiously used in magazine scientific romance: sinister scientist makes discovery; puts it to anti-social use; is destroyed along with his invention; normality is restored. Dozens of such stories were written by numerous writers, but Wells's own versions are never quite as simple as that; they always have an extra layer of irony. 'Filmer' (1901) is perhaps the neatest, featuring a scientist whose aeroplane is lost to the world because his fear of flying prevents him from demonstrating it. It is clear in *The Invisible Man* that Wells has a deal of sympathy with the lone intellectual who can see further than his contemporaries, and can see a measure of tragedy in the idea that such men will not be heard. The failure of Griffin to use his invisibility to attain his ends is in one way reassuring, but the restoration of normalcy is not something that has Wells's wholehearted backing. Several similar stories of advantaged individuals reach similar conclusions, including 'The Man Who Could Work Miracles' (1898) and 'Jimmy Goggles the God' (1898), but the failure of the sighted man in 'The Country of the Blind' (1904) is represented in different terms. It is significant that in 1939 Wells rewrote the ending of that story for a special private press edition, condemning the valley to destruction because its inhabitants will not heed the warnings of impending doom offered to them by the sighted man. By that time, he had come to think of himself as a sighted man in a country of the blind, and though he was far from such vanity in the 1890s, he could not help wondering, in his characteristically sceptical fashion, where the right of the matter truly lay. It is notable that in 'The New Accelerator' (1901) the amoral scientist's decision to make his discovery available to the world, despite its destructive potential, is reported without comment.

Other short stories roughly contemporary with *The Invisible Man* take a more objective view of hypothetical possibility, and have an almost clinical tone about them. Some, like 'The Plattner Story' (1896) and 'The Crystal Egg' (1897), offer enigmatic glimpses of elsewhere, but 'The Star' (1897) eschews such modesty in presenting a laconic journalistic account of a close encounter between the earth and a celestial body that passes through the solar system. Civilisation is destroyed, but the story ends with the conclusions drawn by Martian astronomers, from whose remote viewpoint the earth seems to have suffered remarkably little damage.

The idea that earth might be under observation from Mars, contained in 'The Crystal Egg' as well as 'The Star', is extended dramatically in *The War of the Worlds* (1898), the ultimate future war story and the first of countless horror stories about alien invasions of our world. Other writers, notably Camille Flammarion, had tried to imagine what alien beings might be like, taking their premisses from the theory that evolution would produce beings adapted for life in their particular circumstances. Cosmic tourists had already visited the other worlds of the solar system in various interplanetary stories. Wells, though, was the first man to see the Darwinian struggle for existence as something which could extend across interplanetary space. If Mars, as was sometimes supposed, were a dying world, might not its inhabitants seek to claim a younger and more luxuriant one?

Wells had already observed, in his speculative article 'Intelligence on Mars' (1896) that:

> Granted that there has been an evolution of protoplasm upon Mars, there is every reason to think that the creatures on Mars would be different from the creatures on earth, in form and function, in structure and in habit, different beyond the most bizarre imaginings of nightmare.[10]

In *The War of the Worlds* Wells put flesh on this hypothesis:

> Those who have never seen a living Martian can scarcely imagine the strange horror of their appearance. The peculiar V-shaped mouth with its pointed upper lip, the absence of brow ridges, the absence of a chin beneath the wedge-shaped lower lip, the incessant quivering of the mouth, the Gorgon groups of tentacles, the tumultuous breathing of the lungs in a strange atmosphere, the evident painfulness of movement, due to the greater gravitational energy of the Earth – above all, the extraordinary intensity of the immense eyes – culminated in an effect akin to nausea. There was something fungoid in the oily brown skin, something in the clumsy deliberation of their tedious movements unspeakably terrible. Even at this first encounter, this first glimpse, I was overcome with disgust and dread.[11]

These monsters are, of course, not evil; they are merely playing their part in the cosmic scheme. Just as we have felt no qualms about driving other species to extinction, so they need harbour no particular sympathy for us. Their technology of destruction easily outstrips ours, and when the verdict is finally delivered as to who is fittest to survive in the struggle for existence, it is not we who have out-competed them but plague bacilli. This idea, too, Wells had first broached in an essay on 'The Extinction of Man' (1894), where he had named several possible contenders for the honour of outliving man. The other contenders all featured in his fiction at some stage – crustaceans in *The Time Machine*; intelligent cephalopods in 'In the Abyss' (1896) and ants in 'The Empire of the Ants' (1905).

As with *The Invisible Man*, *The War of the Worlds* has a storyline which follows a pattern which has become a standardised cliché, but it too has considerably greater depth than the many copies of it. Like *The Time Machine* and 'The Star' it emphasises the precariousness of man's dominion, and the ease with which all that we possess – the wealth of knowledge as well as our material heritage – might be swept away. This sense of precariousness was something that Wells was never to lose, and which would be gradually reinforced by the key events of twentieth-century history. Many of Wells's early contemporaries played with the same sense of precariousness without apparently feeling it very deeply, but Wells's own urgency was eventually to prove infectious.

By this time, signs had begun to appear of a change of

direction in Wells's imaginative fiction. He was still exploring possibilities in an entirely open-ended way, but he had also begun the work of trying to find solutions for the problems he was exposing. His earliest long stories of future society, 'A Story of the Days to Come' (1897) and *When the Sleeper Wakes* (1899), are still sceptical in the same fashion as *The Time Machine*, deliberately taking a pessimistic view of likely developments, but in each story the question is broached of whether there is a better way to do things, and whether the rot might be stopped. 'A Story of the Days to Come' is weak enough to fall back on the hoariest of Victorian literary clichés, salvation by inheritance – a *deus ex machina* used to introduce a concluding note of hope into so many 'realistic' novels of industrial squalor. *When the Sleeper Wakes* attempts a more radical exploration of the possibility of progress. Like *Caesar's Column* by Ignatius Donnelly, *When the Sleeper Wakes* can easily be read as a reaction against the comforting optimism of Edward Bellamy's *Looking Backward*, developing the thesis that in the future class divisions will become more marked and exploitation more extreme. Just as there is no real hope to be found in Caesar Lomellini's revolution in Donnelly's novel, so there is no real hope to be found in Ostrog's *coup d'état*, which replaces one set of masters by another. Here there is no escape but rather a symbolic self-sacrifice as the sleeper, Graham, tries to bring down Ostrog's aeroplane in the midst of a great aerial battle, by crashing his own craft into it.

The ending of *When the Sleeper Wakes* is enigmatically cloaked in ambiguity, and there is little in the story that might be reckoned constructive social speculation. The war against dystopian possibility is begun, but hardly carried forward towards any alternative vision of Utopian possibility. In his speculative essays, though, Wells was soon to embark upon this task. The sceptical journalist playing with exciting ideas gave way to the earnest extrapolator trying to discover the actual shape of the future, and to discover in that future the social salvation of mankind.

Anticipations of the Reaction of Mechanical and Scientific Progress Upon Human Life and Thought (1901) is the first significant work in the genre of 'futurology' – though Wells does not use that term, referring instead to 'quite serious forecasts and inductions of things to come'. In a footnote referring to the very first page he made it quite clear that what he was doing in this book was something different from what he had done in his futuristic fiction, and something for which fiction was ill-adapted:

> But from its very nature, and I am writing with the intimacy of one who has tried, fiction can never be satisfactory in this application. Fiction is necessarily concrete and definite; it permits of no open alternatives; its aim of illusion prevents a proper amplitude of demonstration, and modern prophecy should be, one submits, a branch of speculation and should follow with all decorum the scientific method. The very form of fiction carries with it something of disavowal; indeed, very much of the Fiction of the Future pretty frankly abandons the prophetic altogether, and becomes polemical, cautionary, or idealistic, and a mere footnote and commentary to our present discontents.[12]

There is much in this statement that is sensible, and there is a certain tragedy in the fact that having made this observation Wells then proceeded to forget it, or to ignore its implications. After 1901 there was always a confusion of motives in Wells's speculative fiction; although he never fell into the simple trap of trying to cast his 'quite serious forecasts and inductions of things to come' in a fictional mould he nevertheless imported something of the purpose of his futurological writing into his fiction, and thus transformed it subtly in character. Previously, he had been a pioneer in the *terra incognita* of the scientific imagination, looking to see what might be found there with no real thought of a destination or target. After 1901, though, his exploration was guided by a sense of mission; his scepticism was tainted by a creed, and that creed became a cage confining and perverting the instinct of his vaulting imagination. It is therefore not surprising that the last of his truly great scientific romances was one that he composed almost in parallel with *Anticipations: The First Men in the Moon* (1901).

To some extent, *The First Men in the Moon* carries forward themes initiated in *The Island of Dr Moreau* and *The War of the Worlds*. In the description of the society of the Selenites which Cavor sends back from the moon Wells offers another post-Darwinian nightmare: a species which has taken over from the forces of natural selection the task of adapting its individuals to their mode of life. Here is a society which has 'solved' the problem which faces all human societies: the problem of integrating individuals into a complex political hierarchy, specialising without complaint in many different kinds of work, which offer very different experiential rewards and penalties. This is the imaginative prototype for a nightmare view of the human future which was to appear in several later scientific romances, most notably Aldous Huxley's *Brave New World*.

There is, however, another element in the story which connects it also to other stories which Wells published that year: 'Filmer' and 'The New Accelerator'. Like those stories it poses a question regarding the social role and social responsibility of the scientist. Here there is offered a careful contrast between two characters, Bedford and Cavor. The former is a down-to-earth, *practical* man, a modern entrepreneur. The latter, by contrast, is detached from the ordinary currents of social life, operating in an abstract world of thought. In a sense, the two men have very different adventures on the moon. Bedford's is a tale of dramas and disasters, threats and escapes; there is something in his exploits for him to enjoy, but his only eventual goal is to get back safely to the comforts of home and the restoration of normalcy. It is entirely appropriate that he should return from the moon while Cavor remains there, and similarly appropriate that when *his* story is complete Cavor should then take up the tale in his broadcasts, adding a new dimension to it. Cavor's goal is discovery and the increase of knowledge, and the comforts of home and normalcy mean little to him. Unfortunately, his chosen detachment is only partial, because what he does in the pursuit of his personal quest inevitably rebounds upon the world of his fellow men; though his invention – unlike Gibberne's New Accelerator – is lost, his attempts to explain the ways of men to the Grand Lunar have their effect. When his messages to earth are cut off, his fellow men can only wait and wonder what the consequences of his recklessness might be.

It is interesting that *Anticipations* takes a rather different view of the likely impact of the activities of scientists upon the wider society. (This is, indeed, the first instance of the general rule that while fiction about the future has always been predominantly anxious, non-fiction about the future has always been predominantly hopeful.) Although he imagines a situation which will probably get worse (in the sense of becoming more chaotic) before it gets better, Wells nevertheless imagines that the seeds of a new order are already planted. As far as its technological prophecies are concerned the book has enjoyed mixed fortunes – there are some perceptive comments about the probable nature of future wars, though these are weakened by the slightly surprising statement that 'I do not think it at all probable that aeronautics will ever come into play as a serious modification of transport and communication'[13] – but the core of the argument is really concerned with the evolution of social classes. In striking contrast to the Marxist analysis Wells proposes that four main social classes will emerge, albeit unclearly and overlapping one another:

> Here, then . . . are the main social elements of the coming time: (i) the element of irresponsible property; (ii) the helpless super-seded poor, that broad base of mere toilers now no longer essential; (iii) a great inchoate mass of more or less capable people engaged more or less consciously in applying the growing body of scientific knowledge to the general needs, a great mass that will inevitably tend to organise itself in a system of interdependent educated classes with a common consciousness and aim, but which may or may not succeed in doing so; and (iv) a possibly equally great number of non-productive persons living in and by the social confusion.[14]

Wells's principal interest is, of course, in the third class: the socially responsible scientists who could and might assume command of the world as idealistic technocrats, guiding it to safety and happiness. In the later chapters of *Anticipations* he proposes that such men will become the custodians of a New Republic, espousing a rationalist religion which will permit moral conviction without superstition. In this New Republic there will be an educational system designed to cultivate both the minds and bodies of men, allowing a transcendence, if not an extirpation, of the 'mean and ugly and bestial' aspects of their character.

All of Wells's subsequent futuristic fictions are coloured by this judgment of future probability and future necessity. It is not simply that he used fiction to display such a historical pattern, as in *A Modern Utopia, Men Like Gods* and *The Shape of Things to Come*, but that whenever he undertook a purely hypothetical endeavour it would only soar so far into the unknown before being captured by the gravity of this idea and brought into orbit about it.

Wells followed up *Anticipations* with *The Discovery of the Future* (1902), a pamphlet containing a lecture delivered to the

Royal Institution in January of that year. Here he begins by contrasting two kinds of men: those whose view of things is determined by their past experiences, and those whose view is determined by their expectations of the future. Bedford was surely an example of the former kind of man, but the latter is a transfigured Cavor: a Cavor brought back to earth and transfused with a quasi-messianic quality. Wells goes on to compare the knowledge which we have of the past, through the agencies of memory and history, with our ignorance of the future, and alleges that although we can never have any insight into the future which mirrors memory, we might be able to build up a set of expectations which will provide a futuristic equivalent of history. This is, in its way, a fatal conclusion; having reached it, Wells could hardly help committing himself to a search for the *real* future instead of being content to wander in infinite possibilities. His fantasy novel of 1902, *The Sea Lady*, is a bitter-sweet confection about the lure of exotic romance. Its protagonist forsakes the opportunities of conventional marriage to follow his lovely mermaid, but at the end of the chapter whose title declares 'Moonshine Triumphant' we are reminded that he has chosen death. Wells was to remain permanently suspicious of the allure of the extraordinary, though he recognised its power well enough: 'The Door in the Wall' (1906), which is a companion-piece to *The Sea Lady*, remains one of his most touching stories. The same suspicion is responsible for his remarkably uncharitable and dismissive commentary on his early scientific romances in his Preface to the Gollancz omnibus of 1933.

It is perhaps appropriate that after writing *The Discovery of the Future* Wells should produce the most prophetic of his short stories, 'The Land Ironclads' (1903), which foresees tank warfare. His next full-length scientific romance, however, is something rather different. *The Food of the Gods and How it Came to Earth* (1904) takes up, in a way, where 'The New Accelerator' left off, exploring the social consequences of the reckless release of a new discovery: the nutrient *Herakleophorbia*, which makes all creatures grow to giant size. In the early part of the novel there are many melodramatic encounters between men and giant vermin, but the real theme of the story is the metaphorical and actual division of mankind into two species: 'little people' and giants. The giants become the future-orientated men of *The Discovery of the Future*, standing for science and wisdom against the superstitious conservatism of their parents. The new men are literally too big to be confined by the traditions of the past and the institutions of contemporary society. The tone of the story changes markedly as it extends, from relatively amiable satire to spiteful sarcasm, but it ends with a visionary rhapsody that recapitulates (using the same metaphors and some of the same words) the fiercely optimistic rhetoric that closes *The Discovery of the Future*.

The Food of the Gods was written while Wells was briefly involved with the Fabian Society, and it helps to highlight both the kinship and the conflict between his ideas and those of the Society. The technocratic aspects of his thought are here de-emphasised, and there is much talk instead of fraternity – the *brotherhood* of the giants. On the other hand, there is an impatience in the story which did not sit well with the Fabian insistence on gradual evolution towards socialism, Although it is in no sense Marxist, Wellsian socialism was revolutionary rather than evolutionary, and he always believed that the new order could not emerge unless or until the old one was dis-solved or smashed.

The Food of the Gods was followed in 1905 by an explicit attempt at Utopian design, *A Modern Utopia*, whose presenta-tion is a peculiar amalgam of essay and fiction. In an introduc-tory note Wells offers it as the concluding work in a series begun with *Anticipations* and continued with *Mankind in the Making* (1903), a polemic on the appropriate nurture and educa-tion of the citizens of the future. It presents an image of an alternate world (incarnated for convenience on a hypothetical planet 'far in the deeps of space') run by the New Republicans of *Anticipations*, here formalised into an Order of Samurai. Of the other developing social classes mentioned in *Anticipations*, 'the element of irresponsible property' has here been elimin-ated; the 'non-productive' speculators have been banished; and the poor inessential toilers are a dwindling minority of educa-tional failures. Wells tries to prevent the picture from becoming utterly flat and static by injecting passages of argumentative dialogue between the person who has glimpsed Utopia and a sceptical botanist, and also dissociates himself as actual author from the narrative voice, or hypothetical author, of the text. The element of scepticism thus introduced, however, is a pale shadow of the robust scepticism that had characterised his work only a few years earlier.

The first line of the 'Note to the Reader' and the last line of the text of *A Modern Utopia* both strive to give the impression that Wells had got Utopia off his chest and would not need to trouble himself with it again. He quickly turned instead to *Kipps* (1905), the second and more successful of his attempts to write effective contemporary fiction and bid for a reputation as a serious novelist. The earlier attempt was *Love and Mr Lewisham* (1900). But he was not done with Utopia by any means, and in a curious fashion *Kipps* led him straight back to it. *Kipps* was a very popular book, painting a picture of the life of the lower middle classes that many readers found charming and appealing, but in order to achieve that effect Wells had had to don rose-tinted glasses. In his next book, *In the Days of the Comet* (1906), another scientific romance, Wells began by offering a much bleaker image of the world from which he had escaped – a dark world direly in need of redemption. Here, redemption comes, in the shape of a miraculous cometary gas which suffuses the air men breathe with an agent of moral purification. Evil impulses are wiped out at a stroke, and the brotherhood of man is secured in an instant. The remainder of the story tells of the reconstruction of social relationships.

The magical comet is the least convincing of all the literary devices that Wells used in his scientific romances, though it is no more impossible than the time machine, the food of the gods or Cavorite. The use of such devices has always stirred up controversy among the readers of scientific romance, calling forth the censure of would-be speculative purists (like Jules Verne, who objected strenuously to Cavorite in a famous interview[15]), but scientific romance could not survive without them. It appears, though, that Wells had grown a little weary of the business of constructing a jargon of apology to give his inventions an aura of verisimilitude. When a writer has a strong sense of purpose like Wells's, he is bound to come to regard such devices in a purely utilitarian light, and it is noticeable that most of Wells's later fantasies are quite careless in their deployment of fanciful ideas. *In the Days of the Comet* differs from the early scientific romances in that the comet's properties are simply a means invented to secure an end, whereas the creativity of earlier stories was at least partly invested in working out what the logical consequences might be of a particular invention. The direction of the speculative argument in *In the Days of the Comet* is the reverse of that in, say, 'The

71

Man Who Could Work Miracles' – it is a matter of sentence first and verdict afterwards.

Wells was not finished, though, with the more familiar mode of speculative fiction. By now he was aware that he had made a mistake in *Anticipations*, and that the coming of the aeroplane really was going to make a big difference to the world. He realised, in fact, that George Griffith – a writer of whom he did not hold a high opinion – had been more perceptive than seemed likely. Wry acknowledgement of this fact is made in the first chapter of *The War in the Air* (1908), where Bert Smallways is given a glimpse of things to come by reading *The Outlaws of the Air*. (Alas, Griffith was already dead, and hence unable to accept the compliment.)

The War in the Air begins, like *In the Days of the Comet*, in the world of the lower middle classes, and deals with a dramatic transformation of that world. It is a remarkable rarity in being a future war novel which uses the viewpoint of ordinary people, and deals primarily with the effects of aerial warfare on those ordinary people. Although Bert Smallways gets involved in the action, he is basically a spectator at the carnival of destruction, and he sees it from a perspective very different from that adopted by George Griffith or William le Queux. Because of this, the shape of Wells's argument brings him to a conclusion very different from that characteristic of the future war novels written before 1914: civilisation is virtually obliterated, and the Scientific Age is brought to an end.

This anxiety lingered in Wells's mind for a little while – he published an article in the New York *World* in 1909 called 'The Possible Collapse of Civilisation' – but it did not stick long. Though *The War in the Air* ends with Old Tom stubbornly asserting that the war 'didn't ought ever to 'ave begun', Wells was too wrapped up in the idea of a new order rising from the wreckage of the old to maintain an anti-war stance. Six years were to pass before Wells wrote another future war novel – six years during which he devoted his creative energies to the quest for literary respectability, producing in succession *Tono-Bungay* (1909), *Ann-Veronica* (1909), *The History of Mr Polly* (1910), *The New Machiavelli* (1911), *Marriage* (1912) and *The Passionate Friends* (1913), and six years during which the world crept to the very brink of the actual Great War – but when he did, it was a novel which accepted wholeheartedly the idea of a war to end war, despite the fact that it anticipated not merely aerial bombing, but the use of atomic bombs.

Wells's atomic bombs, in *The World Set Free* (1914), are not the cataclysmic explosives which were later to be widely imagined (and eventually to be invented); he imagined that a chain reaction would produce a *series* of explosions, so that the bombs once dropped keep on exploding and force the evacuation of the affected cities. In the ruins, though, is forged the international league of one-time rulers and intellectuals which sets out to exploit the constructive possibilities of atomic power and hence make the world a place fit for men to live in.

When the war actually began, Wells greeted it with enthusiasm. His pamphlet *The War That Will End War* (1914) collected a series of newspaper articles representing the war as a great opportunity and not a disaster:

> This is already the vastest war in history. It is war not of nations, but of mankind. It is a war to exorcise a world-madness and end an age . . .
> The character of the new age that must come out of the catastrophies of this epoch will be no mechancial consequence of inanimate forces. Will and ideas will take a larger part in this *swirl*-ahead than they have ever taken in any previous collapse . . . This is a time of incalculable plasticity. For the men who know what they want, the moment has come. It is the supreme opportunity . . .[16]

In *What is Coming? A Forecast of Things After the War* (1916) Wells was still singing a similar tune, though he had by then decided that the war would last a lot longer than he expected in August 1914. Here he anticipates that socialism will be forced upon the nations once they have spent themselves in their orgy of bloodletting. In the same year, he wrote his most successful novel, *Mr Britling Sees It Through*, an exercise in moral justification whose protagonist is converted to belief in God, reflecting a similar flirtation with faith that Wells was experiencing, and which was explained in all its unorthodox detail in *God the Invisible King* (1917). Wells was later to regret this phase in his work and his career, and apologised for the belligerence of much of his journalistic writing. His autobiography is highly apologetic about his attacks on conscientious objectors, such as can be found in *War and the Future* (1917). He was in a more constructive mood, though, in the last of his wartime essays, *In the Fourth Year: Anticipations of a World Peace* (1918), which was an important piece of propaganda for the League of Nations. Afterwards, of course, he realised that he had once again gone wrong, and that *The War in the Air* had been a more pertinent book than he had realised; the preface that he added to the 1921 edition claimed that the thesis of the book had not been damaged by the real war, but rather underlined. By that time, though, there was nothing in the least unusual about the observation.

It is ironic that the man who brought scientific romance so swiftly to an early peak of perfection should have come so quickly to despise the genre. While his wonderful early works provided a guiding light for many other writers who aspired to follow in his footsteps he became dismissive of their merits, regarding them almost as embarrassing juvenilia. Partly, this has to do with literary and intellectual prestige. By 1900 Wells had conceived the ambition to be a great man of letters; later he became impatient with the limitations of the literary sphere, and sought simply to be a great man. Neither ambition really seemed, in his eyes or the eyes of the world, to be consonant with a unique talent for writing exotically fanciful adventure stories about time machines, nasty Martians and invisible men. Partly, though, it had to do with changes in Wells himself, when he developed that sense of philosophical purpose which took over his speculative endeavours. He thought that sense of philosophical purpose was necessary to make his work truly serious, but in fact it only served to change the kind of seriousness that there was in his work. It remains a matter of opinion which kind of seriousness is to be preferred, and the fact that the scientific romances have remained much more popular than Wells's later speculative works is not strictly relevant to the decision (it is their playfulness rather than their seriousness which is admired) but there is a case to be made for the assertion that when Wells sacrificed the special kind of innocence which Prendick brought to the island of Dr Moreau his work lost much of its impetus. The purgation of old expectations which, in his case, was achieved during his first year at the Normal School of Science was only a temporary one. A similar pattern will be seen in the biographies of many other writers of scientific romance; their scientific romances often belong to the earliest phase of their careers, and the form is often abandoned thereafter, save sometimes for a brief return late in life.

The Major Writers of the Pre-War Period

M.P. Shiel

Matthew Phipps Shiel was born on 21 July 1865, in Montserrat in the West Indies. He was the son of a Methodist preacher, but turned against the faith of his father in his early teens. He attended King's College, London, for a while, and also studied for some months at Bart's Hospital with the intention of becoming a doctor, but he drifted into the literary world instead. His first short story sale was to the magazine *Rare Bits* in 1889, and he began to place other stories with the new popular magazines of the 1890s. His first book, a trilogy of exotic detective stories, *Prince Zaleski*, was published in 1895. This collection and *Shapes in the Fire* (1896) were issued by John Lane, and were contemporary with Lane's *Yellow Book*. Both volumes share with the work most typical of the *Yellow Book* a self-conscious decadence and an interest in unconventional philosophies of art and life. These affectations are superimposed on stories which may well have been inspired by Poe – the second collection includes some highly-coloured horror stories.

Shiel seems to have been eased into novel-writing as a result of his friendships with other literary men. His first short novel, *The Rajah's Sapphire* (1896), was written at the behest of W.T. Stead, the one-time editor of the *Pall Mall Gazette*, whose exploits in circulation building put even Arthur Pearson in the shade. Stead told this story to Shiel, who produced the written version for a new periodical which Stead had planned, although it failed before the story could be printed there. Stead had been one of the journalists campaigning for the reform of Britain's armed forces and increased naval spending, but he was also a supporter of the international peace movement. It was, however, another friend – Louis Tracy – who suggested that Shiel should jump on the future war bandwagon. Tracy had just written *The Final War* for Pearson, and suggested that some contemporary trouble in China might lend topicality to a tale of East/West war. Shiel wrote 'The Empress of the Earth' for Pearson's *Short Stories*, and it was subsequently reprinted in book form as *The Yellow Danger* in 1898.

'The Empress of the Earth' is England and *The Yellow Danger* is a work bursting with Anglo-Saxon pride in a fevered manner akin to that of the final section of *The Final War*. Here the future war is not merely a war to end war but a struggle between the

75

yellow race and the white to settle the dominion of the world (a struggle that was promised, but never delivered, in *The Angel of the Revolution*). The evil genius who becomes the instrument of the yellow race is Dr Yen How, while the Englishman selected by destiny to oppose him is the midshipman John Hardy. After numerous naval battles, captures and escapes, all Europe falls except England, but the invasion fleet which sets out to capture the island fails in its task, and many of its troop-carriers are fed to the Maëlstrom. Prisoners infected with plague are then released in mainland Europe to wipe out the occupying forces. The novel is ruthlessly nasty minded, and apart from the implicit racism of its theme (backed up in the text by some social Darwinist arguments) it contains some highly unflattering analyses of the Chinese character. (Comment on the supposed alien psychology of the yellow race was not uncommon at the time; Stead had written on the topic and a similar thinking is evident in some of Grant Allen's anthropological stories.)

One must beware of taking the ideas in *The Yellow Danger* too seriously. Shiel was a writer who took great delight in startling his readers. He loved to strike a pose at once casual and provocative, to give offence in a carefree but never unsubtle fashion. The *outré* and the unpopular had a natural attraction for him, and he would avoid orthodoxy at any price. Even more than Wells he was attracted to 'opposite ideas', and was prepared to try them out with all due sincerity.

Shiel's future war stories were very different from Griffith's, paying relatively little attention to the possibilities of new weaponry. But they were different, too, from the kind of story that William le Queux and other, more journalistic writers produced, which made much of the decisions of generals and the tactical movements of forces. Shiel tended instead to a quasi-symbolic format whereby a conflict between nations or races would be crystallised into a duel between individuals embodying conflicting philosophies. *Contraband of War* (1899), inspired by the Spanish–American war, follows this pattern, and so does his second East/West war story, *The Yellow Wave* (1905), which was provoked by the Russo–Japanese war. It is very noticeable that *The Yellow Wave* is purged of the crude racism of *The Yellow Danger*, abandons social Darwinism, and ends with a fervent plea for harmony and the union of races under socialism. In both *Contraband of War* and *The Yellow Wave* there is far less distinction between hero and villain than in *The Yellow Danger*, and this too was to become a marked feature of Shiel's work; he seems to have stopped thinking in terms of good and evil in order gradually to evolve a new moral sensibility. Paul Spencer argues in his essay 'Shiel versus Shiel' that Shiel moved from Christianesque morality towards a Buddhist philosophy, and that even in this early phase of his work it makes sense to talk of *yin* and *yang* rather than good and evil.[17]

Contraband of War was followed by two historical novels, *Cold Steel* (1899) and *The Man-Stealers* (1900), and then by Shiel's most important scientific romances, *The Lord of the Sea* (1901) and *The Purple Cloud* (1901). These two novels are actually parts of a trilogy, the third part of which is *The Last Miracle*. *The Last Miracle* appears to have been the first of the three to be written, probably in 1897, but it was not published until 1906, by which time it may well have been revised – the concluding section, at least, is a late addition. Shiel may initially have planned four books rather than three, as the stories are represented as visions transmitted from the future via a medium in trance; four notebooks are mentioned, though the introduction to *The Lord of the Sea* mentions plans only to publish three of them.[18]

The Lord of the Sea has proved the most controversial of Shiel's works, becoming the subject of a vitriolic attack by Sam Moskowitz on account of alleged anti-Semitism, said by Moskowitz to compare in intensity with Hitler's *Mein Kampf*.[19] There *is* a certain amount of anti-Semitic comment in the text, and the story's villain, Frankl, is portrayed as a grasping Jew after the fashion of Shylock or Fagin. Many other versions of this stereotype can be found in contemporary British fiction, and it can hardly be reckoned unusual, but what makes Moskowitz's opinion highly questionable is the fact that the hero of the book is also a Jew – and no ordinary Jew, but the Messiah who returns to his people their Promised Land.

The Lord of the Sea begins with an influx of Jewish refugees into England, following their expulsion from other European nations. They become a powerful political and economic force, bringing a new prosperity with them, but pride triggers a fierce feud between the rich landowner Baruch Frankl and the young farmer Richard Hogarth. Frankl frames Hogarth for murder, but he escapes from prison and with the aid of a cache of diamonds recovered from a meteorite he finances the building of giant floating fortresses that give him command of the sea-lanes. He uses this advantage to blackmail the nations into peace and social progress.

There are many early scientific romances in which the possessors of new powers of destruction blackmail the world in this fashion, but *The Lord of the Sea* is exceptional in offering an elaborate account of the reforms demanded by Hogarth. The foundation-stone of his socialism is the conviction that all land must be in common ownership and all rents devoted to the Commonweal – a theory closely resembling that proposed by the American economist Henry George in *Progress and Poverty* (1879). For Hogarth and Shiel, however, progress is not simply a matter of economic reforms, it is a basic evolutionary process. Like Herbert Spencer, Shiel saw social and biological evolution as different aspects of the same thing, and believed Nature to have an inbuilt tendency towards improvement. Although he had given up Christianity Shiel was still very much a deist; as a materialist he believed that there is nothing in the world but matter in motion, but his God was the motive force which keeps the material universe in a state of ceaseless change. He would not accept motion as the result of some random Epicurean *clinamen*, but insisted that change is both purposive and progressive: in his non-speculative novel *Unto the Third Generation* (1903) he unhesitatingly declares it 'proved' that 'matter is moral'.[20]

Hogarth's grand plan fails in the novel; he is betrayed by a man he mistakenly trusts. He succeeds, though, on a small scale, because he is encouraged to fulfil a prophecy and return all the Jews to Palestine during his brief span of power. After his fall, he joins them in their exile, and under his progressive leadership Israel becomes a land flowing with milk and honey.

The Purple Cloud is generally – and rightly – considered to be Shiel's finest work. It is as much a theological fantasy as a scientific romance: an apocalyptic tale of a new Adam and Eve, told as a first-person narrative by its guilt-ridden hero. The narrator, Adam Jeffson, is tempted by his fiancée to commit murder in order to win a place in an expedition to the north pole. It has been prophesied that disaster will follow if the pole is reached, because it is in some mysterious symbolic sense the forbidden Tree of the Knowledge of Good and Evil. Jeffson does reach the pole, though he sees it only through a veil of illusion, and is plagued by further hallucinations as he makes his lonely way south into a world depopulated by the volcanic release of a

poisonous purple gas. His search for survivors is a transcendental voyage through an inner hell, interrupted by bouts of
profound despair which alternate with paroxysms of feverish
activity – including his destruction of London by fire and his
looting of the treasures of Europe for his own fabulous palace.
The story is fragmentary, breaking off at one point for a period
of seventeen years.

Jeffson is tormented throughout by opposing forces within
him, whose battleground he seems to have been throughout his
life. He characterises them 'the white' and 'the black', and in the
torment of his guilt considers himself the instrument of the
latter, though the former will not abandon him. He finds in
himself a symbol of the world, his moods and struggles reflecting the plight of all life in its slow and fitful evolution. He
abandons himself to death more than once, but is preserved as
if for a special purpose, which becomes clear when he finds a
second survivor: a girl, younger than the world's emptiness,
born in an airtight chamber where her mother was imprisoned.
He will not let the girl name herself Eve, rebelling against the
scheme by which 'the white' seems intent on making him the
father of a new race. His rebellion fades, though, as the girl's
presence in his private world brings him slowly back to sanity.
Though disaster *has* followed his acquaintance with the Tree of
Knowledge of Good and Evil, the suffering of the world is not
without purpose, and Jeffson learns the force of 'the one motto
and watchword proper to the riot and Odyssey of Life in
general': 'Though He slay me, yet I will trust in Him.'[21]

Though it is heavy with scriptural allusions, the hypothetical
theology of *The Purple Cloud* is by no means Christian. It is a
synthesis of *Genesis* and *Job*, and its motive force – like that of
much of the Old Testament – is the attempt to reconcile the
notion of God's essential benignity with the appalling suffering
of the world. Shiel will not follow the New Testament path of
creating an anti-god; there is nothing at all Manichean about
his imagined contest between black and white, whose dialectical opposition is part of the motor of progress. In order to find
the true knowledge of good and evil Adam Jeffson (whose
surname, of course, is a contraction of Jehovah's son; in his
suffering he is Everyman) must penetrate the veil of illusion
whose too-simple implication is that suffering is evil. He is
reluctant to bear the responsibility for fathering a new race to
live, like the old, under the lash of 'racks, rack-rents, wrongs,

sorrows, horrors', but he must learn that God is, after all, moral, and must be trusted.

Shiel continued to develop this thesis, albeit somewhat obliquely, in his next novels, *The Weird o'It* (1902), *Unto the Third Generation* (1903) and *The Evil That Men Do* (1904), which are riotous stories of moral education through melodramatic adventure. It is in *The Weird o'It* that Shiel first uses the notion of 'overmen', which he borrowed from Nietzsche, though he is careful to differentiate his use of it from Nietzsche's. Shiel and Nietzsche are equally enthusiastic in championing evolution, and in exhorting men to become overmen; but Nietzsche is a moral individualist whose overman must stand aside from and gain power over the common herd; while Shiel is a moral collectivist who insists that overmen must not think of themselves, but of the whole race, and must be ever ready to suffer and sacrifice themselves for the common good. *The Yellow Wave* concludes with a spectacular instance of such martyrdom.

The Last Miracle, which should have begun the trilogy of futuristic romances, becomes instead a kind of conclusion to this phase of Shiel's work, though it becomes awkwardly broken-backed in so doing, because the main story clearly belongs to the beginning of the chain of thought, and the epilogue to the end. As with so many of Shiel's works it features a duel of wits between two men: Aubrey Langler, a gentle humanist modelled, Shiel later said, on Matthew Arnold; and Baron Kolar, a Nietzschean enemy of Christianity whose villainy ultimately turns out to have some of God's motive force in it. Kolar has imprisoned a priest whom Langler wishes to release, and also stages a series of fake miracles to entrap the trust of unwary Christians, hoping to destroy the Christian faith when he reveals them to be false. The political background of the story includes controversy surrounding a eugenics bill to provide for the sterilisation of 'diseased persons' – an element of social Darwinism which recalls the fact that the story must first have been composed before or alongside *The Yellow Danger*. It is interesting to note that *The Last Miracle* was first drafted some years before Guy Thorne's best-selling *When it was Dark* (1904), which deals with a similar plot to destroy Christianity with contrived evidence, though Thorne takes an opposite view of the merits of the scheme.

In *The Last Miracle* the final confrontation between Langler and Kolar ends badly for both, but their deaths are of no great consequence – the real climax of the story is not their final duel but the appendix which leaps forward into the future to offer a glimpse of the new religious order which rises out of the ashes of demolished Christianity:

Religion is a modern thing like electrometers. Not that Plato, Jesus, the cavemen, were not religious a little in their villager-way, but our religion is a river to their trickle: they hadn't our data, our *means*, to be religious. Isn't religion an attitude of adoration and donation? the donation depending on the adoration? the adoration depending upon knowledge of the Being adored, upon science? Adoration is a compound of (1) awe, and (2) love; and to have it we must *know* that God is (1) great, and (2) greatly good. But no ancient could suspect these: Jesus believed that the stars would some day 'fall from heaven', and that God is littley good, 'loving' village Tom and Dick; *we* know The Gospel, The Tidings of Great Joy, that (1) the stars are suns, (2) that we come from monkeys. Our stars can't 'fall' upon Jerusalem 'like figs'; a thousand million earths can fall into Betelgeuse and be lost, and there are doubtless billions and billions of Betelgeuses in a billion island-universes, of which a few are visible to our eye-pieces. God's great: we have awe. And we are related to snakes: there is a principle of progress in Being leading on to lives that will one day be finer, wiser, more wildly delighted, than ever entered into our little hearts to fancy. Now, how greatly good – Ah, the glad tidings! – we can't help loving: we have adoration. And from adoration springs donation, which is religion in the stricter sense – that which 'binds us back' from living to please our roughest upper-self: so the village-religions said 'live to please the neighbours, Tom, Dick'. But the evolution of this? Is it not 'live to please the distant, invisible: Man, Society'? And the evolution of this? Is it not 'live to please even the non-existent, the still unborn'? [22]

The finalisation of this prospectus for a new religiosity was followed by a decline in Shiel's productivity. He published only four more novels before the outbreak of the Great War, plus a collection of short stories, and then he published nothing at all for nearly a decade. Two of the four novels are scientific romances: *The Isle of Lies* (1909) offers a further development of the Shielian notion of an overman, by producing a curious exemplar; while *The Dragon* (1913; later revised as *The Yellow Peril*) is basically a new version of *The Yellow Danger*, transfigured to update its intrinsic philosophy.

The Isle of Lies is the story of Hannibal Lepsius, the son of an archaeologist who fathers him and nurtures him for the sole purpose of deciphering some mysterious ideographs which require superhuman insight to penetrate their meaning. He is a custom-built overman, reared in isolation and led to believe that the world at large is inhabited by men of great intellect and magnificent physique, to whose hypothetical standard he must live up. The fraud is successful, but the plan goes awry when visitors come by chance to his island, and carry him away. Later, having found out what the world is really like, he schemes to change it, and becomes involved with a bold project to give the earth an artificial satellite to serve as a second sun. He betrays himself by his own recklessness, as so many of Shiel's heroes do. There is no mention of the new religion of evolution here; instead young Lepsius is to be found reading the gospels intently and looking for the true meaning in the life-history of Jesus. This was an intellectual quest that was to occupy Shiel's attention for many years.

The Dragon, though written after a four-year abstinence, is much more of a reaffirmation of the message of *The Last Miracle* than is *The Isle of Lies*. Here the duellists whose personal struggle represents the great world conflict are the Chinaman Li Ku Yu and Prince Teddy, scion of an imaginary branch of the royal family, who rule Britain in place of the actual House of Windsor. Each of the combatants is abetted by a female partner – Li Ku Yu by the ingenious Oyone and Teddy by a commoner to whom he is secretly wedded (and who remains unaware that she has married the heir to the throne). The plot is all melodrama, an astonishing blend of Cinderella and Fu Manchu, replete with conspiracies and fights, captures and escapes, mistaken identities and perilous misapprehensions. There is more use of advanced weaponry than in Shiel's earlier future war stories, but this is not really important to the story. The climax of the plot is a confrontation which reveals that Li Ku Yu and Teddy are both on the side of progress, disagreeing only about which people is best fitted to take the lead in securing it. Like *The Last Miracle* the novel has an epilogue in which the victorious Teddy sets out his manifesto for change in a speech which echoes the political schemes of Richard Hogarth and the metaphysics of Baron Kolar, though in an unusually confused and faltering manner which suggests a loss of imaginative impetus on the part of its author. Shiel must have thought so too, and he was not a man to grind out hackwork simply to keep the pot boiling; he stopped writing, until the mood should take him again.

Shiel never attained anything like the popularity that Wells won, and though *The Purple Cloud* was admired by connoisseurs it was not greatly popular with the public, who found it far too difficult. Most commentators on Shiel have called attention to his remarkable prose style, which is too wild and convoluted for most tastes, and even those readers capable of perceiving the meaning expressed therein probably would not have been receptive to it. Nevertheless, Shiel is in his way as interesting a writer as Wells, and the two are all the more interesting in juxtaposition, because rarely have two writers provided such a striking pattern of similarities and contrasts.

Both Wells and Shiel fell under the spell of evolutionary theory, to the extent that it provided a philosophical frame for their view of entire existence; but Wells's evolutionism was thoroughly Darwinian while Shiel's was Spencerian. Wells had a keen appreciation of the *precariousness* of progress, a desperate anxiety that when the struggle for existence was settled, man might be among the losers. When he came, therefore, to invent a new religiosity for his New Republicans, and to flirt with faith on his own account, he thought of religiosity in pragmatic terms, as a matter of commitment: God was dead and had, in the Voltairean fashion, to be invented. For Shiel, though, faith came into the matter at a much more fundamental level, for his faith in the thrust of evolution and its inherent progressiveness would not let him doubt that man must have a future even if the world be gassed almost to death. There was nothing pragmatic about his new religiosity, nor was it a voluntary commitment: it was discovered truth which compelled belief and could not allow doubt save through foolish ignorance.

Wells and Shiel were similar, too, in their ideas about the nature and purpose of literature. Wells disputed fiercely with Henry James in order to defend the novel of ideas – the novel as a philosophical vehicle which must not become too introverted in its pursuit of psychological intimacy. Shiel argued in a long essay printed as an introduction to *This Knot of Life* (1909) that the object of art is precisely the same as the object of science and philosophy: to enlarge consciousness of the truth of things, and to serve the sacred cause of Progress. Ironically, though, their attempts to embody similar philosophies in their work led them to cultivate very different methods and merits. Wells, the anxious sceptic, was at his best when he was both anxious and sceptical, in *The Time Machine, The Island of Dr Moreau* and *The War of the Worlds*. Shiel, the victim of a revelation, was at his best when he was most certain, carried along by the fervent celebration of his great discovery. It is no coincidence that Wells wrote plainly, with deadly accuracy, while Shiel wrote explosively, with feverish certainty.

Wells and Shiel were perhaps closest of all in the tenor of their socialism. Both men looked to the emergent class of scientist/intellectual to be the saviours of the world. Both men wanted that class to expand in size to swallow up as great a proportion of the population as could be fitted for it. Wells, though, was always ready to try his hand at modelling the social, political and economic relations of a society of overmen, while Shiel was very reluctant to do so. His overmen are always seen against the background of a world of ordinary men, where they act and appear as villains rather than as heroes because of their lust to change it. Shiel's very certainty about the progressive thrust of evolution made him awkward and ambivalent when he came to assign roles to individuals, while Wells's basic unease made him look for men of unshakeably firm purpose to snatch order from the jaws of chaos. Wells, desperately unsure of the future, was always trying to make it concrete. Shiel, convinced of the morality of matter, was content to discover progress, and yet leave its future course unmapped.

Arthur Conan Doyle

Arthur Conan Doyle was born on 22 May 1859 in Edinburgh, the son of artist and civil servant Charles A. Doyle. His grandfather had also been an artist, and his uncle was the famous illustrator Richard Doyle. He was educated at the Jesuit school, Stonyhurst, where the teachers wanted to prepare him for holy orders, but he resisted (in spite of an offer to his hard-pressed family of free schooling) and became an agnostic materialist. He studied medicine at Edinburgh University, taking his MB in 1881 and eventually becoming an MD in 1885. He was greatly impressed by two of his teachers at Edinburgh – Drs Bell and Rutherford – and was later to borrow aspects of their character in portraying Sherlock Holmes and Professor

Challenger. He was physically strong and an enthusiastic sportsman – he boxed, played rugby, and was very fond of cricket.

While he was still qualifying as a doctor he undertook two trips as a ship's surgeon, and also sold some early short stories. His first sale, 'The Mystery of Sassassa Valley', was to *Chambers' Edinburgh Journal* in 1879, and this was quickly followed by 'The American's Tale', about a giant Venus fly-trap capable of consuming a man. For most of the 1880s he had a medical practice in Southsea, on the south coast of England, but it never really thrived. His literary career gradually gained ground, though, and he placed stories with various literary journals. Some were fantastic, including 'The Captain of the Polestar' in *Belgravia* in 1883 and 'The Great Keinplatz Experiment' (1885), a story of identity-exchange with pseudo-scientific trimmings. He did not make much impact with his early novel-length Sherlock Holmes stories, *A Study in Scarlet* (1887) and *The Sign of Four* (1890), but fared better with his historical novels, *Micah Clarke* and *The White Company* – the latter was serialised in the *Cornhill* in 1890–1. It was, though, with the founding of *The Strand* that he really came into his own as an author, when he began the first classic series of Sherlock Holmes short stories and became a legend along with his hero.

Doyle's first significant essay in scientific romance was the short novel *The Doings of Raffles Haw* (1891), which he apparently wrote in seventeen days. It tells the story of a reclusive scientist who discovers a way to manufacture gold. He wants to use his instant wealth for the benefit of his fellow men, but cannot figure out quite how to go about it. He receives some well-intentioned advice, but his attempts at philanthropy all go wrong. He decides in the end that he is doing more harm than good, laboriously transmutes his vast hoard into the dust from which it came, and destroys his invention. The story may be taken as the archetype of the 'no-good-will-come-of-it-all' school of scientific romance, so widely practised by lesser magazine writers like Cutcliffe Hyne. A similar spirit can be seen in the short story 'The Los Amigos Fiasco' (1892), in which the progressive inhabitants of Los Amigos install the world's first electric chair to replace the obsolete hangman's noose. Unfortunately, the chair not only fails to kill its victim but charges him with electric vitality, making him virtually invulnerable to the traditional methods of lethal dispatch. It was in this period, too, that Doyle wrote 'The Terror of the Blue John Gap', eventually to be published in *The Strand* in 1910, about the exploits of a cave bear mysteriously left over from prehistoric times in northern England.

Doyle seems to have regarded his fantastic tales and his detective stories as hackwork, and something of a distraction from his more serious literary endeavours. He was always anxious to be done with Holmes, despite the ever-increasing fees which the Holmes stories brought in, and eventually sent him to his premature death over the Reichenbach Falls (though of course he was forced to relent in this decision after the turn of the century). It is perhaps surprising that after Wells was so successful in the mid-1890s Doyle deliberately avoided scientific romance for many years; during the genre's finest early years he was virtually silent, and it was not until the other major writers of the period had nearly finished that Doyle returned to scientific romance to show what he could do. He did publish some supernatural fantasies, though, including the novelette *The Parasite* (1894), about a sceptic who is reluctantly forced to concede the power of a medium when she takes a fancy to him and sets out to make him the prisoner of her will. When her passion becomes murderous he is helpless to interfere, and her plans are thwarted only by her timely death.

There are marginal elements of scientific romance in one or two of the Sherlock Holmes stories, notably 'The Adventure of the Creeping Man' (1903), in which a supposed rejuvenation serum based on the blood of langur monkeys has a quasi-theriomorphic effect on its user, but it was not until 1911 that Doyle again became interested in the genre. In that year he published the Wellsian story 'The Great Brown-Pericord Motor', in which the engineer who builds a marvellous new machine takes a much more down to earth approach to its possibilities than the intellectual who first conceived the idea of it. Again, no good comes of it all: the dreamer kills the engineer and uses the fabulous engine to dispose of his body, spending his remaining days in an asylum where he draws the most wonderfully intricate designs for flying machines.

In 1912 Doyle decided to do something different in the way of work slanted to the commercial market. He decided to 'do for the boys' book what Sherlock Holmes had done for the detective story', and produce a Vernian romance that would rejuvenate a literary species that had become sterile in the hands of the likes of Fenton Ash and George C. Wallis. The boys' papers of the day were replete with stories of journeys into the last unexplored regions of the earth, populated by savage tribes, exotic animals and lost civilisations. These stories were reckoned to be 'boys' books' partly because they were often crudely written, but also because they were so determinedly masculine: they comprised a celebration of courage, toughness, honour and veiled misogyny.

Doyle's awareness of the fact that this species was already in its decadent phase has much to do with the style of presentation of *The Lost World*, which is always close to self-parody. It revels in its own audacity and exaggeration, and the first book edition underlined this flamboyant irony by carrying as a frontispiece a photograph of 'the members of the expedition' with Doyle posing in a monstrous false beard as Professor Challenger. There are other fake photographs among the illustrations, and Challenger's image is inlaid into the cover in gilt, above the inscription 'Yours truly [to use the conventional lie] George Edward Challenger'. These devices provide a caricature of the convention by which such novels often masquerade as sober reportage.

The characterisation in the book is consciously over the top: Challenger is a hyperbolic version of the extrovert variety of eccentric genius; Roxton is a hero out of Rider Haggard; Summerlee is the introverted version of the clichéd man of science; even the innocent Malone – the 'straight man' of the circus – joins the mission according to the dictates of the classically absurd cliché, to prove his manhood to his beloved Gladys (who marries a solicitor's clerk while he is away). The parody, however, is kept under careful control; it is a decorative border around an adventure story in the grand manner.

The Lost World was by no means the first story to feature a relic fauna left over from prehistoric times, but it was the first to attack the notion with such conviction. Although it has thematic echoes of Verne's *Journey to the Centre of the Earth* it is by no means a Vernian story; the account of the journey *to* the lost world is very sketchy, and once there, the characters are anything but mere tourists. On the other hand, Doyle is both clever enough and conscientious enough to show restraint in parading before the reader his monstrous survivors. There is none of the crude routine of staged battles which is characteristic of the film made from the novel in 1925 and has remained the staple diet of Hollywood dinosaur epics ever since. Doyle is also careful to pay proper heed to what was actually known at the time about the particular species he displays, and is careful to stress that there must have been several invasions of the plateau in different eras to allow men and ape-men to co-exist with one another and with the dinosaurs.

It is obvious that Doyle thoroughly enjoyed assuming the *persona* of Professor Challenger for the purpose of writing *The Lost World*, and it is not surprising that the role continued to attract him. It was natural enough that he should write a sequel, and that the sequel should be somewhat different from its predecessor. By 1913, when he published *The Poison Belt*, he was aware that he had a much wider audience at his disposal than the boys' book audience he had originally had in mind when planning *The Lost World*.

Like George Griffith's *Olga Romanoff*, *The Poison Belt* illustrates the problems involved in following up a work whose appeal is based on the spectacular scope of its fantastic imagination. Nothing less than the threat of probable world destruction will do, and there is almost an obligation to carry out the threat. Challenger, having warned an unbelieving public about the impending sterilisation of the world, invites his friends to join him as witnesses to the catastrophe, sustaining themselves for a few extra hours with cylinders of oxygen while other men breathe air saturated by 'poisoned ether'. When their oxygen runs out, though, they find that the Earth has cleared the poison belt and they undertake an odyssey through the silent world, which is interrupted when the effect of the poison turns out to have been cataleptic rather than lethal. In order to avoid ending on this anticlimactic note, Doyle goes on, in rather uncharacteristic fashion, to draw a moral from the story and to emphasise it strongly. Malone, as narrator, and a quotation from a *Times* leader both insist that the brief passage through the poison belt has revealed to men what they had previously been unable to accept: their own insignificance in the cosmic scheme of things. Thus, the adventure story begun as pure entertainment is forced to close as an affirmation of what Peter Nicholls and others have called 'conceptual breakthrough'.[23]

The idea of a conceptual breakthrough is that a particular realisation, discovery or event serves to bring about a wholesale transformation of the way the world is seen. The Copernican theory of the solar system and Darwin's theory of evolution are the most frequently quoted examples of conceptual break-throughs in the history of science. H.G. Wells clearly experienced a personal conceptual breakthrough at the Normal School of Science, which led eventually to the production of his remarkably original scientific romances. It is hardly surprising that a great deal of speculative fiction is concerned with conceptual breakthroughs, given that it is such events which liberate the speculative imagination from fetters which have previously bound it tightly. There *is* something surprising, though, about the emergence of such a theme in the work of a writer like Doyle, who had previously been a paradigm case of a writer whose use of speculative scientific notions was conservative and non-serious. Doyle was a professional writer who regarded fantastic ideas of all kinds simply as melodramatic flourishes to decorate literary confections. *The Poison Belt*, however, had an inertia of its own which carried him on from the sheer clowning of the episode when the characters feel the first effects of the poisonous ether as a kind of intoxication, through the sober descriptions of the narcotised world to a serious consideration of the implications of the hypothesis.

Doyle's other speculative fictions of the immediate pre-war period also had more bite than his early efforts. 'The Horror of the Heights' (1913) is basically a shocker about the horrible things that happen when aviators first fly high enough to encounter the monstrous denizens of the upper atmosphere, but it has a conviction which such stories as 'The Los Amigos Fiasco' and 'The Great Brown-Pericord Motor' lacked. Doyle seems to have decided that he need no longer be apologetic about exercising his imagination in this fashion. This became much more obvious when he came to write – at a very late stage – his first future war story, 'Danger!' (1914). Though this novelette does not feature any futuristic weaponry, it nevertheless caused something of a stir when it was published in *The Strand*. It dealt with the menace posed to merchant and passenger shipping by submarines. By the time the story actually appeared the possibility of a real war was becoming strong, and officials in the Admiralty felt compelled to issue a statement to the effect that there was no possibility of any nation breaking the rules of war by launching sneak attacks. It was only to be a matter of months before this assurance was made to look hollow by the depredations of the U-boats.

When the war came, Doyle was ready for a complete change in his way of life. He became involved with work connected with the war. He wrote about it, in the mammoth account of *The British Campaign in France and Flanders*, research for which involved numerous visits to war zones and constant correspondence with military men. He was a founding member of the Volunteer Force that was the Great War's version of the Second World War's Home Guard, and he put parts of his home at the disposal of the military men based nearby. It was during the war that he, like Wells, suffered a religious conversion which drew him away from materialism into unorthodox faith. He achieved his own peculiar conceptual breakthrough in becoming convinced of the proven truth of survival after death, and became an enthusiastic propagandist for spiritualism. This conversion may have been aided by, but was not initiated by, the death of his son in the war. Wells's brush with God the Invisible King was a temporary one, but Doyle acquired the characteristic zeal of the convert, and became unshakeable in his new faith.

The conversion ruined Doyle, of course, as a writer of scientific romance, though he did return to it in later years. Before 1913 he had found it too difficult to be serious while being playful; after 1917 it was the playfulness that no longer had any verve or vigour. Challenger *was* to return, but he was but a shadow of his former self, and he was to learn an earnest humility very different in character from that which the world was hypothetically supposed to have learned from its passage through the poison belt.

Perhaps Doyle does not really warrant separate concern as one of the 'major writers' of early scientific romance. He wrote less of it, after all, than Cutcliffe Hyne or Robert Cromie, and the ideas which he used in his work of this kind do not have the same *outré* fascination as the ideas deployed by M.P. Shiel and John Beresford. He does provide, though, an illustration of the way that the popular writers of this period were attracted to the themes of scientific romance, and he was more successful than anyone else except Wells in demonstrating how to get real *excitement* out of scientific romance. *The Lost World* provided a beautiful example of the accomplishments of a disciplined imagination, displaying with admirable panache the melodramatic potential in the fanciful use of scientific knowledge.

William Hope Hodgson

William Hope Hodgson was born on 15 November 1877 in an Essex village. His father, Samuel Hodgson, was a rather unorthodox Anglican clergyman, with whom he quarrelled fiercely. The family was a large one – there were twelve children, though three died in infancy – and was always poor. Hodgson ran away from home and school on more than one occasion, and became determined to get away by going to sea. He was eventually apprenticed as a cabin boy in 1891 and remained at sea for eight years despite appalling conditions which made his early years aboard ship almost unbearable. Because his family was in desperate straits following the death of his father in 1892 Hodgson was forced to assume much of the burden of support. He studied for his mate's papers, and took up body-building and photography. He became very strong, and remained an enthusiastic propagandist for physical culture; he also achieved some notable successes in connection with his other hobby, taking remarkable pictures of storms at sea.

By 1899 he had had enough of the sea, and turned to his other skills in search of a means of support. He opened a school of physical culture in the north of England, but it never became commercially successful. He had always been an avid reader, especially of fantastic material, and an early fascination with the supernatural had partially given way to an enthusiasm for scientific romance. In the early 1900s, therefore, he began to investigate the possibilities offered by the popular magazines. He began by writing articles (illustrated by his own photographs) for a magazine of physical culture, but rapidly moved on to the general magazines. He joined the Society of Authors and became an enthusiastic member, often contributing to its journal, *The Author*. Although he was a long way from the literary world of London he corresponded with other writers, including Wells.

Hodgson's early fiction sales included a far-fetched murder story, 'The Goddess of Death' (1904) for Pearson's *Royal Magazine*, and a sea-serpent story, 'The Tropical Horror' (1905). He was more successful, though, with his articles about the sea, and he began doing lectures built around the photographs which he had taken aboard ship. It was for the American *Monthly Story Magazine* (later retitled *Blue Book*) that he started writing fantastic stories in some quantity. His first story published there was 'From the Tideless Sea' (1906), the story of life aboard a ship which has been trapped in the floating weed of the Sargasso Sea, and which is menaced by various creatures of the deep, including giant octopodes. The story was reprinted in Alfred Harmsworth's *London Magazine* in 1907.

'From the Tideless Sea' established a pattern which Hodgson was to follow in many later stories. He did more than any other writer to popularise the myth of the Sargasso Sea – a mid-Atlantic region clogged with weed where sailing ships could be entrapped for ever. The idea was not introduced into popular fiction by Hodgson – Thomas Janvier's novel *In the Sargasso Sea* had appeared in 1898 – but he was the man who developed the legend into its most fantastic form. The first story was followed up by a sequel, 'More News from the *Homebird*' (1907; retitled for English publication in 1911 'The Fifth Message from the Tideless Sea'), and by an unconnected but similar story 'The Mystery of the Derelict' (1907). All these stories are essentially tales of *haunting*, but not haunting by ghosts: the monstrous things which lurk in the damp darkness on and aboard these stricken ships are living creatures, exaggerated in size and ferocity from their natural counterparts. 'More News from the *Homebird*' has giant crabs, 'The Mystery of the Derelict' giant rats. In these stories Hodgson was simply ringing the changes after the fashion of writers connected with the modern boom in horror stories, but his imaginative range was to expand very considerably.

Hodgson's enthusiasm for physical culture seems to have been correlated with a preoccupation with hygiene. Certainly, the psychology of his horror stories is based very strongly in anxieties about personal pollution. Attention is frequently called in his stories to noxious odours and to the uncomfortable presence of slimy substances. This aspect of his work is particularly clear in three works which saw publication in the latter part of 1907. In 'The Terror of the Water Tank' a series of puzzling deaths turns out to be due to a ribbon-like monster that emerges periodically from a filthy water tank; while 'The Voice in the Night' – Hodgson's most famous short story – features the strange tale of a castaway and his wife forced to eat a strange addictive fungus whose appearance and texture their own flesh gradually acquires.

In between these two short stories Hodgson published his

first novel, *The Boats of the 'Glen Carrig'*. This too is an account of the adventures of a group of castaways, written in a mock-archaic style. The *Glen Carrig* is wrecked and the survivors drift through weed-choked waters. The first land they reach appears to have no animal life, although the plants crowding it seem to have animal forms embedded in their flesh. Even human faces can be found, possibly those of people absorbed by the plants, which attack the castaways and scream and bleed when their attack is repulsed. This section was presumably intended originally as a short story, which Hodgson then elected to continue to novel length. Having left the first island the shipwrecked sailors drift on through the Sargasso, encountering derelict ships, giant crabs, octopodes and a beaked humanoid face. Eventually, they come upon a second island, which proves to be the home of the beaked creatures with man-like faces: Weed Men like 'human slugs' with slimy bodies and tentacles instead of fingers. Another ship lies close to the island, fortified against the Weed Men, and the men of the *Glen Carrig* succeed in reaching it before their final climactic battle with the monstrous creatures.

The Boats of the 'Glen Carrig' is primarily an exercise in teratology, made highly effective by the careful combination of the realistic details derived from Hodgson's own experiences at sea and the particular horrific *frisson* connected with the mingling of human and animal characteristics. Tales of wolf-men and ape-men were already commonplace, but slug-men were something new; man-eating trees were also familiar, but not man-*absorbing* trees.

Hodgson was now keen to become a novelist, and to develop his ideas much more elaborately. In his next short stories of the sea he abandoned teratology in favour of a peculiar mysticism: in 'The *Shamraken* Homeward-Bounder' (1908) he made elaborate use of his experience of the meteorological phenomena associated with cyclones to colour a very eerie story about a ship whose crew feel that the Day of Judgment is at hand. In 'Out of the Storm' (1909) a man aboard another ship that is going down feels that the world he is in has been deserted by God and that the sea itself is a monstrous cruel force whose dominion is absolute. But Hodgson's creative efforts in these years were almost wholly devoted to two novel-length stories which display a much less conventional mysticism: *The House on the Borderland* (1908) and *The Ghost Pirates* (1909).

The House on the Borderland consists mainly of a manuscript purportedly found by two tourists in the west of Ireland. They discover it in the ruins of an almost-obliterated structure on the brink of a great chasm beneath a waterfall, and it is the account of the visionary experiences of a man who lived in the building when it was whole, with his sister and dog. Part of the story deals with the writer's attempts to protect himself and his sister from the effects of forces of decay which are focused in swine-like humanoid creatures which invade his environment from below. (In the end, he is infected by this decay by the dog, which has been in contact with the swine-things.) The story also includes visionary sequences. In the first the writer describes a vast and desolate plain surrounded by high mountains, where there is a transfigured version of his house and the chasm which it overlooks. Behind the mountains are glimpsed the apparitions of ancient gods, including Kali and Set, and the swine-things appear to be avatars of one member of this evil pantheon. Other visions carry the writer to a more peaceful place, the Sea of Sleep, where he can renew contact with a long-lost loved one, but one of these episodes gives way to a sensation of accelerating time, which seems to hurtle him into the distant future. Although the house remains inviolate things in it crumble to dust and the earth itself dies as the sun burns out. Disembodied, the writer watches the house taken over by the swine-things and consumed by a pillar of flame. The solar system collapses and falls into a giant Green Sun, from which white globes then emerge, transporting the writer with joy to the Sea of Sleep and reunion with his loved one. Then a Dark Sun appears to separate the lovers again, and from a dark nebula come more globes, this time pregnant with sorrow and anguish; one of them engulfs the writer and returns him to the plain of his earlier vision. Entering the house there he is finally brought back to its 'real' counterpart. It is after this that the 'infection' from without is brought into the house to destroy him.

This story seems a very radical break from Hodgson's previous work, though he was later to argue that it was the centrepiece of a trilogy begun and ended with the much more conventional novels that preceded and succeeded it. It also seems to be radically different from previous fantastic literature, though it has some strong echoes of Poe in it, and the cosmic vision sequence recalls in some respects Poe's visionary essay *Eureka* (1848). (There are also some echoes of Wells's *Time Machine* in this sequence.) The story's closest links to the burgeoning tradition of scientific romance seem to be forged by the cosmic perspective embraced by this vision: a perspective even greater in its temporal sweep than that of *The Time Machine*. Hodgson's purpose, though, is not simply to widen imaginative horizons; the whole plot is an allegory displaying a world-view as elaborate and as eccentric as that embodied in Shiel's *The Purple Cloud*.

Hodgson added to the novel an introduction in which he assumes the guise of editor in order to call attention to the allegory and suggest how it might be decoded:

> From a *seeming* 'fantasia' there grew, to reward my unbiassed concentration, a cogent, coherent scheme of ideas that gripped my interest more securely than the mere bones of the *account* or *story* . . . I found a greater story within the lesser – and the paradox is no paradox . . .
>
> I cannot but look upon the account of the Celestial Globes as a striking illustration (how nearly had I said 'proof'!) of the actuality of our thoughts and emotions among the Realities. For, without seeming to suggest the annihilation of the lasting reality of Matter, as the hub and framework of the Machine of Eternity, it enlightens one with conceptions of the existence of worlds of thought and emotion, working in conjunction with, and duly subject to, the scheme of material creation.[24]

The world into which Hodgson's writer is carried by his visions is a quasi-Platonic world of Ideas, where the innate moral order of the cosmos is displayed in a series of physical representations and transactions. The house is the home of consciousness – the psyche – which exists both in the mundane world and (in a grander form) in the world of Ideas. The 'two central suns of creation', the Green and the Dark, are neither Good and Evil nor Life and Death, but rather Growth and Decay, the former associated with love and ecstasy and the latter with emotional pain. This redefinition of the fundamental opposition is not so very different from Shiel's characterisation of the black and the white which are at war in Adam Jefferson's soul, but in Shiel's evolutionary scheme both black and white are the instruments of progress, and the forces of destruction, however one may regret the suffering they bring, are ultimately to be construed as positive. Hodgson, by contrast, embraces a deep pessimism. The oasis of consciousness is set in a bleak Plain of Silence, behind whose protective boundaries lurk the forces of Decay, symbolised by the malevolent gods of ancient pantheons (Kali from the Hindu pantheon and Set from the Egyptian). Evil is here represented physically as swinishness, and in the mundane world it seeks to invade consciousness from below. It is opposed by affection, whose power is weakened by the dream-like quality of erotic passion, which tends to attach itself more to images than to real people. In the end, man – individually and collectively – is bound to be consumed by the forces of decay, and so are the earth and the sun. Even the world of Ideas, it seems, must suffer dereliction.

One should perhaps refuse the temptation to psychoanalyse an author by means of complicated interpretations of his work, but in connection with Hodgson's association of love with remote objects of memory rather than real individuals some other points might be mentioned. One of his early stories, 'The Valley of Lost Children' (1906), is a sentimental story about an imaginary land where dead children are preserved, and one wonders if, like J.M. Barrie, Hodgson found himself competing on uneven terms for his mother's affection against his siblings who died in infancy. Hodgson did not marry until five years after he published *The House on the Borderland*, and may well have had little experience of love in 1908. His devotion to physical culture certainly suggests a determination to resist the ravages of bodily deterioration, but any such victory could only be temporary. Men die, and in the life and death of every man there is reflected in microcosm the *kalpas* – a term which Hodgson borrowed from Hindu metaphysics to describe the entire cosmogonic cycle which is witnessed by his visionary. In this sense Hodgson is in total opposition to Shiel; whereas Shiel saw individuals as unimportant within the great scheme of things, the morality of matter being concerned only with the progress of the entire race, Hodgson took the individual as his measure of all things, the Moral Order of the universe reflecting the inevitable death of the individual in the ultimate victory of the archetypes of malevolence.

The explication of this 'greater story within the lesser' helps to illuminate some features of *The Ghost Pirates*. Hodgson's preface to this work claims that it concludes a trilogy begun with *The Boats of the 'Glen Carrig'* and continued with *The House on the Borderland* and that 'though very different in scope, each of the three books deals with certain conceptions that have an elemental kinship'. This elemental kinship has not been obvious to commentators on Hodgson's work, and is not explored in Sam Moskowitz's long essay on the writer,[25] but it does exist.

The Ghost Pirates is, like its predecessor, a tale of the Borderland separating two worlds. It is the most elaborate of Hodgson's tales of haunted ships, telling the story of the last voyage of the *Mortzestus* (the name has an obvious significance), which is first invaded by humanoid creatures which come up out of the sea, and then sails out of our world altogether, into a peculiar zone of separation. Here the narrator (who is telling his story to the captain of another vessel, having been picked up as the sole survivor of the disaster which ultimately overwhelms the ship) sees a fleet of ghost ships sailing in the 'mirror world' beneath the surface of the sea. Eventually, the humanoid denizens of that world swarm forth in force to slaughter the crew of the *Mortzestus*.

Although this is superficially a tale of parallel worlds not too different from other such tales, Hodgson's deliberate association of it with *The House on the Borderland* suggests that the 'other dimension' inhabited by the malevolent humanoids is to be given more significance. The monsters emerging from the 'underside' of the sea are easily associated with the swine-things that menace the house in the earlier novel. They are not simply nasty creatures but embodiments of the forces of destruction. The ship here takes the same symbolic role as the house, and the sea the same role that it has in 'Out of the Storm'. Hodgson apparently intended this symbolism to extend retrospectively to the ships in *The Boats of the 'Glen Carrig'*, and by implication to all his other stories of vessels doomed to dereliction and destruction by their entrapment in slimy weed and their invasion by monstrous creatures.

Hodgson had begun his writing career as a relatively hard-headed professional, but the direction he had taken in 1908 had carried his writing far away from the world of the popular magazines. None of his novels was serialised, and it appears that none of them made a significant amount of money. In 1910, therefore, Hodgson made a conscious effort to change gear, and to confine his work according to strictly commercial priorities. He became a prolific producer of short pieces, including numerous non-fantasy stories of life at sea. For *The Idler* he produced a series of stories about Carnacki, a consulting detective specialising in supernatural visitations. Carnacki is clearly modelled on Algernon Blackwood's 'psychic detective' John Silence, several of whose adventures were featured in a book published in 1908. The stories published in 1910 are mediocre, but Hodgson wrote others that did not sell then. These do not appear in the book *Carnacki the Ghost Finder* published in 1913, but are in the similarly titled collection published by Mycroft & Moran in 1947. The last of these, 'The Hog', is an inter-dimensional fantasy which is clearly associated with the allegory of *The House on the Borderland*.

Some of the stories belonging to this period, including 'The Thing in the Weeds' (1912), are lacklustre pastiches of his earlier sea-monster stories, but in the main the short stories of 1910–12 were of a very different character from his early fantasies. Two of them – 'The Island of the Ud' (1912) and its sequel 'The Adventure of the Headland' (1912) seem to be attempts to write sea stories in the more jocular vein of Cutcliffe Hyne's popular stories of Captain Kettle. Alongside these stories, though, Hodgson was writing something else – something not in the least commercial, in whose composition he permitted himself to be absolutely self-indulgent. This was the long novel *The Night Land* (1912), one of the most bizarre and eccentric fantastic novels ever produced.

The novels of the earlier trilogy are all set in the past. Both of the sea stories are set in the eighteenth century (though there are no dates in *The Ghost Pirates*) and the manuscript in *The House on the Borderland* is said to have been found in 1877, though obviously composed much earlier. Hodgson adopted a deliberately archaic style for all of them, and in *The Night Land* he indulged this affectation further. The story begins in an unspecified time, in an apparent medieval setting, and the narrator tells the story of his love affair with one Mirdath, whom he marries after saving her from a mad dog which wounds her. She subsequently dies, after giving birth to a child, condemning the narrator to 'an utter and dreadful pain of longing' from which he is liberated only in sleep, when he experiences an astonishing vision of the distant future in which he and she can be united, as he puts it, 'in the Womb of Time'. The main part of the book – which is longer than the three earlier books put together – is an account of this futuristic vision.

In this distant future the last remnants of mankind live in a huge pyramid called the Last Redoubt, under the benevolent rule of the Monstruwacans. The pyramid is defended by the Electric Circle, and needs to be, for in this decadent earth the barriers separating it from other dimensions have long broken down, and the forces of destruction are free to roam the world in a multiplicity of physical forms, ranging from the gargantuan immobile Watchers to serpentine creatures, all hidden by the cloak of perpetual darkness.

The inhabitants of the Last Redoubt discover that their refuge is ill named when they receive a call for help from a Lesser Redoubt whose existence they had not suspected. Naani, who is a 'reincarnation' of Mirdath, appeals for rescue, and the narrator's dream-self sets out across the haunted landscape to reach her. The journey is very long and arduous, and is described in such great detail that its countless bizarre incidents ultimately fuse into a monotonous catalogue. He arrives to find the Lesser Redoubt already fallen, though Naani is still alive, and they begin the equally long-drawn-out return journey. Now the menace of the monsters from the eternal night is punctuated by their decorous love-making, in a series of scenes which cannot help but strike the modern reader as appalling in their sickly sentimentality and their reflection of Victorian sexual mythology. Naani is ultimately killed – struck down by an evil spiritual Force – but is then resurrected by the 'Earth-Current' which sustains the Electric Circle. The story ends with the very archetype of a happy ending, and displays its moral like a triumphant banner:

> And I to have gained Honour; yet to have learned that Honour doth be but as the ash of Life, if that you not to have love. And I to have Love. And to have Love is to have all; for that which doth be *truly* LOVE doth mother Honour and Faithfulness; and they three to build the House of Joy. 26

The Night Land is a literary curiosity. Such are its idiosyncrasies that it is virtually unreadable – in terms of literary style it must be one of the worst books ever published – but it also has an imaginative intensity that could belong only to an extremely personal book. It is highly enigmatic, disdaining even the token gesture of explanation that is to be found in the introduction to *The House on the Borderland,* and presents a puzzle to would-be commentators which none has really tried to solve. The book has had its admirers, though – Moskowitz quotes several very favourable press notices that the book received, and H.P. Lovecraft spoke very highly of it in his classic essay on 'Supernatural Horror in Literature'.[27]

There is not space here for any detailed examination of the book's symbology, but the broad outlines of its plot fit in well enough with the allegory in *The House on the Borderland*. It imagines the world approaching the end of a *kalpas*, with the forces of decay all but triumphant, though their ravages can still be held at bay by the careful cultivation of the forces of growth: physical culture, love and the force of the Earth-Current. The optimistic note on which the story ends seems to contrast with the pessimism of the earlier novel, but it results from a change of perspective rather than a change of mind. *The House on the Borderland* brooded on the inevitability of death; *The Night Land* accepts that, and concentrates on the personal triumphs which can be won in spite of it.

A condensation of *The Night Land*, less than a tenth of the length of the original, was published in America as *The Dream of X*, in a volume containing some other material, mainly poetry. This may have been done in order to obtain an American copyright for the book, but it seems highly probable that Hodgson had to pay for this publication himself. The book made no money to speak of, and Hodgson continued to turn out hackwork for the magazines, mainly for Alfred Harmsworth's *London Magazine* and *Red Magazine*. Some of these stories recapture the spirit of his early works, including 'The Derelict' (1912), about the spontaneous generation of life aboard a decaying ship, and 'The Stone Ship' (1913), about a petrified vessel thrown up from the sea-bed with a monstrous collection of deep-sea creatures by an underwater volcanic eruption. The only really significant story of the period, however, was one which the magazines would not take, though it eventually appeared posthumously in 1919 as 'The Baumoff Explosion'. Originally entitled 'Eloi, Eloi, Lama Sabachthani' (under which title it is reprinted in the collection *Out of the Storm*, 1975), this tells the story of a chemist who reproduces the meteorological anomalies which occurred at the time of the crucifixion, and crucifies himself in order to form a psychic link with Christ. The alien consciousness which invades him as the experiment reaches its climax, though, is a bestial one: it is the swinishness of the dark gods that possesses him, not the loving spirit of

Christ. Thus Baumoff learns, in the cruellest possible fashion, the metaphysical intuition which Hodgson had long ago found to justify his own apostasy.

Hodgson married in 1913, and went to live for a while in the south of France. In the next few years he was to publish several collections of his short stories, but he wrote little new material. He did begin another novel – another sea story involving faces in the water that belong to monstrous humanoids – but did not get far with it. When the Great War began he and his wife returned to England and he enlisted in 1915, receiving a commission in the Royal Field Artillery. While serving in France in 1916 he was thrown from a horse and badly injured, but he returned to the front when he had recovered. He was killed in action in April 1918, near Ypres.

As a writer, Hodgson was a remarkable amalgam of hard-headed professional and inwardly driven amateur. Historians of speculative fiction usually regard him as a writer of horrific fantasy and not as a writer of scientific romance. but this is to neglect certain important elements of kinship which link his work to that of Wells, Shiel and John Beresford. There is nothing in his work which is authentically supernatural; his metaphysics is just as thoroughly dis-enchanted as Wells's, though it is certainly baroque. What distinguishes him from the other three writers just named is that they all built their new metaphysical systems around ideas derived from evolutionary philosophy. Their cosmic schemes, whether optimistic or pessimistic, dealt with possibilities of change in the human species. Hodgson was *not* an evolutionist, and did not think in such terms at all. His model of change was taken entirely from the life-history of the individual, and his macrocosmic visions embody the Renaissance principle of 'As above, so below'. His idea of the fundamental, impersonal Force that must stand in for God is therefore very different from that formed by Shiel. In Shiel's view, that basic Force imported a progressive *élan vital* into the history of life and the career of mankind; in Hodgson's view the Force that must ultimately win was the force of decay – ashes to ashes, dust to dust – and the individual's battle was to win an essentially temporary and partial victory. Had he been familiar with the concept of entropy, and had he known how the order of life on Earth is dependent on the influx of energy from the sun to mount its temporary defiance of the entropic decay of the universe, he would surely have made much more use of scientific language in his work, rather than borrowing ideas and images from Hindu mythology. His self-education was too selective to make such ideative resources available to him, and this limited his mode of expression, but his limitations should not obscure the spirit of his endeavours.

J.D. Beresford

John Davys Beresford was born on 7 March 1873, in a small Northamptonshire village where his father was the rector. He contracted infantile paralysis when he was three years old, and always attributed this to the carelessness of his nurse. He remained lame for the rest of his life. When he left school – he attended Oundle and Peterborough – he was articled to an architect, and spent some years as a draughtsman, though he eventually decided that he had no future in that profession. He tried his hand at advertising, and held various other odd jobs, but increasingly invested his efforts and his hopes in literary work. In 1907 he became a regular contributor to the *Westminster Gazette*, an evening newspaper which published literary articles and reviews, but it was not until 1911 that he published his first novel, *The Early History of Jacob Stahl*, which drew heavily on his own experiences.

This first novel was reasonably successful, and became the first part of a trilogy continued with *A Candidate for Truth* (1912) and *The Invisible Event* (1915). These novels constitute an intense autobiographical appraisal, describing and evaluating the career of a man crippled in infancy, who rebels against his father's religious faith, is articled to an architect and eventually becomes a novelist, making his mark with an autobiographical trilogy of novels begun with *John Tristram*. The detailed realism of these novels is the product of obsessive introspection, and though they won Beresford a considerable early reputation he never managed to recapture the same intensity again – at least, not in his mundane fiction. His later work in that vein is characterised by a cool objectivity and lack of involvement, and though it is unfailingly competent and earnest it is also unexciting.

Beresford did, however, maintain a strong personal interest in his more imaginative fictions. Once he had translated his own life-story into fiction he had used it up, but he never used up his spirit of philosophical inquiry, which he poured into a series of imaginative stories produced between 1911 and the end of the Great War. He was a great admirer of H.G. Wells, and in 1915 he produced the first full-length critical appraisal of Wells's work for Nisbet & Co.'s 'Writers of the Day' series. This essay includes a scrupulous analysis of the method of Wells's scientific romances, and it is significant that he singles out for quotation a passage from *The War of the Worlds*:

> *The War of the Worlds* (1898), although written in the first person, is in some ways the most detached of all these fantasies; and it is in this book that Mr Wells frankly confesses his own occasional sense of separation. 'At times,' says the narrator of the history, 'I suffer from the strangest sense of detachment from myself and the world about me, I seem to watch it all from the outside, from somewhere inconceivably remote, out of time, out of space, out of the stress and tragedy of it all.'[28]

This is significant because what especially characterises Beresford's own essays in scientific romance is precisely this 'sense of separation'. Beresford seems always to have considered himself a man apart, possessed of a disinterested objectivity which qualified him to pass judgment on man's place in the universe. No doubt his lameness, and the sense of grievance which he felt because of it, assisted him in feeling detached, though in other ways he seems to have enjoyed a much more comfortable existence than Wells, Griffith or Hodgson did – he seems never to have been really poor, and he married shortly after his initial literary success, settling thereafter into conventional domesticity.

Beresford came relatively late to the writing of scientific romance, though he was only seven years younger than Wells, but he began with more serious intentions than any other writer. He set out to use imaginative fiction as an arena for a contest of ideas, and as a means of exploring and attempting to grasp the implications of the new world-view which he espoused after rejecting his father's religion and politics. When he began writing *The Hampdenshire Wonder*, which he published in 1911, he was still trying to find his intellectual bearings.

The Hampdenshire Wonder is one of the great scientific romances. It is the first important story based on serious speculation about the intellectual nature of a human who has reached a 'higher' evolutionary stage. It tells the story of a freak child, possessed of intellectual capacities that will one day be the common property of man's descendants. This wonder-child becomes an observer who can comment on the affairs of men from a detached and superior viewpoint. There had been earlier novels which imported such superior observers into the contemporary world, including Wells's *The Wonderful Visit* and Grant Allen's *The British Barbarians*, but Beresford's wonder-child is a much more ambitious creation than Wells's innocent angel or Allen's smug time-travelling anthropologist. He has something in common with the giants of *The Food of the Gods* and with 'The Man of the Year Million', but goes well beyond these Wellsian precedents.

Beresford's narrator first encounters the Wonder on a train, as a babe in arms with a huge head and a disconcerting stare. This encounter is juxtaposed with a quotation from a book which the narrator is reading, which sets the scene for the commentary which the Wonder will ultimately deliver on the limitations of human knowledge. In the first edition of the story the book in question is Henri Bergson's *Time and Free Will*, and the quotation equates free will with irrationality, but in later editions Beresford substituted a more apposite quotation from Hegel's *Phenomenology of the Spirit*.

The early part of the novel describes the curious circumstances of the Wonder's conception, in a marriage of convenience contracted by a professional cricketer (this may be an ironic homage to Wells). The child then attracts the attention of the local squire, Henry Challis, and the rector of the parish, Percy Crashaw. Crashaw is the villain of the book: the embodiment of anti-scientific religious fervour and fanatical intolerance. This extremely unflattering portrait presumably reflects Beresford's rejection of the views of his father – who was a rector in a similar village. Challis, on the other hand, takes the Wonder under his wing and gives him the run of his library, where the child familiarises himself (by the age of five) with the entire heritage of human knowledge. Beresford is careful to make the Wonder a taciturn individual who makes only a few substantial pronouncements, but who succeeds in implying much more than he actually states. He cannot explain to the narrator his own view of the world, because he has not the words to do so, and his one substantial debate with Challis is reported only in the vaguest terms, because Challis deliberately puts it out of his mind.

In spite of this obliquity, the reader is left in no doubt about the scorn in which the Wonder holds our science and philosophy. He is free of the burden of emotion and the craving for faith which drive men to the worship of all manner of Baconian idols. He has no place in our world, though, and is eventually murdered; the reader is left at liberty to choose between the two suspects who may have committed the crime: the rector and the village idiot.

The effect of the Wonder's visitation is to confirm in the narrator a sense of alienation, of helplessness in the face of the newly revealed human condition. He becomes pessimistic about the prospects of the modern quest for understanding, feeling that man has not the intellectual equipment to meet the demands of positivist philosophers like Ernst Mach, who ask us to strip away our preconceptions, or metaphysicians like Bergson, who require us to adopt a radically new perspective on time and mind. It is not the narrator, though, who has the last word. His friend and squire offers him instead a counsel of contentment:

> You and I are children in the infancy of the world. Let us to our play in the nursery of our own times. The day will come, perhaps, when humanity shall have grown and will have to take upon itself the heavy burden of knowledge. But you need not fear that will be in our day, nor in a thousand years.[29]

Challis criticises the opinion of the Wonder that the utility of knowledge is simply to be acquainted with the truth. Challis takes a much more pragmatic line, suggesting that illusion too might have its utility, and that human beings may need mystery to give intellectual life its colour and purpose. Beresford certainly seems to have found colour and purpose in his own intellectual life through his engagement with mystery and speculation. He was to be constantly attracted by pseudo-scientific fashions – spiritualism, psychoanalysis, ESP and faith-healing among them – though the only one he could ever bring himself to believe in was the last.

Beresford's second full-length scientific romance was *Goslings* (1913), which describes the progress of a new plague whose effects are sexually selective. All but a handful of men are killed throughout Europe, and women inherit the world. The activities of the suffragettes had stimulated the production of a whole series of futuristic works investigating the hypothetical question of whether women really could assume the privileges and prerogatives of men, from Walter Besant's outrageously Victorian *The Revolt of Man* (1882) to F.E.M. Young's dream fantasy of a world without men, *The War of the Sexes* (1905). Most of these stories had been written by men, and most concluded that women were not equipped by nature for running the world. Beresford, characteristically, tried to take an entirely fresh approach to the hypothesis, treating it as reasonably as possible. His account of the problems faced by women nurtured for dependence when they try to take over the reins of agricultural and industrial production is well balanced, and his suggestions as to how the women might treat and use the few remaining men carry a certain conviction. In the end, though, the story ends weakly, failing to carry through its project by proposing that the plague's virulence declines as it marches westward; the miraculously preserved men of America arrive to save the day.

As a commentary on sexual politics *Goslings* seems very tentative by today's standards, but this is only to be expected. In its own day, it was a thoughtful and fairly perceptive work, and it has a good deal more finesse than Wells's strident propagandistic novels in support of the liberation of women.

In the wake of these two speculative novels Beresford began to produce short stories in some quantity. Some appeared in the *Westminster Gazette*, but many of them proved difficult to place. To some extent this reflects a growing conservatism in the popular magazines, which were not as receptive to scientific romance as they once had been, but the stories themselves were often quirky, many being visionary vignettes without much in the way of narrative structure.

Many of these short stories were eventually assembled in two collections, *Nineteen Impressions* (1918) and *Signs and Wonders* (1921). The second of these was not issued by a commercial publisher, but by the Golden Cockerel Press, one of the most famous British private presses. In the introduction to the first volume, Beresford laid claim to a double purpose in writing these pieces:

> In certain of the items that make up this collection, there are two motives. The first is undisguised, and is displayed as the distraction

of a common story; the movement of modern life in an ordinary setting. The second motive is never explicit. It does not represent the discovery of separation, nor attempt any indication of what that moment might reveal . . . all that the second motive stands for is the hesitating suggestion that the other thing is there, the essential reality behind every expression, the immanent mystery of life independent of space or time.[30]

This quotation concludes a discussion where Beresford suggests that one of the uses of fiction is to provide 'an instant's separation', by which the reader is removed temporarily to a stance of objectivity, from which the ordinary looks different. Characters in the stories which follow frequently have momentary glimpses of past or future, which relocate their experiences within a much wider perspective. Three of the author's earliest essays along these lines are grouped together under the collective title of 'Flaws in the Time-Scheme' (1912) – a title which could easily embrace others, too, including 'The Escape' (1913) and 'The Ashes of Last Night's Fire' (1914). *Nineteen Impressions* also includes some odd allegories, including 'The Little Town', whose narrator visits the Kosmos theatre where marionettes go through a painfully clumsy routine on stage while the members of the audience struggle desperately to help the animator by the ineffectual exercise of their own collective will.

The stories in *Signs and Wonders*, which are not individually dated after the fashion of the earlier collection, are in very much the same vein as those in *Nineteen Impressions*, and probably belong to the same period. Many were obviously written during the war years, and for the most part they offer a cosmic perspective more greatly expanded than that occasionally suggested in *Nineteen Impressions*. The collection opens, in fact, with 'The Appearance of Man', a playlet in which two men and a woman exchange polite platitudes on the theme of 'it's a small world', while projected behind them is the panoply of cosmic history, from the birth to the death of the universe. 'Signs and Wonders' is a vision story in which a man sees the heavenly host parading across the sky, but more effective stories in the same vein are 'The Cage', in which a modern man briefly exchanges perceptions with his prehistoric ancestor; and 'Enlargement', about a vision which relieves the immediate horror of an air raid. The collection also has several stories based on psychoanalytic theories: 'The Hidden Beast' is Freudian, while

'The Barrage', 'The Introvert' and 'The Barrier' are all character studies based in Jungian ideas.

The most impressive story in *Signs and Wonders* is 'A Negligible Experiment', a story of approaching cosmic disaster recalling Wells's 'The Star', in which the imminent destruction of the earth is taken as proof that man has only been one of the universe's negligible experiments, of no real significance at all. Equally effective in its coolness is the neat horror story 'Young Strickland's Career', in which an experiment in precognition is held to be a failure when all that can be seen is an improbably desolate landscape where a man is apparently digging up a turnip. Young Strickland does not understand what he has seen until he goes off to fight in the Great War, and finds that the blasted landscape was not so improbable after all, and that what he took for a turnip is actually a human head.

As with the other important writers of early scientific romance, the war years proved to be a turning point in Beresford's career. He was the only writer who was actually provoked to produce stories of scientific romance by his experience of the war, but these were few in number and like Wells, Shiel and Doyle he seems eventually to have been deflected away from scientific romance. Curiously, it was the coming of the Second World War that diverted his attention, late in life, back to the production of scientific romance, and he appears to have found the storm and stress of war something of a provocation to his imagination. In the short term, though, he put scientific romance behind him in or shortly after 1918. By that time, the genre's first formative phase was over. Scientific romance is, in the main, a young man's genre, and by 1918 there were very few young men left; the war had aged those it had not killed. Beresford certainly had not brought his intellectual explorations to any sort of conclusion, but he was willing to take the advice which he had offered himself through the voice of Henry Challis, and let well enough alone. Doyle, the most frivolous of the first-rank writers of early scientific romance, lost his frivolity; Beresford, in an ironic reversal, lost his seriousness.

4

PATTERNS AND TRENDS IN
EARLY SCIENTIFIC ROMANCE

The Carnival of Destruction

THE BOOM in future war stories produced by the circulation-boosting efforts of various popular periodicals in the 1890s helped to launch the careers of other writers besides George Griffith. The species was particularly attractive to journalists who wanted to turn their hand to serial-writing, because the subject matter lent itself readily to a narrative style very close to reportage. The art of nineteenth-century journalism had developed hand in hand with war reporting since the days when William Russell's dispatches from the Crimea had first paraded a carnival of destruction before the public in the pages of *The Times*.

Even before *The Angel of the Revolution* commenced its serialisation, Pearson's rival, Alfred Harmsworth, had begun a future war serial in his *Tit-Bits* imitation, *Answers*. This was 'The Poisoned Bullet' by William le Queux, and it was very much a piece of fake journalism – not so much a novel as an exercise in 'speculative non-fiction'. The story involves no new weaponry, ostensibly providing a realistic account of a war fought with available resources. It was, though, reprinted in book form by Tower Publications, the publisher of Griffith's early work, in 1894 as *The Great War in England in 1897*. Le Queux and Griffith were acquainted, and it is possible that Griffith introduced le Queux to Tower, which also issued his lost race fantasy *Zoraida* in 1896. When Tower failed, le Queux went with Griffith to F.V. White, who published another lost race story, *The Great White Queen* (1897) and the 'shilling shocker' paperback *A Madonna of the Music Halls* (1897), featuring an evil scientist who uses disease as an instrument and

109

controls the emotions of his patients with drugs.

William le Queux was born on 2 July 1864, in London. Though his mother was English his father was French, and he spent many of his early years in Europe, later travelling extensively in Europe and Africa. Accounts of his life by himself and others relying upon his statements tend to be rather colourful, and one suspects a certain embroidery. As well as his formal career as a journalist he claimed to have been employed as a secret agent, and to have been involved in vital espionage work for anything up to thirty years before the Great War. Whatever his exploits in real life, he was certainly the great pioneer of spy fiction, from the publication of his novel *Guilty Bonds* (1890) onwards. In his thrillers he turned away from the description of imaginary future conflicts on a large scale to the description of action behind the scenes in the contemporary world, where German plots were forever being thwarted by British agents, who thus prevented the enemy from achieving advantages that would make actual hostilities profitable. *England's Peril* (1899) set the pattern for this kind of work.

Le Queux was not content to write stories about the exploits of spies; he wanted to alert the British public to the menace posed by the 'Invisible Hand' – the German 'fifth column' that was supposedly already at work in England. It was in pursuance of promoting this kind of alarm that he may have laid claim to knowing far more about the secret world of espionage than he actually did. The actual outbreak of hostilities made him even more vociferous, and he was able to follow up such speculative non-fictions as *Spies of the Kaiser* (1909) with the novel *The German Spy* (1914) and the supposedly non-fictional *German Spies in England* (1915) as well as more lurid propaganda along the lines of *German Atrocities* (1914).

Alfred Harmsworth had been sufficiently impressed by 'The Poisoned Bullet' to turn to le Queux again when he planned a much more spectacular circulation-boosting exercise for the most significant of all his publishing ventures, the *Daily Mail*. Le Queux spent some months researching the story, aided by a naval writer, H.W. Wilson, and the redoubtable Lord Roberts, leader of the political campaign for increased defence spending. In the event, though, it was Harmsworth who decided the tactics of the imaginary German invasion with an eye to circulation, sending the troops through various major towns. I.F. Clarke records that Harmsworth even dressed sandwich-board men in German uniforms to advertise the paper.[1] The serial began in March 1906, and was reprinted later in the year in book form as *The Invasion of 1910*. It became a bestseller and may have been the most widely read of all the British future war stories; Clarke notes that it was translated into twenty-seven different languages, and that the German edition had a different ending, in which the invaders won.[2] Needless to say, the 'Invisible Hand' is prominently featured, and alarm was so widely promoted that questions were being asked in Parliament about the government's inaction regarding this supposed enemy within.

Le Queux seems to have been one of the few writers who were delighted by the advent of the Great War, feeling that it justified all his warnings. He was one of the few speculative writers to write future war stories while the war was actually in progress. *The Zeppelin Destroyer* (1916) castigates the government for failing to prepare an adequate defence against Zeppelin raids, and features the timely invention of a miraculous ray-gun which can shoot them out of the sky. This was virtually the only occasion on which le Queux bothered to devise new weaponry, although *The Terror of the Air* (1920), a thriller about the exploits of Teutonic air pirates, has an advanced flying machine and features biological warfare on a limited scale.

Unsurprisingly, in view of his paranoia about German spies, le Queux was also preoccupied about the exploits of Bolsheviks in our midst, and his other important future war story is an account of a hypothetical socialist uprising in England, *The Unknown Tomorrow* (1910).

Another journalist who was already involved with the future war sub-genre before Griffith was W. Laird Clowes, whose *The Captain of the 'Mary Rose'* (1892) had been serialised in *The Engineer* and launched Tower Publications' series of future war novels. Clowes (1856–1905) worked for the *Army and Navy Gazette* and wrote several books on the navy. He had earlier written, in collaboration with A.H. Burgoyne, a hypothetical account of *The Great Naval War of 1887* (1887) and he was later to collaborate again with Burgoyne to produce a centenary account of *Trafalgar Refought* (1905). *Black & White*, which had run Colomb's serial 'The Great War of 1892', commissioned its follow-up serial from Clowes, *The Great Peril and How it was Averted* (1893). This fanciful story represents an obvious attempt by Clowes to diversify, and involves a plot by an

American Trust to take over England with the aid of devices similar to those later featured in le Queux's *A Madonna of the Music Halls*. Clowes followed this with another thriller, *The Double Emperor* (1894), which is more Ruritanian romance than futuristic fiction, and seems to have derived its main inspiration from Anthony Hope's *The Prisoner of Zenda* (1894).

Griffith seems also to have provided the initial stimulus for another journalist who did a great deal of work for Arthur Pearson, Louis Tracy, to become a writer of scientific romance. Like le Queux, Tracy – who was born in 1863 in Liverpool – was partly educated in France, and travelled widely in Europe and India. His journalistic career was a very successful one, and he eventually served on the editorial staffs of *The Times* and the *Daily Mail*, but he also pursued a secondary career as a writer of popular fiction.

For Arthur Pearson, Tracy wrote *The Final War* (1896), a fervently militaristic book which is one of the most jingoistic of the major future war novels, and one which subscribed very heavily to the notion of a war to end war. The plot tells how the British Empire manages to survive an evil conspiracy directed against it by other European powers, with the aid of some innovative weaponry and astonishing fighting spirit. The last chapter of the novel is a virtual sermon which builds to a rhetorical crescendo:

> For the message which Science gave the world was that that race alone would conquer in the struggle for existence which showed greatest adaptability, which could easiest accommodate itself to the countless variations of earth's wayward moods. It was the cruel law of the survival of the fittest. There was need of some versatile people who feared no change of climate or contradiction of condition, for whom heat and cold, desert and fertile land, sea and plain, peace and war, luxury and indigence, struggle and ease were alike – whose temperament had infinite degrees passing from sanguine heat to phlegmatic torpor. For such a race the earth lay open, offering its dominion . . .
>
> This, then, is the mission of the Saxon race – slowly but surely to pour itself over the earth, to absorb the nations, to bring to pass that wonderful dream of a world united in a single family and speaking a common speech.[3]

Tracy was a close friend of M.P. Shiel, and it was he who persuaded Shiel to write 'The Empress of the Earth' for Pearson.

The ideology of 'The Empress of the Earth' – so different from the kind of religious evolutionism that Shiel later embraced – is very close to that of *The Final War*, and it may well have been Tracy's influence that was responsible for Shiel's brief acceptance of social Darwinism.

Shiel appears to have been perennially willing to help Tracy out with his hack writing, and had a hand in many of the detective thrillers which he wrote as Gordon Holmes between 1905 and 1919. Shiel also wrote at least one episode of Tracy's second *Pearson's Weekly* serial, *An American Emperor*, issued in book form in 1897. In this story the rich American hero becomes the darling of the French public, and despite strong opposition from the ruling élite is granted imperial power, which he uses to launch an ambitious scheme to irrigate the Sahara, thus vastly increasing the worth of France's colonial holdings. The casual preposterousness of the plot is out of line with Tracy's subsequent work, and it may be that Shiel had a hand in the planning of the story as well as the writing of it. The sequel, *The Lost Provinces* (1898), reverts to a more conventional future war theme. The advanced armaments featured in the story are relatively modest, though they do include forerunners of the modern armoured car (this was, of course, some years before Wells published his description of 'The Land Ironclads'). Tracy's last serial for *Pearson's Weekly*, *The Invaders* (1901), is more conventional still, with German and French fifth columnists revealing themselves by attacking and taking control of various English towns.

In his later work Tracy did attempt to diversify into other areas of genre fiction, and produced some fantasies of other types. In the thriller *The King of Diamonds* (1904) he borrowed from Shiel's *Lord of the Sea* the idea of a diamond-studded meteor whose discovery makes its finder phenomenally rich, but his hero is much more modest in his schemes than Richard Hogarth had been. *Karl Grier, the Strange Story of a Man with a Sixth Sense* (1906) is an early story of telepathy, but as in *The King of Diamonds* the hero finds only the most modest of uses for his talent, saving the girl he loves from a villain out of Victorian melodrama.

Even more successful as a journalist, in the fullness of time, than Tracy was Max Pemberton (1863–1950), who ultimately became a director of Northcliffe Newspapers. (Alfred Harmsworth became Lord Northcliffe in 1905.) On the way to this pinnacle of success he founded the London School of Journalism, and was for a while editor of *Cassell's Magazine*. In 1893, though, he held the humbler position of editor of the boys' paper *Chums*, and it was for this publication that he wrote his Vernian romance of modern piracy, *The Iron Pirate*, which was reprinted in book form in the same year. This was to become one of the most popular of all the Victorian boys' books, with its remarkably charismatic anti-hero Captain Black, who murderously terrorises the seas with his gas-powered golden ship, keeping his vicious crew in check by sheer force of personality.

Pemberton went on to write numerous other thrillers, mostly aimed at the adult market. The ones which border on scientific romance are often stories of the sea which feature Vernian refuges from the greater world, secluded and heavily fortified. *The Impregnable City* (1895) is one such, and *The House Under the Sea* (1902) another. He also wrote some stories of aborted wars after the fashion of le Queux, including *Pro Patria* (1901), in which the French build a channel tunnel for nefarious purposes, and *The Giant's Gate* (1901), in which submarines are used to evade Britain's sea defences. When the anti-hero of *The Iron Pirate* returned in a belated sequel, *Captain Black* (1911), he too had a submarine, but it had not the dash of the *Nautilus* or the golden ship. The most interesting of his speculative works is *The Phantom Army* (1898), an alternate history story set in 1893, dealing with an imaginary Napoleonic uprising – a story which, by its very nature, required no scientific innovations.

It is only to be expected that these journalistic writers, into whose hands the future war sub-genre was very largely delivered, would be relatively unambitious in their further ventures in scientific romance. Imaginative innovation was not their style; as newspapermen they were no strangers to invention, but their inventions were always confined by narrow horizons of probability. There was nothing Wellsian about their work; they did not partake of any new perspective opened up by nineteenth-century discoveries in science, Tracy's racist social Darwinism notwithstanding. Those who followed in their footsteps in later years developed their own curious sub-genre of frustrated wars and fantastic plots – thrillers and spy stories in which the world is frequently threatened with disastrous disruption, but always saved from it. Practitioners of this dubious literary art included J.S. Fletcher, E. Phillips Oppenheim, Edgar Wallace, Sydney Horler and Sax Rohmer, and there is hardly a writer of popular thrillers flourishing in Britain between the wars who did not borrow a little from the mythology of Invisible Hands, terrorists armed with new weapons, and foreign plots to plunge Europe into war.

On the whole, very few writers indeed followed George Griffith in suggesting that the shape of the war that was to come would be very different from the wars that had gone before. Wells realised this, a little belatedly, and Shiel had some sense of it too, but the great majority of writers remained stuck in a contemporary rut. Outside *The Angel of the Revolution* and *The War in the Air* one can find hardly any mention of aerial bombing, even by Zeppelins. Edward Douglas Fawcett was prepared to produce a quick copy of *The Angel of the Revolution*, dissenting from Griffith's political ideology, in *Hartmann the Anarchist; or, the Doom of the Great City* (1893), but he did not attempt to follow up this lead – his other scientific romances, *Swallowed by an Earthquake* (1894) and *The Secret of the Desert* (1895) are Vernian boys' books. The future war stories which continued to roll off the production line between 1893 and 1914 were reflections of a national paranoia rather than attempts to glimpse future possibilities.

I.F. Clarke's bibliography *Tale of the Future* indicates that 1907 was a particularly good year for future war stories, with more than half a dozen appearing, and it is not surprising that two years later P.G. Wodehouse published his carefree parody of the species, *The Swoop*, in which an alert boy scout puts paid to invaders from Germany, Russia and several other nations, not to mention the Swiss Navy and the hordes of Islam. The species was not completely without artistry, though, producing on the very eve of the Great War H.H. Munro's excellent story of defeated England, *When William Came* (1913). This is a 'Wake up, England!' novel like so many others – its most similar predecessor was *The Message* (1907) by A.J. Dawson – but it is delicately executed, with a carefully understated sense of urgency, and it turns the tables on Wodehouse by giving the small, symbolic gesture of rebellion which closes the story to the boy scouts.

There is no way of telling how much difference these stories of imminent war made to probability that a real war would be fought. They can hardly have been crucial, though it is likely that they did make a contribution to the relish with which many Britishers welcomed the beginning of the Great War, queuing up to fight in it. In reflecting anxieties about the danger of invasion, the activities of fifth columnists, and the malice of the German imperialists these stories also fed those anxieties, creating something of a positive feedback effect. In popularising the myth of a war to end war, the stories helped the prosecutors of the war to give it that image.

What George Griffith might have thought of the actual carnival of destruction which ran for four years in the blasted landscapes of France we can only guess. Some of his contemporaries seemed relatively unaffected by it – le Queux seemed not at all disturbed. On the other hand, there were several who, for whatever reason, never returned to the writing of futuristic thrillers afterwards. Tracy, who held a commission during the war, was one of these. One, at least, had second thoughts about what he was doing even before the war began, and had a complete change of heart afterwards. This was Erskine Childers, author of one of the finest stories of frustrated invasion plans, *The Riddle of the Sands* (1903). In the 1913 edition of the book Childers regretted any anti-German feeling that he might have stirred up, and expressed 'the hope that nobody will read into this story of adventure any intentions of provoking feelings of hostility to Germany, with whom, happily, far friendlier relations have recently been established'.[4] Later still, in the posthumous edition of 1931, M.A. Childers added a more explicit comment:

> In *The Riddle of the Sands*, first published in 1903, Erskine Childers advocated preparedness for war as being the best preventive of war. During the years that followed, he fundamentally altered his opinion. His profound study of military history, of politics, and later of the causes of the Great War convinced him that preparedness induced war. It was not only that to the vast numbers of people engaged in the fostered war services and armament industries, war meant the exercise of their professions and trades and the advancement of their interests; preparedness also led to international armament rivalries, and bred in the minds of the nations concerned fears, antagonisms, and ambitions, that were destructive to peace.[5]

Erskine Childers had died by firing squad in 1922, after a secret trial and with his appeal unheard. He was executed because of his activities in the Irish Republican Army, whose chief propagandist he had become. The only other important author active in the future war sub-genre who actually became a casualty of war was H.H. Munro, who was killed in action in 1916.

The Discovery of the Future

H.G. Wells's pamphlet *The Discovery of the Future* (1902) announced the advent of a new kind of man, orientated in his thinking towards the future rather than the past, and also expressed his conviction that the future was knowable: that it *could* be explored and discovered if only people would try. This was a more novel suggestion than it now sounds, and it represented an attitude that called forth several sceptical responses. The meditative French writer Anatole France wrote an excellent fictional essay, *The White Stone* (1905), on the difficulties of prognostication, and observed in the course of its discussion that Wells was the only man who really had set out to explore the future, ready and able to be surprised by what he found there, instead of merely projecting into it his hopes and fears. Even Wells, as we have noted, became a backslider in this regard.

Wells was right in pointing to the existence of future-orientated men; the world was full of reformers of various kinds. By the time he wrote his little essay, there *had* emerged, too, a vague consensus about what the future would probably be like. Attention had been focused upon various trends which seemed well set, and no matter whether people approved or disapproved of these trends they were prepared to concede that they constituted signposts to the future. The main prop supporting this consensus was not so much the idea of constant technological advancement, but rather a notion similar to that expressed in Auguste Comte's law of the three stages: the idea that human thought and social life was passing out of an era when it had been dominated by metaphysical theories, and into an era where positivistic and materialistic theories would hold dominion. There was a widespread conviction that as men became more knowledgeable and more technically competent they would also become more 'rational'. The word 'rational' has to be placed in inverted commas in this context, because it has a special meaning not particularly well related to its literal one. Within this uneasy consensus 'rational' was taken to imply a lack of emotion, a calculative utilitarianism, and an overweening respect for order. This kind of 'rationality' has its own morality, which rejected many of the taboos of traditional morality as mere superstition and substituted a pragmatic humanism.

Wells was one of the main subscribers to this consensus, and one of the main popularisers of it. He was by no means an originator of it, though, and a few earlier enthusiasts had employed fiction to dramatise it. One was Grant Allen (1848–99), another of those clergyman's sons converted to freethought, whose career anticipated that of Wells in many ways, albeit feebly. He became a populariser of evolutionism, though he favoured Herbert Spencer over the narrower Darwinian creed of Thomas Henry Huxley. He made his living in the 1880s as a scientific journalist and short story writer, though he found it hard without the markets that Wells later had open to him. He was a member of the Fabian Society and an ardent champion of the sexual liberation of women: his bestseller *The Woman Who Did* (1893) brought him belated notoriety.

Allen's first scientific romance was 'Pausodyne' (1881), a story of suspended animation in which a man awakened from a sleep of generations cannot persuade his new contemporaries of the truth of his story. Of much greater significance, though, is 'The Child of the Phalanstery' (1882), in which he took his stand as a champion of the new mythology of progress. The story revolves around a moral dilemma faced by members of a Fourieresque future society, and pleads the case for reasonable infanticide. It is a story designed to shock, but also to provide an ambitious parable in support of the new ideology. Most of the other parables which he wrote to attack traditional morality and superstition, and to put forward his theories of cultural determinism, have a contemporary setting but in his one speculative novel, *The British Barbarians* (1895), he tried to see the world from the hypothetical viewpoint of an anthropologist of the future, simultaneously amused and appalled by our stupidly primitive ways.

Allen subtitled *The British Barbarians* 'a Hill-top Novel', and claimed in the introduction to be raising 'a protest in favour of purity' to counterbalance the 'stories of evil tendencies' with which the world had recently been flooded. This is, of course, mockery, reflecting the prejudices of those who had condemned *The Woman Who Did* as an immoral work, but Allen goes on to explain his own idea of 'purity', with the aid of liberal quotation from Herbert Spencer. The story is frankly artless, and Allen's anthropologist must seem to modern readers to be a vain fool – but then, so were most of the anthropologists of the day, offering judgments on the life of distant societies from the security of their armchairs, relying entirely on hearsay evidence. The book appeared as part of John Lane's 'Keynotes' series, alongside the early works of M.P. Shiel and a novel by another unorthodox champion of progress, John Davidson. The central character of *Earl Lavender* (1895) acquires his pseudonym by disguising the title Earl de l'Avenir, which he assumes when he decides that he is the *übermensch* favoured by the progressive thrust of evolution, and that he can therefore trust fate to look after him. Although Davidson was an authentic Nietzschean, *Earl Lavender* is not intended to be taken seriously, and makes its main appeal to the reader in its portrayals (supported by an Aubrey Beardsley illustration) of aesthetes revelling in flagellation. In such company, Allen could hardly hope that his message would be received in the right spirit. Allen's premature death prevented his making further use of scientific romance for propagandist purposes, though he did a neat disaster story for *The Strand* in 1897, 'The Thames Valley Catastrophe'.

Following Allen's death in 1899 Wells and Shiel were left in a rather isolated position as writers of scientific romance who were firmly committed to the cause of progress. Even Wells, in *The Time Machine* and *The War of the Worlds*, can hardly have seemed enthusiastic about future prospects. The majority of writers, contemplating the 'rational' future, were uneasy, and a few were quite appalled. Many felt that if this was to be the shape of the future then the time was more than ripe for the second coming of Christ and the Day of Judgment. Clarke's *Tale of the Future* lists more than a dozen novels with that theme from the early years of the twentieth century.

The most spectacular novel of this kind was *Lord of the World* (1907) by Robert Hugh Benson but the writer who made most capital out of this kind of work was 'Guy Thorne', who published the bestselling *When it was Dark* in 1903. In this novel an evil humanist fakes evidence to prove that Christ's resurrection never took place, and shatters the Christian faith. There follows a virtual breakdown of civilisation as moral anarchy threatens, but the world is saved when the fraud is exposed. This success was followed up by *Made in His Image* (1906), in which a future world made in the conventional mould is saved from its degradation by a resurgence of Christian faith, and by *The Angel* (1908) and *And it Came to Pass* (1916), both of which featured superhuman moral exemplars. The last novel, published in the taut years of the war, awoke an echo of the fervent welcome given to *When it was Dark*.

'Guy Thorne' was actually Cyril Arthur Edward Ranger Gull (1876–1923), the son of a clergyman who definitely had not turned against the faith of his father. By profession he was a journalist, and quite a successful one – he worked at various times for the *Saturday Review*, the *Daily Mail* and the *Daily Express* – although he ultimately gave up that work to become a novelist, retiring to seclusion in Cornwall. By the time he began writing fiction the popular magazine boom was over, but le Queux was still available as a model. Under his own name he wrote a fantasy for F.V. White, *The Soul-Stealer* (1906), and an Invisible Hand conspiracy novel, *The Enemies of England* (1915). Oddly, he chose to put the Guy Thorne pseudonym on his own Zeppelin-destroyer novel, *The Secret Sea-Plane* (1915), published a year before le Queux's, and to a number of borderline fantasy thrillers which he published after the war. He signed his own name to his most important post-war scientific romances, *The Air Pirate* (1919) – again, published just ahead of le Queux's similar *Terror of the Air* – and *The City in the Clouds* (1921), in which a wealthy scientist builds a floating pleasure palace over London. His posthumous *When the World Reeled* (1924, as Thorne) is a world-blackmail story involving weather control, after the fashion of George Griffith's *The Great Weather Syndicate*.

Gull's peculiar career lends emphasis, if any were needed, to the observation that one did not need any real interest in future possibility to qualify as a writer of popular scientific romance. Like his model, William le Queux (with whom, of course, he was presumably acquainted and probably friendly), Gull was in no sense a 'future-orientated man' of the kind described in Wells's essay. The apparatus of scientific romance, which had become familiar and conventional by the time he began writing, was for him simply a set of available literary devices for enlivening hack thrillers. Whenever he became serious in commenting on the significance of the march of technological change, he was steadfastly loyal to the 'no-good-will-come-of-it-all' school.

In between the extremes represented by Allen and Gull, though, there were writers who were prepared to approach the future in a more enquiring spirit, whose 'discoveries' there were thus enabled to become rather more interesting. One such writer was Robert Cromie (1856–1907), an Irishman who left his career in banking during the 1890s to become a professional writer. A substantial fraction of his output was scientific romance, and had he not died, like Grant Allen, shortly after his fiftieth birthday, he might well have done more.

Cromie's first futuristic novel, *For England's Sake* (1889), was a mundane future war story, significant only in its unfortunate timing – it was published a year or two before the boom in such fictions. This was followed, though, by the interplanetary novel *A Plunge into Space* (1890), which pleased Jules Verne well enough for him to be persuaded to write a preface for the second edition of 1891. In view of Verne's enthusiasm for this story his subsequent acid comment about *The First Men in the Moon* seems uncharitable, because Cromie uses a means of propulsion very similar to that devised by Cavor. Cromie's voyagers find a desert Mars where an advanced quasi-Utopian society is entering a decadent phase. The story is relatively uneventful by comparison with many later Martian fantasies, and follows what was later to become a clichéd line, focusing on a romance between the hero and a Martian girl. This plot is bound to seem weak to modern readers, though it has an unusually grim conclusion following the discovery that the spaceship has not enough air to bring all its passengers safely back to earth, but it serves as the vehicle for some thoughtful discussions about the rewards and costs of material progress. Unusually, the characters find Utopia not to be to their taste, but the author judges that their perspective is distorted:

> And yet if there was nothing of future novelty possible under the Martian sun, nor beneath his twin moons; if material and philosophical science had been long centuries back perfected, till every natural force had been subjugated to man's service; if knowledge had grown until by its own excess it had rent the veil from every secret in the boundless fields of hitherto untrodden truth and destroyed the possibility of its farther grasp; if literature and art by constantly mending had finally ended themselves in a grand domain of sublime achievement further than which no created man might go; if idyllic social economy had followed in the wake of individual refinement till there was nothing left to fight for on Mars,

hardly anything to sigh for; if the daily round of life was as even and undisturbed as the slow-recurring seasons of the planet itself, there was much that might have recompensed these restless men of Earth for the sweet monotony of absolute perfection. There was much, could they but have read the lesson aright.[6]

There follows, of course, a painstaking enumeration of the advantages of such an existence. In the end, though, the structure of the story requires the questions raised to remain open. Cromie's next scientific romance, published in the same year as *The Time Machine*, was *The Crack of Doom* (1895), an even more ambitious attempt to fuse a melodramatic plot with thoughtful consideration of future possibilities for mankind. Set a hundred years in the future, the plot concerns the exploits of an amoral scientist who has discovered the secret of atomic energy, and proposes to apply it in the service of his highly eccentric interpretation of the Darwinian message. This strange anti-hero embraces a pessimism as deep as that of William Hope Hodgson, but a great deal more callous. His metaphysics elevates the idea of Nature red in tooth and claw to a universal principle, and he proposes to intervene in the course of history by triggering his own orgy of destruction. Some modern readers find the book utterly stupid (Suvin judges it 'incoherent', and provides a very uncharitable plot summary in his bibliography[7]) and it must be conceded that as an amateur philosopher Cromie fails to carry much conviction. Nevertheless, it represents an exploratory spirit that has much to commend it.

The Next Crusade (1896) is a more modest effort, set firmly in the conventional mould of contemporary future war stories, but it represents itself as the second volume of a 'history of the future' – the first volume being *For England's Sake* – and thus might be regarded as a preparation for more ambitious work. That more ambitious work, though, never did materialise. It was at about this time that Cromie devoted himself to full-time writing, and it may be that the pressure of making a living from his pen forced him to be more conservative in what he wrote. Whatever the reason, though, he produced only one more futuristic story – a stereotyped thriller about a secret society conspiring to obtain world dominion, misleadingly entitled *A New Messiah* (1902).

Cromie's exploratory fervour was actually rather ill-matched with the vehicles he used to contain it. There is so much in his plotting and dialogue that is solidly Victorian, utterly dominated by the conventions of the day, that his attempts to reach out for new horizons can hardly help but seem eccentric. Wells managed to escape this trap – though not without difficulty, as the awkward format of *The Time Machine* demonstrates – by casting off much of the dead weight of literary convention. His creativity was adequate to that task, but there were very few people who could have hoped to emulate him.

The conventions of Victorian fiction were easier to cast away in stories which took themselves less seriously than Cromie's. It was what passed for 'realism' (though it was not at all realistic) in the representation of conversation and sentiment that was the real dead weight. Accounts of hypothetical futures could actually be more neatly composed if, while not reducing to mere farce or ordinary satire, they were content to be moderately lighthearted. A quaint example is provided by the anonymous paperback novelette *The Coming Era; or, Leeds Beatified* (1900), signed 'A Disciple' (of Wells), whose hero borrows Wells's time machine to see what fate has in store for his home town. The accounts of the time-traveller trying to raise a supply of future currency by pawning the time machine are amiably silly, but they do provide a suitable context for observations about the effects of progress on an industrial city.

A much more sophisticated exercise in this spirit is Rudyard Kipling's first essay in scientific romance, 'With the Night Mail' (1905), which uses the ingenious tactic of offering glimpses of the future via its trivia – advertisements, snippets of news and the like. The story takes advantage of the fact that it is possible to imply much more than is actually stated by deft selection of detail. The basic futuristic vision of the story – of a world revolutionised by air travel – is both sober and serious, but the sobriety and seriousness are not undermined, as they are in so many early stories of the future, by deadly earnest narration. Kipling – who had already shown an interest in the implications of new technologies in such stories as 'Wireless' (1902) – went on to flesh out the image of future society presented in 'With the Night Mail' in the more orthodox story 'As Easy as ABC' (1912).

Kipling was, however, exceptional among writers of prestige in being prepared to dabble in scientific romance even to this limited extent. In a way, this is surprising, because Wells was not only a very popular author but a much-respected man in the literary community. He had many admirers among his peers, and several significant literary friendships (though some of these were soured by feuding), but very few really capable writers were attracted by the prospect of writing scientific romance. Henry James was prepared to dabble in stories of the supernatural, but not in speculative fiction; Arnold Bennett left scientific romance alone; and even Joseph Conrad, who was wildly enthusiastic about some of Wells's efforts, only introduced a very tiny measure of speculative fiction into one of his collaborations with Ford Madox Hueffer, *The Inheritors* (1901). This reflects the fact that Wells's prestige within the literary community was of a peculiar kind. He was seen as a man who had achieved great successes *in spite of* the character of his work; his feat in winning respect for extravagant fantasies was considered almost paradoxical; a freak performance which could not stand as a precedent. Wells himself became a subscriber to this view, and despite his prickly egotism he determined to put his early work behind him and cement his reputation by proving that he could write 'real novels' too. Writers who had been prepared to contest this view of the doubtful legitimacy of scientific romance and science fiction have always been few, and other writers followed in Wells's footsteps first in taking to scientific romance with enthusiasm and then in dropping it from their repertoire.

What also has to be taken into account, though, is that the great literary men of Wells's day – and, for that matter, of almost every day – were the kind of people that he criticised in *The Discovery of the Future* for being enmired in the past, looking backwards instead of forwards. The nature of literary tradition probably makes this inevitable. It was for this reason that Wells tended to fall out with his friends, as he did with Henry James – because there was a sense in which they were his enemies, too. They could not go along with his ideas, and one or two of them even adopted his methods purely in order to express their dissent. One such exercise, now established as a classic, was E.M. Forster's 'The Machine Stops' (1909), which is a very artful piece of anti-Wellsian propaganda, deploring the ideology of material progress by predicting that it must ultimately lead mankind to disaster.

A much more profound dissent from Wells's views is found in the first novel written by his great intellectual antagonist

G.K. Chesterton, *The Napoleon of Notting Hill* (1904). In the elegant essay which precedes the text, Chesterton offers a flat contradiction of the thesis of *The Discovery of the Future*. According to this cheerful and ironic argument, the future *cannot* be discovered, because the actors in history are engaged in a ceaseless game of 'Cheat the Prophet', asserting and celebrating the power of their free will by defying all expectations. In his devotion to 'opposite ideas' Chesterton gaily put Wells and Shiel in the shade. He was born in a slightly later age (on 29 May 1874), and while the older generation of clergymen's sons were busy converting to freethought he converted all the way back to a romanticised version of medieval Catholicism

While the consensus was all for a thoroughly 'rational' future, Chesterton looked forward with enthusiasm to an 'irrational' one. Just as the conventional 'rationality' was metaphorical in character, so was his 'irrationality', which was, in its own way, thoroughly reasonable. Where others stressed the virtue of ratiocination, he stressed the virtues of intuition – and was thus able to write detective stories very different in character from those of Conan Doyle. *The Poet and the Lunatics* (1929) features a detective whose successes are achieved because he is certifiably insane. *Manalive* (1912) is the novel which explains most fully his championship of spontaneity in human affairs, but he followed up *The Napoleon of Notting Hill* with other futuristic novels pleading the same case. *The Ball and the Cross* (1909) features a Shielian duel between two larger-than-life eccentrics; *The Flying Inn* (1914) describes the rebellion of the champions of intoxication in an England made dull by faddish sobriety; *The Return of Don Quixote* (1927) tells of the triumph of one of Wells's past-orientated men in changing the world.

Chesterton's work is calculated to subvert the subversiveness of scientific romance, to defy the modern iconoclasts by casting down *their* idols. It is satisfying, though, to note that the table-turning did not stop even with Chesterton; one of the Anglican churchmen with whom he and Hilaire Belloc debated, G.G. Coulton, also adopted the form of fantastic fiction to carry forward his case, in the time-travel novel *Friar's Lantern* (1906).

It is curiously difficult to decide, with the aid of eighty years' hindsight, whether Wells or Chesterton was right about the predictability of the future. If forced to offer a verdict, one would have to say that there was a little justice in each of their claims. In the world around us we can see elements of the 'rationality' in which the *fin de siècle* consensus placed its faith, but we can also appreciate the extent to which that developing pattern has been compromised by the kind of factors Chesterton would have pointed out: the personalities of certain individuals and a certain stubborn spontaneity of human response to circumstance.

There *is* a sense, though, in which both Wells *and* Chesterton discovered the future. Their real discovery was not the discovery of prophetic power, nor can they really qualify as indexers of plausible possibility, but they did achieve something more than merely projecting their hopes and fears into imaginary eras yet to come. They each used the future as a medium for experiments in thought, where they were able to subject their ideas about what *might* happen to a form of testing. This 'testing' bore little resemblance to the rigorous proof that is entailed by actual experiments, but it had a degree of detachment about it, and an insistent curiosity within it. *The Napoleon of Notting Hill* is, like *The Time Machine*, an inquiry into the kinds of forces which will shape the future of mankind, and the possibilities which those forces permit. We already know that Chesterton's 1984 is not at all like the real one, but even though 802,701 AD is still a long way in the future we can probably say with confidence that *that* year will not be much like Wells's image of it. Neither story, though, can be ruled incompetent or insignificant on this account. Their real meaning is untouched by such considerations. In so far as they are didactic, the lesson they have to offer may still be attended to (though, like all the best lessons, one need not swallow them whole) and their aesthetic elegance – their playful aspect – has not faded with the years.

The early writers of scientific romance did not 'discover the future' in that they found it for the first time as a location for their stories; that discovery had already been made. Nor did they 'discover the future' in the sense that they found out what it would really be like; that discovery could not be made. Even so, there was something new in the way that the best scientific romances set out to explore the future: a new awareness of and sensitivity to the motive forces of social change. It *is* possible to write stories set in the future without any trace of such an awareness or sensitivity – as some of the lesser practitioners of the future war sub-genre demonstrate – but it is mostly differences of degree that distinguish writers. One of the reasons why it makes sense to write a history of scientific romance, rather than simply offering a catalogue of authors and their works, is that as scientific romance progressed this awareness and sensitivity altered and matured according to a more or less consistent pattern.

The Allure of the Extraordinary

The particular fascination exerted by stories of bizarre and extraordinary events has never been quite respectable. It is rather like putting freaks of nature on display in a fairground: people are willing to pay to look at midgets, bearded ladies and seven-legged calves, but feel slightly ashamed of that willingness. There is an element of shame, too, in being willing to listen to and be captivated by tales of the unreal. Such tales always have to overcome a certain generic disreputability before they can be applauded, and it is almost always as *exceptions* that they win respectability.

It is because of this that fantastic fictions are often treated in a condescending fashion. Jules Verne's novels were considered – in England, at least – entirely suitable reading *for boys*. Charles Dickens managed to foist upon the Victorians a tradition of Christmas ghost stories, cunningly putting across the idea that in the holiday season a relaxation of normal standards could be forgiven, and even welcomed.

The great success of Wells's scientific romances was not considered to constitute a redemption of scientific romance *per se*, but rather a testimony to his artistry in being able to write stories that were worthy of applause *in spite of* their nature. As we have seen, Wells came to feel rather ashamed of the works that made his reputation, and prestigious writers were reluctant to follow his example. The other men who became wholehearted contributors to the making of the genre were almost all possessed of a determined independence of spirit, and even then, many of them failed to preserve that spirit in the face of subtle disfavour.

There were surprisingly few writers active between 1890 and 1914 who submitted unashamedly to the allure of the extraordinary, taking up the new vocabulary of ideas outlined by Wells purely for its dramatic potential. For a few brief years, though, scientific romance *was* fashionable as the new periodicals went through their experimental phase. That period began in 1893, reached its height around 1898, and had petered out by 1905. While it lasted, a great many magazine writers were permitted a measure of self-indulgence without stigma – a licence to play with some exciting new ideative toys without too much embarrassment.

The writer who took most copious advantage of this licence was C.J. Cutcliffe Hyne. Hyne was born on 11 May 1865 in Bibury, Gloucestershire, the son of a clergyman. He attended Clare College, Cambridge, where he studied natural science, and took his MA in 1891. By that time he had already been writing for some years, placing material in *All the Year Round* and several less prestigious markets. His first novel was *Beneath Your Very Boots* (1889), which features a subterranean race living under England, whose totalitarian theocracy easily puts down a rebellion sparked off by the narrator – an invader from the world above.

When the new middlebrow periodicals appeared in the 1890s Hyne was ready to take the opportunity thus presented. He had travelled widely, and spent a good deal of time at sea while in his twenties, and he used this experience as background for numerous stories set in far-flung outposts of the British Empire. His greatest success was with a series of stories featuring the redoubtable Captain Kettle, who became *Pearson's Magazine's* answer to Sherlock Holmes. This series of picaresque adventures is exotic, though only a handful of its tall tales are actually fantasies, but in other work Hyne was prepared to be much more extravagant. Indeed, he seemed determined to run the entire gamut of speculative notions, in so far as these could be accommodated within the anecdotal framework of his short stories.

He wrote another early speculative novel in *The New Eden* (1892), in which a scientist isolates a boy and girl on a desert island for experimental purposes, but for several years thereafter his scientific romances were all short fictions. Significantly, many of them were produced under the pseudonym Weatherby Chesney. His production reached its peak in 1898, when two Chesney collections appeared – *The Adventures of an Engineer* and *The Adventures of a Solicitor* – each containing several scientific romances, and he also published a number of magazine stories under his own name. The Chesney stories feature airships, submarines, invisible men, Martian invaders, prehistoric survivals and robots, all of which make their appearance and are destroyed, restoring the world to normality (usually without its ever suspecting that it has been disrupted). Of the stories published under his own name in this period, the most notable scientific romances are 'The Lizard', about a prehistoric monster surviving in a deep cave; 'The Mummy of Thompson-Pratt', about a stiff-necked scientist who establishes a mental link between a feckless demonstrator and his mummified ancestor; and 'London's Danger' (later retitled 'The Fire'), about a great fire that devastates London and ruins England as a world power.

Hyne's most famous fantastic novel is *The Lost Continent* (1900), written – like 'London's Danger' – for Arthur Pearson. This is the best of several novels published in the wake of Ignatius Donnelly's *Atlantis: the Antediluvian World* (1882), which popularised the mythology of the sunken continent for Victorian readers. With tongue slightly in cheek, Hyne treated the myth as it really deserved to be treated: as a grandiose exercise in imaginative sensationalism.

When the fashion for scientific romance waned, Hyne reverted to more conventional fare, though he did produce a routine future war novel, *Empire of the World*, in 1910. This is solidly within the Griffith tradition, involving a lone inventor who tries to blackmail the world into peace. Hyne's hero was one of the last to succeed in such a mission; later versions of the formula take a more pessimistic line as regards the world's ability to withstand such pressure.

Hyne continued to produce books until the 1940s – he died in 1944 – and wrote the occasional light-hearted fantasy, including the novel *Abbs: His Story Through Many Ages* (1929), in which an immortal remembers a few incidents from his centuries-long career. Like the ancient Egyptian in 'The Mummy of Thompson-Pratt', Abbs is an amiable and fun-loving character whose memory for things that other people consider historically important is none too strong. His refusal to take things very seriously is an obvious reflection of his creator's outlook on life and literature.

Despite the number of speculative motifs which he introduced into his work, Hyne always retained a certain restraint and discretion. Not everyone who took advantage of the fashion for scientific romance was similarly inclined. Some were tempted to cast off the shackles of imaginative conservatism entirely. One such was Fred T. Jane (1870–1916), who was also the son of a clergyman, and who first got involved with scientific romance by extending his efforts from journalism into pseudo-journalistic consideration of near-future conflict.

Jane differed from the other journalists who turned into war correspondents in that he was an illustrator as well as a writer. He was on the staff of the *London Illustrated News*, and was eventually to lend his name to the famous catalogue of naval silhouettes, *Jane's Fighting Ships*. (Updated versions of this publication and the later *Jane's Fighting Aircraft* have survived into modern times.) He was the illustrator of Griffith's *The Angel of the Revolution* and *Olga Romanoff* in the Tower Publishing Co. editions, and he went on to produce his own future war story for Tower, *Blake of the 'Rattlesnake'* (1895), in which he drew upon his considerable knowledge of naval affairs to present a realistic account of the use of torpedoes in war. The relative sobriety of this novel was not altogether in keeping with the extravagant visions of airships in combat that he provided for Griffith's books, and he quickly followed it up with a more exotic romance, *The Incubated Girl* (1896), in which the 'lost science' of ancient Egypt enables a female homunculus to be manufactured. The story is a romance, but the girl does function to some extent as an innocent observer, after the fashion of Wells's angel in *The Wonderful Visit*.

The lost science of ancient Egypt figures much more prominently in Jane's next novel, *To Venus in Five Seconds* (1897), where it is revealed that it enabled its users to migrate to Venus by matter-transmission. The hero, a medical student, is abducted to Venus by one of their descendants, and while there he also encounters the Venerian indigenes – intelligent elephantine insects. This plot provided ample scope for the author to employ his illustrative talents, as did the last and wildest of his fantasies, *The Violet Flame* (1899). Possibly inspired by Cromie's *The Crack of Doom*, this 'story of Armageddon and after' throws together several fabulous motifs: the super-scientist who tries to blackmail the world; an impending cometary strike; the last survivors of the catastrophe becoming a new Adam and Eve. All this is further complicated by the transmutation of elements and the revelation that the heavenly bodies are living and intelligent. After this, it seems, Jane's attention was wholly absorbed by more serious projects –

130

though it may be that there was simply no way to follow a story as incredibly eventful as this one.

Another writer enabled to produce some strikingly unusual work by the fashion for scientific romance was George C. Wallis, who was primarily a writer for the boys' papers, producing numerous lost race adventure stories. In the later 1890s he did several stories for Arthur Pearson's publications, including a series of Atlantean fantasies antedating Hyne's *The Lost Continent*. It was for Alfred Harmsworth, though, that he produced his two best stories, 'The Last Days of Earth' (1901) and 'The Great Sacrifice' (1903). The first is a curious parable in which the last man and the last woman face death together, the latter an extravagant story in which the inhabitants of Mars sacrifice their own world to save Earth from annihilation by a meteor shower. There were to be no more opportunities for writers of Wallis's rather mediocre abilities in this stratum of the market, though, and he went back to the boys' papers. Interestingly, Wallis was the only writer who contributed to the magazines in this period who subsequently became a contributor to the pulp science fiction magazines.

Other popular magazine writers of this period who dabbled in scientific romance while it was fashionable included Owen Oliver and Fred M. White. Oliver wrote a good deal for Pearson and Harmsworth, most of his short stories being in a rather sentimental vein, but in 'The Black Shadow' (1903) he presented an anecdote about a scientist's soul temporarily displaced from his body by a lunar entity, and then went on to write the amazing 'Out of the Deep' (1904), in which six-foot flying fish with teeth terrorise the sea and ultimately invade the land, smashing civilisation. White was given more to travellers' tales, though these often become exotic, as in 'The Red Speck' (1899), about nasty spiders, and 'The Purple Terror' (1899), about a homicidal tentacled tree. He published one speculative novel, *The White Battalions* (1900), in which a shift in the Gulf Stream brings Arctic winter to Europe, interrupting the course of a future war. This was done for Pearson, as was a series of disaster stories modelled on Hyne's 'London's Danger'. In each story of the series London is threatened with catastrophe, and saved in the nick of time. Some are mundane, like 'The Four White Days' (1903), about a harsh winter, and 'A Bubble Burst' (1903), about a stock-market panic. The great fog in 'The Four Days' Night' (1903) has to be dispelled by aeroplanes, though, and the great plague in 'The Dust of Death' (1903) has to be arrested by an electrical treatment. The other stories in the series are 'The Invisible Force' (1903), about the consequences of an explosion in the Underground, and 'The River of Death' (1904), about a drought.

Another writer who, like George Wallis, slanted most of his work towards a juvenile audience, but was able to gain some advantage from the brief fashion for scientific romance, was Francis Henry Atkins (1840–1927), who signed his earlier works Frank Aubrey and his later ones Fenton Ash. As Aubrey he produced *The Devil-Tree of El Dorado* (1896), an interesting forerunner of Doyle's *The Lost World*, whose main fantasy element is the eponymous man-eating tree; *A Queen of Atlantis* (1899), a Sargasso Sea fantasy; and *King of the Dead* (1903), another South American romance which has some curious (but presumably coincidental) parallels with W.H. Hudson's classic *Green Mansions* (1904). As Ash – which pseudonym he may have shared with his son – he wrote numerous fantastic adventure stories for the boys' papers, most interestingly the interplanetary stories 'A King of Mars' (1907) and 'A Son of the Stars' (1907–8), the first of which was reprinted in book form as *A Trip to Mars* (1909). Ideas used in the Aubrey novels are frequently redeployed in Ash novels: the Sargasso Sea is featured again in *The Black Opal*, serialised in 1905 and reprinted in book form in 1915, while *The Radium Seekers* (serialised 1904, in book form 1905) is a South American romance with numerous fantastic elements.

Ash's *A Trip to Mars* was one of a whole series of imaginative novels published in rather handsome book editions with pictorial covers. Early books of this kind were mostly earthbound Vernian fantasies featuring exotic flying machines: *The Log of the 'Flying Fish'* (1887) by Harry Collingwood and *The Cruise of the Crystal Boat* (1891) by Gordon Stables are examples. As scientific romance became more popular, though, quite a number of these upmarket boys' books took their heroes on interplanetary journeys. Examples include Charles Dixon's *1500 Miles an Hour* (1895), which features a rather improbable propeller-driven spaceship, and Edwin Pallander's *Across the Zodiac* (1896). Pallander went on to write one of the first novels about a human shrunk to microscopic size, *The Adventures of a Micro-Man* (1902), and also collaborated with the American writer Ellsworth Douglass on a short story for *Cassell's Maga-*

zine, 'The Wheels of Dr Gynochio Gyves' (1899), in which an inventor devises a machine which will stand still in space while the earth speeds on. Douglass also wrote an interplanetary novel, published by Arthur Pearson, called *Pharaoh's Broker* (1899), in which Mars is a world whose history is running parallel to that of Earth but delayed by several thousand years.

Despite the examples set by Wells and Griffith in *The First Men in the Moon* and *A Honeymoon in Space*, interplanetary stories remained much more the fare of juvenile fiction than of adult fiction. It was far less easy — as Fred Jane demonstrated — to take trips to Venus as seriously as one could take futuristic stories about torpedo warfare. Earnest attempts were made to continue the tradition of interplanetary stories to which Lach-Szyrma's *Aleriel* belonged, but only J.J. Astor's *A Journey in Other Worlds* (1894) achieved much success in this line, and the trend was to abandon the metaphysical elements of such fiction. All too often, though, what was left was somewhat lacklustre. *A Trip to Venus* (1897) by John Munro, extended from a short story, 'A Message from Mars' (*Cassell's Magazine*, 1895), has a moderately crowded plot but fails to generate excitement. Rather more interesting is Robert William Cole's *The Struggle for Empire* (1900), which took the future war story into space and burst the boundaries of the solar system with the first ever vision of interstellar warfare.

When scientific romance ceased to benefit from its temporary faddishness in the mid-1900s, interplanetary romance was the first subspecies of scientific romance to beat a retreat back into the juvenile market, to which it remained virtually confined for many years. After 1905 none of the major writers of scientific romance made any significant use of interplanetary fiction until the 1930s, when Olaf Stapledon wrote his extravagant visionary novel *Star Maker*. Even then, most of his contemporaries left interplanetary fiction alone: S. Fowler Wright, Neil Bell and John Gloag, the other major writers of scientific romance to emerge between the wars, wrote none of it. This is one of the main points of contrast between the development of British scientific romance and American science fiction. In the former, interplanetary fiction became, with a handful of exceptions, irrelevant; in the latter, it became increasingly important.

Interplanetary romance, though, never disappeared entirely from the British scene, but it remained the property of writers like John Mastin, author of *The Stolen Planet* (1905) and *Through the Sun in an Airship* (1909), purveyors of utterly improbable melodramas for boys whose powers of scientific discrimination were very weak. Interestingly, Mastin's publishers made much of his scientific publications (in the field of biology) when advertising his works – as well as the fact that the king 'graciously condescended' to accept copies as free gifts (for H.R.H Prince Edward) – although the imaginary physics in which they are based is patently absurd. The last really effective interplanetary romance to come out of Britain for twenty-five years was a book which did not take the idea of space travel at all seriously – the exotic dream-fantasy *Lt Gullivar Jones – His Vacation* (1905) by Edwin Lester Arnold, a lush and captivating adventure story which anticipates many aspects of the interplanetary fantasies of the American writer Edgar Rice Burroughs.

This break in the history of interplanetary fiction is perhaps the most obvious result of the decline in the fortunes of scientific romance. Wells was already an institution in his own right, and the fact that he ceased to patronise the genre must be attributed to other factors, while Doyle perversely left it alone during its peak years and returned to it when it was no longer in fashion, and Shiel was always very much his own man. Lesser writers, though, were clearly affected by the changing market forces, and those who persisted in producing scientific romance found it difficult to reach a public. George Griffith was not the writer he had been in his later years, but this was not the only factor involved in his shift to the production of potboiler books which apparently went largely unread. Other writers in his vein, who came along too late to catch the boom, have lapsed into total obscurity. One such is William Holt-White, who wrote six sub-Griffith novels between 1906 and 1914 without acquiring the least vestige of a reputation even among the indefatigable historians of science fiction.

Not everyone, of course, took the boom in scientific romance seriously even while it was happening, and it called forth a good many parodies. Particular works were often mocked after becoming successful: Allen's *The British Barbarians* was followed by H.D. Traill's *The Barbarous Britishers* (1896) and Wells's *The War of the Worlds* by C.L. Graves and E.V. Lucas's *The War of the Wenuses* (1898). The entire enterprise was also subjected to some sarcastic treatment. *The Ludgate Monthly*, a cheap imitation of *The Strand*, carried in its first Christmas

Annual (1891) a short novel by Henry Herman called 'The Woful Story of Mr Wobbley, Comedian; or, the Dangers of Modern Science', whose hero has some unhappy experiences after offering himself as an experimental 'odic battery'. For Arthur Pearson the humorous writer Barry Pain produced a series of articles on 'Nature's Next Moves', caricaturing the inventions of scientific romance with accounts of such useful innovations as Chameleonica (the perfect medicine for hypochondriacs); Treble-X-rays (powerful enough to show up the thoughts inside the brain); and the Poom (a new all-purpose pet). Pain himself, though, submitted eventually to the allure of the extraordinary in some of his later, more serious works, notably *An Exchange of Souls* (1911), which describes a scientific experiment to trap and control personality which goes tragically wrong.

The fad for scientific romance was so very largely based in the middlebrow magazines and the penny weeklies that it was bound to be checked by the great changes that affected the periodicals around the turn of the century. The founding of Harmsworth's *Daily Mail* in 1896 and Pearson's *Morning Herald* – later the *Daily Express* – in 1900 did not directly affect the monthly magazines, but they did displace a good many of the more frequent ephemeral journals which would now seem to us 'hybrid' entities, half-newspaper and half-magazine. These new daily papers divided the world of popular newspapers from the kinds of journalism that remained associated with the monthlies and the weeklies. Quite apart from the fact that these new papers absorbed much of the attention of Harmsworth and Pearson, taking their personal influence away from the business of discovering new writers of fiction and commissioning extravagant serials, the very success of the *Mail* and the *Express* spelt the doom of the kind of enterprise with which *Pearson's Weekly* and the *Pall Mall Budget* had been so heavily and so profitably involved. Both the *Mail* and the *Express* were to run some serial fiction, including future war material, but for them such exercises could not be a part of their staple diet, merely an occasional whimsy.

The transformation of this lower stratum of the middlebrow market changed the shape of the market which confronted writers of popular fiction, and economic power over fiction production came to be vested much more in book publication – books were becoming much cheaper now that the old three-deckers had been swept away – and in the more upmarket magazines, which were rapidly accumulating their own burden of tradition. *The Strand, Pearson's Magazine* and the *Pall Mall Magazine* had all attained respectability (and economic security) by 1905, and their experimental phase was over. Scientific romance never really touched the more sedate and long-established periodicals, though isolated stories did appear in the *Cornhill, Belgravia* and *Temple Bar*. Even the Scottish journal *Blackwood's*, which had a long tradition of presenting supernatural stories, and in the 1880s had serialised Curwen's *Zit and Xoe* and Minto's *The Crack of Doom*, remained virtually aloof, though in 1901 it published 'The Captivity of the Professor' by A. Lincoln Green, in which a scientist is captured and temporarily enslaved by intelligent ants. Blackwood also published Green's longer excursion in scientific romance, *The End of an Epoch* (1901), though the journal did not carry the story as a serial. *The End of an Epoch* is a great plague story whose protagonist, Adam Godwin, has experiences which often parallel (literally and allegorically) those of Shiel's Adam Jeffson.

In strictly commercial terms, therefore, the extraordinary had lost much of its allure long before the outbreak of the Great War. Writers drawn to the genre after 1905 again had disincentives to overcome, and it once again became problematic placing such works before the public. The tide was never really stemmed, though, and writers continued to emerge whose personal motivation and sense of purpose were adequate to make them careless of the slight disreputability and esotericism of speculative fiction. There had always been such people, of course, because the extraordinary has an allure of its own that can often transcend commercial considerations. To a certain extent, Wells *was* an opportunist who took advantage of a market space that opened up for him, but he was not at all the same kind of opportunist as Cutcliffe Hyne. The fanciful ideas which fascinated him exerted an enormously powerful force upon his imagination, which demanded expression. It must be remembered that he began, essentially, as a hobbyist writer playing with ideas for his own edification in 'The Chronic Argonauts' which were only reworked by degrees into the viable popular fiction of *The Time Machine*.

There were other hobbyist writers of this kind, who made little impact on the public or on their fellow writers, but who can be seen in retrospect to have been possessed of remarkable powers of imagination. Often, such writers were not blessed with any conspicuous stylistic elegance – sometimes they were frankly inept – but they do warrant attention for the sheer idiosyncrasy of their creativity.

The cardinal example of this kind of writer is the author of *Scientific Romances* himself, Charles Howard Hinton (1853–1907), a professional mathematician who became fascinated with the idea of four-dimensional space. He published his first essay on the topic, 'What is the Fourth Dimension?', in 1880, four years before another mathematician, Edwin Abbott, published his classic dimensional fantasy *Flatland*. His first work of didactic fiction, though, was unconnected with this interest, dramatising instead a thesis held by his father, the surgeon James Hinton, about the virtues of pain. 'The Persian King' describes a hypothetical world where one individual becomes an animating and progressive force by accepting a burden of pain from its inhabitants, thus precipitating them out of a balanced situation by 'donating' a surplus of pleasure to their endeavours. His efforts are facilitated by some clever mathematical figuring about how to establish a situation where the maximum motion can be elicited from the minimum removal of pain. The thesis bears, of course, on the significance of Christ's redemptive suffering on the cross.

Stella & An Unfinished Communication: Studies of the Unseen (1895; later reprinted in *Scientific Romances: Second Series*) presents two novelettes closer in theme to Hinton's own interests. The first is the story of an invisible girl of a rather moralistic bent, who has various adventures; the second is a much more baroque tale in which the fact that duration can be represented as a fourth dimension is used to support the supposition that interference from a higher space-time entered after death might allow the record of a lifetime to be productively reconstructed. Hinton died while his last scientific romance, *An Episode of Flatland* (1907), was in press. This very strange story describes a two-dimensional world rather more complicated than Abbott's, and features a startling plot in which the inhabitants of a two-dimensional planet avoid collision with another by diverting their 'world' in the third dimension, taking advantage of the fact that – like the human hero of 'An Unfinished Communication' – their souls have access to more dimensions than their bodies.[8]

Another learned man who employed scientific romance for a very strange exposition of some of his theories was James

William Barlow (1826–1913), the son of a clergyman who became professor of modern history at Trinity College, Dublin. He published several books on history, theology and ethics, and attempted to dramatise his ideas in *History of a World of Immortals Without a God*, published under the pseudonym Antares Skorpios in 1891 and reprinted under his own name as *The Immortals' Great Quest* in 1909. Although framed as an interplanetary story this resembles Hinton's 'The Persian King' in describing the history of a hypothetical world from its inception. The immortal inhabitants of a Utopian society depend for their existence on their happiness; when it fails they are disintegrated and re-embodied on another continent. As in Hinton's story, the inhabitants of this hypothetical world try to reason from what they know of the conditions of their existence to the nature of their Creator, thus providing a comparison for our own theological efforts.

No biographical details are available in relation to R.A. Kennedy, who was arguably the most adventurous of the writers who used scientific romance as a framework for thought-experiments in metaphysics. His first book was an essay, *Space and Spirit: a Commentary Upon the Work of Sir Oliver Lodge Entitled 'Life and Matter'* (1909), but he followed this in 1912 with *The Triuneverse: a Scientific Romance* (1912), which is built around the hypothesis that there is a hierarchy of universes, whereby the atoms in our universe are worlds in their own right, and our own solar system is but an atom in a greater perspective. It also embodies the notion that worlds might be living organisms, and in the course of the story Mars undergoes repeated binary fission before its clones begin devouring other bodies in the solar system.

As novels these various works leave much to be desired – such matters as characterisation are hardly relevant to their concerns – but it is wrong to try to evaluate them as if they were novels. They are not even stories, despite their token gestures in the direction of conventional plotting. They are really, to borrow a phrase from Olaf Stapledon, 'essays in myth creation' which construct imaginary worlds in order to embody particular metaphysical theses. Each of the three authors attempts to incorporate into his work some kind of presumed insight into spiritual truth, which is as relevant to our lived-in-world as to the bizarre alternative realities which are described, and in so doing they attempt to place *our* world in a greater context, as part of a much more elaborate whole which is the cosmos. This is an essential element in the allure of the extraordinary: the adoption of an extraordinary viewpoint can renew the strangeness of the world which we actually inhabit, and can help us avoid the trap of taking it too much for granted. One of the functions of scientific romance is to jolt us out of an intellectual and imaginative somnolence which can too easily take possession of us and institutionalise us within the pattern of our everyday lives.

PART TWO
The Imaginative Legacy of the Great War

5

FUTURISTIC SPECULATION BETWEEN THE WARS

The Divergence of Scientific Romance and Science Fiction

THE DECLINE in fashion which affected scientific romance after 1905 continued until the outbreak of the Great War, and then was further emphasised by changes in the literary marketplace that were encouraged by the disruptive economic effects of the war. The magazines gradually lost the economic power which they enjoyed in the literary marketplace because it was eroded by competition from cheap books. In the 1890s the new periodicals had played a vital role in the careers of a new generation of professional writers, enticing them to produce short stories in abundance, and to write longer works primarily for magazine serialisation. This decade, though, also saw the rise of the literary agent and the growing power of the Society of Authors. Along with the three-decker novel there died many of the economic arrangements which had made book publication so unprofitable for the great majority of authors. The standardisation of royalty agreements meant that authors of very popular works no longer ran the risk of remaining penniless while publishers who had bought their copyrights grew rich. Payments for serialisation grew relatively less important to professional writers, and the practice of serialisation declined in consequence.

Most of the middlebrow magazines survived the Great War, though there were many casualties, but they emerged into a world where they had become marginal in their economic importance. After 1918 the literary marketplace was first and foremost a market in *books*. Writers of short fiction found themselves with fewer opportunities and – perhaps more significantly – narrower sets of expectations to meet. The phase of development which the popular magazines now entered was anything but experimental, and writers of a more liberal imaginative bent frequently complained about this. In his third collection of short stories, published two years after *Signs and Wonders*, John Beresford included a casually embittered foreword advising would-be authors that if they wanted to sell short fiction to high-paying markets they must at all costs exclude any *meaning* from their work (and he tried very hard to take this advice himself, never again producing anything as ideatively lively as the material in his first two collections). Of the new writers of scientific romance, S. Fowler Wright was able to sell short fiction only during the brief years of his celebrity, and Neil Bell – an indefatigable writer of conversational prefaces – described at some length his great diffficulty in placing his more adventurous work. John Gloag, all of whose early novels were speculative, or at least unusual, wrote only a handful of imaginative short stories, the rest of his work in that medium clinging, like Bell's later stories, to a conventional shallowness.

The principal medium for cheap fiction in Britain between the wars was the cheap hardcover book. A new novel which acquired wide popularity would usually be issued in its early editions at 3s 6d, then reprinted as often as the market would stand in a 2s edition. Eventually it might work its way down to the cheap 1s series like Collins Shilling Fiction Library or Hutchinson's Universal Library, though these were mostly filled with reprints of works initially published before the war, as were the cheapest lines of all – Newnes' Sevenpenny Series and Hodder & Stoughton's Sevenpenny Library. These were the forms in which the popular authors of the period, from Edgar Wallace to John Galsworthy, thrived.

Post-war scientific romance is conspicuous by its absence from these cheap series of books. A good deal of pre-war scientific romance is to be found there: Wells, Doyle, and even Cutcliffe Hyne were published prolifically in this form; but none of the major scientific romances of the 1920s ever reached such editions. Among contemporary writers only Edgar Wallace and E. Phillips Oppenheim routinely had their (rather marginal) imaginative works released in very cheap editions. New scientific romances were not regarded by publishers as books likely to be commercially successful; they were considered esoteric. E.V. Odle, author of what is perhaps the outstanding scientific romance of the 1920s, *The Clockwork Man* (1923), wrote in 1936 that an enthusiastic critical reception (from J.B. Priestley among others) had encouraged him to continue his work in this vein, but that the publishers would have no more of it.[1] Nor, during the years that he was editor of *The Argosy*, did he himself show any particular favour to the genre.

Of the new writers who were to establish themselves as major writers of scientific romance between the wars only one (S. Fowler Wright) made his debut before 1930, and that with books which he initially published himself. The most interesting scientific romances of the 1920s – *The People of the Ruins* (1920) by Edward Shanks, *Theodore Savage* (1922) by Cicely Hamilton, *The Clockwork Man*, and *The Emperor of the If* (1926) by Guy Dent – all remained their authors' sole contributions to the genre, though Hamilton did issue a heavily revised version of her novel as *Lest Ye Die* in 1928. Apart from Fowler Wright the only significant writers of scientific romance whose careers extended from the twenties into the thirties were Muriel Jaeger and Shaw Desmond. Of the writers who began before the Great War, neither Shiel nor Beresford produced any significant scientific romance in the twenties, and it was not until the thirties that Wells's enthusiasm for the genre was reignited in any real measure. Doyle's scientific romances of the twenties were produced with the ulterior motive of popularising his spiritualist ideas.

If the peak of the fashion for scientific romance was reached in 1898, then its trough was reached in 1918 or thereabouts, and its climb out of that depth was a slow one. It was not until 1931 that scientific romance entered a new phase of popularity and a new generation of writers established themselves in the genre. Most of the futuristic works produced in the interim were modest in scope, and the more adventurous ones usually remained obscure (an obscurity which has stayed with most of them until the present day).

In the United States of America, the situation developed very differently. The domestic literary marketplace evolved in an entirely different manner, and the place of futuristic fiction within it was just as different. This resulted in a sharp divergence of characteristic theme and manner between British and American speculative fiction. It is this divergence which justifies the use of different terms – in America, of course, speculative fiction had by 1926 acquired the label 'scientifiction', later modifed to 'science fiction'.

In the years before the Great War most of the major works of British scientific romance were reprinted in America, though Griffith's anti-Americanism kept out many of his works. The USA had its own equivalent writers, most notably Jack London. In America, though, books were already relatively cheap before the 1890s; there was no three-decker price fixing there, and the widespread pirating of English novels helped American publishers to keep their costs down. The conspicuous 'middlebrow gap' which existed in Britain in 1890 was not in evidence in the USA, and the advent of American editions of magazines like *The Strand* and *Pearson's Magazine* made very little difference to the economic situation of American writers.

The boom in US publishing which ran parallel to the periodical boom in Britain was much more closely connected with new technologies allowing the production of cheaper magazines – especially with the mass-production of cheap paper from woodpulp. Pulp magazines began to proliferate in the 1890s, gradually driving out the 'dime novels' which had previously been America's version of the British penny dreadfuls and twopenny novelettes. In Britain the kind of fiction associated with the penny dreadfuls – crude, action-packed melodrama – almost faded away, its genres retired into the boys' papers. In America, by contrast, such lurid material continued to thrive in the pulps, where it underwent only the slightest sophistication. The fiction in the pulps was by no means uniformly awful, and in fact it remained reasonably heterogeneous in character and style, but the marketing of popular fiction in America clearly reflected the more aggressive entrepreneurialism of American marketing in general. The pulp publishers wanted to reach the largest possible number of readers, including as many of the semi-literate as could be enticed into the reading habit, and they were keen to give those readers anything which they showed the least inclination to buy in quantity.

It is frequently alleged that this kind of strategy inevitably reduces the quality of popular fiction to the 'lowest common denominator of popular taste', but the implication that it imports into the fiction a kind of uniformity is misleading. What actually happened was that the publishers of pulp magazines followed the dime novel publishers in adopting a kind of fictional brand warfare. Like the penny dreadful publishers in

Britain, the American dime novel publishers had discovered that people frequently hungered to consume many different examples of the same kind of story, and that many readers would become virtual specialists if given the chance, favouring one species of fiction to the exclusion of others. Dime novels had already diversified into detective novels, westerns, and rags-to-riches romances, and each major publisher had his own line of each particular kind of fiction. There was even a species of dime novel fiction that was speculative in character: fiction about the fanciful exploits of young inventors, aimed primarily at a juvenile audience.

The major pulp publishers began eventually to produce detective pulps, western pulps and various other 'specialist' fiction magazines, but the most successful magazines in the early years – before 1910 – were general fiction magazines which did not specialise, like *The Argosy* and *Blue Book* (originally the *Monthly Story-Teller*). These magazines published a certain amount of speculative fiction, initially importing the bulk of it. *Argosy* reprinted serial stories by Verne, F.H. Atkins and Griffith, while *Blue Book* carried material by William Hope Hodgson and others. The first important American writer to specialise in speculative fiction for the pulps was William Wallace Cook, who wrote a number of serial stories between 1903 and 1907, mostly light in tone but with some propaganda for social reform and a keen awareness of the rapidity of social change.

Cook was rapidly followed by George Allan England, who began publishing serial fiction in 1909. His early works recapitulated familiar fantastic themes, but began to cultivate a more distinctive tone in his novel of rejuvenation, 'The Elixir of Hate' (1911). A good deal of his work exhibits strong socialist sympathies, especially *The Golden Blight* (serialised 1912; in book form 1916) and *The Air Trust* (1915), but he scored his most spectacular success with a trilogy of serials about the adventures of a man and a woman who wake from a long period of suspended animation to find America devastated, inhabited by savages. The trilogy was collected in a single volume as *Darkness and Dawn* (1914), the first serial having appeared under that title in 1912.

Darkness and Dawn is a crude piece of work, rather less impressive in its writing than some of England's other works, but it traded heavily on the daydream appeal of the notion of one man and one woman surviving in an empty world, setting up cosy housekeeeping while undergoing periodic melodramatic adventures. The preposterousness of the story is offset by the deliberate naivety of its fantasy, which is carefully cultivated at great length. At this particular literary game, though, England had to take second place to an undoubted master who made his debut in 1912: Edgar Rice Burroughs. Burroughs published his first two novels in that year, both in the pulp magazine *All-Story*: 'Under the Moons of Mars' (retitled in the book version *A Princess of Mars*) and *Tarzan of the Apes*. As a writer of daydream fantasies Burroughs had no peer, and this was eventually to lead him to unparalleled success as a professional writer. He founded his own publishing company to issue his books when he became impatient with exploitation, and may well have been the first person ever to become a millionnaire by writing fiction; eventually the citizens of his home town renamed it Tarzana in his honour. Burroughs was to have as much influence, in his way, on American imaginative fiction as Wells had on the British version, and he did as much as anyone to give fantastic fiction in America the impetus and direction which was to determine its evolution over the next twenty years. He revitalised interplanetary fiction by using other planets as lush, exotic *milieux* where men could fight monsters, meet extremely beautiful women, and win their way to the command of empires. His fiction was robust, fast paced, colourful and unashamedly innocent of any vestige of intellectual sophistication. It was perfect escapist fantasy, and it exposed a whole new dimension of potential use for the vocabulary of ideas built up by the British and French writers of scientific romance.

The advent of Edgar Rice Burroughs coincided with an important division of the American magazine market, under the influence of advertising agencies. Many magazines moved upmarket and became very heavily dependent on advertising revenue. These were magazines printed on better paper, and they tended to be larger in size, in order to show off their advertisements to the best advantage. Market research had shown that it was women rather than men who determined patterns of purchasing, and these magazines increasingly slanted their material towards a female audience. The pulp magazines, whose economic fortunes depended on their sales rather than their advertisers, continued to base their circulation on the appeal of their fiction. Fantastic fiction remained associated with the pulps, and was largely squeezed out of the higher paying markets, along with most other kinds of adventure-orientated fiction.[2]

Burroughs inspired many imitators, who produced a glut of exotic interplanetary fiction in the pulps after 1918. Writers in this tradition included J.U. Giesy, Homer Eon Flint and Ray Cummings. Writers who diversified their work across a wider spectrum of fantastic themes included 'Francis Stevens' (Gertrude Bennett) and 'Murray Leinster' (Will F. Jenkins), but the only new writer who managed to attain great popularity in the 1920s was Abraham Merritt, who outdid Burroughs in the lavish decoration of his imaginary worlds – usually parallel worlds reached from the surface of the earth rather than other planets – and in the intensity of his narration. He never attained the width of Burroughs' appeal, but he produced the most vivid of all the odysseys in exotica.

The first pulp magazine to specialise in fantastic fiction, *Thrill Book*, appeared in 1919 to coincide with this boom in daydream exotica, but it proved unsuccessful. *Weird Tales*, which initially featured all kinds of imaginative fiction, did manage to build up a viable audience after its debut in 1923, but it eventually became a supernatural fiction magazine as it abandoned futuristic and interplanetary fiction to the science fiction magazines. The first such magazine, *Amazing Stories*, was founded by Hugo Gernsback in 1926. This was a period of feverish proliferation in the pulp magazine market, when publishers were trying out all kinds of new genres in the hope of finding new species capable of holding a corner of the market – there were magazines specialising in railroad stories, sea stories, yellow peril stories, the exploits of crime-fighting superheroes, and even a short-lived pulp called *Zeppelin Adventures*. Most of the genres were inevitably stillborn, but science fiction *did* secure and hold an audience of its own, and though it remained economically precarious for some years the genre was healthy enough to support a number of competing magazines issued by rival publishers.

The sharp differences between British and American speculative fiction which developed after 1918 were by no means solely attributable to the different development of the two nations' literary marketplaces. The fortunes of the two nations were very different in a much larger sense, and this inevitably coloured the outlook of their people.

The Great War was a decisive break in world economic history: the end of an era of European economic dominance. The world monetary and trading system, centred in Europe before 1914, was smashed by the war, and a new era of instability, uncertainty and unprecedented change began, which saw a remarkable financial and industrial upsurge by the US. The United States had sent its soldiers to fight in the war in 1916, but the people who remained at home were largely untouched by the experience, in stark contrast to the people of Europe. It transpired, too, that the United States was the only real winner of the war, enjoying an economic boom throughout the 1920s while Europe was in economic decline. The USA was not without its political upheavals and industrial disputes in the twenties, but there was nothing to compare with the British Labour Party's ascent to power in 1924 or the General Strike of 1926. In these years US productivity was unparalleled, and a whole range of machine-made products became available to ordinary consumers. Automobiles became commonplace, the telephone network spread rapidly, and the consumption of electricity soared. Modern technology really did seem to be bringing about a social metamorphosis in the USA, while Britain remained enmired in economic chaos, seemingly abandoned by progress. It is hardly surprising that speculative fiction began to boom in America, producing a kind of science fiction which rejoiced in the limitless opportunities of futuristic adventure and looked forward to a plethora of new inventions, while the British public remained unmoved and unreceptive.

The economic situation in America was changed dramatically following the Wall Street Crash of 1929, when the great boom ended and the Depression began. But so powerful had America become as a force in the world economy that the Depression spread like wildfire, and in Europe things went from bad to worse. The kind of speculative fiction which began to appear again in some profusion in Britain after 1930 was not at all like the American science fiction of the late twenties: it was an anxious and often deeply embittered kind of fiction, in which the world of the future loomed as a nightmarish threat far more frequently than it beckoned as a wonderland of opportunity. One might have expected American science fiction to move in the same direction, and in fact a note of anxiety did begin to sound within it, but for the most part it held its course.

The reasons for this relative buoyancy of tone retained by

American science fiction in spite of the Depression are not too hard to see. One sector of the American economy which did well in spite of the Depression was the pulp magazine market, especially in so far as it dealt in escapist fantasies. Pulp fiction was very cheap, and there was plenty of demand for reading material which could distract people from their plight. There was no particular increase in the demand for speculative fiction as such, though the influence of Burroughs and Merritt made much American speculative fiction eminently suitable for escapist purposes, but science fiction already had its corner of the pulp market, and had no difficulty in hanging on to it. Near-future fiction was, however, de-emphasised, and the years after 1929 were dominated by 'space opera' – extravagant costume-dramas which turned the entire galaxy into an adventure playground, pioneered by the heroes of series of stories written by Edward E. Smith, Edmond Hamilton, Jack Williamson and others.

It is surprising, in a way, that there was so little fiction produced and published in England which was of the same kind as American science fiction. Edgar Rice Burroughs' novels were published in Britain, but like Verne in an earlier era he was seen as an author of boys' books. His imitators, like Verne's, found themselves constrained to write for the juvenile market. There were some British books whose content resembled American science fiction more than Wellsian scientific romance, but they were very few. G. McLeod Winsor's *Station X* (1919) is an alien invasion thriller which was, in fact, reprinted in an early science fiction pulp. Stacey Blake's *Beyond the Blue* (1920) is an interplanetary adventure story combining elements of Verne and Burroughs. Bohun Lynch's *Menace from the Moon* (1925) and Francis Grierson's *Heart of the Moon* (1928) are both alien menace stories. Such stories, though, virtually ceased to appear in Britain at the moment when they began to appear in such profusion in specialist American pulps. Interplanetary fiction – even fiction with a slightly more serious purpose, like Ella Scrymsour's *The Perfect World* (1922) – vanished from the British scene for some years.

One reason for this is that the American pulps became the obvious market for British writers interested in futuristic and interplanetary adventure stories. The pulp publishers never showed any interest in Britain as a market, and there was no organised exporting of pulps on any real scale, but pulp magazines did reach Britain, where they were sold in bins in Woolworth's as 'Yank Mags' (having reportedly been used by transatlantic ships as ballast). Several British writers began writing for the pulps, most prolifically John Beynon Harris and John Russell Fearn. Little of their work appeared in book form in Britain, though Harris – writing as John Beynon – published a lost race novel, *The Secret People*, in 1935 and an interplanetary story, *Planet Plane*, in 1936. The latter was reprinted as a serial in the boys' paper *Modern Wonder*, with the leading female character replaced by a boy to enhance its suitability. Another pulp novel reprinted in Britain was *The Green Man of Kilsona* (1936; known in the US as *The Green Man of Graypec*) by Festus Pragnell, a microcosmic fantasy which had the distinction of drawing a complimentary letter to its author from H.G. Wells.

By the mid-thirties, when these books began to appear, there was a substantial community of science fiction fans in Britain. They started their own amateur magazine, *The British Scientifiction Fantasy Review*, in 1937, under the editorship of Walter Gillings. Later that year Gillings persuaded *The World's Work Ltd* that there was enough interest in Britain to sustain a science fiction magazine, and he became the editor of the first domestic science fiction pulp, *Tales of Wonder*, which published sixteen issues in five years from 1937 to 1942. This reprinted some material from American pulps, and provided a market for the handful of British science fiction writers: Harris, Fearn, Eric Frank Russell, Benson Herbert and the veteran George C. Wallis. *World's Work* became the first British publisher to issue a line of science fiction novels in 1943, beginning with reprints from the pulps by Fearn and Russell, but the earlier volumes did not carry the 'science fiction' label. It was not until after the war that stories began to be written in profusion for publication under that heading in Britain.

Just as some American science fiction reached Britain, so some British scientific romance reached America. In its early days Gernsback's *Amazing Stories* used a great deal of reprinted material by Wells and Verne (and often, interestingly, work translated from German). By 1930, though, this flood of reprints had stopped, and the number of contemporary scientific romances which were published in the pulps was very tiny. Writers like Neil Bell, John Gloag and Olaf Stapledon all had difficulty in marketing their works in America, though some of their books appeared there, and S. Fowler Wright's *Deluge* was a bestseller. Such works apparently had no influence on American writers, perhaps because they were regarded as examples of British idiosyncrasy.

Coincidentally, when pulp science fiction began to be reprinted in book form in Britain in 1943, a complementary development did take place in America. The pulp magazine *Famous Fantastic Mysteries*, initially established to reprint material from older pulps owned by Frank Munsey (including *Argosy* and *All-Story*), found itself cut off from this material by a legal tangle, and switched instead to reprinting material that had appeared only in book form. Because of the dearth of American material the editor frequently had recourse to British scientific romance. J. Leslie Mitchell's *Three Go Back* was reprinted there (in abridged form) in 1943, to be followed by G.K. Chesterton's allegorical spy story *The Man Who Was Thursday*, William Hope Hodgson's *The Ghost Pirates* and *The Boats of the 'Glen Carrig'*, Cutcliffe Hyne's *The Lost Continent* and many others. Exercises such as these helped pave the way for the eventual mingling of the traditions of scientific romance and science fiction, but between 1918 and 1943 those traditions remained essentially separate.

The British science fiction fans did pay some attention to scientific romance. Eric Frank Russell, who lived close to Olaf Stapledon, visited him and took some science fiction magazines to show him. Walter Gillings later interviewed Stapledon for *The British Scientifiction Fantasy Review*, and asked what he had thought of them. Stapledon expressed surprise that so much work of that kind was being done, having never suspected that such things as science fiction pulps existed, but felt that the stories were 'terribly crude'.[3] The books reviewed in that issue of the *Review*, though, are Stapledon's *Star Maker*, Wells's *Star Begotten* and an eccentric mind-control story, *Men Are Like Animals*, by Donald Macpherson. The British science fiction fans were clearly interested in domestic scientific romance as well as American science fiction, though – as Stapledon observes in the interview – they tended to evaluate it from their own distinctive point of view.

It is reasonably safe to say that for the entire period between the two world wars British scientific romance and American science fiction, within the spectrum of speculative fiction, were poles apart, with only a tiny measure of overlap between their themes and methods. While American speculative fiction, confined to what many of its historians have referred to as a 'pulp ghetto', became intensely playful, British scientific romance became just as intensely serious in its fierce anxiety and social criticism. Even where scientific romance was orientated towards pure entertainment its thrillers tended to deal almost exclusively in threatened or actual catastrophe rather than in exuberant interplanetary adventures. This observation should not be taken to imply that all the virtues were on the side of scientific romance. Even before 1938, when the editorial influence of John W. Campbell jr began to force the leading American pulp writers to write and think in a more sophisticated manner, American science fiction had an exploratory verve which expanded considerably the vocabulary of ideas available to speculative writers. In the meantime, the writers of scientific romance often seemed fettered by imaginative caution. When they set out to explore the consequences of a single hypothesis, they often did so much more carefully, sensitively and convincingly than any science fiction writer could have done, but their very conscientiousness set limits on their ambition. Their canons tended to develop in the direction of introspection – several produced early work of great scope but remained much more closely confined in their later work. One may complain of early American science fiction that its authors wrote very crudely, and took no account of contemporary speculative thought regarding the advancement of science and the developing pattern of social change; but one might argue also that British scientific romance remained a little *too* dependent on such contemporary discussion, and was overly constrained by its anxieties.

Speculative Essays of the Twenties and Thirties

The period between the two world wars was an unusually fruitful one as far as speculative non-fiction was concerned. The prolific production of speculative essays has a clear connection with the renewal of interest in scientific romance in the thirties, and much of the scientific romance produced between the wars consists of further and more fanciful developments of ideas that were topics of discussion in these essays. The fact that so very many such essays were published in Britian owes something to the example of Wells the futurologist and social commentator, who remained a prolific pamphleteer and journalist. It is no coincidence that two of the most accomplished and adventurous of the new essayists were, like Wells, 'biologist-philosophers': Julian Huxley and J.B.S. Haldane. Huxley (the grandson of Wells's mentor Thomas Henry Huxley) collaborated with Wells on his summary of contemporary biological knowledge, *The Science of Life* (1930), and also collaborated with Haldane on a similar overview of the science.

Julian Huxley shared with Wells a sense of the special relevance of biological knowledge to the human situation, and was keen to alert people to the possibilities inherent in the advancement of the science. In the Preface to his collection *Essays of a Biologist* (1923) he observed that:

> As the grasp of principles in physico-chemical science led speedily to an immense new extension both of knowledge and of control, so it is not to be doubted that like effects will spring from like causes in biology. But whereas the extension of control in physics and chemistry led to a multiplication of the number of things which man could do and experience, the extension of control in biology will *inter alia* mean an alteration of the modes of man's experience itself. The one, that is to say, remained in essence a quantitative change so far as concerns the real life of man; the other can be a qualitative change. Applied physics and chemistry bring more grist to the mill; applied biology will also be capable of changing the mill itself.[4]

The essays in the collection mostly examine the implications which discoveries in biology have, or seem to have, for human society and man's attitude to himself. The book opens with an essay on Progress, and goes on to talk about 'Biology and Sociology'. It closes with two essays on the clash of ideas in modern science and religion. Two more were initially published in the literary journal, *Cornhill* – one of them an essay on the presumed psychology of birds, the other a remarkable imaginative extravaganza, 'Philosophic Ants: a Biologic Fantasy' (1923). The latter article tries to imagine how the world would seem if viewed through the sensory equipment of an ant, and constructs a hypothetical philosophy and theology based in these perceptions. It closes with a synopsis of a Wellsian fantasy about the experience of a man whose mode of perception is radically altered. Huxley subsequently went on to write a fully fleshed-out Wellsian fantasy in 'The Tissue-Culture King'

(1926), also printed in the *Cornhill* (and subsequently reprinted in one of the American science fiction pulps). The bibliography appended to 'Philosophic Ants' in the book version is as whimsical as the essay itself, referring the reader not only to a textbook on ants but to Bergson's *Time and Free Will*, Clerk Maxwell's *Collected Papers*, Lewis Carroll's Alice books, *Gulliver's Travels* and George Meredith's oriental fantasy *The Shaving of Shagpat*. The same spirit that animates this essay can be seen, albeit in more modest form, in many other of the speculative essays produced during the following fifteen years in Britain.

J.B.S. Haldane's work in this vein was a good deal more journalistic than Huxley's. Haldane was primarily a populariser of science, who usually employed whimsy merely as a sugar-coating for short educative pieces that appeared in newspapers. (He was for a while the science editor of the *Daily Worker*, the newspaper of the British Communist Party.) He admitted to writing most of these articles on train journeys. Some of his more extended pieces are, however, classics of their kind, and were to prove very influential. His first important collection of essays was *Possible Worlds* (1927), which includes articles on 'The Future of Biology' and 'Eugenics and Social Reform', and which builds to a startling climax in the two concluding essays, 'Possible Worlds' and 'The Last Judgment'. 'Possible Worlds' resembles Huxley's 'Philosophic Ants' (to which it refers) in presenting the world viewed from a radically different angle, through different senses. As Huxley had constructed the world-view, philosophy and religion of the ant, so Haldane constructs the world-view, philosophy and religion of the barnacle.

There is no synoptic Wellsian fantasy in 'Possible Worlds', but 'The Last Judgment' is, in its entirety, a blueprint for a Wellsian vision of a scope which even Wells had not dared to tackle since *The Time Machine*. It begins with Flammarionesque speculations about the possible ways that the world might end, giving special consideration to cosmic accidents, describing one particular sequence of events in which the surface of the earth becomes uninhabitable after the moon's orbit becomes unstable. Haldane suggests, though, that man might survive the earth's destruction by migrating to Venus, and then embarks upon an elaborate discussion of the possible future evolution of man as he is forced to adapt himself to new physical circumstances, first on Venus and later (when forced to migrate again because of changes in the sun) on Jupiter. The essay ends with the suggestion that even the end of the solar system might not put an end to the human story, if the knowledge and adaptability of man is adequate to the task of taking him to the worlds of other stars. Though no one ever set out to write a full version of the fantasy sketched out in 'Philosophic Ants', *this* story was eventually incorporated into Olaf Stapledon's ambitious future history of man's descendants, *Last and First Men* (1930).

Haldane's optimism regarding the adaptability of man had already been displayed in another essay, which began as a paper read at Cambridge in 1923 (Haldane was a Reader in Biochemistry at Cambridge at the time). It was published the following year as *Daedalus; or, Science and the Future*, a little booklet of some 93 pages, by Kegan Paul, Trench, Trubner & Co. Ltd. This essay argues robustly that the advancement of biological science will transform the human world before the century is out. In particular, it argues, when biologists find out more about the fundamental processes of life and reproduction, it will be possible to carry out various kinds of biological engineering, to create new species and modify existing ones. Armed with this kind of knowledge, Haldane suggests, disease will be abolished, new edible organisms will solve the world's food supply problems, and human babies will be born ectogenetically, in artificial wombs. Scientists will have such power to influence the development of these ectogenetic babies that elections might one day be fought on such issues as whether to equip the next generation with prehensile tails. The last suggestion is, of course, entirely whimsical, but it does serve to exemplify in a dramatic manner the kind of potential to which Haldane was referring.

Nowadays, when the possibility of genetic engineering is much more widely discussed, it is easy to appreciate how much more far-sighted than his contemporaries Haldane actually was, but at the time his speculations seemed simply to be one more development of a basic thesis about the role of science in human affairs. The real purpose of this essay is to defend science against the gathering anxiety of the time. In the wake of the Great War the British intelligentsia had become very suspicious of the idea of progress. They had lived through a terrible war which had been fought by machines rather than men, and in which the capacity of scientific knowledge to equip men with frightful forces of destruction had been demonstrated in no uncertain terms. This lesson seemed to many people to lend a new emphasis to old suspicions about the effects of mechanical production on the quality of life, and the loss of ideals which might be corollary to the spread of materialism.

Daedalus begins, significantly, with memories of the Great War:

> As I sit down to write these pages I can see before me two scenes from my experience of the late war. The first is a glimpse of a forgotten battle of 1915. It has a curious suggestion of a rather bad cinema film. Through a blur of dust and fumes there appear, quite suddenly, great black and yellow masses of smoke which seem to be tearing up the surface of the earth and disintegrating the works of man with an almost visible hatred. These form the chief parts of the picture, but somewhere in the middle distance one can see a few irrelevant looking human figures, and soon there are fewer. It is hard to believe that these are the protagonists in the battle. One would rather choose these huge substantive oily black masses which are so much more conspicuous, and suppose that the men are in reality their servants, and playing an inglorious, subordinate, and fatal part in the combat. It is possible, after all, that this view is correct.[5]

Haldane adds a note to the effect that had he been present at a similar moment in 1918, there would have been even fewer men and more shell bursts, but the men would have been running 'with mad terror in their eyes, from gigantic steel slugs, which were deliberately, relentlessly, and successfully pursuing them'.[6] The second scene to which he refers took place in India, where he and some other Europeans were distracted from a dance by a nova, which might, he suggests fancifully, have been 'the last judgment of some inhabited world'.[7]

These two scenes seem to Haldane symbolic of a gathering resentment against the march of science. His optimistic essay about the salvation of man by the advancement of biology is an answer to those who feel that modern inventions threaten the destruction of man, and that the cosmic perspectives of astronomy and geology render man hopelessly insignificant in the scheme of things. He castigates earlier prophets on the grounds of conservatism, commenting scornfully on Chesterton's *Napoleon of Notting Hill*, and condescendingly on Wells's *Anticipations*. He does not mention George Bernard Shaw, but it is important to note that the biological speculations contained in *Daedalus* are framed in opposition to the Shavian view, developed at length in the preface to *Back to Methuselah* (1921), that hope for human progress depends on a rejection of Darwinism and a commitment to a philosophy of evolution which assumes that acquired characteristics are transmitted from one generation to the next. Haldane's biological engineering proposes that man might take control of his own physical evolution without any such reckless philosophical commitment, and it is worth noting that though his early essays on Lysenko were laudatory it was the Communists' adoption of the doctrine that acquired characteristics could be inherited that led him to quit the party.

Although the form of Haldane's essay is slightly clumsy, much of the futuristic material being presented in the form of an essay written by an undergraduate student in 2073, it is nevertheless a very striking work. It was intended to be sharply provocative, and Haldane deliberately tried to outdo even Thomas Henry Huxley in claiming that the advancement of biology would not only force men to remake their mythology, but their morality too. Just as the biological innovations of the past, from milking cows to contraception, had been greeted initially with superstitious resistance, so, he acknowledged, would future innovations be resisted. In time, though, he proposed, such resistance would give way, and men would accept the opportunities given to them by such inventions as artificial wombs and methods of human engineering. The title of the essay derives from an ironic analogy suggesting that the idea of the scientist as Prometheus, stealing the fire of the gods for man to use, was out of date; the scientist of the future might better be likened to Daedalus, whose creation of the Minotaur established him as mythology's first experimental geneticist. This particular joke, though, was bound to rebound, and so it proved when Bertrand Russell took up the case for the opposition, using the title *Icarus; or, the Future of Science*.

Russell argues, elegantly and persuasively, the case which Haldane had tried so forcefully to reject. Men, alleges Russell, are simply untrustworthy. They are governed mainly by their 'collective passions', which are mostly aggressive and evil. The march of science, therefore, will simply give the men who have power more opportunities to indulge in destructive orgies of national rivalry, or to oppress their own subjects.

Russell's was not the only argument used to counter Haldane's prospectus for a brighter future. As with so many Utopians, Haldane found that his own ideas about what constituted an ideal society horrified people who had different ideological commitments. One such was Aldous Huxley, Julian's brother, who elaborated Haldane's ideas into his nightmarish vision of *Brave New World* (1932), the best known of all the scientific romances of the thirties.

Icarus, like *Daedalus*, was issued as a pamphlet by Kegan Paul, Trench, Trubner & Co., who then decided to follow them up with a whole series of essays under the general heading *Today and Tomorrow*. Between 1924 and 1930 more than a hundred titles were issued in this series, most of them borrowing their titles from figures in mythology to explore the future of the sciences, the arts, various nations, Churches and moral philosophies. Other early titles in the series were *Tantalus; or, the Future of Man* by F.C.S. Schiller, *The Passing of the Phantoms: a Study of Evolutionary Psychology and Morals* by C.J. Patten, *Narcissus: An Anatomy of Clothes* by Gerald Heard, and *Wireless Possibilities* by A.M. Low (all 1924). Not all the essays were serious, by any means – Robert Graves contributed two essays on the future of swearing (*Lars Porsena*, 1927) and the future of humour (*Mrs Fisher*, 1928). Many, though, retained the ambition of the original contributors to make some decisive statement about the relationship of man and the products of his science, and to anticipate the way in which that relationship was likely to develop. These essays include *Ouroboros; the Mechanical Extension of Man* (1925) by Garet Garrett, *Prometheus; or, Biology and the Advancement of Man* (1925) by H.S. Jennings, *Hephaestus; or, the Soul of the Machine* (1925) by E.E. Fournier d'Albe, and – most ambitious of all – *The World, the Flesh and the Devil* (1929) by Haldane's fellow Marxist, J.D. Bernal. Bernal's book looks forward to the conquest of space, and the extensive self-modification of future men by means of what would now be called cyborgisation (the integration of organic and inorganic systems); as a piece of visionary writing it is at least the equal of *Daedalus* and 'The Last Judgment'.

Both the original protagonists in the *Today and Tomorrow* debate were later to dabble in scientific romance. Haldane wrote the greater part of a Wellsian novel, *The Man with Two Memories*, though this description of a Utopian other world, named Ulro in honour of one of William Blake's visionary fantasies, was not published until 1976, twelve years after his death. Russell produced two volumes of short fiction late in life – *Satan in the Suburbs* (1953) and *Nightmares of Eminent Persons* (1954). Nearly all the stories in these volumes, and some of the fiction in his *Fact and Fiction* (1961), are scientific romance. Even more significant, though, is the number of later contributors to the series who already were or became significant writers of scientific romance.

Gerald Heard, whose early *Today and Tomorrow* essay *Narcissus* was his first book, went on to become an important essayist in the thirties. His books *The Ascent of Humanity* (1929) and *The Emergence of Man* (1931) influenced Olaf Stapledon, and he followed the example of so many other speculative writers in trying to produce a philosophical revision of the theory of evolution in *Pain, Sex and Time* (1939). He turned to fiction late in his career, when he had left Britain to live in California, but his stories in the collection *The Great Fog and Other Weird Tales* (1944) and various later works are very much in the British tradition.

A.M. Low, another of the earliest contributors to the series, went on to write many more works of enthusiastic futurology, mostly aimed at a juvenile audience. He was highly optimistic about the future rewards of mechanical technology, and in such books as *Our Wonderful World of Tomorrow* (1934) he wrote about interplanetary travel, robots, television and weather control. He de-emphasised the biological innovations which Haldane talked about, but argued that the men of the future would be more sensitive and more agile, and that eugenic control of births would be inevitable. Low wrote two scientific romances for younger readers: *Adrift in the Stratosphere* (1937) and *Mars Breaks Through* (1937).

John Gloag's *Artifex; or, the Future of Craftsmanship* (1926) begins by citing several scientific romances as visions of future possibility, extracting from them the question of whether modern men would have the constructive skills necessary to keep themselves alive and supply their needs if a destructive war smashed the industrial system. Gloag went on to write several excellent scientific romances, mostly preoccupied with this same question.

J. Leslie Mitchell, author of *Hanno; or, the Future of Exploration* (1928), went on to write two fine scientific romances, *Three Go Back* (1932) and *Gay Hunter* (1934), elaborating Russell's side of the initial debate, and might have become a major writer in the field but for his premature death in 1935, a mere eight days after his thirty-fourth birthday. Although his real name is now virtually forgotten he is still remembered for the novels of Scottish rural life which he wrote under the name Lewis Grassic Gibbon.

Muriel Jaeger, author of *Sisyphus; the Limits of Psychology* (1928), had already written two interesting scientific romances, *The Question Mark* (1926) and *The Man with Six Senses* (1927), and she was to go on to write two more thoughtful speculative novels, more notably *Retreat from Armageddon* (1936), which summarises many arguments which can be found in the *Today and Tomorrow* essays. *Retreat from Armageddon* includes a vision of 'a Biologist's Utopia', but it is a rather feeble eugenic fantasia with none of the ambition of *Daedalus*, and is easily satirised in the story. Otherwise, though, the exemplary positions taken up by the characters represent very well the spectrum of contemporary debate about the ills and prospects of modern civilisation.

Robert Graves, author of *Lars Porsena* and *Mrs Fisher*, also went on to write some speculative fiction late in his career, including the novel *Seven Days in New Crete* (1949) and some short stories.

C.E.M. Joad, author of *Thrasymachus; or, the Future of Morals* (1925) and *Diogenes: or, the Future of Leisure* (1928), became a prolific essayist and populariser of philosophy. He contributed the leading article, 'Is Civilisation Doomed?' to the first issue of a short-lived journal, *Today and Tomorrow*, which tried to take up where the pamphlets left off in 1931. His one venture in fiction was the satirical story of *The Adventures of the Young Soldier in Search of a Better World* (1943), which recalls the Alice books as well as George Bernard Shaw's *Adventures of the Black Girl in her Search for God* in reviewing again all the arguments about the way to save civilisation which were the real substance of the *Today and Tomorrow* debate.

In view of all this work it is perhaps surprising that the only one of the *Today and Tomorrow* pamphlets which actually took the form of a scientific romance was not by a British writer at all. This was *The Next Chapter, or the War Against the Moon* (1927) by the French writer André Maurois. This was one of several 'fragments from a Universal History', supposedly written in 1992, which are included in his collections of essays.

Maurois did spend a great deal of time in Britain and the USA, and he wrote two speculative novels closely akin to British scientific romance. One – *The Weigher of Souls* (1931) – is set in London.

The kinds of argument developed in the *Today and Tomorrow* series were carried forward into the 1930s by numerous books similar in spirit. Perhaps the most successful futurological book of the period was *The World in 2030 AD* (1930) by the Earl of Birkenhead, who was at the time High Steward of Oxford University and Rector of Aberdeen University. This was a handsome volume, with *avant-garde* illustrations by E. McKnight Kauffer. The text covers every aspect of life in the twentieth century, and borrows heavily from several *Today and Tomorrow* volumes, especially *Daedalus*. The best of several Flammarionesque essays on possible ends of the world, Geoffrey Dennis's *The End of the World*, also appeared in 1930. (An identically titled volume by Joseph McCabe had appeared in 1921, and another was to be produced by Kenneth Heuer in 1953.)

The speculative essays of the period were not, however, restricted to futurological adventures in prophecy. One of the most impressive collections of essays of the 1930s was *If it had Happened Otherwise* (1932), edited by J.C. Squire. This was a series of exercises in alternate history, inspired by the historian G.M. Trevelyan's essay 'If Napoleon Had Won the Battle of Waterloo' (1907). The contributors included G.K. Chesterton ('If Don John of Austria had Married Mary Queen of Scots'), André Maurois ('If Louis XVI had had an Atom of Firmness') and Hilaire Belloc ('If Drouet's Cart Had Stuck'). All these writers produced works of scientific romance, as did Harold Nicolson ('If Byron had Become King of Greece'), author of the early atom bomb story *Public Faces* (1932), and Fr Ronald Knox ('If the General Strike had Succeeded'), author of the satirical *Memories of the Future* (1923) and *Other Eyes than Ours* (1926). The star of the collection was, however, Winston Churchill's 'If Lee had not Won the Battle of Gettysburg', in which a historian in an alternate world tries to imagine how *our* history might have turned out.

It must be stressed that many essays in the *Today and Tomorrow* series were not actually concerned with prediction at all. Although they were written with an eye to the future, many were simply attempts to appraise and evaluate the present state

163

of civilisation. They reflected a widespread feeling that civilisation needed such a careful analysis – that a new *theory* of social and intellectual development was required in order to cast light on the puzzling aspects of the contemporary situation. Gerald Heard went on to produce such a theory, and Bertrand Russell's one-time collaborator A.N. Whitehead was busy on a similar project, in his trilogy *Science and the Modern World* (1926), *Process and Reality* (1929) and *Adventures of Ideas* (1933). After writing *Brave New World* Aldous Huxley moved into this area too, with *Ends and Means* (1937), to whose themes he was to return at intervals of about a decade, in *Science, Liberty and Peace* (1947) and *Brave New World Revisited* (1958). C.A. Beard edited two large anthologies of essays, *Whither Mankind?* (1928) and *Toward Civilisation* (1930), in which eminent men offered their appraisals of various aspects of modern civilisation, and the prospects for future progress. Both of these volumes were deliberately optimistic, in defiance of what Beard considered to be the contemporary trend, and in his introduction to the former volume he appointed himself a kind of crusader against the type of pessimism that was so extensively developed in Oswald Spengler's *Decline of the West* (1918–22), a widely cited work first translated in the late twenties, when it fitted in very well with the British *zeitgeist*.

These essays helped to draw up the agenda for the serious scientific romances of the thirties, though only a handful of them were directly influential to any degree. *If it had Happened Otherwise*, though of considerable interest in its own right, did not lead to any boom in scientific romances of alternative history, though R. Egerton Swartwout wrote an interesting full-length alternate history of early twentieth-century Britain, *It Might Have Happened* (1934). There was one work of speculative non-fiction, though, that was very influential, stimulating the production of many works of fiction. This was *An Experiment with Time* (1927) by J.W. Dunne, which attempted to account for prophetic elements in dreaming by means of a multidimensional theory of the universe not unlike the one proposed by C.H. Hinton in some of his essays. This book was very successful, not only commercially, but in terms of attracting the attention of scientists and intellectuals. It helped give birth to a widespread fascination with the idea of twists and slips in time, and several authors who otherwise showed little interest in speculative fiction wrote stories based on Dunne's theory. These include J.B. Priestley, author of the three 'time plays' *Dangerous Corner* (1932), *Time and the Conways* (1937) and *I Have Been Here Before* (1937), and Ralph L. Finn, author of three time-twist novels, *The Lunatic, the Lover and the Poet* (1948), *Twenty-Seven Stairs* (1949) and *Time Marches Sideways* (1950). The influence of Dunne's theory of the 'serial universe' is seen in many other works published in the two decades spanned by these works, and *An Experiment with Time* is more often cited by characters in scientific romance, when they try to come to terms with extraordinary happenings, than any other book. Dunne felt that his theory provided 'irrefutable proof' of human immortality, and by giving a pseudo-scientific gloss to that idea he took over, for many people, where the spiritualists left off.

It is very noticeable that almost all of this speculative non-fiction was the work of British writers. Although the *Today and Tomorrow* series was reprinted in the USA, only a handful of Americans figure among its authors. Some of Huxley's essays and Haldane's articles first appeared in American periodicals, but very little in a similar vein was produced by American scientists. The reasons for this have much to do with the cultural differences between the British and American scientific communities, and their traditions. There have always been unashamedly unorthodox British scientists who have made every effort to communicate directly with the lay public, without necessarily losing the respect of their peers by so doing. American scientists have usually been conservative by comparison and have characteristically observed a different etiquette.

The absence in America of this kind of tradition in speculative non-fiction correlates with the absence in America between the wars of any substantial tradition of serious speculative fiction. The most important writer of scientific romance to emerge in the thirties, Olaf Stapledon, was as much essayist as storyteller, and his unique achievement was to blend together techniques of fiction and non-fiction in a new way. The other major writers of scientific romance who began their careers between the wars – Fowler Wright, Gloag, Bell and C.S. Lewis – also clearly showed in their work the influence of speculative non-fiction. They were all, in their fashion, sceptical appraisers of the state of contemporary civilisation, and analysts of its prospects.

6

THE MAJOR WRITERS
BETWEEN THE WARS

The Survivors: Doyle, Wells, Shiel and Beresford

FOUR OF THE writers who established themselves before the outbreak of the Great War as important writers of scientific romance survived the war years. Not one of the four, though, did anything to compare with his early work for at least fifteen years after the war's end. There are elements of scientific romance in their work of that period, but it is always subdued and tentative. In one or two of the writers this might be credited to personal idiosyncrasy, but in all four it clearly reflects a more general and more fundamental rejection of the genre. The individual manifestations of the rejection are at least partly symptomatic of the intellectual climate of the day.

By 1918 Conan Doyle had ceased to regard his literary work as the main focus of his endeavours. He had become instead the ardent champion of Spiritualism – perhaps its most prestigious evangelist. In such books as *The New Revelation* (1918) and *The Vital Message* (1919) he tried to persuade the world that personal immortality had been proved beyond the shadow of a doubt. So hungry was he for evidence that would confound the sceptics that by 1922 he was ready to be taken in by the faked photographs of the Cottingley fairies, which he publicised in his book *The Coming of the Fairies*. He became an enthusiastic receiver of spirit messages, and obviously felt himself to be on intimate terms with many inhabitants of the other world. When S. Fowler Wright achieved brief celebrity with the publication of *Deluge* in 1927 Doyle wrote to him, saying that he had long had it in mind to write a book with exactly such a plot and that Fowler Wright must have been told the idea by his spirit acquaintances. When Fowler Wright's son, feeling that the joke was too good not to share, quoted extracts from the letter in a newspaper article, Doyle sued for breach of copyright, and won damages, though he did send Fowler Wright an autographed copy of *Pheneas Speaks* (1927) – a book of messages from the Other Side – in the vain hope of convincing the ardent sceptic that the matter was not so absurd as he thought.

By this time Doyle had actually returned to the writing of speculative fiction. Professor Challenger, having been slightly unhinged by the death of his beloved wife, was drawn into the world of mediums and messages from the dead in *The Land of Mist* (1926). This novel is a rather lifeless exercise in propaganda, but Doyle followed it up with a story that began as the kind of adventure story that *The Lost World* had been: *The Maracot Deep* (1927; in book form 1929). This story begins as Vernian romance, but following the discovery of the relics of Atlantis it rapidly becomes occult romance rather than scientific romance, its climactic confrontation bringing Professor Maracot face to face with Baal-Seepa, the Lord of the Dark Face – an incarnation of evil. This short novel appeared in a volume with three short stories, two of which feature Professor Challenger. One, 'The Disintegration Machine', follows the pattern made familiar in so many early magazine stories, in which the nasty inventor and his nasty machine are destroyed together. 'When the World Screamed' is a more adventuous piece, in which the drilling of a hole through the crust of the earth reaches the tender flesh of the living organism inside, which reacts to the pain by triggering a series of volcanic eruptions. The story is presented as an amusing fancy, narrated in a tone of apologetic irony.

Whether Doyle would have continued to produce stories of this kind one can only speculate. He died on 7 July 1930 after a series of heart attacks, at the age of seventy-one. He was quite considerably outlived by his three fellow writers of scientific romance – who were all, of course, younger men. By coincidence, they died within six months of one another: Wells on 13 August 1946, Beresford on 2 February 1947, and Shiel on 17 February 1947. All three, therefore, lived just long enough to see the Second World War through to its conclusion.

Like Doyle, Wells got religion during the Great War, though he recanted his temporary faith in a personal God by the mid-twenties. His first post-war novel, *The Undying Fire* (1919), was an attempt to explore and dramatise the new theology which he had developed in *God the Invisible King* (1917). It is a reformulation of the book of Job, in which the sorely tested hero is a schoolteacher, whose situation is partly modelled on that of Sanderson of Oundle, whose biography Wells was later to write in *The Story of a Great Schoolmaster* (1924). Job Huss – named after Jan Huss, the reformist heretic who anticipated Luther – is driven to the edge of despair by disaster and near-fatal illness, and has a visionary dialogue with God and Satan while under anaesthetic during the operation which saves his life. Although God was later written out of the script the ideas in this dialogue, most importantly the demand for man to maintain the pace of progress, remained central to Wells's philosophy.

The use of a schoolteacher as protagonist in *The Undying Fire* reflects Wells's keen concern in the post-war years with education as the key to social improvement. He was eager to provide new tools for teachers to use, that might instil in students an appropriate way of thought. The most important of these instruments was published in 1920: *The Outline of History; Being a Plain History of Life and Mankind*. The most important novel features of this text are its concern in the early chapters with the early evolution of man, emphasising the role of natural selection in the making of mankind; its rebellion against ethnocentricity by dealing conscientiously with cultures other than Western Christendom; and the futuristic slant of its final chapter, which calls for the future unification of human communities under a world state. The emphasis on education can also be clearly seen in the next of his revised blueprints for that world state, *The Salvaging of Civilisation* (1921).

As he had done in the past, and would do again in the future, Wells supplemented his latest blueprint for world salvation with a Utopian novel, in this case *Men Like Gods* (1923). Here, three carloads of people are mysteriously transported into another dimension, where they find a world of a kind that earth may become in a thousand years, if only men will commit themselves to the cause of progress. Its inhabitants are demigods, physically perfect and long-lived, and theirs is a garden world in which nature is entirely under human dominion. They have long practised eugenics and strict birth-control, and they have little trace of any governmental system. 'Our education is our government,' one of the godlike informs the visitors. Among the visitors are representatives of all the presumed evils of the human present – a caricature capitalist, the Secretary of State for War, and a narrow-minded preacher, with various hangers-on. They begin scheming, inevitably, to take over this Utopia and reform it, but they are betrayed by the hero. He returns along with them, though, to our own world – Utopia has no place for him, and his task in the scheme of things is to work for the cause of progress in Britain. The story is distinctly turgid, showing none of the narrative flair that characterised Wells's early work.

In the preface to the omnibus volume of *Scientific Romances* published in 1933 Wells commented that *Men Like Gods* was 'almost the last' of his scientific romances, adding that: 'It did not horrify or frighten, was not much of a success, and by that time I had tired of talking in playful parables to a world engaged in destroying itself.'[1] He concedes, though, that in between *Men Like Gods* and the preface he had written two other 'sarcastic fantasies' – *Mr Blettsworthy on Rampole Island* (1928) and *The Autocracy of Mr Parham* (1930). Actually, there is a little more scientific romance in his works of the later twenties than is indicated by these remarks. *The Dream* (1924) is a novel of contemporary working-class life, but it is told from the hypothetical viewpoint of a dreamer who lives in a Utopian world of the 40th century. There is also the first of Wells's several film stories, *The King Who Was a King* (1929), which is basically an adventure story but involves the fight to control a hypothetical metal named calcomite.

In spite of these marginal elements, and the assembly of almost all his shorter scientific romances in *The Short Stories of H.G. Wells* (1927), Wells seems to have partaken of the aversion for scientific romance which was a feature of these years. *Mr Blettsworthy on Rampole Island* is not a scientific romance but a story of mental derangement in which the hallucinating protagonist, in rather Swiftian fashion, sees the inhabitants of New York as stupid savages whose social institutions are analogically related to giant sloths. *The Autocracy of Mr Parham* is also a story of derangement, this time attributed to his quasi-demonic possession by a Martian which infuses him with the Master Spirit of Manhood and Dominion and Order. This Spirit transforms Parham from an obscure academic into the Lord Paramount of England, a parody of Mussolini. Wells wrote several other novels about characters suffering from strange delusions, including *Christina Alberta's Father* (1925) and *The Bulpington of Blup* (1932), and a similar interest in abnormal psychology can be found in the work of other leading writers of scientific romance. John Beresford and Neil Bell both wrote several stories of this general type.

Wells continued to revise his plans for the salvation of the world in the twenties, first in the long semi-fictional appraisal of the state of the world *The World of William Clissold* (1926) and then in *The Open Conspiracy* (1928). The 'open conspiracy' is a loose alliance of the scientist-intellectuals who, in Wells's view, must take the future in trust, but in these two books they are not really called to action, but rather to educate themselves in the appropriate ideology. These works provide further evidence of the fact that Wells was suffering at this time from a kind of imaginative enervation. This did not last long, though, and he began to work with greater enthusiasm and effect in the early thirties. After planning the textbook of biology which was to be a partner for *The Outline of History*, *The Science of Life* (most of the actual writing was done by Julian Huxley and by Wells's son G.P. Wells), he produced the most substantial of all his sociopolitical studies, *The Work, Wealth and Happiness of Mankind* (1931). This was the definitive summary of his ideas about the present and future of society, and represents the final crystallisation of those ideas. Although he was to write many more essays and books his position remained essentially the one outlined here.

It is clear that Wells felt that he had reached a kind of conclusion in his career at this time. By 1934 he was ready to write his autobiography, albeit in typically eccentric fashion. When he wrote the preface to the *Scientific Romances* he obviously believed that he was done with that side of his work. 'The world in the presence of cataclysmal realities has no need for fresh cataclysmal fantasies,' he wrote. 'That game is over.'[2] He could not resist the temptation, though, to write one last future history to accompany his last 'working analysis of our deepening social perplexities', and so he produced *The Shape of Things to Come* in 1933.

The introduction represents the main text of *The Shape of Things to Come* as another revelatory dream, and the author further distances himself from it by inserting himself into the introduction as a character, roundly criticised by the supposed dreamer as a 'Dealer in the Obvious'. The introduction also makes lengthy reference to Dunne's *Experiment with Time*, which is credited with inspiring Wells to write one of his very few short scientific romances of the thirties, 'The Queer Story of

Brownlow's Newspaper', which appeared in *The Strand* in 1932. Despite the apparent ambivalence of the introduction, though, Wells described *The Shape of Things to Come* as 'as deliberate and laborious a piece of work as anything I have ever done' and considered that 'I have contrived to set out in it my matured theory of revolution and world government very plainly'.[3] He also commented on the difference in the intellectual climate between the time in which he wrote *The World of William Clissold* and the time he wrote *The Shape of Things to Come*, in a way which sheds some light on the enervation of the former and muscularity of the latter:

> *The World of William Clissold* was written during a 'boom' phase in the world's affairs, the profound rottenness of the monetary-credit system was still unrealised, and so Clissold turned to social boredom and the irritation of seeing industrial and mechanical invention misused, in order to evoke the discontent necessary for a revolutionary project. But by the time *The Work, Wealth and Happiness of Mankind*, which was, so to speak, the workshop in which was built *The Shape of Things to Come*, was in hand, the artificiality and unsoundness of those boom conditions had become glaringly obvious. The realisation was spreading through all the modern categories of workers, the men of science, the men of invention, the big-scale industrial organisers, the engineers, the aviators, the teachers and writers, the social workers, every sort of skilled artisan, every honest and creative-minded man, indeed, everywhere, that if the new mechanical civilisation by which they lived was to carry on, they had to be up and stirring. The Open Conspiracy of William Clissold was essentially speculative, optional and amateurish; the Open Conspiracy of De Windt which took possession of a derelict world, was presented as the logical outcome of inexorable necessity.[4]

This observation may stand not simply as a background to the re-animation of Wells's interest in scientific romance, but as background to the revitalisation of scientific romance in general. It was not that the twenties saw anxiety about the future laid to rest – far from it – but for many people it was a resigned anxiety, expressed mainly in passive cynicism. Between 1926 and 1933, though, anxiety had been awakened into a much more active form of expression. The Wall Street Crash and the rise of Fascism in Europe were seen as symptoms of a rapid process of deterioration that was taking the world from comfortable decadence to the brink of collapse. It is significant that Wells chose to subtitle the first section of *The Shape of Things to Come* – which deals with the world before 1933 – 'Today and Tomorrow: the Age of Frustration Dawns'.

The 'Age of Frustration' lasts, in *The Shape of Things to Come*, into the 1960s, when its development is shown as a gradual and general failure of 'social nucleation' – the world order disintegrates. A new outburst of wars in the 1940s fails to bring about the destruction of the world as envisaged in *The War in the Air* because the nations that are fighting are in a state of virtual exhaustion. The widespread hunger and depletion of sanitary provision resulting from the wars, however, opens the way to a series of plagues, culminating in an epidemic of 'maculated fever'. From this terrible plight the world is rescued during the later decades of the twentieth century by intellectuals, inspired by the prophetic writings of Gustave De Windt, who contrive to enforce world peace by means of Air and Sea Control, which they achieve by virtually monopolising the remaining fighting aircraft and fighting ships. After a period of benevolent but firm dictatorship the architects of the new World State gradually transform the business of government. Initially the Air Dictatorship embarks upon a ruthless 'mental disinfection' of the world, which banishes bad ideas along with destructive plagues, but in so doing it removes the need for its own tyrannical puritanism, making way for a world where, as in *Men Like Gods*, education replaces government as the agent of social control and the protector of social order. The Age of Frustration gives way, in the fullness of time, to an Age of Abundance, and man himself is transformed by 'adaptation' into a new being:

> By means of education and social discipline the normal human individual today acquires characteristics without which his continued existence would be impossible. In the future, as the obscurer processes of selection are accelerated and directed by eugenic effort, these acquired characteristics will be incorporated with his inherent nature, and his educational energy will be released for further adaptations. He will become generation by generation a new species, differing more widely from that weedy, tragic, pathetic, cruel, fantastic, absurd and sometimes sheerly horrible being who christened himself in a mood of oafish arrogance *Homo sapiens*.[5]

It is hardly surprising, given Wells's background, that he

should close his most ambitious account of the shape of things to come with a summary chapter which assimilates the historical changes he describes to fundamental changes in human biology. Nor is it surprising that in imagining a biological transformation of mankind he should compare this to religious ideas of transfiguration. As this chapter closes his imaginary historian observes that 'The body of mankind is now one single organism . . . We are all members of one body',[6] and scrupulously adds a footnote crediting the latter phrase to St Paul, linking his own Utopian philosophy to that of Christ. Echoes of this kind of thinking can be found in the work of many other writers of scientific romance during the thirties, where analogies are very frequently drawn between biological and spiritual evolution – analogies which occasionally border on confusion. Wells undoubtedly understood the theory of evolution by natural selection better than contemporary futuristic writers, yet in the passage quoted above even he blurs the issue of how changes might actually come about in human nature with vague talk of 'eugenic effort' as the means by which acquired characteristics can ultimately be imprinted more deeply in the genes.

Ideas from *The Shape of Things to Come* were incorporated into the second of Wells's film books, *Things to Come* (1935), which actually became a film in the following year, directed by William Cameron Menzies and produced by Alexander Korda. Two of Wells's books had already been filmed in Hollywood – *The Island of Dr Moreau* as *The Island of Lost Souls* (1932) and *The Invisible Man* (1933) but *Things to Come* was a very different project, much closer to Wells's idea of what a film of his work ought to be like. He began producing more film scripts, based on his early short stories, and in 1936 he produced *The Man Who Could Work Miracles* and 'The New Faust', the latter deriving its basic premiss from 'The Story of the Late Mr Elvesham' (1896). Although a film was made of the former, directed by Lothar Mendes, 'The New Faust' was never filmed, nor was the script reprinted in book form until publication of *The Man with a Nose and the Other Uncollected Short Stories of H.G. Wells* in 1984. This is a pity, because this identity-exchange fantasy would have made a very effective film, and as an example of story-telling it is more readable and more interesting than any of Wells's other late works.

Having finished his autobiography Wells relaxed into a more

173

playful attitude to his works. As well as the film stories he wrote the consciously eccentric *Anatomy of Frustration* (1936) and three long stories which might best be classified along with *Mr Blettsworthy on Rampole Island* as 'sarcastic fantasies'. The first and best of these is the novelette *The Croquet Player* (1936) in which a self-satisfied man of leisure fails to be impressed by a 'ghost story' told to him by a neurotic medical man. This is the story of 'Cainsmarsh', an allegorical village whose inhabitants are under a kind of curse which has come down through the ages from their prehistoric ancestors (whose bones are sometimes exhumed from the marshes), The doctor's delusion is then reinterpreted by his psychiatrist, who finds in it a statement of the predicament of the world, but the protagonist still cannot swallow the story.

Star Begotten (1937) is subtitled 'A Biological Fantasia', and presents a similar allegory. The protagonist, an unthinking writer of popular tales from history, is disturbed by the idea that cosmic rays from Mars are creating mutant children who will inherit and transform the world. He begins looking for these 'Martians' in the world around him, harbouring suspicions about his wife and his own child, but it is not until his wife charges *him* with being a member of this superior alien species that he realises the potential for change which lies within himself, and awakens to his duty. In *The Camford Visitation* (1937) an alien visitor really does appear, though only in the form of a sceptical voice which disturbs the tranquillity of a British University by challenging its time-honoured ideas about education.

This playful phase in Wells's writing passed, and in 1939 he published the last of his exercises in future history, a long character-study of a man who becomes a revolutionary, and then a dictator: *The Holy Terror*. Although it is generally regarded as a poor work there is much of interest in the book, which develops the premiss that the kind of man who might smash a corrupt world order is likely to be possessed of a certain kind of paranoia. Rud Whitlow is an English equivalent of Hitler and Stalin – a charismatic leader who accomplishes much that is worthwhile in the ascendant phase of his career, but once in power becomes ever more the victim of the infantile behaviour traits which made him a 'holy terror' in the nursery. It echoes again the conviction of so much of Wells's work that before civilisation can be put to rights the old order must be utterly dissolved, but adds to this the thesis that such a dissolution can be carried out only by a 'recklessly destructive man' who must then be put away before his destructiveness can blight the prospect of a new order. Wells had interviewed Stalin in the early thirties, just as he had interviewed Lenin more than a decade before, and he had a keen interest in analysing the sad fate of the Russian experiment with socialism. *The Holy Terror* ends with the world put to rights, but it has a keen awareness of how easily the path of progress might be lost. This awareness is also seen in the pessimistic *The Fate of Homo Sapiens* (1939), which suggests that there are too many forces preventing mankind from making the kind of crucial adaptation to circumstance that Wells had long considered necessary to survival.

The Fate of Homo Sapiens was revised slightly and combined with a new blueprint for revolution, *The New World Order* (1940), in *The Outlook for Homo Sapiens* (1942). This prospectus was again revised into the substance of the last of his blueprints for the future, revealingly entitled *Phoenix* (1942). In the meantime he had produced one more playful allegory, *All Aboard for Ararat* (1940), in which Noah Lammock lays down some sensible conditions before he will consent to built a second Ark to preserve a fragment of civilisation from the Deluge. The story told in *All Aboard for Ararat* is deliberately left unfinished, in recognition of the fact that the Second World War had begun, and that its outcome was unknowable. Wells's last writings veer from cheerful idiosyncrasy to nihilistic pessimism, and for his last brief book he chose the title *Mind at the End of its Tether* (1945) – ostensibly to describe the situation of the human species, though it should perhaps rather be taken as self-description. In a chapter entitled 'There is no "Pattern of Things to Come" ' he concludes that 'Our doomed formicary is helpless as the implacable Antagonist kicks or tramples our world to pieces'.[7] Such a descent into despair is not altogether surprising in a man nearing his death, living out his last years in the midst of a world war, but it must also be recognised as a capitulation to what Wells believed to be the spirit of the age: a perversely self-indulgent acceptance of Frustration.

Like Wells, M.P. Shiel left scientific romance more or less alone during the 1920s, but returned to it in the 1930s. Like Wells, too, Shiel used some of his later works to present a kind of grand summary of his philosophical position – but his method of presentation was as different from Wells's as was his position.

After a ten-year holiday from writing novels, Shiel resumed his career with the Haggardesque adventure story *Children of the Wind* (1923), but it was in the second novel after his comeback, *How the Old Woman Got Home* (1927), that he took care to plant a series of monologues and dialogues which lay out in full his eccentric socialism, his evolutionism and his impersonal theology. There is some similar didactic argument in *Dr Krasinski's Secret* (1929), but in both books the discussion runs parallel to the plot, which is in each case a highly peculiar but non-speculative story. The only scientific romance which Shiel wrote during the 1920s was 'In 2073 AD', which was serialised in the *Daily Herald* in 1928. This is a trivial and quaint love story set in a future when whole towns and cities have taken flight and aerial transport is commonplace.

In 1933 Shiel produced *This Above All* (reprinted ten years later in Britain as *Above All Else*), a religious fantasy in which several Biblical characters, including the Wandering Jew, are imagined to be still living in the modern world, blessed or cursed with an immortality granted them by Jesus's miraculous power. It was not until the following year, though, that Shiel returned to scientific romance with 'How Life Climbs', a dialogue between a scientist kidnapped aboard a flying saucer and an intelligent egg, first published in an anthology of new stories edited by Shiel's friend and admirer John Gawsworth. This dialogue recapitulates Shiel's evolutionist ideas, and adds many new comments on modern knowledge and belief. Like several other writers of scientific romance Shiel puts his own ideas into the mouth of the superior alien being, who teases and castigates the earthly scientist. The dialogue reveals Shiel's physics to be as idiosyncratic and unorthodox as his metaphysics; the egg calmly rejects both the theory of relativity and the theory of gravity as superstitions. There is not much in the style or content of this discourse to link it to Wells, but on one crucial point the two writers agree. The egg, like Wells, calls for a renewal of mankind, characterising men's present ideas as decadent barriers to essential change, and calling for an intellectual awakening that will transform human affairs and human institutions.

Shiel subsequently placed 'How Life Climbs' into the novel *The Young Men Are Coming* (1937), where the egg donates to the scientist a rejuvenating serum which allows him to be physically and spiritually transformed. He becomes young in body and in mind, possessed of an irresistible enthusiasm which makes him an analogue of Wells's Holy Terror. He founds a social movement, the Young Men, which quickly becomes such a threat to the Establishment that the government assumes totalitarian control of Britain and arms for civil war. The force that drives him to change the world, though, also drives him to make reckless errors in his personal life, which disrupt his revolutionary career. It is interesting, though, to contrast the personalities of Wells's Rud Whitlow and Shiel's Wallace, because they are in one sense polar opposites. While Wells's protagonist is fundamentally selfish to the point of paranoia, Shiel's is fundamentally selfless to the point of self-destruction. Their recklessness is of two very different kinds. In the climax of Shiel's novel, though, Wallace achieves exactly the kind of preparatory destruction of civilisation that Wells thought necessary before the process of renewal might begin. With a characteristic imaginative flourish, Shiel involves him in a duel with an evangelist, both men undertaking to raise a storm to prove their respective faiths. The evangelist's God fails to deliver, but Wallace's alien abductors respond to his appeal, and disturb the earth so profoundly that it is all but wrecked.

Shiel, fourteen months older than Wells, was seventy-two when *The Young Men Are Coming* was published, and it is understandable that a fantasy of rejuvenation should appeal to him. The imaginative scope of this novel – the last which he managed to publish before his death – cannot, however, be attributed simply to self-indulgence. Its recklessness is calculated, and it is as much a response to the temper of the times as *Star Begotten*, which was published in the same year. Although Shiel published no more, he did not stop writing, and by the time of his death had finished his study of the career of Jesus (though part of the manuscript is unfortunately lost). This is basically a new translation of the Gospel according to Luke, with a commentary thereon which attempts to strip away superfluous mythology to reveal the 'true' meaning of the document. It should be remembered that Shiel was one of the converted sons of clergymen who used their literary work, in part, to explain, elaborate and justify their apostasy. There is a definite propriety in the fact that on the one hand we find Shiel's hypothetical rejuvenated Young Man challenging a champion of the Old Time Religion to a decisive storm test (and winning), while on the other hand the aging Shiel searches the gospels meticulously for a new Jesus who will fit into his scheme of faith.

We find something rather similar in the later career of the other clergyman's son with whom this sub-chapter must concern itself: J.D. Beresford. His post-war career has a form similar in some important ways to Shiel's.

In 1921 – the same year that his collection of wartime fantasies *Signs and Wonders* appeared – Beresford published the only futuristic novel which he produced in the twenties. This was *Revolution*, which tells the story of an abortive socialist revolt in Britain. It employs as narrator a young man recovering from shellshock, who is virtually 'reborn' into the world, innocent of all prejudice. Through the medium of this outsider Beresford tries scrupulously to give an even-handed account of the political issues behind the rebellion. The story ends, though, on a note of tired disappointment, fitting in closely with the post-war mood of enervation displayed by Wells's *World of William Clissold*. Beresford wrote little more fantastic fiction in the twenties or thirties, and his three novels of that period which have some fantastic content are all stories of individuals who are forced to try to cope with the unexpected intrusion into their lives of a supernatural experience. *All or Nothing* (1928) is the story of a man who has a *bona fide* religious experience, but finds that his revelation will not fit in comfortably with the doctrines of the established churches. *Real People* (1929) embeds the story of a doctor who discovers that he has extra-sensory powers within a conventional novel of manners. *The Camberwell Miracle* (1933) is a story about a faith-healer.

The personal significance of stories of this type, so far as Beresford was concerned, is most obvious in the last-named. Here the beneficiary of the miracle is a girl crippled in infancy owing to the carelessness of a nurse (this being, of course, Beresford's opinion of his own situation). He followed up the novel with a non-fiction book, *The Case for Faith-Healing* (1934), becoming a propagandist for the cause much as Doyle had become a propagandist for Spiritualism. Whereas Doyle had had no trouble in receiving messages from the spirits, though, Beresford remained obstinately lame, and his faith faded in consequence. None of these three novels is very good, and a much more successful exercise from the same period was

Peckover (1934), a careful and realistic account of the experiences of an amnesiac which is the best of his 'case-study' novels.

In 1938 Beresford wrote the first of a series of books on personal philosophy for Heinemann, *What I Believe*. The general prospectus of the series was to explain why 'materialism is not enough', and some other contributors to it were authors of serious fantasy novels, including Gerald Bullett and Charles Williams. Beresford pointed out in his own essay that Aldous Huxley and Gerald Heard had undertaken similar exercises, and Olaf Stapledon was also to do so. All these writers were seeking to discover a way to put the mundane world into a proper metaphysical context, and all used fiction as a way of dramatising their arguments. Writing this book may have been one of the factors that led Beresford back to writing scientific romance; the descent of Europe into a new world war was certainly another.

The only item of scientific romance which Beresford published between the wars (*Revolution* is a political fantasy with no hypothetical innovations, and is as marginal as *Real People*) was a short ecological parable, 'The Man Who Hated Flies', in his collection *The Meeting Place* (1929). After the outbreak of war, though, he returned to the kind of visionary speculative fiction which he had produced in abundance in the early phase of his career. 'What Dreams May Come ...' (1941) relates the experiences of a conscientious objector concussed by a bomb while working in the fire service. He is comatose for three weeks, which time he spends in the Utopian world of Oion, which he has previously glimpsed in his dreams.

In Oion, physically perfect beings live according to the philosophy of One Mind and One Body, in social harmony. Beresford's protagonist learns their ways, and when he returns to his body he has acquired their powers of control, able to remould himself physically in their image. He embarks upon a messianic career, trying to teach the principles of One Mind and One Body, but the only convert he wins is a soldier – with the consequence that he is charged with incitement to desertion. When he is sent to prison he chooses to die, returning by this means (he hopes) to his dream Utopia. He leaves an account of his vision with the soldier, in the hope that it may yet be able to influence people when less troubled times return.

To some extent 'What Dreams May Come ... ' is an escapist

fantasy, similar in some ways to Arthur Machen's classic *The Hill of Dreams*. In this sense it reflects a comment made by Beresford in filling in a questionnaire for a contemporary dictionary of British writers, where it is stated that he 'Believes European civilisation is disintegrating and that readers will turn to romance to forget their losing battle with life.'[8] There is no doubt, though, that Beresford took the philosophy of life which his hero embraces quite seriously, and his vision of the nature and life of 'evolved' humans is consciously corrective of his earlier account of the Hampdenshire Wonder.

A Common Enemy (1942) is a disaster story in which a wave of earthquakes puts an end to the world war and faces the people of the various nations with a more elementary war to secure the means of their survival. The shake-up brings the old social institutions tumbling down, in true Wellsian fashion, and the process of reorganising a new political community allows the voice of common sense to prevail. This is a cosier novel than any of Wells's, though, and its hero – always referred to with telling politeness as Mr Campion – makes a far gentler dictator than Rud Whitlow or the Air Dictatorship during the transitional phase. The story ends with the reformulation of international relations, and with the announcement that a new human race is beginning to appear, after the fashion of the Hampdenshire Wonder, with the advent of a host of miracle births. (The text refers to Shaw's *Back to Methuselah* to provide theoretical justification for this happening.) Thus, the book ends, like *The Shape of Things to Come* and 'How Life Climbs', with a vision of future mankind transformed and renewed:

> And the future would produce a new race. Those gifted children of Stepansky's would be the forerunners of men and women differing physically, mentally and morally from those of today – physically, in that they would develop a simpler organism and be immune from disease; mentally, in that they would have a clearer, far wider vision of life as a whole; morally, in that they would not be so dominated as men had been in the past by the various desires of the flesh.
>
> Oh! yes, he saw so clearly tonight a time when those forerunners of a finer humanity would increase in number until they became undisputed masters of a world in which all the evils and abuses of the old civilisation would seem like the horrors of barbarism, and the men of today primitive, gross, bestial.[9]

At this point in the text a footnote scrupulously refers the reader to '*What Dreams May Come . . .* ' for a description of this new human race. As with Wells, though, Beresford seems to have lost faith in the probability of this reconstruction, and though he did not give way to despair he certainly became much more anxious about the actual direction of history. The last of his three Second World War scientific romances was *The Riddle of the Tower* (1944), written in collaboration with Esmé Wynne-Tyson. Here, another concussed protagonist has a panoramic vision of the future of man. He sees the failure of a Utopian experiment, followed by a slow decay into 'automatism', whereby individuals surrender their moral will to central authority and artificial determinism, until the human world is completely mechanised, analogous to a termitary. This vision is the unfolding of a hypothesis rather than a glimpse of destiny – 'automatism' is first introduced as the subject of a book whose author claims that human nature includes a negativistic desire to surrender moral prerogatives, a craving for submission to authority. Beresford is thus playing devil's advocate to his own hopeful beliefs, anxiously identifying parallels between the regimented state glimpsed here and the world of Oion (One Mind and One Body, guaranteeing harmony). As usual, Beresford's narrator feels a strong sense of separation from his fellows, and tries to retain an earnest neutrality in evaluating the implications of his experience. He accepts the hopelessness of converting the present-day world to a saner view of things, but can at least express his own commitment to the cause of 'divine anarchy'. In the last of their collaborations, Beresford and Wynne-Tyson further elaborated this idea: *The Gift* (1947) is the biography of a man who is one of nature's own 'divine anarchists', who meets the same fate as the hero of '*What Dreams May Come . . .* ' when he tries to spread his message. It is here that one is required to draw a parallel with Shiel, for this last novel of Beresford's is very close in spirit to Shiel's last, unpublished work. It is very much the story of a new and different Jesus, the meaning of whose life is transfigured so as to fit in with an unorthodox religiosity formed in uneasy reaction against the precepts of a doctrinaire father.

Beresford's later scientific romances can be regarded as a bridge between the later works of Wells and Shiel. By providing such close parallels with both, Beresford emphasises the extent to which all three writers were engaged in a common endeavour. All three had a vision of future mankind – of a 'higher' species that would and must replace our own, so that a transformation of social institutions would be accompanied by a mutation of human nature. All three were Utopians, but all three accepted that contemporary men were not made for Utopia, and could not expect to live in it without undergoing an adaptation that was probably beyond their powers. In the meantime, they could only look for new models to show them how to behave in a manner that would at least point the way toward the transcendent tomorrow. The two clergymen's sons, Shiel and Beresford, naturally found the character of Jesus haunting their attempts to replace him; Wells, who adopted Thomas Henry Huxley as *his* father-figure, found his visions haunted in a very different way, by the spectral brutes of Cainsmarsh.

S. Fowler Wright

Sydney Fowler Wright was born on 6 January 1874. He was little more than seven years younger than Wells, less than a year younger than Beresford and nearly four years older than William Hope Hodgson. While these contemporaries were making their names as writers of speculative fiction in the years before the Great War Fowler Wright was working as an accountant. He was successful in this profession, and though he apparently wrote a good deal of lyric poetry before 1918 (in which year his first wife died) it was not until after that date that he became more intimately involved with literary endeavours.

Fowler Wright came from a family of devout Baptists – his father was a lay preacher and one of his sisters became a missionary – but he became a freethinker, abandoning the dogmatic apparatus of his father's faith in favour of a religious and moral philosophy which he worked out for himself. This independence of mind began early in life, when he left King Edward's School in his teens to take charge of his own education. He was very fond of animals and passionately devoted to all things natural. He did not eat meat, did not smoke and was very moderate in his use of alcohol; this asceticism was coupled – as asceticism so often is – with firm moral convictions. He had a very strong commitment to individual freedom and responsibility, and disliked intensely what he saw as the progressive erosion of freedom and responsibility by legislation and bureaucracy. He was a strong believer in natural justice, and very suspicious of the police, whose role seemed to him unjustifiably intrusive. His love of nature had as its counterpart a determined antipathy towards technology in general and the motor car in particular. His attitude to contemporary social changes was thus unusually hostile, and he found it easy to conjure up nightmarish images of a future where the trends he deplored had been carried to extremes. He found it equally easy to glorify primitive and pastoral settings, which he often used in his imaginative works.

Fowler Wright's involvement with the literary world began in 1917 when he became one of the founding fathers of the Empire Poetry League, whose function was to promote cultural endeavour through the English-speaking world. Other prominent members of the League were G.K. Chesterton, L.A.G. Strong, H.E. Bates and Humbert Wolfe. The organisation was philanthropically funded, and Fowler Wright took a leading part in its affairs. He became the administrator of the League's own publishing imprint, the Merton Press, and the editor of its journal, *Poetry* (later *Poetry and the Play*). He compiled numerous anthologies for the Merton Press. His own first published work, issued under the name Alan Seymour, was a small volume of poems, *Scenes from the Morte d'Arthur* (1919). This was part of the grand project which was to be the core of his life's work in the literary field: a rendering of the whole body of Arthurian legend in blank verse. He worked on this constantly, occasionally publishing small sections of it. It was complete in 1940 but the manuscript was destroyed in the Blitz, and he had to do it all over again. It has never been published in full.

Shortly after publication of the *Scenes* Fowler Wright wrote his first novel, *Deluge*, but failed to find a publisher for it. He used the Merton Press, though, to publish in 1925 his second novel, *The Amphibians*, a work comparable in its scope only to *The Time Machine* and *The Night Land*. It is set in a future so remote that man has disappeared from the earth, to be replaced by other intelligent species, including the gentle, telepathic Amphibians and the giant troglodytic Dwellers. The story's narrator is projected into the future by a scientist in order to search for two other men who have previously been dispatched and have failed to return.

In this remote future the narrator finds himself in a bizarre artificial environment, where his emergence from hiding so startles an Amphibian that 'she' (the Amphibians are actually hermaphrodite, but seem feminine to the narrator) is seized by a carnivorous plant. This unfortunate accident triggers a sequence of events which causes trouble between the Amphibians and the Dwellers. In the quest to repair the damage, the narrator joins forces with a troop of Amphibians in the quest to release one of their number who has been captured and imprisoned by the ferocious, semi-intelligent Killers. Because he has more in common with the Killers than the Amphibians have, he is commissioned to take a leading role in the assault, destroying the Killers' arsenal.

A key element in the story is the narrator's attempts to see himself as the Amphibians see him, and to explain his world to them. At one point he is allowed to 'see' into the mind of one of the beautiful, gentle and high-minded creatures, and is appalled by the repulsion which he senses there. Later, she comments on his account of his own world as follows:

> I think there are two ways of life which are good. There is the higher way, which is ours, in which all are united; and there is the lower way, of the shark or the shell-fish, of freedom and violence, which only greater violence can destroy, and which nothing can bring into slavery. But the vision which you give me is of a state which is lower than either of these, of blind servitudes and oppressions, to which you yield without willingness.[10]

This reproduces a common image in scientific romance of this period, by which the human world is seen as an unfortunate intermediate state, neither wholly natural nor wholly civilised, with man himself half ape and half angel. Fowler Wright was, however, more outspoken than anyone else in his scathing account of the degradation of such a state. This makes him seem, occasionally, to be a vitriolically misanthropic writer, though the impression is somewhat misleading.

Another project on which Fowler Wright was working while he was writing *The Amphibians* was a translation of Dante's *Divina Commedia*, and some imagery from the *Inferno* spills over into it. The climax of the story is a bizarre episode in which judgment must be passed on a group of bat-winged creatures (resembling Doré's illustrations of Dante's devils) who have been delivered to the Killers by the Dwellers for execution. They are members of a race which once ruled the earth, and were preserved by the Dwellers for research, but have been condemned as too vile to live. When the narrator releases the trapped Amphibian, he must decide whether or not to release them too, and thus becomes a court of appeal. The character of these beings – and the specific crime with which they are charged – is a parody of human nature and conduct, but the narrator does finally concur with the judgment that they are too vile to be allowed to live. After this digression, the book comes abruptly to a halt, with some mysterious new accord apparently having been reached between the Dwellers and the Amphibians. The last line, though, promises a continuation in another volume.

Fowler Wright was far from being the only writer of scientific romance to imagine a kind of 'higher man' whose nature would be superior to our own, though the Amphibians are physically more different from us than most versions – Beresford's inhabitants of Oion, for instance. Where he does stand apart from other writers, though, is in his idea of their environment. The idealised Amphibians do not live in a comfortable Utopia, but in an environment closer to Hell than to Heaven. Fowler Wright was flatly opposed to the kind of 'Utopia of comforts' favoured by Wells and Beresford, and was willing to argue against Heaven itself. His reverence for nature was in no way based upon the misapprehension (common among modern ecological mystics) that nature is harmonious. He accepted its redness in tooth and claw, and presumed that struggle and strife were necessary features of a healthy way of life. He felt that his contemporaries, in trying to avoid that struggle, had elevated an undesirable set of goals – idols whose worship was bound to lead them to ruin.

The Merton Press became defunct soon after *The Amphibians* was issued (or, rather, reissued – a tiny first edition was quickly followed by a more substantial second). Fowler Wright was encouraged, however, to carry on with some similar ventures on his own account. He established a new publishing company, Fowler Wright Ltd, to issue *Deluge* and the first part of his translation of Dante, the *Inferno*. *Deluge* appeared in 1927, to a very enthusiastic reception from the newspaper critics. Arnold Bennett, Edward Shanks and Gerald Gould all praised the work highly, and the fact that the book was self-published added to the interest that was taken in it. Such was its celebrity that the American Cosmopolitan Book Corporation were encouraged to invest in it as a potential bestseller, and their promotion of the book assured its success. Film rights were quickly sold and Fowler Wright (who had relatives in California) cheerfully set off to assist in making the film. Within the space of a few months his life was transformed, as he rose from the obscurity of hobbyist self-publisher to celebrity status.

Deluge is a disaster story, in which a series of earth tremors alters the contours of the planet's surface. Almost all of the civilised world is inundated, but part of England is elevated so that the Cotswolds become a tiny chain of islands. The storms accompanying the tremors kill many people, and the survivors find themselves uncomfortably born out of the womb of civilisation into a hostile world to which they are ill adapted. The story of their struggle for survival is told with a brutal realism which had few precedents. The novel's chief protagonist is Martin Webster, who loses his wife and two children in the storm, and later forms an alliance with another woman, believing her dead. After pledging himself in marriage for a second time, though, he discovers that his first wife is still alive. In a world where there is a drastic shortage of women it seems he must give up one or the other, but in the novel's conclusion he persuades the community which has made him its leader that the decision of the women to share him must be accepted.

As with many other disaster stories *Deluge* has much to say about the fragility of civilised mores and the ways in which civilised life makes people incompetent to keep themselves alive once the supportive apparatus of social institutions is swept away. Fowler Wright is exceptional, though, in the extent to which he blames the defects of human nature *on* Civilisation. His philosophy is rather Rousseauesque in that he believes the state of savagery to be (potentially, at least) a noble rather than a brutal one. Many people misinterpreted the end of *Deluge*, considering that the establishment of the hero's *ménage à trois* was a shocking victory of immorality, but Fowler Wright was almost the last man in the world to speak out in favour of immoral self-indulgence, and the real significance of the ending is very different. As befits a Rousseauesque Libertarian, Fowler Wright considered that the real basis of social life is to be found in the contracts made between free individuals. For Fowler Wright the most fundamental and most sacred of these contracts was the marriage contract, and Martin's acceptance of his two wives is not a manifestation of sexual greed but a recognition of the vital necessity of honouring contracts which he had made in good faith. (It might also be noted that Fowler Wright married again in 1920, at about the time he wrote *Deluge*, and the way in which Martin Webster's first wife welcomes his second may reflect, in part, an earnest desire to believe that his much-loved first wife would not have resented his marrying again after her death.)

Fowler Wright's third novel was presumably complete when *Deluge* took off so spectacularly, and it was published very quickly in order to cash in on the wave of publicity. This was *The Island of Captain Sparrow* (1928), and it was rapidly followed by *The World Below* (1929), which reprinted *The Amphibians* along with the promised sequel. In the meantime, Fowler Wright Ltd continued in its own eccentric pattern with more volumes of poetry and a pamphlet entitled *Police and Public*. This last work suggests that Fowler Wright aspired, like Wells before him, to become a twentieth-century sage as well as a fantastic novelist – he was perhaps encouraged by the fact that an article in the *Daily Express* nominated him as one of 'the ten best brains in Britain'. Other titles which he optimistically announced for publication were 'The Problems of Motor Traffic', 'The Case against Birth Control', 'The Safeguarding of Industries', 'The Ethics of Taxation', 'The Votes of Women' and 'The Channel Tunnel', but none ever appeared and Fowler Wright Ltd lapsed into inactivity. His celebrity also allowed him to sell some short stories of a highly individual nature to periodicals in Britain and America. 'The Choice: an Allegory of Blood and Tears' (1929) appeared, oddly, in the upmarket women's magazine *Eve*, as did 'P.N. 40 – and Love', when the magazine had absorbed another to become *Eve and Britannia*. This breakthrough did not lead to any immediate renewal of interest in fantastic fiction in the British magazines, though, and after a handful of initial successes even Fowler Wright could no longer sell such items to them.

The Island of Captain Sparrow is the story of a man cast away on an island whose inhabitants include the last survivors of an antediluvian civilisation (presumably Atlantis), a race of nonsentient satyrs, and the descendants of a pirate crew. There have been other recent castaways, one of whom is a young girl who lives naked, wild and free in the forest, forced to evade the satyrs and the pirates alike. The hero's coming, though, sets off a chain of events which leads to her being captured, and he must rescue her before she is made the bride of the bestial pirate leader. This he achieves, with the aid of the last of the elder race, but he is wounded, and in the end he and the girl are left alone on the island, with a baby donated by the Atlantean, conveniently cut off from their means of escape. The girl will therefore induct the hero into her way of life rather than *vice versa*, and the implication is that this is the only possible happy ending. The story is basically an escapist dream-fantasy, ending with a symbolic re-entry into an Edenic garden.

The population of the imaginary island with ambiguous characters, who combine human and bestial traits in different ways, relates *The Island of Captain Sparrow* to *The Island of Dr Moreau*. If the story is to be seen as a parable, then it subverts and contradicts Wells's parable in much the same way that the portrayal of the Amphibians and the Dwellers in *The Amphibians* subverts and contradicts Wells's image of the Eloi and the Morlocks in *The Time Machine*, though this is not what Fowler Wright had consciously in mind as his purpose. Whereas Wells saw the bestial element in man as a hangover from his remote ancestry, Fowler Wright saw it as part of the corruption of civilisation. Thus, Prendick flees his island but finds his later life haunted by what was revealed to him there; Fowler Wright's hero can revert to the innocence of nature once the degenerate pirates have been expelled – the morally innocent satyrs can remain, because they are the opposite of Moreau's Beast Folk.

Marcelle, the heroine of *The Island of Captain Sparrow*, became the prototype for a whole series of Fowler Wright heroines (though she herself might be regarded as simply a new version of the narrator's Amphibian companion in *The Amphibians*). She is similar in many ways to Rima, the heroine of W.H. Hudson's *Green Mansions*, but much more robust. Hudson, of course, was the first great ecological mystic, whose view of Nature was highly romanticised, and whose female nature-spirit was correspondingly ethereal. Fowler Wright, who recognised well enough that the natural life was *hard*, made his nature-spirits correspondingly tough.

When he became successful Fowler Wright also became frenetically active; new works of various kinds flowed from his pen. By 1931 he had produced not only the sequel to *The Amphibians* but a sequel to *Deluge*, a historical novel, a crime story and a novel of contemporary life. Such energy is astonishing from a man in his late fifties, and it is not surprising that the quality of his work was not assisted by such a rate of productivity. (Nor did it help his reputation, although he published his crime novels under the pseudonym 'Sidney Fowler'.) *The World Below* had probably been written some years before its publication – probably before the publication of *The Amphibians* in 1925 – and was arguably not in a satisfactory state for publication. Certainly it is not in any real sense a conclusion to the story, and it ends with a synoptic rush that makes it seem as if what had been intended as a much longer work had been hastily wound up in order to get it out of the way.

The World Below takes the time traveller and an Amphibian companion into the subterranean territory of the Dwellers, where much more is revealed about this strange future world by the 'living books' – artifical organisms impressed with telepathic recordings – which they discover there. The Dwellers seem to be beginning a war against the insectile Antipodeans, glimpses of whose progress are caught via images projected on corridor walls. The protagonist is eventually captured and imprisoned, finally encountering the sole survivor of those he came to find – quite mad, alas. Before his release he must offer the Dwellers' Seekers of Wisdom an account of his own world, which they find almost as absurd and disgusting as do the more gentle Amphibians.

Dawn, the sequel to *Deluge*, is a more substantial work than *The World Below*, but succeeds in adding little to its predecessor. Most of its story runs parallel to the one told in the earlier book, and when it does move on to a further time it virtually recapitulates the crisis that was faced by the community of survivors in *Deluge*. The major elements of the book that are new constitute an examination of the roles of two men: the entrepreneurial trader Henry Butcher who cleverly corners the market in various desirable commodities by careful scavenging and artful bartering; and the fiercely independent farmer John Burman. Martin Webster, in trying to formulate a political system for his little empire, must find a way to control the anti-social enterprise of Butcher's kind without compromising the freedom of Burman's.

Dawn is perhaps the book which encapsulates more neatly than any other Fowler Wright's essential pessimism. It has a good deal to say about the unpromising nature of human beings, even when those most perverted by civilisation have been weeded out. It asks not only whether a man of intelligence, resolve and goodwill could possibly organise a sane and happy society, but the more fundamental question of whether he has any moral right to try. Fowler Wright, as a Libertarian, conceded that people must be free even to be foolish, indolent or wicked. He recognised too the need for working communities to establish some form of social contract to limit or contain foolishness, indolence and wickedness. He had no real confidence, though, that people could actually be trusted to honour such a contract, because the capacity for such honour was just not in them. Unlike *Deluge, Dawn* ends on a very sober note, with a meditation which brings Martin almost to the edge of despair, from which he is roused not by any triumphant renewal of hope but by the conviction that *whatever* the future may hold, he must do his best. The symbolic dawn which is referred to in the last line of the text is, significantly, 'the indifferent dawn'.[11]

The pessimism of *Dawn* is given rather more bitter expression in Fowler Wright's novel of contemporary life, *Seven Thousand in Israel* (1931), a relentlessly downbeat story whose hero is financially ruined and eventually dies. Oddly, though, the narrative is frequently interrupted by awkwardly self-conscious passages in which the author wonders whether he is doing the right thing in allowing his plot to develop so bleakly. The leading character of *Dream; or, the Simian Maid* (1931) also begins her story deep in the slough of despond. She is a depressed socialite, Marguerite Leinster, who seeks release from her condition in dreams conjured up for her by a 'magician' – a scientist who sends her consciousness back through time to experience other lives. She has already visited Babylon and Atlantis, and now desires something even more remote and primitive. She finds herself incarnated as a tree-dwelling furry primate.

The plot of *Dream* is complicated when two others follow her into the dream. One is Stephen Cranleigh, who is ambitious to marry Marguerite, the other his sister. They are incarnated as members of another species, the 'cave-people'. Although this race is more technologically advanced, Rita (Marguerite's new self) considers it a lower species. There is also another, even lower – the Ogpurs, a mongrel race so brutal and vile that (the author suggests) they are presumably the ancestors of modern man. The three dreamers eventually find themselves in a curious kingdom where they receive a highly ambiguous welcome, and become embroiled in complicated schemes and affairs of the heart. In the end, the kingdom is being destroyed by an invasion of giant rats, while Rita and her would-be lover become lost in a maze of caves and ultimately die on opposite sides of a stone wall, able only to touch by means of a narrow breach. This frustrating ending stands as a slightly enigmatic symbol of the relationship which Cranleigh and Marguerite have with one another and with their own world once the dream is dissolved.

Dream is in no way an attempt to re-create the actual circumstances of man's pre-human ancestors. It belongs neither to the anthropological tradition of Wells's 'A Story of the Stone Age' and J.H. Rosny the elder's *La Guerre du Feu*, nor to the small group of moral fantasies, including J. Leslie Mitchell's *Three Go Back* and William Golding's *The Inheritors*, which contrast the supposed natures of Cro-Magnon and Neanderthal Man in order to promote theories about the supposed corruptness of human nature. *Dream* relegates its comments on the corruptness of human nature to a couple of throwaway lines, and has much stronger links with *The Island of Captain Sparrow* and *The Amphibians*, presenting an argument about the principles on which the natural world operates, regardless of the presence or efforts of man. It is a book about the struggle for existence, though Fowler Wright has his own notion of the implications of that phrase, distinct from the ways in which Spencer and Darwin used it.

All Fowler Wright's longer scientific romances from *The Amphibians* to *Dream* deal with worlds remote from our own where, one way or another, the laws of nature (as he saw them) hold more obvious dominion. His shorter stories of the same period, by contrast, follow the opposite tack – they deal with worlds where culture has overwhelmed nature and obliterated its rule. Ten short stories are gathered together in the collection *The New Gods Lead* (1932), the first seven of which are grouped together as glimpses of the future where the 'new gods' of twentieth-century man will take him. The best of these stories constitute what is perhaps the most vitriolic vision of the future ever produced; they have an imaginative savagery of tone and content that is quite unparalleled. All of Fowler Wright's anxieties and preoccupations regarding the march of progress are here subjected to bitterly sarcastic extrapolation.

In 'Justice' the widespread use of birth-control has resulted in a society with a relatively large number of dependent old people; when a law is passed to regulate the penalties imposed on reckless motorists according to the age of their victims, this quickly becomes a licence to murder the old. 'Brain' tells the story of an attempt to seize power in the technocratic world of the future, by a scientist armed with various brain-controlling drugs. 'P.N. 40', set in the 93rd year of the Eugenic Era, tells of an attempt by a love-struck couple to defy the laws of their orderly and rational society.

The last story of the 'New Gods' sequence is 'Automata', which is a philosophical commentary on man's use of machines, predicting the slow usurpation of all human endeavour by mechanical devices. After an expository section which takes the form of an imaginary speech delivered to the British Association, two other brief sections leap forward in time, the first to describe a tea party at which middle-aged matrons compare their mechanical children, the second to consider the plight of the last man in the world as he is condemned to be scrapped for inefficiency.

The other three stories in the collection are not dissimilar in spirit. 'The Rat', which has been widely reprinted, is the story of the discovery of a serum of immortality by an inconspicuous country doctor. After proving its efficacy by rejuvenating an old, sick rat, he thinks about the consequences of releasing it, immortalising the evil as well as the good that is in the contemporary world. He decides, in the end, that the transformation of human life that would ensue would not be for the better, but he learns that new discoveries can be as difficult to suppress as to make.

The New Gods Lead closes with 'Choice' (originally subtitled 'an Allegory of Blood and Tears'), a fable which offers the most explicit expression of Fowler Wright's basic philosophy. A man and a woman who have suffered a great deal in life are reunited after death in the Christian Heaven. They settle down to enjoy the rewards of virtue, courtesy of the mercy of God, but find that Heaven is so pointless in its peacefulness as to be literally soul-destroying. They ask to be reincarnated in a world fit to live in, and God sets squarely before them the prospect they will face:

Birth will be a darkness behind and a darkness before you. You will forget all that you are or have been. You will endure the night of the womb, as your body grows from the current of another's blood, and her thoughts control you; knowing panic when she fears, and causeless joy when she pleasures. You will know the terror of birth when you are cast out with a body which is not yours, but has been made weak or strong by the passions of others. You will live through helpless years under the controls of those who may be foolish or brutal. You will be scourged by the customs of the tribe that breeds you, and enslaved by instincts that you cannot kill, though your mind may hate them. You will know remorse and shame. You will desire things which you cannot reach, or you will find your gains to be worthless. You will know pain that is more dreadful than any sorrow, and sorrow that is more dreadful than any pain. You will do evil to others, and you will suffer evil continually. At the last, you will die miserably, facing the curtain of death without assurance of immortality. For if you go, you go blindly.[12]

Even though they know that rebirth will part them, and that they may never meet again, the man and the woman elect to take their chances. The simple heroism of their decision gives the story a superficial uplift which helps to conceal what a harsh message it is actually delivering.

A rather different view of 'Heaven' is provided in *Beyond the Rim* (1932), in which a small group of adventurers discover a warm valley in the Antarctic, inhabited by religious fundamentalists whose ancestors left England hoping to reach the New World some three centuries before. Despite the sternest efforts of these hardy puritans their ideal society is threatened from within and without by heresy, and the visitors from outside, as living proof of the truth of some heretical ideas, are most unwelcome. Even so, one of the travellers ultimately decides to stay in the valley rather than try to escape.

Power (1933) was Fowler Wright's first novel of the near future, and is a scrupulous attempt to develop a premiss found in several novels of the period. It belongs to the tradition of stories extending from Griffith in which enlightened individuals armed with powerful new inventions try to force peace and social reform upon a reluctant world. Other examples include E. Charles Vivian's *Star Dust* (1925), C.S. Forester's *The Peacemaker* (1934), Francis Beeding's *The One Sane Man* (1934) and S. Andrew Wood's *I'll Blackmail the World* (1935). It is relatively rare in such novels for the blackmailers to achieve any measure of success, but *Power's* Stanley Maitland is actually given temporary command of Britain's ship of state, compelling Fowler Wright to spell out exactly what can and must be done to save the world from its ignominies and injustices. Like Martin Webster, though, Maitland proves to be hesitant in exercising his authority and less certain than he anticipated of what to do with it. In addition, of course, he has the problem of powerful forces plotting against him – aided, unfortunately, by his own wife – and as their plans begin to succeed the plot is drawn back into a more conventional thriller framework. In the end, as in so many such novels (including virtually all of those published between the wars), 'normality' is restored. This is, it hardly needs to be emphasised, a less than happy ending, when we have already been given Maitland's assessment of that normality:

> We are looking at a civilisation without control, and without the freedom that control gives. We are a nation of slaves, and slaves to a tyrant that we cannot kill, being beyond our reach. Our new rulers are the aggregate folly and the aggregate weakness of mankind. Comfort and cowardice are the new gods.[13]

By this time Fowler Wright's period of success was over. He was still producing books prolifically, but they were no longer reaching a wide public. Although his hopes were briefly reignited when one of his crime stories, *Three Witnesses*, was made into a film in 1935, he did not do well out of his writing in the later thirties. Several of his works took years to find a publisher; others were never published at all. He planned a further sequel to *Deluge*, but never wrote it, and his sequel to *Dream*, *Vengeance of Gwa* (1934) was presumably rejected by Harrap, who had published *Dream*. It appeared from another publisher under the pseudonym Anthony Wingrave, with the prefatory material that would have linked it to the earlier story removed.[14]

As in *Dream*, the strong-willed heroine of *Vengeance of Gwa* – another version of Marguerite Leinster, though not so identified in the extant text – enters into an uneasy alliance with savage folk of another kind, and eventually witnesses their destruction by another, more rapacious species. Although the setting is again prehistoric the heroine this time is a refugee from a great city inhabited by a highly civilised people. The people of the city echo the Atlanteans of *The Island of Captain Sparrow*, and their sterile 'Utopia' parallels the Heaven of 'Choice' and the future world later to be described in *The Adventure of Wyndham Smith*. This juxtaposition of prehistoric and futuristic imagery emphasises the fact that Fowler Wright thought of the distant past and the distant future in much the same terms. He had no faith in Shielian progress.

Fowler Wright's career enjoyed another temporary boost following a visit to Hitler's Germany, as a result of which he produced a series of alarmist newspaper articles about the threat to the world posed by the growth of the new state. He was not simply worried by the rise of Fascism; his anxiety was deeper than that because he saw in the new hyper-organised Germany the kind of tyrannical and technocratic society that he feared. He had apparently long planned to write a future war story, and now he was inspired to set about it. His futuristic thriller '1938' was serialised in the *Daily Mail*, the paper which thirty years earlier had run le Queux's 'The Invasion'. It was reprinted in book form as *Prelude in Prague; a Story of the War of 1938* (1935).

Prelude in Prague begins prophetically with the proposition that Germany would embark on the road to war by manufacturing an excuse to invade Czechoslovakia in order to reclaim part of her 'traditional territory'. It rapidly develops, though, into a horror story which put the actual events of 1938 (and even those of 1939) in the shade. The final chapters present a clinically horrific catalogue of atrocities, imagining the effects of devastating aerial bombing and the use of a new chemical weapon – a 'freezing gas'. *Prelude in Prague* ends with the delivery of a German ultimatum to Britain, and its sequel, *Four Days War* (1936), takes up the story with its rejection. The book goes on to describe the devastation of Britain by bombers which carry not only explosives but chemical and biological weapons. The war becomes a world war – and eventually takes on the semblance of a Holy War, with the Christian nations (led by America) arrayed against the forces of a new paganism, symbolised by Germany's new military dictator, Prince von Teufel.

Fowler Wright had intended (in 1933) to call his future war story *The Splendid Curse*, and there are fragments of dialogue in *Four Days War* which concentrate on the degeneracy of contemporary society and the possibility of its corruption being cleansed by the war. The horror of the vision of destruction, though, overwhelms this cynical thread of argument, and it has quite disappeared by the time the story extends into the third volume of the trilogy, *Megiddo's Ridge* (1937). This is the poorest of the three novels, presenting striking but rather implausible images of life within the transformed pagan Germany that recall the stories in *The New Gods Lead*. The rival armies and air fleets mass for their vital confrontation, but the story ends before the battle is fought or decided. The conclusion, though it promises death for von Teufel, refuses even to ask questions about the possibility of a new dawn beyond the riot of Armageddon.

While writing these future war novels Fowler Wright returned briefly to the *milieu* of *The New Gods Lead* to produce the short story 'Original Sin', though he failed to sell it at the time. This story is set in a future world where the conquest of disease has led to strict birth-control, and ultimately to the creation of a pain-free Utopia of comfort and ease, like the one briefly mentioned in *Vengeance of Gwa*. Into this perfect world has come a new ideology – the Doctrine of Futility, which is elevated to sacred writ as men acknowledge the pointlessness of their lives and elect to commit mass suicide. One man and one woman elect to save themselves, to become a new Adam and Eve, but in doing so the man is forced by the woman to commit a crime which, he fears, will extend its shadowy blight over their new version of the story of mankind. When he failed to place the story Fowler Wright expanded it – somewhat uncomfortably – into the novel *The Adventure of Wyndham Smith* (1938). The sharp moral is lost as the early part of the story is intensively re-complicated, and the narrative then follows the two survivors through the early stages of their battle to survive in a world now dominated by the monstrous machines which once served the city-dwellers.

By this time Fowler Wright was slowing down his production, and his plots were coming to seem increasingly ragged. The books which he wrote during the war years were all mediocre crime stories, and though one of them – *The Adventure of the Blue Room* (1945) – is futuristic it is of negligible interest as a scientific romance. This decline is not entirely surprising, given that he was in his seventies by the time he wrote this book. His career was not quite over, and its story will be taken up in a later chapter, but the war interrupted it as decisively as the Great War had interrupted the careers of all the early writers of scientific romance. As with those early writers, it makes sense to offer a 'preliminary summation' of his achievement as it stood at the time of that interruption.

Fowler Wright was in some ways a highly idiosyncratic writer. One commentator on his work, Sam Moskowitz, finds him so idiosyncratic, and his ideas so uncongenial, that he brackets him with M.P. Shiel as a writer possessed of a 'radicalism verging on the insane'. He goes on to speak of the two writers perhaps pandering to a 'streak of prejudice and viciousness' in their readers.[15] This is a mistaken judgment (of both writers) but it does reflect a difficulty which some readers have in coming to terms with the peculiar brand of misanthropism in Fowler Wright's stories. While they are certainly not 'verging on the insane' there is undeniably something highly unusual in his accounts of the world of *The Amphibians* and the future society of *The Adventure of Wyndham Smith*. The second is a portrait of an insane society, while the first suggests strongly that *ours* is an insane society, and in both cases there is a certain relish taken in the description.

It must be recognised, though, that although these are among the most extreme images produced in the period between the wars, they are not out of tune with works produced by many other writers. They reflect, albeit in a particularly striking fashion, an attitude not uncommon in their day. They are expressions of what Wells cannily chose to call an Age of Frustration, when a great many people were seized by the idea that civilisation had somehow gone wrong. This sensation of wrongness was felt all the more deeply because of the hopes that had been entertained before the Great War, and the promises which had been made (in the line of propaganda) during that war. Before it, people had thought of it as a war to end war, a war to save civilisation. Afterwards, looking back on four years of appalling slaughter, remembering scenes of horror that they had never glimpsed even in the wildest of nightmares, people found war unended and civilisation unsaved. Many, indeed, thought things were worse than before, and getting worse still. Small wonder that their frustration turned frequently to despair, and that they looked for scapegoats.

Where Fowler Wright stands virtually alone among writers of scientific romance is in his choice of scapegoats. The sickness of civilisation – for which he could issue only the most gloomy prognosis – was for him symbolised by the motor car and the idea of birth-control, and this symbolisation did indeed make his view seem a little eccentric. But these were only symbols, mere exemplars of much more fundamental trends. The motor car stood for the march of science and the mechanisation of the human world; birth-control for a whole attitude of mind by which men opposed themselves to nature. In deciding that science and the ideologies that marched in its train were evil, Fowler Wright was by no means alone – he was simply more extreme than anyone else, except perhaps J. Leslie Mitchell.

Fowler Wright may be seen as the great ideological opponent of H.G. Wells. In the *Today and Tomorrow* pamphlets the scientific Utopianism of J.B.S. Haldane was countered rather modestly by the scepticism of Bertrand Russell, and in fiction Wells found similarly prestigious and cultured opponents in E.M. Forster and Aldous Huxley. It was, however, Fowler Wright who took up the position which is actually the polar opposite of the one adopted by Wells and Haldane. Fowler Wright argued not that scientific progress was bad because it would deliver more power into the hands of the evil or misguided men who run the modern world, but that it was bad *per se*. He attacked the Utopia of comforts on more radical grounds than Forster or Aldous Huxley, and lent his support to a much more radical alternative, but within his work there is much the same structure of feeling. His philosophy of life may be a harsh one, celebrating the struggle *of* existence (rather than the struggle *for* existence) in a remarkably uncompromising manner, but it had clear connections with the ideas of other writers of this period, and it is most readily understandable as a product of its time.

Olaf Stapledon

William Olaf Stapledon was born on 10 May 1886 in Wallasey on Merseyside. His grandfather had a business in Port Said and Suez supplying ships going through the Suez Canal; because his father worked for the firm Olaf spent his first six years in Port Said. Denied in these early years the company of other English children, he seems to have developed an isolation of spirit which he never quite shook off.

Stapledon was the first major writer of scientific romance to reverse the pattern of intergenerational ideological conflict so common among his predecessors. His father was an agnostic, and though he initially followed this example he eventually struggled long and hard in rebellion against it. Though he never became a Christian he did ultimately become a deist. His scepticism, though, forced him to tackle the job of inventing God all over again, much as M.P. Shiel did. Most of his fiction can be seen as part of this exploratory quest. This intellectual and imaginative task was complicated, first by the fact that it is much harder to make a faith than to lose one, and second by the fact that in Stapledon's case – unlike, apparently, many of the others – a second parental influence must be taken into account. His mother was a Unitarian, professing a strong belief in the ethical teachings of Christ while de-emphasising the metaphysical mythology surrounding his career. His mother is said to have been unusually possessive, and it may well have been her passion for Ruskin that first infused Stapledon with his socialist ideals.[16]

Stapledon returned to England to go to school, and ultimately progressed to Balliol College, Oxford, where he took his degree in History. He went to work as a shipping clerk, but was unenthusiastic to the point of incompetence, and fared little better when he tried his hand at teaching at the Manchester Grammar School. He took more readily, though, to teaching adults for the Workers' Education Authority, and this remained a part-time vocation of his for many years. He dabbled in poetry during his twenties, and published *Latter-Day Psalms* in 1914, already toying in its pages with the idea of God. Later, he was to contribute to volumes of poetry edited by Fowler Wright for the Merton Press, and to the Poetry League journal *Poetry*.

The coming of the Great War changed his life, as it changed the lives of all the men of his generation. It brought upon him a crisis of conscience, and he refused to enlist, serving instead in the Friends' Ambulance Corps, a volunteer organisation run by the Quakers. His actual experience of the war, therefore, was not dissimilar to John Beresford's – Beresford is the writer with whom he has more in common than with any other.

After the war Stapledon married a cousin from Australia, and remained uneasily dependent on his parents – his father eventually bought the couple a home. He did a good deal of work for the WEA and maintained loose connections with the University of Liverpool (from which he obtained his PhD) but never really earned a living for himself. He published numerous articles on human science and philosophy – philosophy was the chief subject which he taught for the WEA – and in 1929 published his first full-length book, *A Modern Theory of Ethics: A Study of the Relations of Ethics and Psychology*. Despite its title the book eventually tries to support ethical theory by reference to metaphysics – not to any supposed commandments laid down by a Supreme Being, but rather to a supposed exceptional mode of human experience which he here calls 'ecstasy'. The idea of such an exceptional mode of consciousness, giving glimpses of a special insight into the nature of things, was to remain central to his work, and was to be fundamental to his gradually reconstituted faith.

A Modern Theory of Ethics was followed in 1930 by Stapledon's first work of imaginative fiction, *Last and First Men*, a future history of all the descendant species of *Homo sapiens*, extending over some two billion years. The 'blueprint' for the book appears to have been supplied by Haldane's 'The Last Judgment'. In a preface, the author offered the following apologia for the work:

> To romance of the future may seem to be indulgence in ungoverned speculation for the sake of the marvellous. Yet controlled imagination in this sphere can be a very valuable exercise for minds bewildered about the present and its potentialities. Today we should welcome, and even study, every serious attempt to envisage the future of our race; not merely in order to grasp the very diverse and often tragic possibilities that confront us, but also that we may familiarise ourselves with the certainty that many of our most cherished ideals would seem puerile to more developed minds. To romance of the far future, then, is to attempt to see the human race in its cosmic setting and to mould our hearts to entertain new values.
>
> But if such imaginative construction of possible futures is to be at all potent, our imagination must be strictly disciplined . . . We must achieve neither mere history, nor mere fiction, but myth . . . This book can no more claim to be true myth than true prophecy. But it is an essay in myth creation.[17]

All of Stapledon's work in the field of speculative fiction can be regarded as one grand 'essay in myth creation', and the phrase encapsulates the sense in which he was trying to go beyond the scope of most previous futuristic thought. He was not content to be a 'mere' historian of the future, in the way that Wells tried to be in *The Shape of Things to Come,* nor a 'mere' fantasist after the fashion of Fowler Wright in *The Amphibians.* He had a different attitude to the future, implicit in which was the conviction that the future of man would not simply be an extension of past history, but must involve some kind of gradual spiritual awakening to consolidate the hold of consciousness on those fleeting moments of mystical intuition which he had earlier called 'ecstasy'. The phrase 'alternative states of consciousness' was not current in Stapledon's day, but that was really the focal point of his interest – all his novels are attempts to explore hypothetically the possibility of such altered states, which might one day give the descendants of men an intuitive hotline to enlightenment. The Last Man who is the notional narrator of *Last and First Men* represents his mission in *his* introduction to the text by observing that 'Somehow . . . I must help you to feel not only the vastness of time and space, but also the vast diversity of mind's possible modes.'[18]

Stapledon's picture of human history extends as follows:

A world state is established by the end of the twentieth century. Disease is banished. Religious truth absorbs the new science and is reconciled with it. The average lifespan is more than doubled and population is strategically limited, though without the use of artificial contraceptives. Various eugenic schemes are operated, some of them rather bizarre. This state eventually collapses because of a resource crisis, and a long Dark Age ensues, in which men revert to barbarism for more than a hundred thousand years.

By the time that a new civilisation emerges, based in Patagonia, man has changed physically, aging more quickly. The sexual impulse has become weak. Atomic disaster wipes out the new civilisation, but survivors establish colonies in Siberia and Labrador. The latter colony undergoes an evolutionary retrogression, and its sub-human descendants repopulate most of the world.

A new species of man which emerges two hundred thousand years in the future, the Second Men, resembles *Homo sapiens* physically but has a radically different psychology, fundamentally altruistic with an innate appreciation of the aesthetics of mathematics. When they become civilised they come into conflict with a primate species which has enslaved the other descendants of the First Men, and this conflict leads to a cycle of rise and fall which persists for a quarter of a million years, various disasters being responsible for the phases of decline.

An invasion from Mars ten million years hence helps to precipitate another long Dark Age, and it is not until a further ten million years have passed that the Third Men emerge, mentally inferior to the Second Men but having acquired a certain telepathic ability – a 'taint' absorbed from the Martian invaders. The Third Men are devoted to the Vital Art, a kind of biological engineering, which eventually produces a Great Brain who tyrannically rules over them and presides over the creation of the Fourth Men. They in turn create their own successors, the Fifth Men, who have no instincts and whose emotions are strictly under the control of reason. In this species neoteny is exaggerated and individuals live for thousands of years. As befits a species fitting so closely the conventional twentieth-century model of superhumanity the Fifth Men develop a technologically advanced world society, sustained by atomic energy, where labour is abolished and everything is produced mechanically. When the sun grows cooler they prepare for a migration to Venus.

In new physical conditions the Venerian men degenerate, and evolve first into the Sixth Men, who are obsessed with the idea of flight, and then into the tiny Seventh Men, who are capable of it. The Seventh Men live an apparently idyllic existence, but eventually commit suicide *en masse*, leaving as descendants a quasi-avian but flightless race which becomes the Eighth Men. As the sun continues to cool they begin to prepare Mercury for human habitation, but have to change their plans when it flares up again, migrating instead to Neptune, adapting themselves to conditions there as the Ninth Men.

Like the emigrants to Venus, the new Neptunians degenerate, and the narrative has by now built up such a pace that the Tenth, Eleventh, Twelfth and Thirteenth Men are described only in brief terms. The Fourteenth Men recall in their condition the First Men, but they give rise to the Fifteenth, whose control of their own evolution allows them to progress by design through three more stages until they have re-created themselves triumphantly as the Eighteenth and Last Men, whose culminating being and society are given more careful and extended coverage. They are said to be 'more human and more animal' than the First Men, having multiple physical forms and complex sub-sexual differentiation. Although 'psychologically ill-fitted' for interstellar travel they mount a project to send 'spores' to seed the worlds of the other stars. They communicate by telepathy and have an enormously extended lifespan – their childhood lasts a thousand years, and their personal development is correlated with a series of cultural phases. Their end is foreseen in a distant cosmic disaster – an unusual nova – whose consequences will include the disruption of the sun.

The sheer ambition of *Last and First Men* gives it a glamour which tends to obscure certain faults in its execution. It is unfortunate that Stapledon should have set out to describe the future evolution of man with the aid of an understanding of evolutionary theory that was at best vague and at worst mistaken. In its details, moreover, the story shows nothing like the imaginative range suggested by the grandeur of its time-scale. Nevertheless, it is a book which one can hardly help but find impressive. It embraces more completely and more effectively than any preceding work the new cosmic perspective. It presents a radical reappraisal of man in his cosmic context, offering a much more invigorating vision of the human situation than the sad warnings of eventual extinction contained in other far-ranging works from *The Time Machine* through *The Night Land* to *The Amphibians*, despite the fact that it embraces in its climax a bitter pessimism, hardly ameliorated by a few uplifting closing lines.

Last and First Men achieved a modest success, including enthusiastic comments by several reviewers. It was published in the USA in 1931 and reprinted twice by Methuen in cheap editions before enjoying the unusual distinction of being reprinted as one of the earliest Pelican Books in 1938. (Pelican Books were – as they still are – the non-fiction line set up in parallel to Penguin Books; *Last and First Men* was thus treated in this reprint as a philosophical work rather than a novel.) This success encouraged Stapledon to devote himself to writing as a vocation, and he ceased to be concerned about the possibility of earning a living. When his father died in 1932 his inheritance was sufficient to provide him with an adequate private income, and in spite of his socialist convictions he was content to let this income sustain him.

He followed *Last and First Men* with *Last Men in London* (1932), in which the Neptunian narrator of the former book offers a more detailed picture of his own world, and then embarks upon a lengthy anthropological and historical account of life in the early twentieth century, derived from his personal researches and those of his contemporaries. This narrative is thus akin to Wells's *The Dream*, though the Neptunian is a much more obtrusive commentator than the observer in the earlier novel. The main focus of the story is the biography of 'Paul', an individual who is said to exemplify the 'spiritual crisis' of the age. In constructing Paul's life story Stapledon drew heavily on his own experiences, and there are sections of the text which are deeply introspective. Despite its great scope and speculative content much of Stapledon's fiction is, in fact, intensely personal, and he constantly constructs very elaborate analogies between the existential situations of his characters and his own. This has encouraged some commentators – particularly Leslie Fiedler[19] – to offer convoluted psychoanalytic accounts of his work, finding evidence of an Oedipus complex, incipient schizophrenia and various other neurotic tendencies. There is little doubt that through the medium of some of his fictions Stapledon was, indeed, engaged in the work of reinterpreting and re-evaluating his own experiences, but it is a mistake to see this as a symptom of any unique anxiety or peculiar obsession. In scrutinising himself so closely he was more interested in his embodiment of the 'spiritual crisis' of his time than in his own idiosyncrasies, and his characters should not be seen as caricatures of himself but rather as exaggerated representations of that supposed spiritual crisis.

Readers of Stapledon, especially the aficionados of science fiction, have generally found *Last Men in London* a disappointing book, and it certainly has not the breathtaking qualities of its predecessor. From Stapledon's own point of view, though, it was a necessary companion piece, because his real interest was, after all, in modern man as seen from a separated viewpoint (after the fashion of some of John Beresford's vignettes in *Signs and Wonders*), and not in the adventures of the Venerian flying men.

Last Men in London serves to underline the great importance of the Great War in determining the intellectual climate of Britain in the twenties and thirties, and its dramatic effect on evaluations of human nature and expectations of the future. The Neptunian narrator reveals that researchers from two billion

years hence concentrate their attention on this historical episode because 'in the war itself and its consequences, the whole
drama of your species finds its climax'.[20] The lesson which
these observers learn from the war is presented here in terms
only marginally less striking than in the judgment delivered
upon mankind by Fowler Wright's Amphibian:

> From one point of view ... they could not but regard your species
> as not yet human; a thing incredibly stupid and insensitive,
> incredibly distorted and tortured by the fantastic habits, the
> rudimentary 'culture' which alone distinguished it from the lower
> beasts; a thing in some ways further removed from true humanity
> even than ox or tiger, because it had strayed further down the
> wrong path; a thing incomparably more filthy than the baboon
> because, retaining brutality, it had lost innocence and learned to
> affect righteousness; a thing which was squandering the little
> powers that it had stumbled upon for ends essentially the same as
> the ends of monkeys, and in its frantic grabbing, devouring,
> voiding, had fouled the whole planet.[21]

But that is not the whole story; like Wells at the end of *The
Shape of Things to Come* and Beresford at the end of *A Common
Enemy*, Stapledon also has his Neptunian find in the men of the
Age of Frustration the seed of something finer. In his version it
is characterised as 'the first blind restlessness of the spirit,
which ... wins its beatitude only in the full human estate.'[22]

This idea of the essential spirit of man was to recur throughout Stapledon's works, characterised in slightly different ways
at different times. The aftermath of the war, with its disillusionment and 'profound moral disheartenment', is later represented
by the Neptunian as 'a grave act of treason against the spirit',
precipitating a conflict between 'the forces of decay and the
forces of rebirth'.[23] Rhetoric of this kind is repeated at several
points within the narrative as Stapledon returns to the point to
labour it again and again, but eventually he arrives at a point
similar to one reached by many others of the period, in
concluding that there may already be exceptional individuals
among us who embody a higher consciousness – who can, in
Stapledon's terminology, keep faith with the spirit of man and
display more extravagantly its potentialities. Most writers stopped with the promise, and *Last Men in London* does no more in
its final chapter than sketch out the brief and tragic life-history
of a misfit proto-superman called Humpty, but the Neptunian

does say that in a future work he might offer something more elaborate. Even though Stapledon discarded the Neptunian as a narrative device, he did go on to attempt to make good this promise, in *Odd John: A Story Between Jest and Earnest* (1935).

Before writing *Odd John* Stapledon produced *Waking World* (1934), a long essay in which he tried to clarify the philosophical position which he had reached, summarising his ideas on human nature, human knowledge, and man's cosmic context. Having unburdened himself of this material, he then seems to have found it possible to try to make *Odd John* into a novel rather than a philosophical tract, and so the narrator who tells John's story is an ordinary man whose commentary has not the same aloof contemptuousness in regard to *Homo sapiens* as the Neptunian had. This is necessary, because John has an entirely adequate supply of it. In effect, the roles of narrator and central character are reversed between *Last Men in London* and *Odd John*.

Odd John takes its blueprint from *The Hampdenshire Wonder*, and there are several textual references to Victor Stott, who is bracketed with a whole series of Nature's failed experiments in superhumanity. John is one of the most successful, and eventually becomes the natural leader of a small tribe of superhumans whom he gathers from many parts of the world, but in the end even he has to conclude that the time is not ripe for his kind. John's career is, however, much longer and more spectacular than Victor Stott's.

Whereas the Hampdenshire Wonder was a passive commentator on human affairs and pretensions, John is active in the human world, exercising his superhumanity in establishing a whole series of temporary relationships with other people. Although he masters mathematics by intuition and precocious logic while still in infancy he shows little further interest in science. The pursuit of knowledge (regarded by so many fictitious superhumans as the only proper activity) is dismissed as an unimportant, perhaps even puerile endeavour – except in so far as it relates to the cultivation of the special spiritual enlightenment that was Stapledon's main interest. John also learns in childhood how to manipulate other people and exercise power over them; he becomes a master of cunning applied psychology, and develops his own martial art from first principles. He refuses to pursue this line of endeavour also, though he does apply his talents to the business of making money, in an off-hand sort of way, for the sake of temporary convenience.

What chiefly distinguishes John from other supermen in scientific romance is his morality – or, rather, the way that morality is treated by the author. John is just as contemptuous of human morality as of human knowledge, and he will have none of it. Many other supermen take the same basic stand-point, but they tend either to speak for a 'higher morality' which is both gentler and more tolerant (like the people of Beresford's Oion) or to be committed to the kind of ruthless 'rationality' associated mythically with the single-minded com-mitment to science. In the latter case, where supermen or alienated scientists use other people in experiments, without regard to their presumed rights as individuals, the characters so doing are almost always regarded as villains. This is so even in Shiel's stories, which often attempt to show how villainy of this kind can nevertheless play a progressive role, and thus serve the cause of good. John's case is presented very differently. He commits numerous murders, for pragmatic reasons which must occasionally seem trivial to the reader, embarks on a series of gruesome genetic experiments with human subjects, and at one point – feeling the compulsion to demonstrate his superiority to *all* human taboos – commits incest with his mother. The narrator, who appears to relish the contempt in which he, personally, is held by John, endorses all these actions by apologising for his censorious reactions, admitting that his revulsion is merely a symptom of his inferiority.

The narrator's acceptance of John's cruel use of human beings is not quite without parallel in scientific romance. There is something similar in Shiel's concession that such 'overmen' as Baron Kolar and Dr Krasinski are on the side of progress. There is something similar too in Fowler Wright's celebration of the violence of nature, and Fowler Wright left behind several unpublished manuscripts which appear to make much of the contention that given the way we treat other species, we could hardly take exception if alien invaders wanted to use *us* as food or experimental animals. Nevertheless, Stapledon's position is distinct from either of these, and though we must beware of identifying Stapledon too closely with the narrator of *Odd John*, his endorsement of violence and cruelty in the make-up of his superman has seemed highly objectionable to some commenta-tors. Oddly, Sam Moskowitz, who thinks that Shiel and Fowler

Wright were 'verging on the insane', treats Stapledon much more generously, but Leslie Fiedler's *Olaf Stapledon: A Man Divided* (1983) makes much of this sado-masochistic element in Stapledon's work.

It might conceivably be the case that Stapledon found himself prey to certain sado-masochistic fascinations which he could not exorcise – like another writer of dense metaphysical fantasies, John Cowper Powys – but Stapledon's use of the relevant imagery is very different from Powys's. In fact, he seems to be trying to cope with a problem that also lay behind the odd attitude of Shiel's *The Last Miracle* and similar novels. Like Shiel, Stapledon was trying to invent a theology that would fit in with and complement modern scientific knowledge. Not content with a God made in man's image they wanted a Creative Force suited to the cosmic perspective, from whose point of view man, *per se*, must be negligible save in so far as he partakes of the general properties of life and intelligence. All the writers who attempted the 'separation' which would allow them to look back upon men, including themselves, from such a lofty perspective found much to despise in what they saw – this can clearly be seen in passages quoted earlier from Wells and Beresford as well as from Shiel and Fowler Wright.

The writers, though, have different imaginative strategies for dealing with the issue. For Wells and Beresford, this is merely a brutal inheritance to be transcended in time by more admirable descendants. Fowler Wright, by contrast, thought some violence natural (and hence not merely acceptable but admirable whereas the remaining perverse violence was the necessary corollary of civilisation. Shiel accepted the cruelty of nature, and much human cruelty too, as part of the price to be paid for progress – an thus a price well worth paying.

Stapledon, too, could not think of this element of nastiness in the business of living as something which could simply be put away one day. It is very clear in *Last and First Men* that it is not something which can be eliminated from the character of the human species more advanced than ours (though some of those more primitive – especially the flying Venerians – appear to recover a measure of lost innocence). The spiritual awakening which Stapledon looked forward to would not be an awakening into saintliness, but rather to an acceptance of the inherent ugliness of certain aspects of experience. In his personal life, and in terms of his political beliefs, Stapledon was a pacifist, like John Beresford. He did not like or approve of violence (though he later conceded that there was moral justification for the war against Hitler). Nevertheless, when he tried to put things into the greatest possible perspective, he felt required to account for the phenomena of pain and violence, and in doing so he clearly felt unable to take 'the easy way out'. The nasty side of John's character, and the pusillanimity of the character who reports back to the reader, are evidence of the keenness with which Stapledon felt this particular problem.

In the later chapters of *Odd John* reference is made to a document written by John, purporting to be a history of the entire universe. As with the reference forward to *Odd John* in the later pages of *Last Men in London* this was a promissory note, but as in the former case Stapledon substituted a different narrator to tell the tale. The 'I' of *Star Maker* (1937), in fact, might much more readily be mistaken for the author's own voice than the narrators of any of his other stories.

Star Maker begins with the narrator taking refuge on a hillside at night, following a quarrel with his wife. He meditates upon his marriage – an 'intimate symbiosis' and a 'prized atom of community' occasionally spoiled by bitterness welling up within the relationship. In this microcosm he finds something of the essential nature of the world – not merely the human world but the entire universe:

> But could this indescribable union of ours really have any significance at all beyond itself? Did it, for instance, prove that the essential nature of all human beings was to love, rather than to hate and fear? Was it evidence that all men and women the world over, though circumstance might prevent them, were at heart capable of supporting a world-wide, love-knit community? And further, did it, being in itself a product of the cosmos, prove that love was in some way basic to the cosmos itself? And did it afford, through its own felt intrinsic excellence, some guarantee that we two, its frail supporters, must in some sense have eternal life? Did it, in fact, prove that love was God, and God awaiting us in his heaven?[24]

All these questions are answered in the negative, because this microcosm of experience is only 'one out of the many potentialities of existence' to be found amid a 'tumult of hate', and in any case, the entire species of man will one day die just as each of its members must. Nevertheless, the narrator concludes, there is some essential connection between the fundamental nature of the universe and this infinitesimal fragment of one man's experience of it. That connection entraps the man on the hillside in a cosmic vision which displays before him the whole universe – all of space and all of time – and allows him ultimately to see the animating force within and behind it all: the Star Maker.

When Stapledon first set out to write *Star Maker* the visionary caught sight of God immediately, witnessed the very moment of creation, and then watched the evolution of the primal nebulae, living entities in their own right, as they formulated their own community. This story of the evolving nebulae, though, quickly became an allegorical parody of human history, with Marxian stages and characters modelled on Christ and Lenin. Stapledon abandoned it, and it was ultimately published in 1976 as *Nebula Maker*. Instead, he developed the vision through a series of stages, each one of which extends the perspective by a further order of magnitude, and saved the vision of the Star Maker himself for the climax. The published version therefore begins with a fairly detailed description of life on a single other world, where humanoid aliens have derived a society not unlike ours. Then there is a whole series of descriptions of alien worlds, in which many different kinds of creatures have evolved to dominance. This recalls an earlier cosmic vision story, *Lumen* by Camille Flammarion, but its catalogue of possible modes of life is more extensive.

The visionary observes that life and intelligence cannot always triumph over circumstance, and sees many worlds and species overwhelmed by horrific disasters. Flammarion, with his fondness for the idea of cosmic catastrophe, had noted this too, but for Flammarion such disasters were not of much consequence, because intelligent beings had immortal souls which could simply migrate to other worlds and become incarnate again. This allowed Flammarion to retain his faith in the goodness and lovingness of God in spite of the ever-present possibility that whole worlds might die, and species become extinct. Without such faith in personal immortality, Stapledon is forced in the face of this panorama of universal suffering to reconsider the personality of the Star Maker – significantly it is in the chapter which deals with the annihilation of worlds and intelligent races that we first receive 'intimations of the Star Maker'.[25]

The perspective expands again, first to take in the community of worlds, and then to take in the life of the stars and the galaxies, and the primal nebulae. Everywhere, at whatever scale, there is growth of community and developing 'symbiosis'. Utopias emerge at various levels. The stars seem better equipped for this than organic species – theirs is an 'angelic company' – but they too must cope with the phenomena of decay and death, as must the entire cosmos. There is a point of contact here between the cosmic vision of Stapledon and the strange allegory of William Hope Hodgson's *The House on the Borderland*, which emphasises a similar quality in their pessimism. In Hodgson's scheme of things, though, growth and decay are separate and opposing principles, like the God and Satan of Christian mythology and the contending forces of good and evil in John Cowper Powys's Manichean theology. Stapledon – a monist like M.P. Shiel – cannot see things in such dialectical terms. For him, the intrinsic imperfections of Creation represent intrinsic imperfections of the Creator. Just as Shiel reinterpreted the imperfections by invoking a philosophy of progress so too, in the final analysis, does Stapledon – but he does it on a grander scale, by making the Star Maker himself an evolving being, progressing slowly towards his own eventual maturity and perfection. Our imperfect universe thus becomes an early experiment, conducted while the Star Maker is 'still in the trance of infancy'.[26]

This part of the vision is offered very tentatively, not as something the visionary simply sees, but as a kind of allegory which is constructed in his mind, and which may be only 'a trivial dream-fiction'. Stapledon never did manage to achieve the certainty of faith that Shiel had, and was never able to escape from the clutches of doubt. In keeping with this, the narrator is never quite clear exactly what characteristics the Star Maker has. At times his failures do not seem simply to be the unfortunate consequences of incompetence – sometimes he seems to take a 'diabolical glee' in the sufferings of the species he endows with intelligence. Sometimes he has a distinct mode of creation where he divides himself into opposing spiritual forces, one creative and the other destructive. When he glimpses these aspects of the Creator, the narrator experiences a horror akin to that of the narrator of *Odd John* when confronted with some of John's actions, but he feels compelled to set this horror aside, and refuses to accept the excuse that the Star

Maker in his full maturity will no longer have this darker aspect:

> Did barbarity perhaps belong to the Star Maker only in his immaturity? Later, when he was fully himself, would he finally outgrow it? No! Already I deeply knew that this ruthlessness was to be manifested even by the ultimate cosmos. Could there, then, be some key fact, overlooked by me, in virtue of which such seeming vindictiveness was justified?[27]

The narrator considers several hypotheses which might stand as such 'key facts', but in the end he cannot take refuge in any of them. This 'dire and insoluble problem' haunts the final phase of the vision, but has in the end to be carried back to the hillside and to the tiny world of men, into the microcosm of the protagonist's loving but strangely frustrating marriage. Here the problem is put back into what is, after all, its real context:

> It seemed that in the coming storm all the dearest things must be destroyed. All private happiness, all loving, all creative work in art, science, and philosophy, all intellectual scrutiny and speculative imagination, and all creative social building; all, indeed, that man should normally live for, seemed folly and mockery and mere self-indulgence in the presence of public calamity. But if we failed to preserve them, when would they live again?
>
> How to face such an age? How to muster courage, being capable only of homely virtues? How to do this, yet preserve the mind's integrity, never to let the struggle destroy in one's own heart what one tried to serve in the world, the spirit's integrity?
>
> Two lights for guidance. The first, our little glowing atom of community, with all that it signifies. The second, the cold light of the stars, symbol of the hypercosmical reality, with its crystal ecstasy.[28]

Such is Stapledon's summation, after due contemplation of the history and population of the cosmos, and the personality of its Maker, of the human predicament in a world on the threshold of its second Great War. How right Wells was to characterise this an Age of Frustration!

Stapledon reckoned after finishing *Star Maker* that he had done all he could with fiction. He had certainly reached the limit of what might be encompassed by the exercise of his creative imagination in terms of scale. In the next few years, therefore, he devoted himself to the production of essays recapitulating his philosophy and further testing his doubt against the temptations of faith. *Philosophy and Living* (1939), which appeared in two volumes in the Pelican series, is perhaps the most interesting of these because it is a book derived from his WEA teaching as an introduction to the problems of philosophy, and it therefore sets Stapledon's own particular obsession in a general context.

The war, inevitably, intensified Stapledon's anxieties, and eventually drove him back to future history in an attempt to analyse the prospect of recovery after its end. *Darkness and the Light* (1942) is supposed to contrast the opposing potentialities, showing how unfortunate political developments might lead to desolation while the victory of enlightened policies might lead to a spiritual awakening of mankind. Even the second section, however, is replete with confusion and horrific incident. Civilisation is ultimately all but destroyed by catastrophe, and the superhumans who come finally to possess the world are only briefly mentioned in a text whose author prefers to dwell on the hopelessness of their predecessors. The 'will for light' is given more exuberant treatment in a short story published two years later, *Old Man in New World*, but even here the man who describes the Utopia of the future is an aging revolutionary who no longer fits in there, and the climactic commentary is delivered by the World State's court jester.

In the same year as *Old Man in New World* Stapledon published *Sirius: A Fantasy of Love and Discord* (1944), which is certainly his finest novel if one accepts his judgment that *Star Maker* is 'no novel at all'. It is the most sentimental of his fictions, and provides his most wholehearted celebration of the joys and rewards of an 'atom of community' – a relationship between individuals. There can be no more eloquent testimony to the depth of his despair in the meagre possibilities of human relationships than the fact that this intense love affair is between a girl and a dog.

Sirius is, of course, no ordinary dog, but the most successful result of an experiment in the artificial augmentation of intelligence. To some extent he functions in the plot as an 'outside observer' of human affairs, like Wells's angel in *The Wonderful Visit* or the alien visitor in Eden Phillpotts's *Saurus* (which had been published only six years before). This is not Stapledon's main purpose in the book, though, and the chapters where Sirius operates in this way are relatively weak, appearing almost as a distraction from the main theme. The book is really an exercise in hypothetical existentialism, and like many of the classic existentialist novels it chooses a central character alienated by nature from the social world in which he finds himself.

Mention was made in an earlier chapter of essays by Julian Huxley and J.B.S. Haldane in which those scientists, considering the ecology of ants and barnacles, tried to imagine the kind of world-view and theology that such creatures might construct were they conscious. In a sense, *Star Maker* is the same kind of exercise – instead of taking human society and theology for granted, it tries to reconstruct hypothetically what our philosophy *ought* to be, given our relationships with one another and with the universe we have discovered. *Sirius* is also this kind of imaginative endeavour, but with one important difference, in that its protagonist is a hybrid creature, with a quasi-human personality imposed on a canine nature. He is in some respects like, and in others crucially unlike, Moreau's Beast-Folk, but in spite of the fact that his story is told to us by a human narrator we see him from the inside rather than the outside, and we are invited to identify with him rather than with a shocked observer in the mould of Prendick.

The plot of Sirius is principally concerned with an inner conflict between his inherited nature and the culture imposed upon him by his upbringing. This conflict is evolved in connection with the various ways in which he has to try to fit into the human world, seeming at various stages to be a sheepdog or a family pet or the companion of a clergyman, while in reality being something else altogether. In the end, the world is alerted to his strangeness and becomes implacably hostile to him, except for his beloved Plaxy, who is so closely bound to him by spiritual and physical ties that the two constitute a unique and special atom of community, frequently referred to as Sirius-Plaxy.

Much is made in the course of the story of the violence innate in Sirius's character. When he first discovers hunting it strikes him as 'the main joy of life' and it is observed that 'he felt its call almost as a religious claim upon him'.[29] It is this violence which is ultimately implicated in his downfall, because he eventually kills a man – albeit in the face of extreme provocation. As his personal philosophy develops, he has to come to terms with this innate violence, and its analogues in mankind. He is aided in this by reading H.G. Wells, whose opinion he once cites

214

regarding the imperfect socialisation of the human species. His attempts to imagine God lead him, as might be expected, to brief moments of ecstatic vision when he catches frustrating but nevertheless enlightening glimpses of the essence of universal Nature. Once, he is comforted by a sudden conviction that instead of the universal Tiger he had suspected there is actually a universal Master – a much more comforting ideal – but he cannot cling to this conviction and doubt reclaims him. All he has, in the end, is his commitment to 'the spirit' and the urge to make a plea (which falls on deaf ears) for the destiny of mankind to be entrusted to people who can awake from their customary stupidity.[30]

In the end, Sirius, like the protagonist of *Star Maker*, has to take what comfort he can from his one intimate relationship, which is the only spiritual anchorage that he has. His acceptance of this, however, is not the resignation which it appears to be in the earlier story, because in his case it requires such an astonishing triumph over circumstance. Domesticity and love, so easily achieved by human beings, are very different when they are the achievement of a human and a mutated dog. Sirius's final dying affirmation that Sirius-Plaxy has been worthwhile thus carries a paradoxical conviction which is present nowhere else in Stapledon's work.

The spirit of resolution present in the climax of *Sirius* was carried forward into his last wartime book, *Death into Life* (1946), a new essay in myth-creation which (if a hint in *A Man Divided* is to be taken seriously) he later came to consider ill conceived. Like *Star Maker* the story expands through a series of enlarging perspectives, beginning with the crew of a bomber whose essential camaraderie is held to be an atom of community like the narrator's marriage in *Star Maker*. When the bomber is shot down, the surviving spirits of the airmen combine into a single collective spirit, which is then revealed to be an element in a greater spirit, the spirit of Man, whose history and situation is considered in some detail. The spirit of Man then has a vision of the cosmos, including a premonition of its own end. Here, though, there is for once a possibility of salvation, a communion with God – an idea whose attraction is strongly felt. The story is intermingled with, and its uncertain moral emphasised by, rhapsodic autobiographical reminiscences which underline the intensity of the effort to find in atoms of domestic community some reflection of comforting universal

215

truth. As always, though, Stapledon's doubt proves unassailable, and the vision dissolves with its work of moral rearmament only partly done.

Like Fowler Wright, Stapledon produced more fiction after the end of the war, but it is reasonable enough to leave consideration of it to a later chapter. It is not so easy, though, to summarise Stapledon's achievement up to this point. He stands out among writers of speculative fiction, of course, because he ranged so much further in time and space than anyone else had attempted to go. He tried to deal with a future history extending over two billion years, and with the nature and contents of a whole universe that was itself part of a vast series of Creations. *Star Maker* will always stand alone, because there is no greater scale that is possible – in respect of its breadth it can never be outdone. He was driven to such an expansive flight of the imagination, though, by his preoccupation with a problem that originated very close to home – in his perceptions of his own inner nature and his intimate relationships. In essence, this was the age-old problem of evil – the question of why human existence seems fundamentally blighted. Stapledon's imagination took him so far because he could not find an answer to that question close at hand. He was not able to accept the answers that other men found, whether they were to do with original sin, the temptations of Satan, the spectres of Cainsmarsh or the corruptions of civilisation. He went to the very limits of his imagination because there was no answer to be found within those limits, and because he could not free himself from preoccupation with the question. In the end, he could only fall back – every time – on a pragmatic compromise that was inherently unsatisfying. He would not even allow himself the luxury of resignation.

Stapledon was by no means as elegant a writer as Wells even when Wells was not at his best. He was, in fact, a less accomplished stylist than John Beresford and John Gloag. Storytelling was definitely not his forte, and there are sections in all his books that are awkward to the point of risibility. Despite these faults, though, Stapledon's accomplishments in scientific romance place him alongside Wells as one of the giants of the genre. He owes this pre-eminence to the sheer power of the motive force in his work – the force of the doubt which would not let his new doctrine crystallise into a final, graspable form.

Neil Bell

Neil Bell was the principal pseudonym used by Stephen South-wold. 'Southwold' too was an adopted name, borrowed from the village in Suffolk where he was born in 1887; in his autobiography he does not reveal the name that he was born with. This seems to have been one manifestation of a strong sense of resentment which he harboured in connection with the circumstances of his early life. His father had been an accomplished and prosperous boatbuilder, but was also a wastrel and a drunkard. By the time Stephen was ten the business was lost and his father went to work in the naval dockyard at Chatham. Stephen was prepared at school for an apprenticeship in the dockyard, and recalls that the schooling was both narrow and cruel. After years of daily beatings he passed the examination for his apprenticeship in 1901, but his career was cut short when other apprentices attempted to subject him to an 'initiation ritual'. Although he alludes to this incident in his autobiography and in several of his novels (which feature numerous accounts of childhoods based on his own) the details of the affair are never made fully explicit, but the assault seems to have involved attempted buggery. Stephen stabbed his assailant with a chisel, and was allowed to leave the yard without further action being taken when he threatened to make all the details public. He became instead a pupil-teacher (following in the footsteps of Griffith and Wells, the latter of whom he admired very greatly).

Bell stuck at teaching longer than Griffith or Wells, though he was no less miserable in the job. He read widely and began writing, beginning by entering essay competitions run by the boys' papers while he was still in his teens. Later he wrote verses for children, augmenting the small salary which he received once he was qualified. While in his twenties he wrote a short novel which began as scientific romance and continued with the protagonist meeting great literary men in the afterworld, returning to earth with samples of their work – a series of pastiches. He failed to sell the story as it stood, but the Shakespearian sonnet which it included was later abstracted and sold to the *English Review* when he began writing for the popular periodicals. Almost all his early professional work was poetry.

During the war Bell served in the Royal Army Medical Corps.

He published his first volume of poems during the war years, but had to make a contribution towards the cost of its production. The name 'Neil Bell' first appeared on a sketch in *Punch* in 1920, and he became a regular contributor to that magazine, producing humorous verse and some occasional prose pieces. Tired of teaching, he tried to move into journalism, applying for a sub-editorship with the Labour weekly *The New Leader*. He failed to get it, and his comment on this failure in his autobiography is a revealing comment on his personality:

> Possibly he had his eye on someone else. Or he just disliked me. Many people do. I seem to rub them up the wrong way. I blurt out what I am thinking and as we are all bundles of prejudices that is bound to give offence. Most people dislike me on a first meeting and many ever afterwards.[31]

Bell began writing children's fiction, under his own name, for a London evening newspaper, *The Star*, in 1922, and soon became a prolific writer of such stories. As Bell he also wrote a series of combative articles for the *Daily Mail* in 1925, attacking cats, smoking, gardening, and other things to which many people were sentimentally attached. Income earned by such means eventually became steady enough to enable him to quit teaching, and he removed himself to Cornwall to become a full-time writer. By a curious coincidence, he moved into the same lonely cottage in Portscatho that had earlier been 'Guy Thorne's' refuge from the world – Bell reveals in his autobiography that village gossip provided an image of Thorne's morality rather different from that implied by his propagandist fantasies. The year after he moved to Cornwall – 1928 – he married, and records that he immediately lost the urge to write for children. Instead, he began writing stories for adults.

The first stories which Bell produced in the early part of 1929 – 'Sovvy's Babe', 'Slip' and 'The Facts about Benjamin Crede' – were all rejected by the magazines, although they are very striking works which can still be reckoned among the best things he ever wrote. In the preface to the collection *Mixed Pickles* (1935) he records that one editor rejected the first story with the one-word comment 'ruthless', and in a way it is. 'Sovvy's Babe' and 'Slip' both exhibit a harrowing bleak realism which strongly recalls the work of T.F. Powys, showing innocent human beings dreadfully mistreated by the cruelty of others, facing their destruction with a kind of naive bewilderment. The very coldness of the matter-of-fact narration makes the stories affectively powerful. Like nearly all of Bell's writings about himself they give the impression of repressed rage confined by a façade of determined indifference. 'The Facts about Benjamin Crede' is a much more sentimental story about a man who discovers that he can fly, and decides to use his miraculous power in order to become a new messiah, leading the world back to sanity. Unfortunately, he falls in love, and loses the power of flight at the moment of his sexual awakening. This tragic parable is echoed in numerous other stories, ranging from Eric Knight's humorous 'The Flying Yorkshireman' through Ronald Fraser's intense *The Flying Draper* (1924) to Michael Harrison's elegant *Higher Things* (1945).

All three of these stories did eventually sell, but not until Bell began to make a name with longer works. He wrote his first novel after moving to Georgeham, where he lived close to his friend Henry Williamson. It was published under the pseudonym 'Miles', titled *The Seventh Bowl* (1930), and though its extravagance and scope cannot quite compare with *Last and First Men* – published the same year – it is nevertheless a work of great imaginative ambition.

The Seventh Bowl draws heavily on earlier works in constructing its future history. Haldane's *Daedalus* is an important source, and Haldane appears briefly in the plot as H——. There is much comment in the story on Shaw's *Back to Methuselah*, and mention is also made of *The Food of the Gods* and the work of Karel Capek (whose robots, first featured in *R.U.R.*, are the model for the Fermo – android servants).

After introducing one of its key characters, Paul Heller, who is expelled from school for his atheism and becomes a brilliant but eccentric biologist, *The Seventh Bowl* describes the next great international conflict, the Gas War of 1940, when millions are killed by aerial bombing and chemical warfare, but which is followed by the founding of a new League of Peoples and the establishment of a World State. Ectogenetic birth, using methods devised by H——, becomes commonplace by 1960, at which time Heller invents his immortality serum Plasm Alpha. He wants to give this to the world, but it is stolen from him by Lord Burfleet and his World Council, who murder him by dropping him from an aeroplane (this being one of the few ways that a man reinforced by Plasm Alpha can be fatally injured). After Heller's death the main character of the novel becomes the sceptic and would-be rebel Padraic Kerin, an atheist and socialist who echoes many of Bell's own ideas, including some reflections on the significance of the Great War. Speaking of his father's experiences Kerin says:

> And when he was nineteen the War of 1914–18 came, and he went through that long infamy, and came out with no shred or tatter of his former illusions to cover his nakedness.
>
> 'Everything failed the common man in that testing,' he said. 'The church of God, that should have held itself aloof and denounced the rottenness of it all, failed to make that gesture, and setting itself rather to fan the flames, sealed its own fate in the hearts of the men who fought. We saw incompetence that slaughtered thousands shielded by the privilege of birth or wealth or political pull; we saw lying, treachery and greed enthroned and triumphant; we saw lust and cruelty shrieking from safe places the hatred that was unknown to the men who stumbled blindly in the bloody quagmires of mud and pain and hopelessness . . .
>
> 'And so we emerged from that struggle believing in nothing, hardly in ourselves.'[32]

The Seventh Bowl, in its entirety, may be regarded as a reflection of this lack of belief; its view of the ultimate prospects of mankind is as nihilistic as any other work of the period. The World Council eventually decides to permit a favoured fraction of the population – selected on eugenic grounds – access to Plasm Alpha. An edict is passed in 1961 to forbid the bearing of children after 1970, and though this period of grace postpones trouble, conflict eventually becomes inevitable between the immortal Primaries and the Secondaries who are condemned to die. Kerin is one of the latter, condemned for his rebelliousness, and his bitterness is compounded by the fact that his wife becomes Burfleet's mistress when she joins the ranks of the Primaries.

Various phases in the social development of this new world are described before the last child born before the deadline – the physicist Martin Torrelli – defies the law by fathering a baby (whose mother is Kerin's daughter Alison). He has already invented a new source of energy, Energent A, which has opened up the solar system for exploration – now he tries to use its successor, Energent B, to blackmail the world. When Burfleet will not yield to his demands, he tips the earth out of its orbit, and it plunges into the sun. By the time it arrives this ending is no surprise, as it climaxes a plot whose every successive phase is desperately cynical. Even its hero, Kerin, accomplishes nothing and after a few gestures of defiance surrenders meekly to the ravages of cruel fate. There are obvious parallels between this story and the darker aspects of the work of Fowler Wright and Stapledon.

Bell was never to write anything else with the same imaginative scope – or, for that matter, with the same depth of cynicism – as *The Seventh Bowl*. At Henry Williamson's suggestion he did write a second novel as Miles, expanding to book length the account of the Second World War contained in the early chapters of the first book. This appeared as *The Gas War of 1940* in 1931, and after *The Seventh Bowl* was reprinted in 1934 under the Neil Bell name, it was reissued as *Valiant Clay*.

Before writing this sequel, though, he turned out his first novel actually to bear the Neil Bell byline: *Precious Porcelain* (1931).

Precious Porcelain is the story of Richard Blaney (one of Bell's many fictional 'self-portraits', as he acknowledges in a later edition). His life-story begins to diverge from Bell's own when, instead of going to Cornwall to write, he continues teaching, though moving from the metropolis to a small cathedral city. Also newly arrived in the town is the reclusive biologist and psychologist David Hartley, who has briefly been a heretical clergyman as well as a practising doctor. The town is disturbed by a series of odd events, which seem at first unconnected. A mysterious Christ-like character appears to mock the established church and protest against the uncharitable treatment of a prostitute. The Cathedral is vandalised. Blaney's boarding house suffers the 'aphrodisiac invasion' of the seductive Ann Brown; and following her banishment a male seducer representing himself as Roy Hartley, a cousin of the great scientist, creates havoc among the town's women. The last of these strange invaders proves to be a monstrous killer, and it is in tracking this unwelcome visitor to its lair that the source of all the troubles is revealed. David Hartley, outdoing Dr Jekyll, has been dividing his own physical and spiritual substance, 'budding off' fragments of personality embodying pure character traits of various kinds. Hartley is killed with his murderous avatar, but his work has cast a shadow of guilt over Blaney's life – having been seduced by Ann Brown it is only with difficulty that he can form a new romantic attachment. The book's conclusion is left to his fiancée:

> Her thoughts drifted into a confused catechism of life. Did men understand what women gave them; forgave them. Did men understand women at all. Or women men. Is every human being a closed book. Are we all, in Kipling's phrase, solitary islands shouting to one another across seas of misunderstanding. Dick loved her, in a way, after his fashion. Was it the fashion of all men. Would there be other Ann Browns in his life. Could any man resist. Did any man want to. Were women, in this as in all other things, much different. *Any* different. Were not all human beings alike. Wasn't that what this amazing business of Hartley proved. Capable of anything: the heights and the depths. How could we be closed books then. Except wilfully. Or solitary islands, with their seas of misunderstanding.[33]

Precious Porcelain was modestly successful. It helped Bell to attract interest in more novels, and also to begin selling his short stories. 'The Facts about Benjamin Crede' appeared in the *London Mercury* and was selected for inclusion in *The Best Short Stories of 1933*, but other fantastic stories would not sell. Bell's newly acquired agent refused to handle his short scientific romance 'The Mouse', a bitter story of an inventive genius who first produces light without heat and makes the world rich and happy, and then produces heat without light and gives it the power to destroy itself. Typically, this catastrophic ending is presented with the same careful ambivalence as the conclusion of *Precious Porcelain*:

> The world is but slowly recovering from that tremendous slaughter. It is still doubtful whether civilisation can survive. And yet I would not end on too hopeless a note. The earth, burnt up and barren as it is, still exists; human life still exists. Beyond this perhaps there is little, but it is enough to begin anew, to make a fresh start. Maybe it was after all a cleansing fire, sweeping away the evil with the good, the rotten lumber with the prized possessions. And The Mouse? He was among the slain, the swept away, but whether he were part of the rotten lumber or the prized possessions must be left to posterity to decide – if there should be posterity.[34]

'The Mouse' eventually appeared in Bell's first collection, *Mixed Pickles* (1935), along with several other unsold stories. 'The Evanescence of Adrian Fulk' is also a scientific romance in which a scientist is blown by an explosion into a macrocosmic dimension where earth is only a speck under a microscope. After his return to the world he disappears again in an even mightier explosion, which he contrives in the attempt to project himself even further. This story too would not sell to the magazines, and Bell became reluctant after 1932 to write more in the same vein. Though his later collections contain a handful of fairly unadventurous scientific romances they represent a very small fraction of his output. In his novels, too, he put imaginative themes aside while he wrote *Life and Andrew Otway* and *The Marriage of Simon Harper*, but he then reverted to a theme very close to that of *Precious Porcelain* in *The Disturbing Affair of Noel Blake* (1932). Unlike its predecessor this was not well received, partly because of the unsympathetic character of its narrator – a violent rebel against circumstance. It is not too difficult to appreciate what Bell saw in this abrasive character, but it is also easy to appreciate why people rubbed up the wrong way by Bell would react even more strongly to this fictitious person.

As with *Precious Porcelain, The Disturbing Affair of Noel Blake* features a series of puzzling incidents which are ultimately revealed to be the actions of one man, the man named in the title of the story. Under the influence of an inquisitive hypnotist Blake has been made to undergo a series of 'regressions', which first return him to the psychological condition of phases in his own childhood, and then evoke a series of 'ancestral memories'. There is much discussion of psychoanalysis within the story, but it is awkwardly constructed and nothing is concluded as a result of the explication of events, even though we have been led to expect some kind of lesson to be drawn.

Bell was producing fiction at a furious pace in order to make capital out of his growing popularity. Like Fowler Wright he was a fluent writer who made up his plots as he went along, and never revised what he wrote. Like Fowler Wright at almost exactly the same time, he began to find his imagination flagging. He completed two more scientific romances in 1932 as well as other work: *Death Rocks the Cradle*, which apparently took him about a fortnight, and *The Lord of Life*, which occupied him for thirty-six days. Both books show a certain strain, which is not entirely surprising.

Death Rocks the Cradle appeared in 1933 under the pseudonym Paul Martens. It is the story of Morris Ellerby, who makes a fortune selling an alcoholic patent medicine, but then falls prey to a bad ulcer and is put on a strict diet. He meets Eve Arleigh, the 'ward' of an adventurer who has found her wandering in Mexico after an earthquake, apparently a refugee from some other world. She has difficulty coping with earthly food, eating only fruit, and that sparingly. She recalls Rima in W.H. Hudson's *Green Mansions*, and as in that novel she persuades the hero to set off with her in search of a way back to her own world. Miraculously, they find it, and the bulk of the story describes Ellerby's nightmarish experiences in Salabria, where he finds himself in a kind of prison city full of 'degenerates' who dine on rich food all the time (unlike the majority of the inhabitants, who live simply and frugally like Eve, in a kind of pastoral anarchist Utopia). Sickness is rife in the prison city, where self-indulgence takes a steady toll, and Ellerby comes slowly to realise that this apparent good life is actually a kind of hell, and that the ascetic Salabrians indulge their sole vice – sadism – by watching the operations performed in the city's many hospitals. By this time he has a wife and child, and is horrified by the fate which awaits and eventually overtakes them. He too approaches his fateful appointment with the knife, but wakes up to find himself in Charing Cross Hospital, possibly having conjured up the whole plot while under the anaesthetic having treatment for his ulcer. The paradoxes implicit in this conclusion are unresolved – and, in fact, deliberately confused when Ellerby is unceremoniously killed in a motor accident.

Although it is an ill-written work, *Death Rocks the Cradle* contains some very striking material, and its depiction of the hypothetical world of Salabria invites consideration as a metaphysical fantasy in which the role of pain and suffering in human affairs is subjected to a Swiftian wrench of perspective.

The Lord of Life (1933) begins with a long semi-autobiographical section telling the story of the early years of the puny and miserable Sidney Larkins, who eventually ends up in an orphanage, and then joins the Navy. He becomes the least significant member of the crew of an experimental submarine, Q1, whose maiden voyage is unfortunately interrupted by the end of the world, destroyed by a mad scientist whose threat to do so if he is not made world dictator has been unwisely ignored. (The manifesto drawn up by the scientist is not so very unlike the one drawn up by Shiel's Richard

Hogarth, though it shows much more self-indulgence and personal greed, and might almost qualify as a parody, though Bell does not mention in his autobiography having read the recently reissued *Lord of the Sea* or any other Shiel novel.)

As luck would have it, the twenty survivors aboard the Q1 include a single woman, and the second phase of the plot is a rather cruel comedy of morals, describing the negotiations which go on as she is traded as 'wife' from one to another in the hope that her children will become the nucleus of a new human race. Frustratingly, though, she bears only sons. When at last the wretched Sid's turn arrives he refuses to take it, and takes off on his own. (This, too, might be construed as a parody of Shiel – this time of *The Purple Cloud*.) Fate, though, guides him to another female survivor, with whom he settles down. *Her* children are all daughters, and in the end Sid returns with them to the Q1 to kidnap mates for them – though the queenly matriarch and her throng of consorts, symbols of all the rotten-ness of the old world, are left to themselves while the new father of the human race – a Candide rather than an Adam – sets about the cultivation of his garden.

In its own way *The Seventh Bowl* had been just as much a sarcastic fantasy as *The Lord of Life*, but a comparison of the two books clearly shows the extent to which Bell's imagination was losing its vigour. He seems, like Wells, to have reached a point where he could no longer take his premises very seriously. When he had his biggest commercial success to date with *Bredon and Sons* – another novel which begins with a semi-autobiographical section, but which develops more earnestly in a mundane context – Bell put scientific romance aside to concentrate on contemporary fiction, with the occasional venture into historical fiction.

According to the classified lists of his books featured in his later works Bell did not write another scientific romance for twenty years after *The Lord of Life*. There is, however, a speculative element in one of the works which he always included under the heading 'Novels'. This was *One Came Back* (1938), written when he believed that a new world war was imminent, and completed shortly before he moved his family to Brixham because he believed Seaford, where he was then living, to be too vulnerable to bombing.

One Came Back might well be reckoned the best of all Bell's novels were it not for its peculiar theme, though its strong support for socialism probably alienated some contemporary readers. It is set in a coal-mining district of Derbyshire, and the early chapters provide a detailed account of the life of the miners. One of its major characters is a miner who becomes a journalist and leader of a new egalitarian political movement; the other is the blind son of a coal-owner, whose tutor enlists his aid in some experiments in telepathy before they are parted by unfortunate circumstance. While the blind boy grows to maturity the novel follows the other characters through the General Strike and the Depression, but then moves on into the future. The key event of the book is the apparent death and subsequent resurrection at Lourdes of Adrian Keston, the blind coal-owner and philanthropist. While 'dead' he experiences a series of visions which appear to confirm the existence of Heaven, and Adrian becomes a preacher – practically a new messiah – whose benevolent influence seems to hold out the only real hope for the salvation of the world from its dangerous political turmoil. His former tutor, though, realises that the content of the visions actually comes from various literary works that were employed in the early experiments in telepathy – most of the imagery of the dream is borrowed from Shelley. Although the tutor and his ally, the ex-miner, are all in favour of the salvation of the world they believe that it should not be accomplished by a renaissance of Christian faith based on illusion (nor, for that matter, by means of the benevolence of proprietors, no matter how enlightened). They publish the evidence that proves the 'miracle' of Adrian's apparent resurrection to be false.

This plot can readily be compared to *When it was Dark* by Guy Thorne and *The Last Miracle* by M.P. Shiel, though Bell does not mention either book as an influence upon him. (It is possible that he had not read either, though one would suspect that 'inheriting' Thorne's cottage would have made him curious enough at least to read his predecessor's most famous work.) *One Came Back* can, in fact, be put together with these two earlier works as part of an eccentric trilogy. Thorne, the defender of orthodoxy, sees the destruction of faith in miracles as a world-shattering tragedy. Shiel, justifying his own highly unorthodox faith, sees it as a means of clearing away the dead lumber of mythology to permit the growth of a new religiosity. Bell, the committed atheist, considers the destruction of misplaced faith a necessity, but one to be accomplished more in sorrow than in anger. For Bell – and in this he can be contrasted with most of the other writers of scientific romance – if the world is to be saved then it should be saved by ordinary men banding together to effect a massive political reorganisation. The epilogue to his story, however, is highly ambiguous in assessing the probability of such a reorganisation – it takes the form of a series of clippings from the *Morning Tribune* of 24 May 1947 which echo a similar series in the Prologue, dated 24 May 1910. Significant changes can be seen, but so can significant similarities, and the overall suggestion is that the world remains in the balance, still to be weighed and perhaps found wanting.

Bell was a professional writer, and it was partly his professionalism that drew him away from scientific romance to other kinds of work. Also, he probably became aware of the fact that he actually wrote better about mundane affairs. His imagination was always handicapped by the fact that he knew very little actual science, and he could not muster the same conviction in describing hypothetical situations that Fowler Wright and Stapledon could. He was not necessarily a poorer writer than they, but he did not have the intensity of their interest in matters remote from the everyday world of twentieth-century man. Despite the relative weakness of his plotting and imagery, though, one can see obvious resemblances between Bell's reaction against the folly of his time and those of the other major writers of scientific romance active in the same period. Aided by his unfortunate early experiences and his abrasive personality, Bell was just as capable of the sensation of 'separation' from the everyday world as Beresford or Stapledon, and the feelings which he experienced in looking back at it from the outside were akin to theirs.

John Gloag

John Gloag was born in 1896. His mother was Welsh; his father was a 'painfully religious' Scots lawyer. He served in the Welsh Guards during the latter part of the Great War, but returned home in August 1918 in a poor state, having breathed poison gas (mostly British poison gas, as his battalion was ahead of the barrage laid down by the British guns). He later commented that:

What I experienced in the army and on active service had a profound effect upon my imagination, and to some extent coloured my fiction when I wrote short stories and novels after the Great War. (Engraved on one of the routine medals I collected, suspended from what was known as 'the Victory ribbon', are the words: The Great War for Civilisation. That's a laugh, in view of the sort of civilisation we've had ever since!)[35]

After the war, Gloag began to develop several professional interests. He was interested in architecture and design, particularly in furniture, and wrote many books on these subjects. He also worked in advertising and public relations, and by the mid-1930s was building a large and thriving business in this line. He also did a good deal of broadcasting in the thirties and afterwards – many of his short stories were written for broadcasting, and he was a frequent member of the Brains Trust. It is remarkable, in view of all this activity, that he also began to write novels in the 1930s.

Gloag's *Today and Tomorrow* pamphlet *Artifex; or the Future of Craftsmanship* (1926) considers the extent to which our way of life is dependent on the skills of specialised craftsmen. In order to dramatise this, he discusses at some length the ease with which civilisation might crumble in the event of a destructive war, whose survivors might have very few of these skills, and would be unable to co-ordinate them properly. He cites several scientific romances in support of this point, including *People of the Ruins* (1920) by Edward Shanks, *Theodore Savage* (1922) by Cicely Hamilton and *The War in the Air* by H.G. Wells, claiming that these should be recognised as 'thoughtful comments on very real and highly unpleasant possibilities'.[36] Although *Artifex* closes on an optimistic note, there is no mistaking the undercurrent of anxiety within it, and it is not surprising that Gloag later produced futuristic fantasies in much the same vein as those he had cited.

Tomorrow's Yesterday (1932) was originally conceived as a film script, and was converted into a novel by adding a few bracketing chapters of narrative. In the story, the script becomes a production put on by the mysterious New Century Theatre, and the narrative chapters deal with the public's reaction to it – the early chapters describe the advertising campaign which leads up to the premiere, the later ones with the critical response in the press.

The film – a three-dimensional colour projection! – has to do with the observations made by two humanoid creatures trying to understand the sad fate of the species which their kind has replaced: *Homo sapiens*. The opening scenes present a satirical account of the role of the sexual impulse in human affairs, and of its exploitation by advertising. The later ones describe a destructive war and, in its aftermath, the gradual reversion of mankind to savagery. In the last stages of this decadence the wheel has replaced the cross as the key symbol of human worship: an echo of past greatness to which human sacrifices are offered in the hope of placating the gods. The new race, who have evolved from cats, have 'conquered fear and lust', eliminating from their affairs the sexual impulse by mechanising reproduction. In consequence, they have become supreme scientists, and have colonised the worlds of other stars. Now, they can reach back through time not merely to watch their predecessors, but even to rescue a few of them from oblivion. A sociologist from the distant past, though, doubts whether human pride could stand such a resurrection.

The narrative surrounding the script adds a further edge to its satire. The audience is smugly out of reach of the message which it is trying to get across, and the critics are almost all hostile and sarcastically contemptuous. There seems to be no future for the New Century Theatre, and it has no sooner announced the title of its next production, *War Gods Wake*, than it is closed down because of a developing national emergency . . .

Tomorrow's Yesterday shows certain literary influences clearly enough. Gloag was an admirer of Wells, and had also been impressed by Kipling's two tales of the future – the techniques used in 'With the Night Mail' are cleverly re-employed in *Tomorrow's Yesterday*. Gloag was also a friend of Olaf Stapledon, and he probably completed the film script section of his novel not long after Stapledon prepared 'Far Future Calling' – an adaptation of some scenes from *Last and First Men* that was intended as a radio play. (Stapledon read *Tomorrow's Yesterday* in manuscript, and objected that cats had not the evolutionary potential to produce successors for mankind.) Despite these connections with other scientific romances, though, and its participation in the general anxieties of the day, it strikes the reader as a highly original piece of work. What is most exceptional about it is its tone. When Wells turned his hand to satire in his 'sarcastic fantasies' he was unusually heavy-handed, and the satirical aspects of Neil Bell's works are also somewhat rough-hewn, but Gloag contrived to be scathing while retaining the finesse and lightness of touch characteristic of the very best satires. No other writer of scientific romance attacked the follies of the day with this combination of deftness and verve. Gloag's work is unique in combining an underlying pessimism about the future, and anger at all that appeared wrong with the world, with a rapier-like wit that seems almost to relish the prospect of disaster on account of its irony.

Gloag described his second novel, *The New Pleasure* (1933), as 'deliberately optimistic', and it is indeed a Utopian novel of sorts, in which the abandonment of technological civilisation is represented as the social salvation of modern man. The agent which brings about this change is typically ingenious – a much more elegant creation than the morally improving gases featured in Wells's *In the Days of the Comet* and *The Autocracy of Mr Parham*.

The eponymous 'new pleasure' is a drug marketed under the name 'Voe', which stimulates the sense of smell and produces a sensation of euphoria. People who take it for the sense of well-being it brings, though, quickly find that their heightened sense of smell reveals to them the true obnoxiousness of many things in their environment. From the start the marketing of Voe is steadfastly opposed by the tobacco industry, and its users soon turn against petrol fumes, cosmetics and crowds. A new age of discretion slowly dawns as men become capable of perceiving that many aspects of modern life – literally and metaphorically – stink. Their awakened noses lead them to a new promised land, where much greater discrimination in personal relationships has a natural eugenic effect. The inventor of Voe, travelling up the Thames in the closing chapters, reflects that it is all rather like William Morris's *News from Nowhere*, except that the architecture of *his* new world is less vulgar.

The thirties did produce other works which celebrated the possibility of a return to a more 'natural' way of life, and there are several stories in which the destruction of civilisation by war is represented as not altogether a bad thing. There is a world of difference, though, between *The New Pleasure*, whose lyrical comments on the re-establishment of harmony between men and nature are as gently ironic as the rest of the text, and the dogged romanticism of Fowler Wright and J. Leslie Mitchell.

Disenchantment with the quality of contemporary civilisation is here politely veiled by urbane charm and a neat sense of the ridiculous. The final chapter describes the unveiling of a statue to the canonised inventor of Voe:

> It was a naked figure. The right hand was raised to the nose, with the forefinger and thumb touching the nostrils as though conveying a pinch of Voe. The left hand was stretched aloft with the index finger pointing to the sky, for the sculptor had resisted the inspiration of the cartoon-symbolist school, which would have compelled him to put in the figure's right hand a sword with a bowler hat impaled thereon, thus relegating to the left hand the vital Voe-taking gesture.[37]

Winter's Youth (1934) is a political satire set in the 1960s, and though it maintains something of the spirit of *The New Pleasure* it returns to the cynical pessimism of *Tomorrow's Yesterday*. It has some similarities to Harold Nicolson's *Public Faces* (1932) in describing how the vanity, self-seeking and incompetence of politicians leads eventually to the employment of a weapon too dreadful to use.

The plot of *Winter's Youth* concerns the attempts of the Second National Government to sustain its popularity by various underhanded means. After suffering an unfortunate blow in connection with their unwise support for a fake new gospel, the cabinet members decide to recoup their losses by sponsoring a rejuvenation process discovered by one Dr Nordelf. This, too, misfires, when the younger generation realise that with the old rejuvenated their inheritance of wealth and power might be indefinitely delayed. The old opposition party, a rather ineffectual alliance of Communists and Fascists, is quickly eclipsed by the much more dynamic Social Revivalists. In the end, rejuvenation does not serve to save the cabinet members from senility, and their increasingly stupid attempts to stay on top lead the nation into a series of calamities culminating in the three-days war, in which four million people die.

The protagonist who offers a commentary on all this is the one clear-sighted man in the cabinet, Lord Privilege (a descendant of Capt. Marryat's Peter Simple). As foreign secretary his mission in life is to preserve Europe from the horror of war – a horror compounded by the invention of 'radiant inflammatol', against which there is no defence. Privilege always knows that at the best he will only win time, and that in the end radiant inflammatol will be used. His basic fatalism, though, is tempered by his compassion, his sense of humour, and his Epicurean enthusiasm to make the best of life's pleasures while they are there to be enjoyed.

Although it is much more sober than *The New Pleasure*, *Winter's Youth* makes similar use of delicate understatement. Its exploration of the impact of the Nordelf process has none of the melodrama of Neil Bell's handling of Paul Heller's similar discovery in *The Seventh Bowl*. Even the war happens in an interlude between chapters, and the climax of the story itself is far from apocalyptic. Privilege's criticism of the world in which he lives is, though, all the more devastating for its lack of extremism. He refers to the 'mental enervation' of the ruling classes, and to the unfortunate emptiness of the rituals to which men are clinging, 'rotted down' from old religious beliefs. His verdict is that twentieth-century society is doomed because it cannot adapt to Godlessness. 'Only intelligent men,' he says at one point, 'could bear the isolation and spiritual responsibility of scepticism.'[38] The main theme running through all Gloag's speculative work is the failure of that kind of 'spiritual responsibility'.

Gloag wrote little futuristic fiction for some years after *Winter's Youth*. He began writing offbeat thrillers and other novels of contemporary life, but one particular image keeps cropping up in his short fiction, and once in his work at novel length: an image of contemporary civilisation in ruins. We find this in the short story 'Pendulum', in which a man's disembodied consciousness swings back and forth through time. In each 'direction' he sees similar changes overtaking London – no matter whether he is travelling forward or backward in time he sees the city slowly claimed by the forest, its inhabitants degenerating to savagery. The same dual perspective is evident in 'The Slit', where a man using a machine that can look through time thinks he is looking back at fifth-century England, with the Dark Ages closing in after the withdrawal of the Romans, but finds out later that he has actually been looking into the twenty-first century. More depth is added to this idea of historical cyclicity in the interesting novel *Sacred Edifice* (1937), whose main narrative is bracketed by scenes set in the distant past and far future – which are, of course, strikingly similar.

232

The main narrative of *Sacred Edifice* concerns the rebuilding of a damaged Gothic cathedral, by an architect determined to recapture the purpose of the original builders. Rather than simply reconstructing the church he wants to make something that will incarnate the spirit of twentieth-century religion just as the Gothic edifice encapsulate the spirit of medieval Christianity. The worship of men is already under threat, not just from scepticism (which only undermines dogma) but from the Depression and the rise of Nazi Germany, and the whole plot is formulated around the conviction that the new sacred edifice must fall in its turn, to be replaced in time by others much more crude, and perhaps in the fullness of time by others as splendid, in endless sequence.

Like *Tomorrow's Yesterday*, *Sacred Edifice* concludes its contemporary narrative with mobilisation for a new war. Gloag felt that 'with a certifiable lunatic in charge of the most aggressive military nation in Europe' war was inevitable, and it is ironic that his next futuristic novel was actually overtaken by events. *Manna* was written in 1939 and the proofs were passed a few weeks before Hitler invaded Poland. By the time the book appeared, in 1940, Europe was at war, as the story's climax anticipated.

Manna is the story of an artificially created species of mushroom that will grow almost anywhere, and will provide all the nourishment that men need. It might potentially banish from the affairs of men the possibility of starvation, though its creators fear that too sudden a release might only promote a population explosion. The situation is further complicated by the fact that manna has an effect similar to Voe – it promotes a euphoric sense of well-being (though not a heightened sense of smell). The men who have the responsibility of deciding what to do with the discovery – a small conspiratorial group of intellectuals – fear that this tranquillising effect might mean the end of social progress and the death of creativity, and they have no wish to turn mankind into a race of lotus-eaters.

The narrator, a journalist, initially feels that manna will be a great boon to mankind, but he becomes gradually more sceptical and disenchanted. The mushroom escapes from the laboratory, seemingly putting an end to the anxious debate, but the final irony is that Europe is lurching into war, and if Hitler is to be defeated then the possible effects of manna on the armed forces are gravely distrubing. The Prime Minister has to broadcast to the nation an appeal that manna 'must be destroyed, uprooted, burned out, seared from the surface of our fair land'.[39]

As usual, the implications of *Manna* are gently understated, and the narrative has not the vigour of *The New Pleasure* or *Winter's Youth*, but there is perhaps no other novel which sums up so neatly the paradoxical outlook which characterises scientific romance between the wars. It has the customary anxieties, and shares the widespread disappointment in human nature – the shocked realisation that *Homo sapiens* has feet of clay – so consistently reflected in British scientific romance. But it is sceptical, too, of the imaginary 'solutions' which were on offer, and ends up offering, with unusual sobriety, yet another study of the Anatomy of Frustration.

In *99%* (1944), the only speculative work which he produced during the war years, Gloag recapitulated the theme of 'Pendulum', 'The Slit' and *Sacred Edifice*, providing a much more elaborate panoramic vision of human history and possibility. The book describes an experiment in which several individuals are enabled, like Fowler Wright's Marguerite Leinster, to re-live in their dreams an experience of one of their ancestors. Each of the participants finds himself rudely jolted out of his complacency, forced to take a new and more dynamic approach to life.

The early chapters suggest, seductively, that much good will come out of the experiment, with each participant's new attitude profiting him, but Gloag is too subtle – and too pessimistic – to adopt such a simple line (as, for instance, is to be found in Warwick Deeping's time-slip fantasy *The Man Who Went Back*, published in 1940). The new fervour which his characters inherit does not allow them to change the world for the better, and more often than not they are betrayed by their enthusiasm. A politician appalled by his experience of past injustices is led to become a devoted Communist, and goes to Russia to aid the revolution, but Russia cannot measure up to his inspiration, and conditions there drive him into an early grave. *99%* thus contrasts strongly with the most elegant previous example of the novel of magical moral regeneration, J. Leslie Mitchell's *The Lost Trumpet* (1932). Even the man who learns most from his experience can only react by abandoning his life of idle luxury for an ascetic and eremitic existence. The key element in this experience is the vision of a stone-age seer:

Of his own physical collapse, he knew nothing; for he was drawn away from his body, and his own mind merged into something far greater than the mind of a tribal priest. He saw the mind of mankind, growing and contracting; he saw it moving brightly towards light and glittering shapes, and returning, darkened, shrunken and scattered. It was like a luminous cloud; occasionally particles of it were detached, grew promisingly and vividly, and then broke up into innumerable fresh particles that sometimes expanded and flourished, but more often faded and blackened.

He saw *through* the cloud, to an earth, green with vegetation, grey with water, belted and banded with golden deserts, and studded with white-tipped mountains. Everywhere on that varied stage pictures were forming and re-forming. Tribes came out of caves and roamed the forests, and then gave up hunting, and settled down to grow their food. Like an enormous panorama, he saw the spread of human life through the world. He observed the invention of building and the control of shelter changing the ways and thoughts of men, and from huts and hovels, came houses, palaces, great monuments, cities, roads, machines, and a world full of movement. And everywhere, men became strangers to each other, and the luminous cloud of the world mind was attenuated, until only a few wisps of its filmy radiance survived. Men built and destroyed, generation after generation, until at last they built only for destruction, and whole tribes and continents gave their lives and dedicated their arts, to the making of machines that would burn and tear down what they had inherited from the past.[40]

Then, of course, the whole pattern is reversed, and mankind reverts to savagery and wheel-worship. New hunters emerge, new tribes form and expand, and in the end the 'world mind' is reformulated, beginning to glow anew with the spirit of community. Just as the seer cannot communicate the import of his vision to his tribe, so the twentieth-century dreamer can do nothing with it. He separates himself, therefore, from the world of his fellow men, reflecting in his actions the separation that his vision has already achieved. Such a withdrawal hardly constitutes an ideal solution to the predicament of the character, but all of Gloag's protagonists favour this kind of retreat as a last resort.

After the war, *Tomorrow's Yesterday* was reprinted along with a number of short stories in the omnibus *First One and Twenty* (1946), to which Gloag added a reflective preface on the subject of speculative fiction. Although he quotes from a letter written by Olaf Stapledon he offers a justification for his own work markedly different from that which Stapledon offered for his. He defends the practice of writing to entertain, and describes speculative fiction as an essentially playful endeavour. Significantly, he also comments on a change in attitude which seems to him to have followed the end of the war. Like Stapledon, he had by this time encountered American science fiction, and found it looking in a direction rather different from that of his own scientific romances:

> The writers of the popular scientific fantasy fiction have created a golden age of their own, projected into the not too distant future, where everything is streamlined, mechanised and appallingly tidy; where atomic energy has been safely harnessed, and life is organised by an aristocracy of technicians. This literature, with its own conventions and jargon, is a manifestation of the scientific romantic movement of which Jules Verne and H.G. Wells are the great progenitors. It responds to contemporary influences, and since the beginning of the Second World War has seldom featured the catastrophic theme. This theme may not be so popular in the future when so many of us have had first hand experience of large scale catastrophe . . .
> Between the wars political, economic and sociological themes were tried and found wanting in entertainment value. Still, there may well be a healthy, creative reaction against the violence and solemnity of the last thirty years.[41]

In later years, Gloag rejected the suggestion that he had been a propagandist after the fashion of Wells, and stressed that his first concern had always been to tell a story, and not to deliver sermons. He acknowledged, though, that the stories he told were coloured by the fact that they were written 'when my life, and the lives of most people in this country, was shadowed by fear: the fear of war, air raids, and (for a brief space) invasion.'[42] There is irony in the fact that Gloag appears to have come out of the Second World War feeling more cheerful. The advent of the atom bomb, which so horrified some of his contemporaries, was not such a surprise for him. As the inventor of radiant inflammatol, he was no stranger to the idea of weapons too dreadful to use and the logic of deterrents. In several of the stories which he wrote after the war there is an element of scientific romance, most notably the short story 'Petrified', which deals with a drug altering perception of the passage of time. The premiss of the story was inverted in the thriller *Slow*

(1954), in which assorted spies battle for control of a drug which slows down metabolism and perception to an extraordinary extent. Nothing he wrote after the war, though, really qualifies as a novel of ideas in the way that his early work did, and even though he was still writing fiction in the late 1970s he was never, apparently, tempted to try his hand at science fiction. He was content to let his visions of the future gather mould along with the rest of yesterday's tomorrows. Perhaps, to some extent, he was put off by the downmarket image of the American science fiction he read, and the British imitations of it which sprang up in the expanding paperback field, but his loss of enthusiasm for speculative fiction still serves to emphasise the way in which the Second World War, like the first, provided a decisive break between eras of thought.

Like Neil Bell, S. Fowler Wright and many of the minor writers of scientific romance active in the 1930s Gloag has fallen into obscurity as far as this aspect of his work is concerned. He has not been featured in any of the series of reprints of early speculative fiction recently produced in the USA – largely because their selection has been governed as much by the expediency of concentrating on works that have fallen into the public domain in America as by the inherent merit of such works. In Gloag's case this obscurity is particularly undeserved, because he was one of the best and most stylish writers of scientific romance in his day. Stapledon's work remains more interesting because of its scope and intensity, but Gloag is far more readable than his friend, and the rhetoric of his works has lost neither its pertinence nor its bite in the course of the last half century.

Gloag stands with Fowler Wright on the right of the political spectrum over which the four major writers discussed in this section extended. Though neither Stapledon nor Bell was ever a member of any Communist Party, both were socialists of a more radical stripe than H.G. Wells or John Beresford. Even the Libertarian Fowler Wright would never have writtten a novel with a hero called Lord Privilege, however ironically the title might be intended. But Gloag was no political dogmatist of any kind, and his stance on the Russian experiment and socialist ideals was the product of his scepticism, not of any opposing creed. In fact, he gives the impression of being the most objective of all the hypothetical visionaries whose moments of 'separation' seemed to offer them a clear and innocent view of the human world as seen from outside. Though they were all, in the final analysis, indecisive victims of Frustration, Gloag was the one who maintained his calmness, restrained his bitterness, and offered what still seems to be the most level-headed account of the spiritual malaise of Britain between the wars.

7

PATTERNS AND TRENDS
BETWEEN THE WARS

The People of the Ruins

FUTURISTIC WRITERS had looked forward to the Great War as a war to end war, and a war to secure civilisation. Men had been recruited to fight it with the aid of the same slogans. The war ended, though, with civilisation no more secure than it had been before, and the fear of future wars unbanished. Inevitably, those speculative writers who considered the possibility of a second world war in the 1920s had a very different attitude to the probable significance of such an event in human affairs.

One of the most widely read scientific romances of the post-war years was *The People of the Ruins* (1920) by Edward Shanks. In this story a new war begins in 1924, and the protagonist is caught up in the bombing of London. Trapped in a bombed building, he is exposed to a preservative gas which holds him in the thrall of suspended animation for a hundred and fifty years. When he awakes, it is to find England in the grip of a new Dark Age, inhabited by savage tribesmen whose way of life is based on scavenging in the wreckage of a civilisation which has now been all but obliterated.

The hero of *The People of the Ruins* finds himself in a unique position. He is, potentially at least, a storehouse of lost knowledge. In fact, as an ordinary man, he has little enough in the way of practical skills, and he finds the education he has undergone woefully ill-fitted to the task which faces him. The petty dictator in whose domain he finds himself, though, cares little about these inadequacies, as long as he can help in the work of making old weapons work again, so that the conquest of England by war can begin all over again.

The only pre-war work which really anticipated the tone of

The People of the Ruins was *The War in the Air*, and even that book ends on a note which is not entirely pessimistic. The world in Wells's novel is at least settled and regretful about its loss. Shanks, by contrast, allows no glimmer of hope:

> Cities would be burnt, bridges broken down, tall towers destroyed and all the wealth and learning of humanity would shiver to a few shards and a little dust. The very place would be forgotten where once had stood the houses that he knew; and the roads he had walked with his friends would be as desolate and lonely as the Stane Street of the Romans.
>
> Even all this story, his victory and his defeat, his joy and his sorrow, would fade out of the memory of man. But what did it all matter to Jeremy Tuft, who, wonder and portent that he was, strange anachronism, unparalleled and reluctant ambassador from one age to the next, had suffered in the end that common ill, the loss of his beloved? He raised the pistol to his head and fired.[1]

This idea of a continuing series of wars, each making the condition of the survivors worse than the last, was to recur several times more in the period between the wars – as we have already seen, it was to be frequently used by John Gloag, who was very impressed by *The People of the Ruins*, and in a work which repeated its message a few years later: Cicely Hamilton's *Theodore Savage* (1922; revised in 1928 as *Lest Ye Die*). Here the decay of civilisation is placed within the lifetime of a single individual. We first meet its eponymous hero as a young man in the social whirl of London in the 1920s, and then follow his progress during a war when cities are obliterated and their populations flee into the countryside to fight against one another in the battle to avoid starvation. One bad winter is all that it takes to make England a nation of scattered scavengers, with hardly a vestige even of tribal organisation. Communities re-form slowly, but the social order they adopt is nothing like the shattered one; they are bound together by fear and hatred of outsiders. The return to barbarism is followed inevitably by a return to superstition; the scientific habit of thought disappears with its products and science becomes the object of blind fear, stigmatised as the evil which destroyed the world. Theodore Savage guesses that this might be part of a pattern of eternal recurrence, and comes to regard the ancient myths of his own world as a disguised account of a previous ruination of human civilisation. This eternal cycle was not a new idea – it is featured, among other places, in Jules Verne's last novella, 'The Eternal Adam' – but it became fashionable again in this period. Again, we have observed its prominence in the futuristic imagery of John Gloag and S. Fowler Wright.

Stories of awesomely destructive wars were produced at regular intervals throughout the twenties and thirties. As well as titles already credited to the major writers of the period there were more than a dozen others. The most significant are perhaps *The Collapse of Homo sapiens* (1923) by P. Anderson Graham, *Ragnarok* (1926) by Shaw Desmond, *The Poison War* (1933) by Ladbroke Black and *The Black Death* (1934) by M. Dalton. That these works reflect a much more widespread anxiety is emphasised by an article published in *Pall Mall Magazine* in 1924 by the man who, fifteen years later, was actually to take England through the Second World War, Winston Churchill. His article was provocatively titled 'Shall We Commit Suicide?' and raised the question of how the Great War might have developed had it not been brought to a close:

> But all that happened in the four years of the Great War was only a prelude to what was preparing for the fifth year. The campaign of the year 1919 would have witnessed an immense accession to the power of destruction. Had the Germans retained the *moral* to make good their retreat to the Rhine, they would have been assaulted in the summer of 1919 with forces and by methods incomparably more prodigious than any yet employed. Thousands of aeroplanes would have shattered their cities. Scores of thousands of cannon would have blasted their front. Arrangements were being made to carry simultaneously a quarter of a million men, together with all their requirements, continuously forward across country in mechanical vehicles moving ten or fifteen miles each day. Poison gases of incredible malignity, against which only a secret mask (which the Germans could not obtain in time) was proof, would have stifled all resistance and paralysed all life on the hostile front subjected to attack. No doubt the Germans too had their plans. But the hour of wrath had passed, the signal of relief was given, and the horrors of 1919 remain buried in the archives of the great antagonists.[2]

The article goes on:

> Certain sombre facts emerge solid, inexorable, like the shapes of mountains from drifting mist. It is established that henceforward whole populations will take part in war, all doing their utmost, all subjected to the fury of the enemy. It is established that nations who

241

believe that their life is at stake will not be restrained from using any means to secure their existence. *It is probable – nay, certain – that among the means which will next time be at their disposal will be agencies and processes of destruction wholesale, unlimited, and, perhaps, once launched, uncontrollable.*[3]

Churchill discusses in this article the methods of chemical warfare and the possibility of biological warfare, and bombs which will 'concentrate the force of a thousand tons of cordite and blast a township at a stroke', plus flying bombs guided to their targets by radio. Of all these possibilities, the one which seemed *most* horrific to the people of the day was poison gas.

As early as 1907 a pact restricting the use of chemical weapons was made by the signatories of the Hague Peace Conference, but the renunciation extended only to projectiles discharging asphyxiating gases; discharge from cylinders on the ground was not mentioned. During the Great War twenty-five different poison gases were used; the most effective ones were delivered in liquid form and became effective by slow evaporation. Mustard gas did most damage, but arsenous smokes which would have been deployed in 1919 had the need arisen – including Lewisite – would probably have been far more effective, causing terrific pain and distress although rarely killing or causing permanent damage.

It is probable that fear of poison gas was exaggerated. J.B.S. Haldane, whose second *Today and Tomorrow* essay was *Callinicus: A Defence of Chemical Warfare* (1925), certainly thought so. He argued that some chemical weapons, especially tear gases, were relatively humane, and that there is in any case no moral distinction to be made between killing people with poison gases and stabbing them to death with swords. At the end of his essay, though, Haldane predicted that no one would take any notice of his arguments, and he was almost right. Fear continued unabated, and there are very few future war stories which feature humane chemical warfare.

By the time Haldane published *Callinicus* a new agreement forswearing the use of chemical weapons had been made in Washington (in 1922), and this was extended by the Geneva Conference of 1925. Writers of speculative fiction, though, had no confidence in the Geneva Convention and its rules of war. It was taken for granted that chemical weapons would be used, and that in any future war air fleets would immediately be dispatched to bomb civilian populations. Again, such anxieties were by no means confined to fiction. They figured prominently in a speech made by Stanley Baldwin in the House of Commons on 10 November 1932, during the period of the first National Government in Britain, while the Nazis and the Communists were battling for control of Germany:

> What the world suffers from is a sense of fear ... a want of confidence ... My own view is that there is no one thing that is more responsible for that fear ... than the fear of the air ...
> In the next war you will find that any town within reach of an aerodrome can be bombed within the first five minutes of war to an extent inconceivable in the last war ...
> I think it is well also for the man in the street to realise that there is no power on earth that can protect him from being bombed, whatever people may tell him. The bomber will always get through.
> The only defence is in offence, which means that you have got to kill more women and children more quickly than the enemy, if you want to save yourselves.[4]

These are exactly the tactics of war featured in Neil Bell's *The Gas War of 1940* and many other near-contemporary novels. Clarion calls for rearmament and reorganisation of Britain's defences, after the fashion of 'The Battle of Dorking', were produced in some quantity. Several were written by E.F. Spanner, who had retired from the Royal Corps of Naval Constructors with the conviction that ships would be largely irrelevant to the protection of Britain in the event of a new European war, and that heavy investment in aircraft was a desperate necessity. In his *The Broken Trident* (1926) the Germans pay Britain back for the humiliations heaped on them after the Great War, albeit in a sportsman-like fashion, without a whiff of poison gas. Like 'The Battle of Dorking' this novel was quickly translated into German. But this is a relatively optimistic work by comparison with *Invasion from the Air* (1934) by Frank McIlraith and Roy Connolly, which is dedicated to Baldwin and uses his speech as a preface. Here the fleets of bombers use explosives, incendiary bombs and gas bombs, and the conclusion is that the political communities of the contending nations would so quickly disintegrate that by the time governments sue for peace they will all be toppling before a threat of universal Fascism.

Like McIlraith and Connolly, many other writers were deeply

suspicious of the competence of the political establishment to prevent a new war, and to manage it once it developed. The argument of Harold Nicolson's *Public Faces* (1932) is that following the development of incredibly powerful atomic bombs a pattern of diplomatic brinkmanship would develop that would lead inexorably to war. John Gloag's *Winter's Youth* endorses this view. Some later novels accepting the same argument grow so desperate in following through the hypothesis that they become almost surreal. *Chaos* (1938), by the Irish writer Shaw Desmond, dissolves in its conclusion into a semi-incoherent plea for supernatural redemption – perhaps a more eloquent expression of hopelessness than the grim pessimism of Shanks and Hamilton.

Images of future war produced in the 1930s are powerful horror stories, virtually without exception. In stories dealing with the aftermath of such wars, though, the horror is very often modified by a measure of romanticism. There is often a conviction in such stories to the effect that a civilisation which could thus destroy itself could not have been worth having. There had always been a romantic vein in disaster stories from Mary Shelley's *The Last Man* onwards – the idea of being alone in a depopulated world has a certain charm as well as its frightening aspect. Then again, there was the Wellsian idea that disaster might clear away the dross of the old world to make way for the building of Utopia by the enlightened few – an idea developed in striking fashion by the most impressive great plague story of the 1920s, *Nordenholt's Million* (1923). A rather different kind of romanticism, though, lies at the heart of John Collier's *Tom's a-Cold* (1933), which celebrates the return of England to barbarism in a quiet fashion reminiscent of the second part of Richard Jefferies' *After London*. Different again is Alun Llewellyn's *The Strange Invaders*, in which the tribally organised survivors of a great war find themselves being gradually dispossessed by handsome giant reptiles.

The one writer who, more than any other, was prepared to welcome the idea of mankind reverted to savagery was J. Leslie Mitchell (1901–35). His first, non-fantastic novel *Stained Radiance* (1930) is a bitter hymn of hate against the vileness of contemporary social life. There are elements of scientific romance in a few of his early short stories, which were published in two series in *The Cornhill*. 'Polychromata' (1929–30; reprinted as *The Calends of Cairo*, 1931, with an introduction by H.G.

Wells and Leonard Huxley) includes 'A Volcano in the Moon', about a tragic disagreement between two astronomers regarding a new discovery, and 'East is West', which features an ornithopter. 'The Chronicles of Neesan Nerses' (1931–2; reprinted in *Persian Dawns, Egyptian Nights*, 1933) has a story about a yeti-like survivor from prehistory, 'The Last Ogre'. Mitchell was a journalist turned archaeologist, though, and his real interest in scientific romance began when he was inspired by the 'diffusionist' theories popularised by V. Gordon Childe and others, which suggested that all civilisation had diffused from beginnings in Egypt. Mitchell took from this theory the idea that modern civilisation was simply the end result of a causal chain begun by a single unhappy accident. This led him to react strongly against the idea in Wells's *Outline of History* that the brutish elements in the make-up of modern man were residues of the character of his remote antecedents.

In *Three Go Back* (1932) Mitchell dispatched three representatives of modern civilisation – a Militant Pacifist, an armaments manufacturer, and an embittered woman whose true love was killed horribly in the Great War – back to the Old Stone Age to discover that man's ancestors were really innocent noble savages whose life, though hard, was socially harmonious and happy. It is the female character who is the protagonist, observing the opposed ideologies of her male companions while she falls in love with the life of the beautiful hunters. Mitchell followed up this novel with one of the most impressive post-holocaust stories written between the wars, *Gay Hunter* (1934), whose significantly named eponymous heroine is similarly hurled through time with two companions, to find England reverted to the same condition as the prehistoric world of the earlier novel. This time the protagonist's companions are two British Fascists, who are intent on civilising the savages and rebuilding the old world – which, she learns, was destroyed by degrees by warring Fascist hierarchies which fought one another across the centuries with atom bombs and poisonous dusts. She manages in the end to mobilise the noble savages against their corrupt enemies, and to save the world from civilisation. Mitchell's fantasy novel *The Lost Trumpet* (1932) – a continuation of the 'Polychromata' sequence – features an archaeological expedition to locate the trumpet with which Joshua destroyed the walls of Jericho, which is, symbolically, 'the lost trumpet of human sanity'. When it is finally blown, by the only one of the *dramatis personae* sufficiently uncorrupted by civilisation to do it, all the characters discover how demoralised and vicious modern life has made them.

The degree of Mitchell's disenchantment is unusual, though it was almost matched by S. Fowler Wright. He was a more accomplished writer than any of the major figures of the period, though modern critical acclaim is reserved for the novels he wrote under the pseudonym Lewis Grassic Gibbon, and he might have become Wells's most important successor as well as his ideological opponent had he not been tragically killed. He had begun a third fantastic story featuring a triad of characters removed into an imaginary world – this time a relic of ancient civilisation preserved in a curious underworld along with gargantuan insects and other grotesques. Fytton Armstrong, who acquired this along with six other unpublished short stories for use in one of the anthologies which he edited for the *Daily Express* as John Gawsworth, added an abrupt conclusion to the fragment and published it as a collaboration in *Masterpiece of Thrills* (1936) as 'Kametis and Evelpis'. Three of the other six stories are scientific romances, including the rhapsodic romance of prehistory 'The Woman of Leadenhall Street' and the futuristic story 'First and Last Woman' (to both of which Armstrong attached the Gibbon pseudonym). 'First and Last Woman' is similar in theme and spirit to the stories in Fowler Wright's *The New Gods Lead*.

Mitchell deserves special consideration not just because of his lost potential but because he exemplifies in its most extreme form a particular kind of reaction to the anxieties of the thirties. The fear of destruction generated a rather perverted fascination with the idea of destruction – a fascination which has extended through a whole series of British disaster stories extending even to the present day. This tradition is characterised by an underlying ambivalence that American critics interested in speculative fiction have often found puzzling. In American disaster stories, including stories of world destruction by war (though very few such stories were produced in the USA before the advent of the atom bomb in 1945), the problem facing the survivors is always represented as the struggle to rebuild a technological civilisation. In Britain, by contrast, such a recovery is often rejected as an option, and sometimes openly derided.

There is an item of advice popularly attributed to Confucius and often quoted nowadays (usually in unseemly circumstances) to the effect that if rape is inevitable one might as well lie back and enjoy it. In many futuristic works of the 1930s British speculative writers appear to have accepted that some kind of spoliation of civilisation was indeed inevitable, and they tried by means of various kinds of argumentative trickery to make the best of the prospect. Mitchell and Fowler Wright took one possible stand in suggesting that civilisation *per se* is corrupting and that men would be better off returned to a state of nature. Wells, Beresford and Stapledon took the more moderate line that it is only the kind of civilisation that we have built which is corrupt, and that its destruction may pave the way for something better. Even Gloag and Bell, some of whose work is more defeatist in tone, maintain elsewhere the hope of some kind of renewal.

From the viewpoint of the reader whose own hopes for the future are pinned to a gradual progressive evolution of contemporary civilisation, British scientific romance of the thirties is bound to seem deeply pessimistic. In so far as these authors (with the experience of the Great War behind them) all realise what an enormity of human suffering would result from a destructive conflict of the kind they imagined, their work is indeed dark and bitter in tone. Nevertheless, it still represents in large measure a triumph of hope over experience. Even writers who can tie that hope only to the possible survival of some tiny Utopian enclave secluded from a whole world gone to perdition, as in James Hilton's *Lost Horizon* (1933) or Alfred Noyes's *The Last Man* (1940), manage to make a meal of their crumbs of comfort.

There are, of course, some stories of this period which end on a note of total despair – a despair whose tenor is perhaps best summed up by the conclusion of *The People of the Ruins*, when Jeremy Tuft, having seen the future which awaits mankind, shoots himself. If we compare this story, though, with those written between ten and twenty years later we can see many writers struggling to make out a case for the *real* story's extension beyond that symbolic suicide. They accept the act itself, and its significance; the opinion of the overwhelming majority is that there is no future for the likes of Jeremy Tuft – the helpless, imperfect, incompetently well-intentioned men of today. It is accepted that if the world is to be remade then the people of the ruins must give birth to a new race. Stapledon makes far more of this than any other writer, and it might be argued that even he never seemed wholly convinced about the possibility or propriety of the emergence of a new and better mankind, but it is an idea that recurs continually in the speculative fiction of the day. The notion itself will be discussed in more detail in the last section of the present chapter, but in concluding this section it is sufficient to re-emphasise the significance of its chief corollary: the curious ambivalence that one finds so widely distributed in British future war stories and British stories of natural disaster written after the lessons of the Great War had been imaginatively digested.

Because of their reaction against the despair that could so easily well up in connection with their contemplation of a second world war, writers of scientific romance contrived to import into their images of devastation an undercurrent of ambiguity. The symptoms of this underlying ambiguity are often easy to identify: the widespread opinion that if civilisation is destroyed it will only be getting its just deserts; the frequent allegation that a better world and a better mankind will rise phoenix-like from the ashes of the old. Less obvious, though, is a growing fascination in scientific romance, inherited in large measure by the best of British science fiction, with what might be termed the 'psychology and existential significance of disaster'. *Theodore Savage* may be regarded as one of the earliest extended exercises of this nature; a particularly interesting example from the end of the period between the wars is *The Hopkins Manuscript* (1939) by R.C. Sherriff – the author of that enduring dramatisation of the futility of the Great War and the poverty of its myths, *Journey's End* (1929). Here a cosmic catastrophe is followed by a period of enthusiastic and successful reconstruction, eventually interrupted and reversed when international conflicts break out again. As with many earlier examples the conclusion is doom laden, but for much of its length the novel seems almost to be an apology for disaster – earnest, if slightly disguised rhetoric supporting the notion that catastrophe has its good side too.

The Age of Frustration

Three years after publishing *The Shape of Things to Come*, in which he characterised the contemporary phase of history as 'The Age of Frustration', H.G. Wells produced *The Anatomy of Frustration*, in which he attempted to analyse what might be implied by the phrase. Alas, the result is itself a frustrating work, presented as a review of an imaginary work whose supposed comprehensive commentary is offered to us only in a series of annotated glimpses. Were it not for certain disagreements between Wells and his contemporaries about the exact nature of the forces in man's make-up and social organisation which were frustrating progress, almost all the scientific romances written between the wars might also be regarded as oblique footnotes to the same hidden text. There is an ever-present uncertainty about the literary visions of the future produced in this era which is deeper and more quizzical than the essential uncertainty of all attempts to anticipate. It often seems that authors in this period do not know quite how to account for their own attitudes and feelings.

This special uncertainty has a certain implicit irony in it. One can, after all, take a paradoxical delight in pointing out that one of the symptoms of an Age of Frustration will be a frustrating incapacity to analyse the sources of the Frustration. It is therefore not surprising that in many of the political fantasies of the period between the wars we find not only severe doubts about the possibility of reaching any kind of Utopia but a perverse celebration of the fact. This made these visions of future states ambiguous to such an extent that they frequently became surreal.

The idea that the Great War might provide a golden opportunity for the reconstruction of society along happier and more egalitarian lines faded very quickly from futuristic fiction. It is not seen again after the publication of *The New Moon* by Oliver Onions in 1918. The very same year, in fact, saw the publication of a remarkable image of future society very different in its implications: *Meccania the Super-State* by Owen Gregory. In this story a Chinese observer tours a European country (obviously Germany) in the year 1970, and finds there an authoritarian regime obsessed with titles, uniforms and bureaucratic procedures. The society is rigidly stratified, with everyone fully conscious of his exact rank and role. The scientific management of every aspect of life has fostered rapid technological progress, and has brought about a curious analytical modernism in the arts. All life is so rationally ordered that all misfits and dissenters are deemed to have proved their insanity by their inability or unwillingness to fit in, and they are confined to asylums. All of this is, of course, held up to gentle but insistent ridicule by the commentary.

Although *Meccania the Super-State* was by no means the first dystopian satire to have been written in Britain it broke important new ground. Although it has never been reprinted there is a crucial modernity in its outlook and attitude that would make it easily accessible to readers in the 1980s. Indeed, we have now become so much more used to the theatre of the absurd that readers today would find the book easier to tune into than its contemporary readers did. Some of the targets of its satirical analysis no longer seem relevant, but the tenor of its sarcasm is familiar enough. We can find a similar derisory attitude in other political satires published in the year following the end of the Great War, including Rose Macaulay's *What Not* (1919), in which the best-laid schemes of the British Ministry of Brains gang fortunately agley, and Ronald Knox's *Memories of the Future* (1923), in which an amiably innocent old lady looks back with unjustified pride over the years between the first Great War and the second (of 1972–5).

In the early post-war years the sense of the absurd which features in such satires as these left more serious exercises in political speculation – Beresford's *Revolution*, for instance – untouched. Many alarmist fantasies, like Hugh Addison's red menace novel *The Battle of London* (1923) also maintain a deadly seriousness. A sense of cruel irony can, however, be found in one of the more lurid images of future conflict between Labour and Capital, *The Great Image* (1921) by 'Pan'. 'Pan' was a pseudonym used by Leslie Beresford, who had published his first scientific romance under his own name in 1910 – a future war story about a revolt against British rule in India, *The Second Rising*. As 'Pan' he had earlier published *The Kingdom of Content* (1918) about a Utopian enclave that survives the destruction of civilisation, and he was later to write two more scientific romances under his own name, but *The Great Image* is his most considerable work in the genre. Like his namesake in *Revolution*, Beresford tries to maintain a scrupulous neutrality in describing the war that breaks out between the owners and their workers, while really being sympathetic to socialist ideals. In his fantasy he alleges that the leaders on both sides have been betrayed into subordinating ordinary moral considerations to their idols, and that the Great Image of the Commonweal might just as easily be thus betrayed as the worship of private wealth and power. Violence even in a good cause, Beresford argues, liberates chaos in such measure that the best efforts of well-intentioned men cannot hope to contain it. There is ample evidence here of the Frustration that was eventually to become so characteristic of the period.

The spread of this unease made it very difficult for writers of the 1920s to produce Utopias, though some tried. One of the most notable attempts was made by the wife of J.B.S. Haldane, Charlotte Haldane, who produced *Man's World* in 1926 as an explicit development of the debate begun by her husband and Bertrand Russell in the *Today and Tomorrow* essays. (Although the long 'Acknowledgement' which begins the text is an imaginary dialogue between Anatole France and his mentor Ernest Renan, the first quotation in the story proper is from *Icarus*, and it is Russell's doubts about how science may be used that provide the starting point for rhetorical negotiation in the text.) The author's commitment to the possibility of building Utopia need not be doubted, but granted this, *Man's World* is a very hesitant book. The first chapter describes the emergence of the Nucleus, a community of intellectuals strongly reminiscent of those envisaged by Wells as the nuclei of his future Utopias. As with Wells's New Republics the Nucleus comes into its own after a destructive war. After this brief introduction, though, Haldane chooses to organise her story around the career of an atavistic child who fails to benefit from the Wellsian ideal education and reintroduces into the affairs of the happy world some of the evils of the old – most notably the senseless quest for occult Meaning which is the core of religious feeling. Haldane's contemplation of the career of this eventually luckless individual is even-handed and regretful.

The idea that the seed of Utopia must be sown in a company of children by sane education also features prominently in another Utopian novel published in 1926: *And a New Earth* by C.E. Jacomb, in which a millionaire recruits a whole population of unwanted babies in order to establish an ideal community on Easter Island. Jacomb's ideas about the ideal community are eccentric, tainted by a kind of racism which would not endear the book to modern readers, but this is a minor issue; what makes the work interesting is the reaction which Jacomb envisages against his sane community, which is first challenged and then attacked by outside forces – Churches and Great Powers in alliance. A world war and a second Deluge appear to secure the world for the Easter Islanders, but this conclusion has been subverted from the very beginning by a frame narrative which reveals that nine hundred years on an apparently thriving world community has had to rediscover the relics of this experiment.

A very different image of a 'newborn' community is provided in a third novel of 1926: *Children of the Morning* by W.L. George. Here is no Utopia but a society formulated from scratch by a group of shipwrecked children, who discover of their own accord most of the ills afflicting the mature civilisation of the day, including superstition and warfare. The story contrasts sharply with the romantic robinsonades so fashionable in the nineteenth century, and provides a remarkable anticipation of William Golding's classic *Lord of the Flies*.

The themes of all three of these novels move uneasily around the question of how, and how far, the development of children is determined by circumstance. All of them are interested in the possibility of rearing individuals possessed of such an innate sanity that they could not help but form a sane community. All three may be regarded as examples of a particular anxiety on this score. In some later works this anxiety becomes much more forceful, as in E. Arnot Robertson's affectively powerful novel *Three Came Unarmed* (1929), in which three children reared as innocent 'noble savages' in the Far East are gradually destroyed by the vicious forces of convention when they are forced to return to the 'protection' of relatives in England. The theme of this story can be seen as an inversion of *The Island of Captain Sparrow*, embodying a view of the relationship of Civilisation and Nature very similar to Fowler Wright's.

One more novel published in 1926 that bears importantly on the problem of educating for Utopia is *The Question Mark* by Muriel Jaeger, one of the *Today and Tomorrow* essayists. This novel, published by Leonard and Virginia Woolf's Hogarth Press, imagines that in twenty-second-century England there has been an economic reorganisation along the lines of that envisaged by Edward Bellamy, where everyone has been made materially comfortable and most labour is accomplished by machinery. A Wellsian education is available to all, but Jaeger borrows from that perennial sceptic Bertrand Russell the hypothesis that most people simply would not want it. Far from using their unlimited leisure time creatively, the vast majority of Normals (contrasted with the small minority of Intellectuals) is content to dissipate its energies in idle pleasure seeking and shallow love affairs, after the fashion of the Bright Young Things of the twenties social scene. In this far-from-perfect world the banishment of poverty has not served to bring people any closer to a sense of personal fulfilment, and its very comfortableness makes the futility of its people seem so much more horrific. Freedom, Jaeger reminds us, must include the freedom to be foolish, indolent, wasteful and stupid, and it is in such indulgences that the people who already have freedom seem to use it. In her introduction to the text, she makes the following observations:

> In the imaginary Jerusalem . . . which prophets have built for me in England's green and pleasant land, Socialism is established; it succeeds; it works well . . . I accept the Bellamy-Morris-Wells world in all essentials – with one exception; I do not and cannot accept its inhabitants. At this point my effort to realise Utopia fails. With the best will in the world, I have found myself quite unable to believe in these wise, virtuous, gentle, artistic people . . .
>
> Other people also have found the Utopians more difficult to swallow than the Utopias. Conditions, no doubt, would modify human nature as they always do; but would they, could they, modify it quite like that? We cannot see it. Very regretfully we are driven to wonder whether some of our philosophers have not here leapt a chasm from what they might deduce to what they would wish. And it seems that others of them, coming to the verge of discovery, have delicately stepped away again, leaving this last and most portentous problem of Utopia still shrouded in veils of mystery.[5]

The evidence of scientific romance shows clearly that other people did indeed share Muriel Jaeger's inability to believe in Utopians – or at least to cast contemporary men in such roles. And without Utopians, should not Utopia itself be reckoned an undesirable place to be? Jaeger herself took up this argument in only one of her other scientific romances, in the section of *Retreat from Armageddon* (1936) in which a feeble mock-Utopia based in eugenicist ideas is easily demolished by satire. The remainder of the novel is content to present an analysis of the failures of contemporary civilisation which is interesting in bringing together ideas to be found in many other contemporary works, but which has little that is particularly new or striking in its presentation. The line of thought opened up by *The Question Mark* was, however, continued by other writers, most notably by Aldous Huxley, who produced in *Brave New World* (1932) the definitive image of a Utopia without Utopians: a happy and well-organised world where all problems of politics and economics are solved, where life itself has become a travesty.

Brave New World is one of two novels which seem between them to have had more impact on the way we think about the future than all the rest put together. It has now become almost conventional to evaluate technological innovations and the proposed political programmes organised around them relative to a '*Brave New World* situation' or a '*Nineteen Eighty-Four* situation'. The two books have become key compendia of images representing all that is undesirable in the possible futures that confront us. The establishment of *Brave New World* as an archetypal nightmare frequently leads modern readers to overlook the fact that it is a rather witty book much of whose parody is amiably comic rather than morally indignant. In the climactic chapters of the book it is, of course, the moral indignation which takes over and becomes paramount, but the story has not quite the moral *certainty* that is sometimes imputed to it. A good deal of its argument is hesitant and rather uneasy, and none of the three characters who function as critics of their world within the plot really achieves a clear victory in justifying his indictment. Mustapha Mond, the defender of his world, comes off better than he is usually given credit for.

The society of *Brave New World* is a clever combination of Communist and Capitalist ideals. Private property is abolished and the state takes responsibility for the welfare of all. On the other hand, a hierarchy of classes has not only been retained but founded in biological engineering; men here are not potentially equal, and the question of their non-equality in practice is therefore set aside. Most importantly of all, though, the people of the new world are *happy*. They are *made* happy by a well-defined process of social engineering which claims to be benign by definition. As in the classic Wellsian Utopia there is not much need of governmental apparatus: 'our education is our government' might be smugly repeated here just as it is smugly reported by Wells's *Men Like Gods*. But these men are not like gods, and only a few of them are much like men. The rest are slaves, not to a system of economic exploitation, but to an efficient technology of direct social control.

Muriel Jaeger's Question Mark attached itself to the problem of what men might reasonably be expected to do with freedom from labour and want, and Jaeger worries about whether those freedoms will really serve to make men happy. Huxley's Question Mark turns the issue around, attaching itself to the problem of whether guaranteed happiness would render the question of freedom irrelevant. When the Savage, the most significant of Huxley's three critics, complains of the lack of freedom he finds in a world where he really did expect to find men like gods, Mustapha Mond points out that the freedoms which have been banished are the freedom to be miserable, the freedom to be hungry, the freedom to be in pain, and so on. Are these really the freedoms that men seek? And if men do not or should not want to be happy, what should they want instead?

Neither Bernard Marx, the restless intellectual alienated by his physical inadequacy, nor Helmholtz Watson, the would-be poet, really pushes through his attempt to find something different. The price of exile is too much for Marx to consider, and Watson cannot answer Mond's observation that the happiness secured for a few by their appreciation of great art is paid for by the suffering of the many which is the emotional substance of that art. The Savage puts up a better show, laying explicit claims to precisely those paradoxical freedoms that Mond mocks, but he fails to carry through his determination. In the end he is seduced by the allure of the hedonistic world, in the shape of Lenina Crowne, and he opts out of the struggle by killing himself. Unlike Jeremy Tuft in *The People of the Ruins*, who despaired of the world and shot himself, the Savage despairs of himself and hangs himself. The climax of *Brave New World*, therefore, is not quite the grandiose rejection of all the perverted Utopia stands for that it sometimes seems to modern readers. Rather, it is a gesture of Frustration occasioned by the intractability of the problem which it addresses.

Huxley's novel now appears to us as one of the most prophetic of all scientific romances, not because our world has come to resemble it but because all the repulsive aspects of its imaginary world now seem more plausible as possibilities, and hence more threatening. It is this increased sense of threat which makes us see '*Brave New World* situations' looming here, there and everywhere. It is ironic that the credit awarded to Huxley for his prescience is really due to J.B.S. Haldane, whose ideas he borrowed in order to attack them. In all his other speculative fiction, from *After Many a Summer* (1939) to *Island* (1962), Huxley showed no trace of any talent for anticipation, and if one looks at the aspects of his future world that were *not* borrowed from *Daedalus* – the religion of Our Ford, for instance – we find them to be slightly silly satirical jokes whose plausibility has not been enhanced at all by the march of time. Even so, Huxley did put flesh on the possibilities that were casually thrown into the arena of debate by Haldane, and he did so in a remarkably striking fashion. It is this ability to give real form to abstract hypotheses that Huxley has in common with the most significant of the writers whose ideology he was attacking: H.G. Wells. Another thing he has in common with Wells is that he was at his best as a speculative writer only in this early phase, when he retained an essential scepticism in his outlook and method. By 1939, when he wrote his mocking account of the horrors of longevity, *After Many a Summer*, he had acquired a new moral certainty, and was prepared to attack the pretensions of scientists on the grounds that no good would come of it all. Like Wells, he was better as an explorer than an explainer, and it is the uneasy uncertainty of *Brave New World* which makes it such a brilliant and fascinating work.

In the years after *Brave New World* was published there appeared a considerable number of works which shared with it a fascination with powerful methods of social control – with the instruments of dictatorship. This was in the main a response to the emergence of Fascism in Europe, and in particular a reaction to the rise of Nazi Germany, but it also reveals a long-standing preoccupation with technology as the means of oppression.

In 1933, the same year that *The Shape of Things to Come* appeared, Michael Arlen published *Man's Mortality*, a rather different account of an Air Dictatorship and its relevance to the evolution of a World State. Here, International Aircraft & Airways have used their monopoly of air power to force peace upon the world after the fashion of George Griffith's Aerians, but its younger officers are becoming disillusioned with the underhandedness of some of its methods of control. Having lost faith in the benignity of the dictators, many of these young men join forces with David Knox, whose invention of a new method of propulsion has enabled him to built aircraft that are faster and more powerfully armed than I.A.&A.'s Unfortunately Knox the revolutionary has messianic ambitions which go far beyond the desire to lighten the yoke of the dictatorship, and he is gradually revealed as a kind of Antichrist who serves the cause of wanton destruction. When the dictatorship is fallen, the only hope for a new world peace seems to lie in the formation of a World State and a better commitment to Christian values (or spiritual values, at least) than men have yet proved able to make. Even the most benign and well-intentioned of the surviving political leaders, though, finds it very difficult to resist the temptation offered to him to take over where I.A.&A. and Knox have left off, by using a monopoly on a powerful new technology to force his own will on the world.

Man's Mortality is interesting not simply because it manifests yet again the uneasiness and uncertainty of the period but because it seems to undergo a gradual transformation of narrative form, beginning as a futuristic thriller but ending as a rather surreal fantasy with an element of peculiar allegory in it. This is a strangely common feature of political fantasies in the 1930s. It is almost as though many writers found an element of bizarrerie in the career of Hitler to which they could not do justice by less elliptical narrative techniques. On the other hand, one can find a tendency to incorporate surreal elements in some novels of the twenties also – sometimes in rather surprising ones. *Kontrol* (1928), for instance, is one of a series of marginally fantastic thrillers written by Edmund Snell. Like the others, it begins as a conventional mystery story, but there clearly came a point at which Snell was seized by the imaginative potential of his central thesis, which involves transplanting brains in order to create supermen. In the later chapters Snell moves far away from his normal fictional orbit in describing an island where the artificial supermen are building a technological Utopia to which they are sinisterly adapted.

A more pronounced surrealism is to be found in a group of political fantasias published in the mid-thirties. In Joseph O'Neill's *Land Under England* (1935) the hero undertakes an Orphean quest in search of his father in a strange underworld where men are enslaved to a collective consciousness. Here is a society which has only one mind and one will, where dissent and division are literally unthinkable. The hero is glad to win eventual release from this place, but there is a distinct ambivalence in the way he looks back at his experience and remembers the warmth of the underworld and its 'suffocating peace'.

A much more complex and enigmatic work is *The Green Child* (1935) by Herbert Read, the noted critic and aesthetic philosopher. Here the hero 'discovers' two highly ordered worlds – one a tranquil pastoral Utopia which he establishes in South America and then deserts; the other a magical underworld whose inhabitants accept a kind of existential petrifaction as the highest good. The intermingling of the hero's story with an ancient folktale recorded by Ralph of Coggeshall in medieval times makes the story a fantasy rather than a scientific romance, and the same is true of some of the other works which manifest this surreal fascination with unnaturally united states. *The Hesperides* (1936), by John Palmer, is obviously allied with scientific romance in placing its totalitarian collectivist state on Venus, but *The Wild Goose Chase* (1937) by Rex Warner uses no such imaginative apparatus, and is content to offer its allegory quite straightforwardly. The same is true of Warner's later novel, *The Aerodrome* (1941), which carefully contrasts the Fascistic glamour of the Air Force officers with the liberal simplicity of the villagers who come under their dominion. A similarly forthright approach to the business of creating allegories is shown by Ruthven Todd in his two fantasies, *Over the Mountain* (1939) and *The Lost Traveller* (1943), in each of which an individual battles with oppressive authority in absurd hallucinatory circumstances. The dates of these last-named novels emphasise that the onset of the Second World War actually encouraged the tendency to surrealise, and one can also see this in Neil M. Gunn's *The Green Isle of the Great Deep* (1944), in which Paradise is taken over by oppressive bureaucrats, and has to be released from its bondage by the human spirit of rebellion and an eventual appeal to the highest authority of all.

Despite the widespread interest in technologies of oppression that is evident in fiction produced between the wars there are relatively few novels which present a convincing account of how such technologies might come into being and be put into operation. *Brave New World* stands almost alone in presenting a complex and multi-faceted technology of social control whose operation is a matter of commonly accepted routine. The great majority of writers followed Michael Arlen in picturing dictators or small oligarchies imposing their tyrannical will with the aid of single crucial inventions on which they have a monopoly. This was an age when people thought of scientific discoveries and inventions as the work of lone eccentrics whose genius gave them a special insight.

This notion of the inventive process is most obviously seen in those novels where lone inventors develop machines of awesome destructive power and use them to blackmail the world (usually with benevolent motives). Stories of this kind are generally framed as thrillers in which secret agents try to locate and identify the blackmailers; examples include *The One Sane Man* (1934) by Francis Beeding (a pseudonym used by two collaborators, one of whom was John Palmer, author of *The Hesperides*) and *I'll Blackmail the World* (1935) by S. Andrew Wood. Some, though, use the scientists as protagonists and give a much more sympathetic account of their endeavours and ambitions. *Star Dust* (1925) by E. Charles Vivian is one novel of this kind, but the best of them is *The Peacemaker* (1934) by C.S. Forester, a heavily ironic tale in which an unhappy and alienated man makes tragic errors in trying to use a ray that prevents electrical apparatus from working to force Britain to disarm. He is eventually torn to pieces by a mob. More than any of the other stories cited, Forester's brings out the idea of a world so perverse that it *will* not be saved, and will instead cling dogmatically to its self-destructive tendencies.

The idea that the mass of men is stubbornly and perversely devoted to its cruel follies was very common in the period, but as we have noted in reference to Bertrand Russell's reply to J.B.S. Haldane's *Daedalus*, it could lead to sharply different attitudes to the advancement of science. The majority opinion was that we ought to be anxious about new discoveries because their destructive potential would be misused, but scientists often saw the situation from an opposed point of view. Some saw the stubborn perversity of men stifling the very inventiveness that might lead them to a better life. The best example of this argument in scientific romance is to be found in *Sugar in the Air* (1937) by E.C. Large (who was a plant pathologist by profession).

Sugar in the Air is the story of a technique of artificial photosynthesis, which allows carbohydrates to be produced cheaply and easily from the carbon dioxide-rich waste gases expelled from factory chimneys. The scientist who makes this practicable (though he builds on theoretical work and techniques developed by others) sees the process as one vital step on the way to solving the world's food problems for ever, but the directors of the company for which he works manage to make an utter mess of things. First they fail to make money marketing the saleable product which results from the early experimental work (an artificial animal feed), and in consequence they will not provide funds for the development of further applications. In the end, the process is taken over by another company, who are prepared to use it to produce animal feed but are completely uninterested in the scientist and the possibility of further developments. He ends up unemployed and disillusioned, and the world goes serenely on.

This is virtually the only scientific romance written between the wars which gives a convincing picture of the social context of scientific research. It is, in consequence, virtually the only one with sufficient sociological acumen to illustrate why it is that new discoveries in science actually do not bring about overnight transformations of the social world. Interestingly, Large followed it by a broadly satirical sequel in which the scientist hero turns his hand to the writing of scientific romance in order to make ends meet. In *this* novel, *Asleep in the Afternoon* (1938), the story which the hero writes is an account of how an apparently trivial new invention does bring about a sweeping change in society, after the fashion of John Gloag's Voe. As with *The New Pleasure*, the ironic amiability of *Asleep in the Afternoon*'s novel-within-a-novel, in which society becomes healthier because its members acquire the means to sleep more restfully, is as much a testament to Frustration as the author's more earnest work.

Apart from surreal satires like *The Wild Goose Chase* and *Over the Mountain*, or ironic fables like *The New Pleasure* and *Asleep in the Afternoon*, there is not a great deal of comedy in scientific romances written between the wars. Despite the general erosion of the more exuberant kinds of playfulness, though, there was one writer who set out to exploit the comic potential of scientific romance's vocabulary of ideas. This was J. Storer Clouston, a Scottish author of humorous novels and spy stories. His first novel in this vein was *Two's Two* (1916), in which a scientist manages to divide himself into his better and worst halves (who naturally disapprove of one another very strongly). Later he wrote *Button Brains* (1933) and *The Chemical Baby* (1934) for Herbert Jenkins, a publisher who produced a great many comic novels, including several fantasies. The former is one of the very few British speculative stories about robots, and features all the mistaken-identity jokes which have since become clichés. It is noticeable, though, that in two novels which he later wrote for another publisher Clouston took a much more sober view of things in extrapolating from speculative premisses. Although he did not entirely forsake his lightness of touch and his sense of humour, *Not Since Genesis* (1938) turns a slightly jaundiced eye on the events which precede an anticipated meteor strike in Europe. (A similarly sardonic contribution to the catastrophe-anticipation sub-genre had been offered earlier by Hugh Kingsmill in 'The End of the World', 1924.) *The Man in Steel* (1939), which is perhaps Clouston's best novel, is a bitter-sweet story about a Scottish clergyman who travels into the remote past, bringing his Presbyterian morality into contrast with the more liberal and more violent morality of the Norsemen., There is an odd echo here of *Two's Two*, where the 'worst half' of the divided scientist is treated far more sympathetically than his dour and intolerant 'better half'; here there is subtle but not unqualified support for the virtues of paganism. Even a humorist like Clouston, therefore, was touched by the imaginative climate of the day, and we can see even in his scientific romance the legacy of the Age of Frustration.

The Transcendent Tomorrow

The major writers of the scientific romance active between the wars produced numerous images of the future in which *Homo sapiens* is replaced by a nobler species. Usually these higher beings are descendants of contemporary men: the new race promised at the end of *The Shape of Things to Come*; Beresford's inhabitants of Oion; Stapledon's Last Men. Sometimes, they are descendants of other creatures, who have overtaken our doomed species in developing a better kind of sentience: Fowler Wright's Amphibians; Gloag's cats. Most of these species look back on our own with contempt, sometimes mingled with disgust and sometimes with tolerant amusement. This is really the function of such beings – they provide new viewpoints from which man can be seen and weighed in the balance. These observers are not necessarily perfect themselves, nor is their appraisal invariably objective, but it is always taken for granted that what they have to tell us is worth listening to. The authors of such fantasies stand four-square with Robert Burns and the sentiment expressed in his poem 'To a Louse':

> O wad some Pow'r the giftie gie us
> To see oursels as others see us!
> It wad frae mony a blunder free us,
> And foolish notion.

Some of the most memorable scientific romances of the twenties and thirties are those which attempt to dislodge 'foolish notions' by means of this kind of imaginative enterprise. Although the dominant view of the time was that the failure of *Homo sapiens* was manifest, there were some writers prepared to take arms on behalf of the species and defend us against these supposedly higher beings. There was, in consequence, something of a debate conducted through the medium of these works.

One of the most influential images of the future evolution of man to be produced in the post-war years is to be found in George Bernard Shaw's play *Back to Methuselah* (1921). Shaw had once, for a brief period, been allied with H.G. Wells when the latter joined the Fabian Society. *Back to Methuselah*, however, was written partly as an explicit rejection of that other faith which confused and almost confounded Wells's socialist ideals: Darwinism. The published version of the play (which is designed to be read rather than performed) is prefaced by a long essay on 'The Infidel Half-Century' which attempts to dismiss the Darwinian theory of evolution as a fad whose day is done. Like so many other intellectuals who found it difficult to believe in the role played by chance mutation in Darwin's theory (Samuel Butler, Hilaire Belloc and Arthur Koestler provide other examples) Shaw became an apologist for a neo-Lamarckian doctrine which would make it possible for men, by the power of the will, to acquire characteristics which they then might pass on, in some small measure, to their descendants. Like so many other writers of scientific romance Shaw wanted to create a new religion appropriate to modern times, and he chose Creative Evolution. His play is an attempt to provide a mythology – or at least a parable – for this new religion.

The new mythos begins, like the old, in the Garden of Eden, where Adam has discovered a terrible dilemma. The terror of immortality has given him the will to die, but he has found himself afraid of death too. In searching for a solution to this problem Eve consults the serpent, who points out that death can be counterbalanced by birth, and that the cycle of birth and death improves on immortality by permitting change and renewal. Change and renewal are not particularly attractive to the conservative Adam, but Eve goes ahead anyhow and conceives Cain. Cain *is* in favour of change and renewal, but his methods are violent; he becomes the parent of warfare. Cain's destructive verve and Adam's dogged materialism become the existential brackets confining the human condition. The rest of the play offers an account of various phases in the transcendence of that condition.

In the later acts of the play the curse of Cain is set aside as men take on the burdensome responsibility of longevity, reorganise their politics, and adopt a new moral philosophy. In the final section, set in 31,920 AD and titled 'As Far as Thought Can Reach', a new Golden Age has arrived, but its oviparous inhabitants are still wondering what it was all *for*. The answer is provided by the prime mover of the story – not God but Lilith, the hermaphroditic being which first divided itself to become Adam and Eve. Having abandoned the burden of Cain, man must now set aside the burden which Adam accepted, and must acknowledge the duty of eternal life as spiritual beings of pure intelligence.

Although very few other writers have attempted to follow Shaw in providing parables for the religion of Creative Evolution it is not too difficult to find echoes of his scheme of human destiny. The idea that future men would first evolve better conscious control over the body, and might eventually free their minds from the restraints of the flesh entirely, is frequently found in British and American speculative fiction. Not everyone, however, had the same attitude to the flesh – its frailties as well as its pleasures – as the ascetic Shaw, and this kind of transcendence by stages was not universally appealing.

A very different evaluation of the human condition is to be found in *The Clockwork Man* (1932) by E.V. Odle, one of the most thoughtful scientific romances of the period. Odle was acquainted with John Beresford, who was apparently instrumental in helping him place his first novel, *The History of Alfred Rudd* (1922), and *The Clockwork Man* may well have been inspired by *The Hampdenshire Wonder*. Both of Odle's novels are bitter-sweet reactions against what he supposed to be the 'rationalist' view of man and his prospects. In the earlier novel this view is attributed to Alfred's father, who comments on the times as follows:

> Everybody's a failure nowadays. Commercial success is only a substitute for the loss of everything that made life worth living a hundred years ago. What we call modern civilisation is simply colossal bungledom, and paying for the mistakes of our ancestors. We're all degenerate and broken down, played out. What we think is progress is nothing but the slough of reaction, the inevitable consequence of sin and folly, and loss of faith.[6]

The clockwork man of the second novel is an accidental visitor from the far future who seems to embody this failure in the most striking possible way. The ordinary faculties of body and brain have been augmented by a mechanism – a 'clock' which regulates his thought and his metabolism, controlling his dreams and supplementing his senses to such an extraordinary extent that he inhabits a multidimensional universe in which there are neither places nor moments, but where all time and space is simultaneously accessible. The malfunctioning of this device has cast the clockwork man back into a world beyond his comprehension. Here, his disruptive appearance brings him into contact with three people who adopt very different attitudes to him.

Gregg, the imaginative captain of the village cricket team in Great Wymering (where the clockwork man appears), is inspired by the idea of future men so wonderfully powerful that they have conquered space-time in this remarkable fashion:

> The clock, perhaps, was the index of a new and enlarged order of things. Man had altered the very shape of the universe in order to be able to pursue his aims without frustration . . . It was a logical step forward in the path of material progress.
>
> This was Gregg's dimly conceived theory about the mystery, although, of course, he read into the interpretation a good deal of his own speculations. His imagination seized upon the clock as the possible symbol of a new counterpoint in human affairs. In his mind he saw man growing through the ages, until at last, by the aid of this mechanism, he was able to roll back the skies and reveal the vast other worlds that lay beyond, the unthinkable mysteries that lurked between the stars, all that had been sealed up by the limited brain of man since creation.[7]

Dr Allingham, the village's general practitioner, is horrified to discover that the visitor is half-machine, and argues bitterly with Gregg about the implications of this. Their debate, though, is ironically resolved when the doctor, trying to help his unconventional patient, finds a plate carrying instructions for the adjustment *and use* of the clockwork man – instructions which clearly suppose a user relative to whom the visitor is only a pet or a puppet. But the story does not end with the deflation of Gregg, for the clockwork man, after his adjustment, returns briefly from his incomprehensible world beyond time to explain himself. Significantly, it is not to Allingham that he reveals his own view of things, but to Arthur Withers, a young bank clerk with no intellectual pretensions, whose contentment with his lot in life is secured by the fact of his being in love.

To Withers the clockwork man explains that he is indeed human, modified into his present condition by 'the makers' who 'came after the last wars' and fitted men with clocks so that they would have the freedom of the multidimensional manifold and would no longer need to fight. People accepted the clock because it solved all their problems (though the amputated sex organs of the clockwork man testify to the nature of this solution). The makers, by contrast, are 'real' and need no such artificial solutions. They live in the real world – which, despite their miraculous perceptions, remains impenetrable to clock-work men. The clockwork man knows that acceptance of the clock represented a retreat from life, and that his security from death and danger is a kind of sterility. His one poignant hope is that one day the makers might perfect the clock and make his kind more like them – but this hope is of necessity illusory. The clockwork man, who now seems a sad creature, unable to love, laugh or cry save as a symptom of breakdown, reveals that he has told all this to Withers because as the youth sits with his girl sleeping in his arms there is something in his eyes which is reminiscent of the makers.

Early in the story, when Gregg and Allingham have their first debate about the clockwork man, Allingham rejects Gregg's thesis by describing it as a myth. 'Even if he is a myth,' retorts Gregg, 'he is still worth investigating.' And so he is. Odle's clockwork man is perhaps the most peculiar of all the alien visitors who come into our world in order to show it to us from a new perspective, and he is worth attending to. The moral of the story is presented a little obliquely, with a scrupulously polite lack of stridency, but this is still one of the most eloquent pleas for the rejection of the 'rational' future and the conservation of the humanity of man. Of the many works of scientific romance that have fallen into utter obscurity, this is perhaps the one which most deserves rescue.

Another fearful vision of what man might become if the present historical trend were to be extrapolated into the distant future is provided by another of the most striking scientific romances of the twenties: Guy Dent's *Emperor of the If* (1926). The 'emperor of the if' is a vain and aggressive scientist, Greyne, who has developed a machine that can alter the phenomenal world in accordance with hypothetical premisses. He first uses this to conduct an experiment in social Darwinism, restoring the world's ecology to the state it would have been in had the last Ice Age never intervened. As his machine slowly triumphs over the 'inertia of custom' various prehistoric fauna and flora invade and conquer the civilised earth, demonstrating the fragility of human dominion. The climax of this section is Greyne's confrontation with the 'men' who evolved in this virile world – camouflaged savages who live in perpetual fear of predators, and who have accomplished nothing. Chastened by this experience, Greyne produces (on a limited scale) the world as it might be millions of years hence if human nature undergoes no fundamental change.

In the twilight zone of an earth which always turns the same face to the sun Greyne and his companion (the narrator) discover a race of dwarfish men kept barely alive by great self-replicating machines which dominate the world and fight endless wars. The usefulness of the humans in serving these machines appears to be almost at an end, and men may soon be wiped out by the murderous carelessness of their mechanical masters. Greyne obtains an account of existence in this world from one of the dwarfs, and draws from this the conclusion that civilisation has been aborted because his own contemporaries were, in the final analysis, unfit to be anything more than slaves to their machines. This moral lesson is emphasised by a vision of the tired and tormented Christ carrying his cross which appears in the sky, and from which the man of the future flees in terror. As it fades away, though, the narrator glimpses a faint light far away in the night-side of the world, and fancies that he hears plaintive music. Because of this, he can carry back to his own world a fragile desire and expectation that, after all, there *might* be hope for future adaptation.

Emperor of the If reflects a much deeper pessimism than *Back to Methuselah* or *The Clockwork Man* regarding the merits of contemporary man, and it approaches the scathing judgments of Fowler Wright and J. Leslie Mitchell, though retaining more conventional views on redemption. Dent shares with Odle, though, a fierce reaction against the 'rational' or 'scientific' view of progress as regulation and mechanisation of the body and the social world. The final dialogue between Greyne and the dwarf concludes when Greyne observes that the fleeing creature seems to have freedom enough. The dwarf's Parthian shot in reply is that 'we're so blasted free that freedom is an intolerable oppression on us.'[8] This emphasises that the opposition to regulation and mechanisation here is not a libertarian one. The clockwork man, after all, had been mechanised in order to be 'freed' from the demands of desire and impulse. This is a kind of conservative opposition, which asks that we should adapt to the future by resisting the loss of that which is in us that is good, and by trying to build on *that* rather than on our scientific and technical competence.

There are other novels which take a sceptical view of 'supermen' of various kinds, and concentrate on the perils of superhumanity. Muriel Jaeger's second novel, *The Man with Six Senses* (1927), is as sceptical about superhumanity as *The Question Mark* was about Utopia. In this early novel of extrasensory perception the man gifted with a new power of perception finds himself frustratingly unable to take advantage of his power, and ultimately suffers severe debilitation because of the demands on his brain made by the extraordinary flow of information. A later, more modest, superman story by Jaeger, *Hermes Speaks* (1933), describes the exploitation of a precociously intelligent child sadly out of place in our world (though not as desperate in this predicament as the Hampdenshire Wonder or Odd John).

A profound ambivalence with respect to the theme of evolving superhumanity can be found in the work of John Hargrave, who became an enthusiastic supporter of the Social Credit Party, which tried to carry an unorthodox economic theory into the political arena in the twenties. His novel of ideas *Harbottle* (1924) is subtitled 'A Modern Pilgrim's Progress from This World to That Which is to Come', although its only fantastic content is a brief visionary sequence near the end. The book is a chronicle of post-war disillusionment – a detailed exploration of

Frustration. It was quickly followed, though, by *Young Winkle*, a novel about the unorthodox education of a young ragamuffin who is gradually inducted into a secret society who are planning the salvation of the world – a more esoteric version of Wells's Open Conspiracy of enlightened intellectuals. Here, too, there is a little rhapsodic rhetoric about a finer world to come, but its hero, even after his awakening to mature responsibility, is not really convincing as an embryo Utopian. When Hargrave did eventually describe a superhuman being in *The Imitation Man* (1931) he did so with very heavy irony, and in contrasting the miraculous homunculus with ordinary men and women he had no difficulty in finding follies on either side. In the end, the amazingly clever (and amazingly sexy) imitation man is dispatched by a delicate *deus ex machina* which is not at all out of keeping with the spirit of the work.

The fact that these stories are sceptical about the superiority of supposed overmen does not signify that they have any particular confidence in the merits of *Homo sapiens*. When they mount their defence of contemporary man against those who might one day replace him they usually do so in much the same spirit that John Beresford's squire showed in *The Hampdenshire Wonder*; they suggest that man's imperfections are a sign of immaturity and may be forgiven in consequence. A more sentimental vein of argument suggests that the human power of love, even if it is 'primitive' (which not all authors are willing to concede), is something to be treasured; it is our best feature, though we are too rarely successful in showing it off. Apologists who seek to defend the human against the superhuman have always taken a similar line, and in most eras they have had a reasonably comfortable time of it – even such apparently obvious improvements as immortality have had a very bad press in fiction since the days of the Gothic novel. The 1930s stands out as the one period in which the defenders of ordinary man have had a very hard time indeed, and it is the one period to have produced wildly enthusiastic accounts of that hypothetical era to come when we and our kind would be swept into the dustbin of history where we belong, so that others more deserving of existence might take our place. The most striking statement to this effect is to be found at the end of *This Was Ivor Trent* (1935) by Claude Houghton, a cryptic story in which the odd behaviour of a writer is finally explained by the fact that he has seen the shape of things to come:

And then I turned and saw – You!

Your figure was shrouded, but your face was fully revealed. It was the countenance of a new order of Being. I knew that a man from the Future stood before me.

Terror overwhelmed me – then. But I do not fear you – now.

I stretch out my arms and invoke you:-

Come!

I do not know whether you stand on the threshold, or whether unnumbered ages separate us from you. I only know that you *must* be: that you are the spiritual consciousness made flesh: that you are the risen man and that we are the dead men. Yet, in us, is the possibility of you.

We are the Old – the dying – Consciousness. You are the New – the living – Consciousness. We have violated earth. You will redeem it. We descend the darkening valley of knowledge. You stand on the uplands of wisdom. We are an end. You are a beginning.

If you are a dream, all else is a nightmare. But I have seen God's signature across your forehead.

Come!

More and more fiercely we deny our need of you. We say you are a fantasy, a lie, an illusion. We madden ourselves with sensation; drug ourselves with work, pleasure, speed; herd in the vast sepulchres of our cities; blind our eyes; deaden our ears; cling to our creed of comfort (Comfort! the last of the creeds!); sink day by day in deeper servitude to our inventions – hoping to numb the knowledge of our emptiness; striving to ease the ache of separation; trying to evade your challenge; seeking to deny our destiny.

Come!

The martyred earth waits for you. Daily, our darkness deepens. Secretly, all are afraid. None knows what to do. To underpin, to patch up, to whitewash sepulchres – these are the substitutes for action. To shout, to boast, to nickname bankruptcy. Prosperity – this is the substitute for leadership. We have glorified ourselves, magnified ourselves, made gods of ourselves. We have served Hate, Greed, Lust. And now darkness deepens around us. And we are afraid.

Come!

Lacking you, there is no solution to any one of our problems. Possessing you, no problems exist. If it be madness to believe in you, the sanity which denies you is a greater madness.

But we who have lived on substitutes; we who have plumbed the abyss of ourselves; we who have glimpsed the magnitude of man's misery – we do not deny you.

From the midnight of madness we stretch out our arms to you. *Come!*[9]

269

This is certainly an extreme reaction, but it is one which was reached by several writers of the day. Even Houghton's quasi-hysterical style is not unique, in that something very like it occurs in some of Olaf Stapledon's later works, and his sentiments echo statements already made in a cooler tone by Fowler Wright and J. Leslie Mitchell.

A more cynical view of the same prospectus for the future is to be found in Andrew Marvell's *Minimum Man; or, Time to be Gone* (1938), which rejects the conclusion of *The Hampdenshire Wonder* and *Odd John* that supermen emerging in our midst would be forced into extinction because of the threat to our self-esteem which they pose. In Marvell's novel a race of tiny supermen is protected by the hero, and later allowed to acquire prestige and power in return for their help in overthrowing a Fascist government. The supermen here are conventional enough except for their small size – they are highly intelligent, mature very rapidly, and have complete control over their emotions, at least in the sexual sphere – and at first the hero is frightened and repelled by them. In time, though, he is won completely to their cause:

> Minimum Man had captured my imagination. Almost in despite of myself I had been impressed by the power which lay in them. Fifteen years of my life had been spent in recording the deeds and utterances of my fellow men, and it had turned me sick. I was not cynical by nature. Doubt had been forced upon me by the universal inanity. My nose had been held down to the mess, and my eyes had been riveted to the futility for fifteen years. It is a long time. Something about Minimum Man had recaptured for me the simplicities and ardours of my pre-reporting days, when my world was a world of brave men and brave women intent upon adventure. I was one of those young people suckled on Wellsian history, and brutally disenchanted by the shape of things as they are.[10]

The original title of this book appears to have been *Time to be Gone* – that is the title that appears at the top of every page in the text – and the slightly disguised argument of the plot is indeed that it is time for our kind to be gone, to give way to a new race whose thoughts are, as the last line of the story assures us, so far removed from ours that we can never hope to 'share or fathom' them. Marvell went on to write another scientific romance, *Three Men Make a World* (1939), in which civilisation is destroyed following the release of an artificial bacterium which devours petroleum products. The three men of the title let loose this scourge deliberately, partly to stop the new world war, but Marvell refuses to see the death of the machine as a kind of salvation. In fact, people are not altered at all, and that is represented as a tragedy.

Like other supermen, Marvell's Minimum Men deliver a fairly elaborate commentary on the limitations and inadequacies of *Homo sapiens*. But it was not only supermen who were recruited to this particular rhetorical task. As we have seen, writers of scientific romance in this period were drawn to look even further afield in search of hypothetical observers who could give us an account of ourselves more clear sighted than we were capable of providing. H.G. Wells introduced an enigmatic alien being in *The Camford Visitation* and Olaf Stapledon employed an intelligent dog in *Sirius*. Another writer who went in search of such imaginary viewpoints in order to provide an appraisal of the virtues and vices of contemporary man was Eden Phillpotts, a prolific writer in several genres. In the twenties Phillpotts produced a series of fantasies drawing heavily upon Greek mythology, in which the ancient gods become unorthodox commentators on our follies. Some of these stories are philosophical commentaries almost devoid of plot, like *The Miniature* (1926), in which the gods watch over the intellectual evolution of man, paying particular attention to the psychological utility of religion, until history reaches its end in a nuclear holocaust. Later, Phillpotts began drawing ideas from the vocabulary of scientific romance as well as mythological fantasy. *The Apes* (1929) is an evolutionary allegory and *The Owl of Athene* (1936) is a peculiar hybrid work in which a divine council tests twentieth-century man by arranging an invasion of the land by gigantic crabs.

Phillpotts followed *The Owl of Athene* in 1938 by *Saurus*, his first 'pure' scientific romance. In this novel earth is visited by a reptilian alien delivered as an egg. The objectivity of this observer of human affairs is guaranteed by his complete lack of emotion, but in spite of his great intelligence he does not immediately assume that he is of a 'superior' kind (which most supermen inevitably do). His is perhaps the most careful and level-headed of all the judgments delivered by hypothetical characters in this period, because he strives more strenuously than any other judge to be fair. He is frequently scathing, but occasionally generous. Despite his lack of emotion he has a well-developed sense of morality, and much of his discourse is devoted to showing how the passions of men draw them so frequently into evil. He sees human history as a war between enlightened rationalism and destructive impulses, and thinks that the natural gregariousness of men (which should be reflected in goodwill towards and respect for others) has somehow been subverted by an atavistic selfishness that ought to be eradicated. The sentimental paternalism of the commentary reflects Phillpotts's own political conservatism – he was as far to the right of the ideological spectrum as Stapledon was to the left – but there is frequently a surprising similarity between *Saurus* and *Sirius*. The two eponymous characters have very different ideas of decorum, and they express themselves in different styles, but they agree about fundamentals like the lack of sociability and charity manifested in the life of man. This agreement is surely testimony to the way in which the period generated its own particular pattern of attitudes in Britain, and encouraged the exploitation of certain kinds of imaginative devices in the speculative exploration of its problems.

The imaginative power of scientific romance is, of course, insufficient really to give us the gift of seeing ourselves as others might see us. Nor can it show us how *Homo sapiens* will one day be superseded by some other species whose way of life might be reckoned a transcendence of our own. In all the stories described in this sub-chapter we are being observed only by ourselves, albeit with the aid of the distorting mirror of the imagination. These supermen and aliens report so harshly on our progress because in the period which produced them, many people in Britain had come to think very harshly of themselves. Their victory in the Great War tasted oddly like defeat, and that taste became more bitter as a second great war – promising to be even more destructive than the first – became ever more likely. The history of scientific romance between the wars is testimony to a dramatic loss of morale which spread like an epidemic through the British intelligentsia. As might be expected of such a flexible medium of expression, it dramatised that loss in many different ways, but underlying its multiplicity there is a decisive shift in its fundamental attitude to the future. It was not simply that the image of the future contained within scientific romance grew more pessimistic, but that writers came to take it for granted that the future would not be and could not be a simple 'linear' extrapolation of the present, but must involve some kind of essential qualitative change in the human condition. This is why it makes sense to speak of 'the transcendent tomorrow' in attempting to summarise and isolate the patterns and trends within the genre.

PART THREE
The Twilight of Scientific Romance

8

AFTER THE HOLOCAUST

Swan Songs and Epilogues

THREE OF THE major writers who came to prominence in the field of scientific romance between the wars produced significant new works of this kind after 1945, though all three were nearing the end of their careers. Olaf Stapledon was fifty-nine in 1945, Neil Bell was fifty-eight and S. Fowler Wright seventy-one. In each case the new work was an extension of arguments and themes introduced in much earlier books.

Olaf Stapledon's novella *The Flames* (1947) is yet another story in which an observer belonging to a 'higher species' offers a new viewpoint for looking at the prospect facing mankind. The higher species here is an alien race of living flames which evolved in the solar atmosphere when the sun was still young. When the planets were formed many such beings were expelled from the sun along with them, gradually to be imprisoned by cold. Now the flames seek release from their suspended animation, with the aid of man. In the fires lit by men the flames can once again become active, and the great firestorms caused by bombing raids in the recent world war have given many of them a taste of freedom. The narrator of the story is asked to become an ambassador, requesting his fellow men to use their new-found control of atomic fire to create enclaves on the earth's surface where flames can make their home.

Because of their gaseous nature flames can mingle and merge with one another, and are much less individualistic than men. Their own highly developed sense of community is something they hope to share with man, as payment for his helping them to return to active life:

'We have a vision,' he said, 'of this planet as a true symbiotic organism, supported equally by your kind and my kind, united in mutual need and mutual cherishing. What a glorious world-community we shall together form! United in the spirit, we shall also be so diverse in our racial idiosyncrasies that each partner will be thoroughly remoulded and revitalised by intercourse with the other . . . you will no longer be the frustrated, bewildered, embittered, vindictive mental cripples that most of you now are . . . with us you can become what, at your best, you are always half-heartedly wishing to be; true vessels of the spirit . . . Without our help, you are doomed to self-destruction, or at best to the life of a beetle vainly struggling to climb out of a basin . . . '[1]

The narrator, though, is suspicious of the flame. He doubts whether the strange being is to be trusted, and his doubt is intensified when the flame tells him that another course of action is open to the imprisoned aliens. They have some measure of telepathic influence over men, and now that men have atomic weapons it will be easy to breed such hatred and mistrust between human nations that an atomic holocaust will become inevitable, annihilating mankind but releasing such a flood of energy that the world would – for a while – provide a new Eden for such beings as they. The narrator responds to this threat with panic, dousing the fire in his grate and banishing the voice of temptation. When he tries to warn the world of its danger he is promptly confined to an asylum, but while there he has a change of heart and comes to accept the benevolence of the flames. He has, however, no chance of persuading anyone else that he is anything but the victim of a peculiar hallucination.

To some extent *The Flames* is simply a dramatisation of an idea that Stapledon had previously laid out in *Darkness and the Light* – the idea that contemporary man had reached an important historical crossroads, facing alternate futures of dreadful darkness or glorious light. Now, though, there is a much clearer consciousness of how that choice might be made. Atomic power suddenly emerges as the instrument of deliverance or destruction. Used in one way, the story suggests, this new power may assist in forging the spirit of community which men so desperately need. Used in another, it will surely secure their annihilation. This was how the atom bomb affected the consciousness of a great many people following its spectacular debut on the stage of history in August 1945. British scientific romance had for many years been anxious about the possibility of a destruction of civilisation, and the advent of the atom bomb could only increase that anxiety by a small margin, but it did give the anxiety a much sharper focus.

The actual course of the Second World War contrasts oddly with the images of such a war contained in the scientific romances of the thirties. In respect of poison gas the Geneva Convention held up. There *was* heavy bombing of civilian populations, and the destructive power of airfleets was amply demonstrated by the firestorming of such cities as Berlin, Tokyo and Dresden, but the capacity of nations to withstand and defend themselves against *blitzkrieg* had been underestimated by the speculative writers. In the main, World War Two was far less destructive than had been feared (despite advanced weaponry, the battle casualties were generally less heavy than in the Great War). On the other hand, some of its horrors had been unanticipated. Even Fowler Wright, who suggested in *Four Days War* and *Megiddo's Ridge* that the new Germany would be capable of some chilling barbarities and violations of the civilised code of behaviour, never imagined anything remotely like Belsen and Dachau. And then, when it seemed that the worst was over, the war was ended by an unparalleled destructive flourish, which made it abundantly clear that although the world had (fortunately) survived World War Two, it was most unlikely to survive world war three. All the fears which had been partially eased returned in full flood.

The atom bomb looked rather different from viewpoints on either side of the Atlantic. In America there had never been the same level of anxiety about the possible destruction of civilisation by war, and that anxiety did not spring into being overnight – Americans, after all, could rest content for a while with the idea that they had the bomb and no one else did. *Their* national paranoia did not blossom until they found out that someone had betrayed their secret to the Russians, and it remained a nationalistic species of paranoia, culminating in the kind of hysterical fear of Communism that was articulated by Senator McCarthy. From British soil, things looked different. Although the atom bomb was in the hands of an ally, it was still in other hands, and there was a long-standing anxiety in the land whose flames only needed a little fanning to make them flare up to apocalyptic magnitude.

From the viewpoint of a man like Stapledon – a committed

socialist with a deep-seated loathing of American capitalism –
the revelation that America had the bomb was a fearful one,
made even more fearful when the Americans reacted so badly to
the discovery that their erstwhile allies had it too. Thus it was
that he achieved brief notoriety in the USA by attending the
Cultural and Scientific Conference for World Peace held at the
Waldorf-Astoria in New York City in March 1949. The conference was regarded by most Americans as a Communist propaganda exercise, and because Stapledon was the only British
delegate he became the target of some very fierce criticism (he
was thus isolated because the other Britons who had agreed to
attend, including the author Louis Golding and the scientist
J.D. Bernal, had all been refused visas by the State Department).
Such was the shock caused by Stapledon's attendance at this
conference that even American literary critics and science
fiction enthusiasts have found it difficult to forgive him – Sam
Moskowitz and Leslie Fiedler both complain bitterly of his
supposed foolishness, and Fiedler's horror colours many of the
scathing judgments he makes about Stapledon's fiction.
Neither critic seems able to comprehend that Stapledon's paramount interest was in the cause of peace, and that from his
point of view it was not so very unreasonable to see the
aggressive paranoia of Americans as a greater threat to peace
than the dogmas of 'the comrades'.

Stapledon's last novel, published posthumously, was *A Man
Divided* (1950), a curious story which begins as another attempt
to see the world as if from a superhuman viewpoint, but which
apparently becomes entangled with matters of idiosyncratic
personal concern. It is the story of a very ordinary man, a slave
to convention and a moderate success within the framework of
bourgeois expectations, who periodically 'wakes up' to become
an altogether different individual. This 'higher self' despises
everything that the lower stands for, appalled by the moral
cowardice and unimaginative blindness that characterise him.
This higher self has, inevitably, a Stapledonian political consciousness, and his greater powers of perception lead him to
grapple with all the metaphysical questions that tormented his
creator. The plot resembles *Sirius* rather than *Odd John*, though,
in focusing very closely on the protagonist's one intimate
relationship rather than his observations on the state of the
world. In his awakened state the divided man finds true love
and happiness with a woman who appears repulsive to his

unperceptive lower self, but the marriage is continually disrupted and strained by the re-emergence of that lower self. This 'dolt' gradually does accept the way of life chosen by his higher self, and by degrees comes to form his own intimate relationship with the wife forced on him by circumstance, but in everything he tries to do he is but a hollow echo of the other, and in the end he can no longer live with his sense of inadequacy. Although the higher self resists this suicidal urge for a time, he too has his own sense of inadequacy – a pessimistic feeling that whatever men might choose to do in search of salvation is 'fatally false', and that mankind is 'a damned species'.[2] Like Odd John, he eventually seems to consent to his own destruction.

Stapledon left unfinished one more work of eccentric philosophy, *The Opening of the Eyes*, which was eventually edited by his wife for publication in 1954. This rather confused work is addressed to a personal God in whom Stapledon, even at the end, could not quite believe. At one moment it declares the necessity of a commitment of faith; at another it accuses the hypothetical God of terrible crimes that can only instil fear and loathing; at yet another it bewails the pressure of 'spiritual lust'. It is useless to speculate as to how Stapledon would have resolved this tortured inner debate had he lived; the overwhelming probability is that he would not have resolved it, because no resolution was possible. His unconquerable scepticism would have prevented him from appending any answer to what was implicitly an unanswerable question.

There is a marked contrast between Stapledon and his contemporary Neil Bell. Bell was every bit as pessimistic as Stapledon regarding the failings of human nature, but he took atheism so much for granted that the issues which so obsessed Stapledon hardly touched him. On him, what Stapledon called 'spiritual lust' exerted no pressure at all. Of all the major writers of scientific romance he was the only one who not only believed that the 'salvation' of man was highly unlikely, but that its unlikelihood made it an issue not worthy of much discussion.

This off-handedness in respect of a matter treated much more reverently by his contemporaries shows up in one of the short scientific romances which he wrote during the war years, 'More than Flesh and Blood Could Stand', which is in his collection *Alpha and Omega* (1946). Here, as in *A Man Divided*, we find an awakened man with unusual powers of perception – a telepath

– but this luckless individual, after a period of childhood celebrity, finds himself a pariah in a spiteful and hostile world. He commits suicide before the world decides to do away with him, and observes in his sarcastic farewell message that 'Once again in its long history of blindness and stupidity the world has failed to accept and use for its benefit a great gift offered it in the person of a man.'[3]

One of the other two scientific romances in *Alpha and Omega*, 'The Crack in the Wall', is just as bitter in telling the story of a young man whose power of precognition is effectively useless because all it can tell him is that he is due to be killed in the war. And if 'The Root of All Evil' is less pessimistic it is no less ironic, describing how the war is ended by the wholesale distribution of fake currency – a tactic which leads inexorably to the collapse of the entire world economic system.

In his last full-length scientific romance Bell returned to the formula of several of his earlier works in that vein. *Life Comes to Seathorpe* (1946) duplicates the pattern of *Precious Porcelain* in presenting a series of puzzling incidents which are finally explained by a manuscript discovered following the death of its author. The idea for the story is taken from an extraordinary document written by one Andrew Crosse, who in the early part of the nineteenth century claimed to have produced artificial insects by administering an electric current to inorganic materials. In Bell's story a modern scientist, having supposedly discovered Crosse's secret, produces a series of remarkable giant insects and crustaceans. The insects tend to decay back into liquid form after a while, thus disappearing from the scenes of the strange events in which they are involved.

Bell's eccentric scientist is killed, like so many of his breed, before his plans come to fruition. Normality is restored – but for Bell as for Fowler Wright that can never really be reckoned a *happy* ending. The manuscript left behind by the scientist reveals that his real goal lay far beyond the creation of gargantuan invertebrates; it was the supersession of man that he was aiming at:

Man, *Homo sapiens*, as evolved by Nature, is, zoologically considered, a failure . . . his organism is so ill-adapted to its environment, his digestive, respiratory, excretory, and reproductive systems so ill-constructed, that millions of his species die at birth, more before reaching maturity, and few attain a bare century of years; while even this brief lifetime is rendered a torment by a succession of ailments and diseases which affect him, from the hideous struggles of parturition to the dreadful convulsions of death. And all through life his physical body is harassed, his emotions racked, his mentality debilitated, by the overriding demands of sex.

I proposed to change all that . . . Profiting by indifferent Nature's mistakes, I should create a being, *Homo splendidus*, who would be worthy of his destiny; that destiny which I foresaw not confined to this planet or system, but reaching out to the uttermost stars. Physically, *Homo splendidus* will be a giant . . . The head will be proportionately much larger and more magnificent than in *Homo sapiens*, and the brain incomparably greater and more complex . . . As the brain will be more complex, so the respiratory, excretory and digestive systems will be more simple . . . But it is in respect of reproductive processes that *Homo splendidus* will differ most widely from *Homo sapiens*. The sex life of man as evolved by Nature dooms him for ever to remain among the beasts. It is an obsession from adolescence until death. It tortures him, humiliates him, degrades him, nullifies the possibilities of his brain, saps his vitality, infests him with the grossest superstitions, and compels him to actions from which in recollection he recoils in disgust and repulsion. These things must pass away if man is to fulfil his destiny.[4]

These statements are, of course, credited to a character who is the villain of the book, in so far as it has a villain, and the reader is not expected to agree with them. On the other hand, there is an element of double bluff in Bell's presentation. He knew well enough that he would not find many readers to sympathise with this kind of creed, but his refusal to endorse it himself is subverted by his similar refusal to defend the *status quo*.

Bell continued to write until near his death in 1964, producing short stories in abundance as well as novels. He wrote a handful of short speculative stories, all trivial but all displaying the same kind of casual cynicism. In 'The Voice' (1951) radio broadcasts are subject to interruption by a sceptical disembodied voice rather like the one in Wells's *The Camford Visitation*, though here the voice succeeds in banishing a good deal of cant from the airwaves. In 'Good Heavens' (1958) an artificial manna is invented; civilisation crumbles when men realise that they need not work to earn the money to buy food, but in the end boredom triumphs and men abandon the manna in order to restore the old days. In 'Fall of an Empire' (1960) the discovery of a vast undersea lode of diamonds causes economic chaos. In the farcical 'Message to Mars' (1961) Martians find that human life has become extinct because of extreme eugenic policies; women disposed of men altogether in favour of sperm banks, and could not recover from the failure of the banks because the last man alive killed himself rather than mate with one of them. All of these stories are deliberately non-serious, but here too there is a double bluff in making an obvious joke out of the moral that the destruction of civilisation is a consummation devoutly to be wished.

Although Sydney Fowler Wright was thirteen years older than Bell he actually outlived him, dying in 1965. Not unnaturally though, he was far less active in the post-war years. His career received a temporary boost when he had a spell editing *Books for Today*, a trade journal published by the London booksellers Hatchards. He used the company behind the journal to reissue a number of his early works, and a new collection of short stories. Shortly afterwards, his early works began to be picked up for reissue in America under the science fiction label. He had stories in a number of hardcover anthologies, and the small specialist publishers which proliferated in the post-war years also took an interest. *The World Below* was reprinted and the stories from *The New Gods Lead* were combined with two other speculative stories to make up the collection *The Throne of Saturn* (1949), which was also issued in England. Thus encouraged, Fowler Wright began turning out new scientific romances aimed at the American science fiction market. Some three or four fantastic novels seem to have remained unsold, but only one novel of this period was actually published: *Spiders' War* (1954), the third in his series of novels of psychic time-travel.

The heroine of *Spiders' War* has married the persistent suitor who followed her in *Dream*, but marriage has not cured her restless spirit, and now she asks to be sent into the far future. Her obliging magician finds no difficulty in doing this, assuring her that past and future are 'all one'. In a striking opening scene she finds herself captured and about to be butchered for meat, but suggests to her captor that he would do better to kill and eat his nagging wife and take her to his bed instead. He agrees, and she takes her place by his side as he leads his desperate tribe (whose crops have failed disastrously) into new lands, fighting for survival against other humans and against a species of giant spider created long ago in an ill-judged biological experiment. As in *Dream* and *The Vengeance of Gwa* this struggle for existence is desperately hard, but for once the fight seems to be won and the ending suggests that the heroine will not return to her own world, having at last found one which suits her better.

Although the brutal opening scene is clearly calculated to offend the prejudices of most readers (Fowler Wright, as a non-meat-eater, often argued that there was less moral difference between using animals for food and using people than hypocritical meat-eaters pretend) the ethical argument which it introduces is a serious one. This is the nearest that Fowler Wright ever came to describing an ideal world inhabited by human beings. It is certainly no Utopia, but it fits fairly closely Fowler Wright's views about how life really ought to be lived. Like so many of his contemporaries, though, the author could not quite believe in his fellow men as fit creatures for an ideal world, and so these tribesmen are credited with telepathic powers, taking decisions by means of telepathic plebiscite. (There is no governmental structure in this Libertarian society, nor any bureaucracy or police force.)

Fowler Wright was quite willing to say straightforwardly what Neil Bell would say only in the apologetic guise of farce: that contemporary civilisation was a historical and spiritual dead end, and would be far better obliterated. Like Bell – but unlike Stapledon – he could not bring himself to consider seriously the possibility of any kind of salvation by transcendence, although there is a sense in which the men of the future in *Spiders' War* have 'awakened' from many of the follies that possessed them in their civilised days. It can hardly be said that Fowler Wright was a more extreme writer than Stapledon, but his rejection of the pretensions of twentieth-century man is no less emphatic for being stated coolly – a point made quite clearly by his last published short story, 'The Better Choice' (1955), which bluntly and briefly makes the point that the life of a cat seems preferable to the life of a wife in the human world.

Neither Bell nor Fowler Wright makes any mention of the atom bomb in their post-war scientific romances, and there is hardly anything in the content of their last works to suggest that they saw things any differently in the 1950s than they had in the 1930s. In a way, this only serves to emphasise how little their views stood in need of correction. For them, the events of the Second World War merely served to confirm what they had long believed. Their cynical views had merely been underlined by circumstance. It was those writers who, like Stapledon, had tried much harder to preserve or discover hope for the future progress of man who were moved to a greater sense of urgency by the disclosures of 1945. This can be seen, for example, in the last fantastic works produced by a writer who had been born four years earlier than H.G. Wells and had come to the writing of scientific romance unusually late in life: Eden Phillpotts.

The Fall of the House of Heron (1948) is a telling moral fantasy about an atomic scientist who commits murder in order to get his hands on the family fortune that will finance his research. He justifies his crime, after the fashion of so many Shielian anti-heroes, by arguing that he is serving the cause of human progress, and that one life means nothing when weighed against the benefits that his research will bring. This account can hardly help but seem hollow, though, when the most evident result of his researches is a great scar hacked out of the land by a nuclear explosion. Though he will not repent after being condemned to death, the epilogue of the book suggests that his attitude is a very dangerous one to be entertained in a world where such destructive powers exist. In the atomic era, it is suggested, science without conscience is a terrible threat.

This moral is repeated in *Address Unknown* (1949), in which Phillpotts deliberately modifies the plot of his pre-war scientific romance *Saurus*. Here two young scientists succeed in contacting a distant alien civilisation much more technologically advanced than ours. The alien super-scientist to whom they talk promises them the means to transform the world to its great advantage, and eventually volunteers to come to earth to help in the task, but an older and wiser man in whom the scientists confide is not at all convinced that this is a good idea.

Despite their cautionary themes, both *The Fall of the House of Heron* and *Address Unknown* conclude with passionate affirmations of faith in the ability of men to solve their own problems and make their own destiny by cementing a link between science and humanism that will allow them to use their knowledge benevolently. *Address Unknown* deliberately abandons the alien viewpoint; the point here is not to see ourselves as others might see us, but to see ourselves as we must resolve to be, when 'the age-long struggles to free mankind from his subconscious self' have at last been resolved and we are awakened to full consciousness:

But this we know: that righteousness travels an upward way

despite the chasms, tempests and high tides of evil that confound its progress among us. Our sense of rectitude persists and the venom poured against it must grow weaker and weaker as reason strengthens to cast out the old idols from our hearts and heads. Within ourselves lie the secrets of salvation: they are not the products of passing ideologies, egocentric philosophies, or the formulae of mutable faiths; nor does need exist to seek awakening by alien beings from any extra-galactic nebula.

Civil war yet rages between the conscious and the subconscious, but ultimate victory is sure though it demands mighty efforts still calling to be made and stern surrender to be suffered. In humanism lies our strength, in an international federation of brotherhood and sisterhood awaiting birth, and only to be born when war is forever banished, selfishness has been vanquished and self-consciousness comes into its own.[5]

In this passage Phillpotts speaks directly to the reader in a forthright manner that Stapledon, Bell and Fowler Wright never duplicated, always preferring to conceal themselves within narrative voices and exemplary characters with whom they never completely identify themselves. But even Phillpotts seems here to have been carried away by the flow of his rhetoric, and he was not immune from the doubts which haunted other writers of scientific romance. In his book of reminiscences *From the Angle of 88* (1951) he repeats the argument quoted above, in different words, but the warning note sounded by the plots of the two novels is here appended to the conclusion:

That our first thought, after atomic fissure was accomplished, should have centred in its application to terrestrial self-destruction is enough in itself to show the abject norm of human mentality and the uses to which we still degrade our supreme endowment of reason; but one likes to believe that consciousness may have won a saner welcome on other planets and that the new astronomy will enlarge our cosmic sympathies, modify our egotism, abate our pretensions and inspire fresh efforts to find for human reasoning power that place in the sun so long denied it.[6]

All the works discussed in this sub-chapter might be seen as late afterthoughts added to *oeuvres* which had previously seemed complete. In each case the experience of the Second World War, and in particular its dramatic conclusion, probably provided part of the imaginative stimulus generating these works. There is a sense in which the explosion of the atom bomb not only marked the end of the war but added a full stop to the discourse which had been conducted through the medium of British scientific romance since 1930. The writers of scientific romance in that period had been dramatising issues and anxieties which, after Hiroshima, no longer needed to be drawn to the attention of the public. Hiroshima put those issues on the agenda of popular thought more economically than a hundred eloquent scientific romances. The writers who came back to the genre in order to issue these swan songs and epilogues were, in a way, merely acknowledging the propriety of their own earlier efforts.

It is not coincidence that the only two writers who warrant attention as major writers of scientific romance who came to prominence after 1938 belonged to the same generation as the writers who came to prominence before the war. They were not young men taking up the torch of the tradition, but middle-aged men who had been preoccupied with other work and had not tried their hand at scientific romance until later in life than was usual. The kind of work they produced is very closely connected to the kind of work discussed in this sub-chapter and but for the absence of earlier work to refer back to could easily have been included under the same heading. The *young* writers of speculative fiction who began to write after the beginning of World War Two were *not* confined by the tradition that was renewed in the 1930s, having been instituted in the 1890s, but took a major part of their inspiration from the American science fiction writers. The tradition of scientific romance had lost a good deal of its impetus simply because its concerns had been too pertinent. The arguments carried on within the genre became commonplace, deployable in a less sophisticated fashion at a less esoteric level.

C.S. Lewis

Clive Staples Lewis was born on 28 November 1898 in Belfast, the son of a solicitor. His mother died while he was still young, and he spent the greater part of his youth in private schools in England. His education was marred by some unfortunate circumstances. His first preparatory school, Wynyard in Hertfordshire, was in a state of rapid deterioration owing to the insanity of its head teacher, and Lewis was no less unhappy at Malvern College, where he was the victim of bullying. He hated the school system, was horrified by the homosexuality that was rife there, and begged his father to remove him. He was eventually sent as a private pupil to W.P. Kirkpatrick, who had once taught his father but had retired from full-time teaching. He benefited from this individual tuition, and thrived on the Socratic methods employed by Kirkpatrick, who was a ruthless rationalist and positivist. These views fitted in well at the time with Lewis's own – he had abandoned the Christian faith of his infancy to become an argumentative atheist with a particular passion for pagan literature and mythology.

Lewis won a scholarship to University College, Oxford, but was interrupted by conscription into the armed forces in the summer of 1917. By the time he saw action the war was almost over, but he was in time to be wounded (apparently by a British shell). Unlike many of his contemporaries he seems to have been relatively unaffected by his experiences in the trenches – which were less hellish, apparently, than Malvern. After the war he 'adopted' the mother of his fellow cadet, Paddy Moore, who had been killed, and took responsibility for her welfare until her death in 1951 – a relationship which, though not sexual itself, seems to have secluded him from relationships with younger women.

After returning to Oxford Lewis graduated in Classics, and then took a second degree in English Literature, clinging on to the university as best he could until he was given a fellowship by Magdalen College in 1925. He settled down to his academic career, perfectly content with his role as an unorthodox intellectual. A year later he met the new Professor of Anglo-Saxon, the equally unorthodox J.R.R. Tolkien, and formed a firm friendship with him.

Lewis's first publication had been a book of wartime poems, *Spirits in Bondage* (1918), which exhibited a calculated pessimism and expressed resentment of a cruel (hypothetical) God. (The book makes an interesting comparison with Olaf Stapledon's *Latter-Day Psalms*, and the subsequent careers of the two men show many interesting similarities and significant contrasts.) In 1925 he published a long narrative poem, *Dymer*, which showed the strong influence on his imagination of ancient European mythology. He shared this interest with Tolkien, who began showing him poems, stories and other fragments dealing with the mythology of his private world, Middle Earth, in 1929. The friendship of the two men became very important to the development of their work in this vein.

Lewis began to drift back from atheism in the 1920s, first embracing a generalised religious viewpoint and an interest in 'the Spirit' very similar to that developed by Olaf Stapledon. He accepted what he called 'joy' as a special dimension of experience much as Stapledon accepted 'ecstasy'. Lewis, however, was able to quell his doubts much more easily than Stapledon. Influenced by arguments deployed by such ingenious apologists as Chesterton, and by Tolkien (who was a devout Catholic), Lewis had accepted the existence of God by 1929. At that stage he still considered Christianity to be a myth, but seized upon a rather peculiar argument enabling him to commit his faith to Christ because of, rather than in spite of, the mythical nature of the gospels. This reasoning came partly from a book by his friend Owen Barfield, *Poetic Diction* (1928), which argued that myths should not be regarded merely as stories, but were central to the development of language and culture by virtue of the fact that primitive man had made no distinctions between the literal and the metaphorical. To this case Tolkien added the observation that myths were not lies, because imaginative constructs no less than physical things must have originated with God and must reflect something of eternal truth. Lewis, always passionately fond of mythology, was delighted to accept the essential truth of the Christ-myth and the more oblique truthfulness of all others. It is not at all surprising, given that this was how he recovered his religious faith, that he became interested in producing his own 'mythopoeic' stories – humble essays in myth-creation that were very similar in kind to, but very different in ideology from, Stapledon's. His first prose fiction, in fact, was an account in allegorical form of his regression to the lost Protestant faith of his infancy, *The Pilgrim's Regress: an Allegorical Apology for Christianity, Reason and Romanticism* (1933).

Lewis's Christianity influenced and controlled his attitude to literature as critic and writer. Authors, in his view, might reflect eternal Beauty and Wisdom, but they were not the real creators. In this he agreed with Tolkien (whose similar ideas are set out in his classic essay 'On Fairy Tales', first delivered as a lecture in 1939), and disagreed strongly with the major contemporary schools of English criticism, most notably the *Scrutiny* group led by F.R. Leavis. Lewis had always disliked T.S. Eliot and other 'moderns', whose efforts were dismissed with casual contempt in *The Pilgrim's Regress*, and he remained doggedly unfashionable in his literary allegiances, unashamedly fond of the fantasies of George Macdonald and the metaphysical extravaganzas of David Lindsay. In a later period he was to join another calculated heretic, Kingsley Amis, in declaring boldly that he found American science fiction much more lively and interesting than the more pretentious kinds of 'literary' fiction.

In 1937, Lewis and Tolkien decided, in following through these views, to write their own mythopoeic stories in the guise of popular thrillers. (Tolkien had already begun to show the way in *The Hobbit*, and Lewis was probably inspired too by the novels of Charles Williams, whom he had not yet met.) Tolkien never finished his time-travel/Middle Earth story, but Lewis did complete *Out of the Silent Planet* (1938). This novel was partly a homage to Wells, but it was partly also a bitter attack on the founding father of scientific romance. Lewis admired the imaginative power and reach of his model, but from his point of view that imagination had been perverted because it distorted instead of reflecting eternal verities. For Lewis, in fact, there was something actually diabolical (in a perfectly literal sense) about Wells's ideology, and the content of his imaginative fictions.

In *Out of the Silent Planet* a placid academic is kidnapped and taken to Mars by a scientist, Weston, and his henchman, Devine. The kidnappers have been instructed to deliver him into the hands of a rather intimidating race, the Sorns, and assume that no good will come to him. Accepting this opinion, the hero, Ransom, escapes and becomes a refugee on Mars. He gradually realises, though, that this Mars bears no resemblance to the world of Wells's (and Weston's) imagination. Wells could only assume that other planets would be ruled, as he supposed ours to be, by the ruthless logic of natural selection. He made his Martians rapacious and cruel, ready to exterminate mankind in order to seize the earth. Lewis's Mars, by contrast, is another of God's creations, more nearly in the image that God intended. There are three races here, but they are not locked into a struggle for existence; rather they live in idealised symbiotic harmony. They co-exist with and are guided by non-material beings whose natural environment is the depths of space, the *eldila*, and the planet is ruled by one of this kind, the Oyarsa.

This Utopian Mars fits in well enough with the assumption
that the universe is the creation of a benevolent God, but Lewis
is then faced with the problem that confronted Stapledon when
he tried to believe something similar: what happens on Earth is
clearly very different from what might be expected when
reasoning from such an axiom. Lewis is forced to recruit an
argument first used by Marie Corelli in *A Romance of Two
Worlds:* Earth, far from being typical of the universe as a whole,
is the one place where God's benevolence is excluded, thanks to
the activities of an evil force (Satan in Christian mythology, 'the
bent Oyarsa' in the mythos of *Out of the Silent Planet*) and by
the weakness of men in succumbing to it. Our world thus
becomes a blot on the face of Creation, due to be erased as soon
as possible by an apocalyptic battle between the forces of good
and evil that will set things to rights.

It is sometimes alleged that *Out of the Silent Planet* is an
allegory after the fashion of *The Pilgrim's Regress*, in which the
hypothetical Creator, Maleldil, simply 'stands for' the Christian
God and the bent Oyarsa for the devil. This is not so. The
metaphysic of the novel is a purely hypothetical construct – an
essay in myth-creation – but Lewis is careful to imply the same
kind of fundamental reality that is implied by the 'true' mythology of Christianity. Thus, though it is pure fiction, it has a
certain essential truthfulness – from Lewis's point of view – that
is lacking in almost all scientific romance. It is for this reason
that Lewis's work occupies a unique and interesting position in
the tradition of scientific romance: it represents a calculated
attempt to 'correct' its mythology.

Weston, the villainous scientist, becomes Lewis's embodiment of all the ideologies which were in his view to be
deplored: social Darwinism and interplanetary imperialism in
particular. Though there are certainly Wellsian elements in
Weston's make-up, and echoes of J.B.S. Haldane can be dis-
cerned in his rhetoric, the idea that Lewis attacks most fiercely
is the idea of the human conquest of the universe – the notion
that man can and must 'plant his seed' on other worlds.
Although not absent from scientific romance, this is an idea
that was much more evident in American science fiction, and
Lewis's scathing mockery of Weston – especially in the confrontation scene where Ransom struggles to translate his
theories into terms that the Martian Oyarsa can understand –
should not be seen as a personal attack on any one individual,

but rather on certain aspects of both genres of speculative fiction.

After the publication of *Out of the Silent Planet* Lewis began work on another imaginative novel – a story of parallel worlds in which Ransom figures as a minor character. Here we are offered an image of a world where evil rules even more openly than on earth, in which the people of earth have *doppelgängers*. When a portal between the worlds is opened, two of these equivalent characters change places, so that an alien evil is released in Cambridge while an earthly academic becomes a disruptive force in the alien world. At the point when the action ought to be getting under way, though, the fragment of the story which survives gets side-tracked into a convoluted exercise in pseudo-Dunneian theory, by which the author tries to rationalise the parallel world and its history. Lewis appears to have become disenchanted with this, and abandoned the novel; it was published in 1977 as *The Dark Tower* in a collection of that title.

For the publisher Geoffrey Bles Lewis wrote a long essay, *The Problem of Pain* (1940), attacking the question that he had neatly evaded in *Out of the Silent Planet*. He followed this attempt to explain why a benevolent God permitted such suffering to go on in the world with a much lighter exercise in apologetics, *The Screwtape Letters* (1942), which used a neatly-inverted perspective to consider the subject of temptation. In a series of letters a worldly-wise demon advises his young and inexperienced protégé on the tactics of temptation. The book is very lively and humorous, and, although Lewis had no doubt about the reality of evil, its demonic characters come across as rather likeable con-men. The book was very successful, becoming a best-seller in America, and it made Lewis's name as a popular writer.

Lewis's exploration of the tactics of devilry continued, in a much more earnest and melodramatic vein, in the second volume of the Ransom trilogy, *Perelandra* (1943). Here Venus, a world of vast oceans and beautiful floating islands, becomes the scene of an attempt by the bent Oyarsa to subvert Maleldil's scheme in a second world. This alien Eden has its own Adam and Eve, vulnerable to temptation and potential victims of a second disastrous Fall. The 'serpent' dispatched by the bent Oyarsa to accomplish this end is Weston, albeit a rather different Weston from the one who took the villain's role in the first novel. Ransom is sent by the Martian Oyarsa and the *eldila* to oppose Weston, and prevent the Fall if he can.

The importance of what is happening on Venus, in *Perelandra*, extends to our own world, because it marks a crucial shift in the form that the battle between good and evil takes. What has in the past been a psychological battle – a contest of moral wills – is now becoming an actual physical contest. Thus, the fight between Ransom and Weston, which begins as a debate, concludes as an actual fight in which the evil must be destroyed. The relationship between this dramatic battle, with its rather horrific conclusion, and the war to defeat Hitler is quite clear. The story is in part a justification for taking up arms to combat active evil.

The ideologies which Weston espouses in *Perelandra* are more subtle and complex than those which he held in *Out of the Silent Planet* – they have to be seductive in order to be used to tempt the alien Eve away from the faith defended by Ransom. They are much more obviously drawn from the tradition of scientific romance – from the metaphysicians Shiel and Stapledon, who had done the same kind of work as Lewis, but had done it (in his eyes) *wrong*. Weston is now a convinced believer in 'emergent evolution':

> The majestic spectacle of this blind, inarticulate purposiveness thrusting its way upward and ever upward in an endless unity of differentiated achievements towards an ever-increasing complexity of organisation, towards spontaneity and spirituality, swept away all my old conception of the duty of Man as such. Man in himself is nothing. The forward movement of Life – the growing spirituality – is everything ... To spread spirituality, not to spread the human race, is henceforth my mission. This sets the coping-stone on my career. I worked first for myself; then for science; but now at last for Spirit itself – I might say, borrowing language which will be more familiar to you, the Holy Spirit.[7]

Weston has acquired a certain eccentric religiosity to supplement and provide a context for his scientific understanding. As Leslie Fiedler points out in *Olaf Stapledon: A Man Divided*, this particular piece of rhetoric is very similar to statements made by Stapledon.[8] As we have seen, however, similar ideas were very widespread in scientific romance, especially in the period between the wars. They are to be found in Beresford and Shaw as well as Stapledon and Shiel. All such quests for a 'new religiosity' that would complement and harmonise with evolutionary theory and new ideas about the scale of the universe were, for Lewis, simply heresies. As such, they were the voice of the devil – and that is the voice that Weston speaks with, as the plot of *Perelandra* makes graphically clear. Significantly, once Weston is destroyed the story is transformed into a rhapsodic celebration of Maleldil's creativity; Ransom has a quasi-visionary experience not so very different from the vision of the protagonist of *Star Maker* or from the flights of the imagination which are sometimes presented in the speeches of Shiel's characters. Ransom is given the means to grasp, in his imagination, the essential morality of matter and to glimpse the Star Maker at work – though *this* hypothetical mythology is 'really' in tune with the infinite, and has resisted the seductive persuasions of diabolical temptation.

The apocalyptic premonitions of *Perelandra* are further developed, though in surprisingly weak fashion, in the last, least and longest of the trilogy, *That Hideous Strength* (1945), which is revealingly subtitled 'A modern fairy-tale for grown-ups' (*Perelandra* was subtitled 'A novel'). Following Weston's death, his erstwhile henchman Devine reappears in a villainous role (he is now Lord Feverstone), but he and all of his motley crew of scientist-usurpers are merely pawns. Their organisation, the ironically titled NICE, has various figureheads, including a famous author, 'Jules' (a parody of Wells), but these are mere front men. Their real commanders are demons who possess some of their number and animate the head of a guillotined murderer which they keep alive for experimental purposes. NICE aims at world domination – or at least the domination of Britain – and its power is secured by artful control of the media. Its plans are, as might be expected, borrowed from the clichés of scientific romance:

> 'What sort of thing have you in mind?'
> 'Quite simple and obvious things, at first – sterilisation of the unfit, liquidation of backward races (we don't want any dead weights), selective breeding. Then real education, including prenatal education. By real education I mean one that has no 'take-it-or-leave-it' nonsense. A real education makes the patient what it wants infallibly: whatever he or his parents try to do about it. Of course, it'll have to be mainly psychological at first. But we'll get on to biochemical conditioning in the end and direct manipulation of the brain . . . '[9]

This creation of 'a new type of man' is something that is revised as the book proceeds and the reader is allowed to penetrate layers of misrepresentation to get at the true heart of NICE's ambitions. Later, a character closer to the inner core of the organisation puts it this way:

> This Institute – *Dio meo*, it is for something better than housing and vaccinations and faster trains and curing the people of cancer. It is for the conquest of death: or for the conquest of organic life, if you prefer. They are the same thing. It is to bring out of that cocoon of organic life which sheltered the babyhood of mind the New Man, the man who will not die, the artificial man, free from Nature. Nature is the ladder we have climbed up by, now we kick her away.[10]

For Lewis, this kind of 'transcendent tomorrow' is, of course, mere illusion. The dupes of NICE, who think they are working towards a goal which is, in their eyes, desirable, are actually conniving with the bent Oyarsa to the ultimate destruction of earth, and to the creation of Hell upon its surface.

The central characters of *That Hideous Strength* are an academic and his wife, Mark and Jane Studdock. Mark is seduced into NICE because its administrators want to get Jane into their power, she having the power of prophetic dreaming. She escapes, though, and is led gradually and a little reluctantly to accept the shelter of Christian faith and alliance with a rival organisation of the well-intentioned, gathered around the person of Ransom. Just as Weston was transformed between the first and second novels, so Ransom is transformed between the second and third, so that he has now become a Magus burdened by holy responsibility, perhaps modelled on the heroes of some of Charles Williams's books, and probably to some extent on Williams himself. (Williams and Lewis had become close friends when Williams's employers, the Oxford University Press, had shifted their main base of operations from London to Oxford because of the Blitz.)

The two rival organisations clash as they attempt to recruit the aid of the magician Merlin, who is due to awaken from his long sleep in order to play his part in the crucial contest of supernatural forces. Despite his pagan origins, Merlin commits himself firmly to the side of right (which is unsurprising, given Lewis's general views on myth and truth, and his affection for ancient legends). In the conclusion he tidies up the villains of NICE with a few flourishes of his magical power. To the reader who was expecting (following the promises made in *Perelandra*) a large-scale apocalypse, this catalogue of petty conjuring tricks is a sad disappointment, and it seems as though Lewis had exhausted his imaginative impetus. It is also significant that the invented mythos of the earlier novels is presented here beneath the veil of a more general eclectic mysticism which tries to assimilate the *eldila* mythos, Christianity and Arthurian legend into a rather shapeless conglomerate. This kind of mystical eclecticism resembles some of the more obscure aspects of Charles Williams's fantasies, and represents a change of direction from the kind of endeavour featured in *Out of the Silent Planet*.

Lewis was to go on to write several more fantasy novels, but he did not return to the form of scientific romance and took little further interest in the ideas of writers of scientific romance. In *The Great Divorce* (1945) he admits to having borrowed an idea from an American science fiction writer in order to help him provide new images of what Heaven and Hell might be like but this novella is basically a follow-up to *The Screwtape Letters*, embedding traditional Christian ideas in imagery rooted in contemporary everyday life. He did set out again to create an entire mythos that would reproduce the truthful features of Christian myth on a more ambitious scale, but this was in his series of children's fantasies set in Narnia, begun with *The Lion, the Witch and the Wardrobe*. His only other full-length story for adults was *Till We Have Faces* (1956), which borrows a story from Greek mythology for a similar purpose, and which achieves a delicacy and conviction that he never quite attained in all his earlier work.

When American science fiction became more sophisticated in the early 1950s Lewis became quite fond of *The Magazine of Fantasy and Science Fiction*, whose editors paid careful attention to the literary quality of the work they published. Lewis felt sufficient affinity with this magazine to write stories for its pages, and his first appearance there was 'The Shoddy Lands' (1956), in which a staid academic becomes able to see the world through the eyes of a flighty young girl, and is appalled by the selectiveness of her perception. This was followed by 'Ministering Angels' (1958), an ideological comment on a proposition that the practical difficulties involved in establishing a base on

Mars would make it convenient for conventional morality to be set aside so that prostitutes could be shipped out for the pioneers. This was not a proposal of which Lewis could approve, but his mode of dissent from it really amounts to little more than an exercise in contemptuous misogyny, along the same lines as 'The Shoddy Lands'. Lewis had married in 1956, though initially this relationship was a marriage of convenience contracted in order to allow the lady in question to remain in Britain (she was an American whose residence permit had been revoked by the Home Office). By 1957, though, the relationship became 'real', and was sanctified by a second wedding in church.

Lewis left behind one scientific romance to be published posthumously – the brief 'Forms of Things Unknown', in which astronauts landing on the moon are turned to stone by Medusa. From the viewpoint of the editors of *The Magazine of Fantasy and Science Fiction* this might have seemed an absurd amalgam of two genres, but from Lewis's point of view the distinction between 'fantasy' and 'science fiction' was a false one – the issue of the probability or realism of speculative fiction appeared very different to him from the way it would have appeared to H.G. Wells. For Lewis, a confrontation between an astronaut and a gorgon could perfectly well be 'true' if it could make a suitably ironic comment on the ambitions of men to conquer the universe. He was prepared to acknowledge forthrightly what some other commentators on speculative fiction dismissed – that speculative fiction, however, 'scientific' its extrapolations, contained a good deal of supernaturalism and carried distinct metaphysical commitments.

Lewis's attempt to subvert the mythology of scientific romance has something in common with the imaginative novels of G.K. Chesterton, which also borrowed the form of Wellsian romance in order to object to Wellsian assumptions about historical determinism. Lewis is, however, much more earnest than Chesterton, and he does not make the defensive move of substituting comedy for melodrama, as Chesterton did in all cases except *The Man Who Was Thursday*. This means that Lewis's work has strong links not only with the tradition of scientific romance, but with the genre of metaphysical fantasy as practised by David Lindsay and John Cowper Powys. He had, of course, much the same attitude to those writers as he had to the writers of scientific romance: he admired their imaginative fecundity, but deplored their heresies. He does not, therefore, provide a bridge between the genres, but rather illuminates an important dimension of similarity between them. The same dimension of similarity exists between modern science fiction and the 'heroic fantasy' genre which flourished in the wake of the belated but spectacular success of Tolkien's *The Lord of the Rings*, and Lewis deserves equal credit with Stapledon for calling attention to the 'mythopoeic' dimension of speculative fiction in general, and scientific romance in particular.

Gerald Heard

Henry Fitzgerald Heard was born on 6 October 1889. He was the son of a prebendary, and thus completes the curiously large set of important writers of scientific romances whose fathers were clergymen. Like the others he drifted away from the faith of his father to become a freethinker; like Beresford and Shiel, though, he retained a strong interest in the metempirical, and he developed an eccentric religiosity of his own. His ideas influenced Olaf Stapledon quite considerably in the early 1930s, and he was impressed in turn by Stapledon's novels.

Heard was educated at Sherborne and Caius College, Cambridge. He took a degree in history, and then went on to do postgraduate work in philosophy. When he left the academic world it was to make his living as a journalist and popular educator. His interests were very varied; he was for a while literary editor of *The Realist* and was a popular science commentator for the BBC, operating through the medium of a radio programme, *This Surprising World* (1930–4; a book of the series was published under that title in 1932). In 1937 he moved to California, where he lived for the rest of his life. There he became familiar with American science fiction, but when he eventually began to write fiction he remained very solidly in the British tradition of speculation.

Heard published very little in book form in the 1920s, except for his *Today and Tomorrow* pamphlet *Narcissus* (1924), but after publication of *The Ascent of Humanity* in 1929 he produced non-fiction books regularly. He became particularly interested in the task of trying to make sense of the pattern of human history, which he attempted to do with the aid of evolutionary theory and ideas gleaned from the sociology of religion. His first major thesis on these lines was *The Emergence of Man* (1931), set solidly in the tradition of Wells's *The Outline of History* but also referring back to Winwood Reade's nineteenth-century classic *The Martyrdom of Man*. His attempts to fit his various resources together into a theory led him to reformulate both the sociology of religion and the theory of evolution, and his work in these disciplines was published in *The Social Substance of Religion* (1931) and *Pain, Sex and Time: a new hypothesis of evolution* (1939). Neither of these works attained any great reputation, and Heard was regarded as a dilettante whose authority to make pronouncements on such subjects was dubious.

The Emergence of Man attempts to find some metaphysical significance in the story of man, and to offer an appraisal of the present situation of mankind. It observes that there has emerged a fundamental conflict of perspectives, represented on the one hand by the mythology of progress promoted by so many nineteenth-century theorists (Heard singles out Spencer as the cardinal example), and on the other hand by anxious discontents associated with the decline of faith. Heard agrees with Reade that when the promise of personal immortality was taken away from men by rationalism and positivism, they were thrust into a state of psychological crisis. Heard's book attempts to negotiate a new compromise between the mythology of progress and the sense of Frustration which is its antithesis. He interprets the history of previous generations in terms of a series of revolutions – the Religious Revolution, the Political Revolution and the Economic Revolution – each of which has led to a drastic reformulation of human communities and a new ideological basis for social control. Although this theory is in some ways similar to Marxist theory (it is dialectical in character, but not materialistic), Heard does not accept that the Economic Revolution can or will be the final one. Like Wells, Stapledon and so many others he believed that there was an important phase in the human story yet to come, which would bring into being a New Man. This fourth revolution would be the Psychological Revolution, which would involve the social deployment of the discoveries of the science of mind:

> Science has penetrated not only to the bounds of space but into the foundations and springs of the mind. Men were humiliated, they

were stripped. But now we perceive that that stripping was as necessary for man as the snake's casting of its skin or the seed its husk. Unless a seed fall into the ground and die it remaineth alone. Man has to cast this final husk of his animal individual self, its uniqueness, worth and dignity that he might realise that man is something more than men and that the mind which is growing in them, they do not own and use, but it owns and uses and it is fulfilled as it uses them up. Their complete emergence is their assumption. There is nothing mystical in this. It is all part of the evolutionary emergence of man.[11]

Later, he claims that 'stage by stage, we can see the being in which we are, the mind which today as it emerges calls itself man . . . rising from the earth and taking of its nature to the sky.'[12] We can easily see this imagery in Stapledon's work from *Last Men in London* to *Death into Life*, but Heard was not in any hurry to dramatise his ideas in fictional form. Because he belonged to that breed of British scientist-philosophers which rejoices in unorthodoxy he did not despise genre fiction in the least, but it was not until he was settled in California that he turned his hand to it, and his first efforts were in the field of detective fiction.

Heard's early fiction consists of exercises in clever, tongue-in-cheek pastiche. He took to detective fiction as a kind of game-playing, but he played the game with all due seriousness and with great style. His first novel, *A Taste for Honey* (1941), has as its hero a man who has long retired from his profession in order to take up beekeeping. His name is not revealed directly to the reader, though he consents to be known to the chronicler of his adventure as 'Mr Mycroft', the name being one with which he has family connections. (His Watsonian colleague does get to hear his real name eventually, but is too crass to recognise it.) The story tells of a remarkably ingenious murder plot, employing an exotic character whose use depends on esoteric scientific knowledge. The plot avoids the conventional pattern of crime-solution-retribution; there is no delivery of the villain, once unmasked, into the hands of the law. In this respect the story strongly resembles G.K. Chesterton's eccentric detective stories, where the key point at issue is often the redemption of the murderer rather than his punishment. Like Chesterton, Heard appears to favour a higher court of justice than a mere court of law. The same pattern is repeated in the sequel, *Reply Paid* (1942), a convoluted puzzle-story which becomes marginally speculative because the mystery turns on the properties of a radioactive meteorite.

Heard was clearly very interested in radioactivity, because it also features prominently in his third and best crime novel, *Murder by Reflection* (1942). This is not a detective story at all – there is no mystery about the crime which is described – but it is an extraordinary study in psychology and morality. A young man with a taste for the elegance of bygone days is seduced by an older woman into a life of carefully crafted illusion which allows him to be what he wants to be but leaves him still unsatisfied with his choice of role and the conditions attached to it. He tries to win his freedom by commiting an undetectable murder, using radiation as a means, but even as he succeeds his weapon backfires. Though there is no question of legal retribution he still pays a terrible price for his crime. As in so much scientific romance, Heard tries to draw a connection between physical theory and morality, binding the two together with metaphor and metaphysics.

A similar kind of thinking underlies most of the short pieces collected in *The Great Fog and Other Weird Tales* (1944; the British edition, first published in 1947, has slightly different contents). The title story is a classic tale of benign disaster, in which a mutant mildew changes the environment of the earth's surface simply but very drastically, by enveloping it in cloud. Travel becomes difficult, war impossible, and civilisation crumbles as the ears replace the eyes as man's chief sensory organs. This is a merciful release from a responsibility which had grown too great to bear:

> We were not fit for the big views, the vast world into which the old men tumbled up. It was all right to give animal men the open. But, once they had got power without vision, then either they had to be shut up or they would have shot and bombed everything off the earth's surface. Why, they were already living in tunnels when the Fog came. And out in the open, men, powerful as never before, nevertheless died by millions, died the way insects used to die in a frost, but died by one another's hands. The plane drove men off the fields. That was the thing, I believe, that made Mind decide we were not fit any longer to be at large . . . We're safer as we are. Mind knew that, and already we are better for our Fog cure, though it had to be drastic.[13]

'Eclipse' (omitted from the US edition) is very similar to 'The

Great Fog', featuring an atmospheric anomaly which screens out most of the sun's visible emissions. The young and the elderly are mysteriously able to cultivate a special night vision, but everyone must remain blind during the prime of life. The scientific basis of the story is preposterous, but it is essentially a parable suggesting that not until men experience blindness will they really learn to appreciate and use sight.

Another story in this collection, 'Dromenon', dramatises some of Heard's ideas about the sociology of religion, and also recalls the environment of his early days – it is one of several stories which he wrote exhibiting an entrancement with churches and church architecture. A dromenon, according to the definition which the story quotes, is a 'pattern of dynamic expression in which the performers express something larger than themselves', and this is the basis of religious experience and religious ritual. The story is similar in important respects to John Gloag's *Sacred Edifice*, and the idea behind it is closely related to the one expressed in the passage quoted in an earlier chapter from Gloag's *99%*.

The only other story in the collection which really qualifies as a scientific romance is 'Wingless Victory', an 'alien viewpoint' story in which the human world is contrasted with a Utopian state established by flightless avian beings in a warm valley near the south pole, discovered by a narrator who appears to be Captain Oates of the ill-fated Scott expedition. The story is heavily ironic, and can best be regarded as an item of Gulliveriana. By contrast, the most deadly earnest story in the book is 'Despair Deferred' (omitted from the UK edition), an exercise in existentialist philosophy which is interesting in the light of Heard's later work because it begins with reflections on the work of the psychologist Kretschmer on the correlation of physique and personality.

Heard published a second collection of fantastic stories in 1947: *The Lost Cavern and Other Tales of the Fantastic*. This consists of four novellas, in much the same veins as the longer stories in the first collection. 'The Lost Cavern' follows 'Wingless Victory' in describing an alien race and its habits, and in suggesting that their existential situation and social order might in many respects be preferable to our own. Here the alien race are cave-dwelling bats, and it represents something of a triumph on Heard's part to use such unlikely material in a sober and very effective *conte philosophique*. The defensive satirical irony of 'Wingless Victory' is very muted here, and the close of the story (when it is revealed that the bats have probably been destroyed in a natural disaster) is positively elegiac:

> For one more of Life's great experiments, who knows, perhaps the greatest, is over. And one more of those strange eyes (of which the mind of *Homo sapiens* is perhaps far from the brightest), those eyes by which the universe has striven to see itself and know itself, has been darkened forever.[14]

The second scientific romance in the collection, 'The Thaw Plan', is the third and least convincing of Heard's benign disaster stories, in which the warming of the earth's surface causes the ice-caps to melt and much land to be inundated. Dense jungle reclaims the tropical zones and human societies survive only in Greenland and Antarctica, completely cut off from one another. There is no repetition here, though, of the earnest moral of 'The Great Fog' and 'Eclipse', as Heard seems to have become interested in the extrapolation of his premiss for its own sake: an unsurprising submission to the aesthetics of thought-experiment.

Of the two occult fantasies which complete *The Lost Cavern* by far the more interesting is 'The Cup', a Chestertonian story of the redemption of a criminal, who finds a priestly vocation after witnessing a dramatic supernatural battle between good and evil. Heard was later to develop a similar model of supernatural conflict in his full-length novel of the super-natural, *The Black Fox* (1951).

While in America Heard had continued to write philos-ophical books, and before turning his hand to fiction had produced an updated version of his interpretation of history in *Man the Master* (1942). This book begins with the forthright statement that the contemporary crisis of man must not be seen as a political or economic crisis, but as a psychologicial one. Heard argues that it must be analysed and solved with the aid of psychological science, and the text goes on to provide an elaborate 'diagnosis' followed by a 'prognosis'. The idea of 'Man' as a collective individual with 'his' own psychology and inherent pattern of development is much more strongly empha-sised here than it was in *The Emergence of Man*. This second work is also more openly metaphysical than the first, conclud-ing its diagnosis in Stapledonian fashion with chapters on

'How and Why Spiritual Power has Failed' and 'The Crisis and Opportunity for Spirituality'. It gives a much more elaborate account of what is to be expected from the fourth revolution – the Psychological Revolution – which is to put mankind (finally) on the high road to fulfilment. The idea of this revolution will be to root social order and the management of life in the 'natural' class-structure of society – a class-structure which is not economic but psychological. In 'The Quadritype Organisation of Society' Heard spells out his theory that there are four basic personality types, fitted for different roles that would complement one another in an ideal society. Actually, the book has very little to say about work in contemporary psychological science, but it has a good deal to say about the social role of religion, and takes a special interest in the role of seers and 'philosopher-saints' in Hindu society. In the evolutionary ideas of Hinduism Heard finds an analogue of his own theories which (he opines) has been sadly perverted in Indian society because of the artificial rigidity of the caste system.

Heard was probably familiar with Kretschmer's work on 'psychophysiological types' before writing *Man the Master*, but did not consider it particularly relevant to his thought. Shortly after writing the book, though, he obviously became acquainted with the work done in elaborating this theory by the American psychologist W.H. Sheldon, who was working at Harvard during the late 1930s and early 1940s. Sheldon tried to associate the three physical types which Kretschmer had identified (endomorphs, mesomorphs and ectomorphs) with a much more elaborate account of their characteristic personalities, calling the three associated personality types viscerotonic, somatotonic and cerebrotonic. With the aid of various co-workers Sheldon claimed to have identified these types of personality in young children, and to have proved a very high degree of correlation between personality and physique. (Others attempting to repeat the work found much lower correlation coefficients, and Sheldon's work has thus been relegated to a footnote in most modern textbooks of psychology.)

Heard was fascinated by Sheldon's work because it fitted in very well with his idea that there were natural social classes whose personalities implied different 'needs' or 'satisfactions', and which if properly sorted into appropriate occupations could make up a balanced society. Sheldon's three personality types fitted reasonably well into Heard's 'Quadritype Organisation of Society', leaving only the 'seers' out of account.

Given the kind of work that was occupying so much of Heard's time in the 1940s it is understandable that he chose to synthesise Sheldon's ideas with his own, not in another non-fictional account of the meaning of history but in a scientific romance that could provide an image of 'the emergence of man' in a hypothetical society of the future where the Psychological Revolution had already happened. This he did in *Doppelgängers* (1947), subtitled 'An Episode of the Fourth, the Psychological, Revolution, 1997'.

Doppelgängers is arguably the most peculiar, most esoteric and least comprehensible of all the important scientific romances. Although it was reprinted by the British Science Fiction Book Club in 1965, and issued as a science fiction paperback in America in 1966, it is difficult to believe that either of the target audiences of those editions could be expected to figure out what on earth the story is about. In certain respects, though, it is a very interesting book – and its themes become much clearer if it is read in association with *Man the Master*.

The world of *Doppelgängers* is ruled by a dictator who styles himself Alpha. By applying Sheldon's insights to the organisation of society he has managed to create a happy and stable society, with people of each of the three personality types given appropriate work and appropriate rewards. Alpha is, however, opposed by an Underground (most of whose operations are indeed subterranean) headed by a mysterious individual titled the Mole. Much is made of the notion that the Mole is Alpha's opposite number, and the two are frequently evoked as paired opposites: Alpha and Talpa; Alpha and Omega; the Bull and the Mole. This is significant in more ways than one, but in the most important way it becomes symbolic of the opposition between the conscious and subconscious parts of the mind. The point is made that Sheldon has provided Alpha with 'something approaching the real map of humanity, instead of those queer selective shadows and profiles of themselves which till then reformers had often honestly taken to be the picture and likeness of mankind'.[15] This metaphor of the map of humanity is extended, so that the whole society becomes a model of the human psyche; in Alpha's world there has been a rationalisation of all that pertains to conscious needs and desires, but the

Psychological Revolution remains incomplete because there has not yet been a final and fundamental synthesis of conscious and unconscious.

The plot of the story concerns an attempt by the Mole to subvert Alpha's rule by replacing him. A member of the Underground who bears a strong physical resemblance to the dictator is made identical by plastic surgery and then released to be discovered by Alpha. Alpha recruits this double, ostensibly for the pragmatic motive of using him as a stand-in to relieve the pressure of public obligation which is beginning to affect him. Actually, though, the fascination Alpha feels in respect of his *doppelgänger* goes deeper than that, and the protagonist becomes his confidant. Eventually the double kills the dictator, and becomes the dictator himself. He begins his rule by defeating a scheme by the head of the secret police to usurp his place, but then finds himself menaced in his turn by the Underground.

Even when he takes control, the double is not really certain what steps can be or need to be taken to change and improve Alpha's world. He has always had difficulty in articulating precisely what he has against it, but he feels that the Sheldonian rationalisation of society has somehow led to a 'castration of the mind'. At the metaphorical level, there is still some force lurking in the unconscious that must be answered: a covert need that is still frustrated and must be met. This force is equivalent to the Freudian libido, though it is not characterised in similar terms here.

The protagonist's criticisms of Alpha's Utopia in *Doppelgängers* bear a close relationship to the criticisms levelled at Mustapha Mond's Utopia in *Brave New World*; they represent a deep-seated conviction that happiness is not enough, and perhaps worthless if it is won by manipulation. Heard's 'natural social classes' are not created by biological engineering like the Alphas, Betas and Gammas of *Brave New World*, but they are manipulated in some of the same ways by propaganda and ritual. Politics in this hypothetical world are organised largely in accordance with behaviourist principles. (*Walden Two*, an earnest prescription for Utopian organisation along behaviourist lines by the psychologist B.F. Skinner, is almost contempory with *Doppelgängers*.) Heard had always believed that there was more to man than is implied by the Sheldonian philosophy, no matter how revealing that account might be. He therefore set out to 'solve' the problems brought into focus by *Brave New World* – his solution bears a strong resemblance to the one which Aldous Huxley was ultimately to formulate in his own Utopian fantasy *Island*.

The climax of *Doppelgängers* is initiated when the new Alpha comes face to face with a new character, who has no name or nickname ('labels are libels,' he observes, though he does describe himself as 'an elevator man') but dresses in a saffron robe. He gives us yet another summary of the achievements of the past, leading up to the fourth revolution, but claims that the world is still in a state of crisis. Although Sheldon's revolution has been the final revolution, the story is not ended, because it remains to put an end to the entire revolutionary epoch of human history and revert to a new evolutionary phase. He assures his listeners that this will not take the adventure out of life, but will rather allow men to see for the first time what kind of adventure faces them. His explanation of what he means – if one can call it an explanation – is an eccentric mixture of physiological psychology and Eastern mysticism, whose conclusion is that Sheldon's three personality types must be supplemented by a fourth, to be created by 'psychophysical training' – Heard's seers, who will use the supposed latent powers of the pineal gland (the 'inner eye' or 'aperture of Brahman') to obtain 'integral thought'.[16]

Once all this has been laid out in discussion the novel moves on to its symbolic conclusion. The new Alpha and the man in saffron descend into the Underworld to confront the Mole, who acknowledges that his task is accomplished and disbands the entire Underground. At the metaphorical level, the unconscious mind capitulates to the demands of the conscious and submits to integration within it. Conflict is ended and a true sense of purpose attained.

Doppelgängers is set solidly in the tradition of British scientific romance, but it differs in one important respect from the great majority of the other works to which it relates: it ends on a note of unqualified optimism. Even Shiel, with his unshakeable faith in the morality of matter and the upward thrust of evolution, could not imagine that the world might be saved before it was torn apart, and most of the other major writers were desperate in their anxiety that it might rather be torn apart *instead* of being saved. Wells, Beresford, Stapledon and Huxley were all equal to the task of imagining the state of society saved, but none could really believe that we could actually attain that end without some radical transformation of human nature. Huxley's *Island*, whose ideal society bears a marked resemblance to the kind of social ideal that Heard sketched out, at least in its reliance on the supposed truth of much Eastern religious mythology, ends with the Utopian enclave threatened with extinction by the forces of materialistic *realpolitik*. Only Heard's contemporary (contemporary in that he too began to write scientific romance at a very late stage) C.S. Lewis exhibited in his work a similar optimism about the possible vanquishing of those social and psychological forces that had brought man to the brink of self-destruction.

It could easily be argued, of course, that Heard's 'solution' to the predicament of man is ridiculous. In fact, the forceful rhetoric which we find in the last three chapters of *Doppelgängers* is really pure nonsense. It has no more claim on the intellect than Lewis's robustly orthodox Christianity, and has not even the excuse of historical inertia to sustain it. But this is not the point. Despite the earnest intentions of men like Wells and Stapledon, the achievements of scientific romance in finding solutions to problems (whether the problems be social or philosophical) are utterly negligible. What is interesting about scientific romance is not that questions are answered but that they are asked, and that the manner of their asking embodies an attitude to the *possibility* of their being answered.

The interesting similarity betwen *Doppelgängers* and the Ransom trilogy is not so much that they are both optimistic, but that their optimism has similar grounds. Lewis and Heard both conclude that there is some essential truth in myth that we have previously overlooked, and to whose significance we must awaken. Lewis supposes that the truth is there because God is the ultimate creator of our imaginary constructs just as he is the creator of the world; Heard supposes that the truth is there because myths, like psychological theories, contain maps of the mind – maps in which the unconscious part of the mind reveals itself obliquely.

Heard also shared with C.S. Lewis an enthusiasm for *The Magazine of Fantasy and Science Fiction*, and he too wrote stories for the magazine. Indeed, his involvement with the post-war expansion and sophistication of science fiction went beyond this. 'The Great Fog' was reprinted in one of the early hardcover anthologies of science fiction, and Heard wrote stories especially for two others, also contributing an introduction to one of them. His first story for *The Magazine of Fantasy and Science Fiction* was 'The Collector' (1951), a man-meets-alien story featuring an aesthetically sensitive giant squid. His second, 'The Marble Ear' (1952), is an interesting fantasy of the 'three wishes' variety which – while not losing the ironic quality of other such stories – is bold enough to suggest an ingenious way of profiting from such a situation. The two stories which he wrote for anthologies are not so elegantly constructed, but they are more adventurous ideatively. 'B + M – Planet 4' (1951, in *New Tales of Space and Time* edited by Raymond J. Healy) describes the first expedition to Mars, where tiny humanoids and giant bees enjoy a symbiotic relationship which is subsequently exported to Earth. The end of the story echoes *Doppelgängers* in declaring the surrender of earth's Underground. 'Cyclops' (1952, in *Future Tense* edited by Kendell Foster Crossen) runs somewhat against the grain of Heard's other speculative stories in reverting to a more conventional cynicism about contemporary man. A man awakened from suspended animation after a nuclear holocaust finds descendants of the survivors radically altered in physique because of the adaptation to new circumstances which they have been forced to undergo. Although their mode of life seems to them infinitely preferable to that of *Homo sapiens* the awakened man refuses to allow them to adapt him to it, preferring instead to return to his endless sleep.

Although Heard did not die until 1971 his last works were written in this period of the early 1950s. He produced one rather eccentric exercise in speculative non-fiction in *The Riddle of the Flying Saucers: Is Another World Watching?* (1951), which includes some fairly elaborate descriptions of what the supposed pilots of the flying saucers might look like, and what their way of life might be. His last scientific romance, though, was an allegory of evolution, *Gabriel and the Creatures* (1952; known in Britain as *Wishing Well*), which attempts to popularise his slightly unorthodox views on evolution through the medium of a tale for children. The 'moral' of the story is that evolutionary progress does not consist of the development of strength, speed or any other specialist investment, but rather in the preservation of versatility and adaptability. This kind of argument is particularly ingenious because it does not need to deny anything in the Darwinian theory, nor to promote any neo-

Lamarckian elaboration of it, in order to stress the *creativity* of the evolutionary process. In the fable, animals other than man use up their power of wishing by investing in some particular faculty – the dog's sense of smell, the porcupine's quills – which then locks them into a particualar way of life and inhibits further development. Man, by contrast, saves his wishes and avoids entrapment (the relationship between this story and 'The Marble Ear' becomes clear on juxtaposing the two). Thus we have a basis for the insistence on the 'openness' of the future that we find in the lecture delivered by the man in the saffron robe in *Doppelgängers*.

Heard's insistence on the necessity of retaining flexibility and the capacity for further adaptation coloured all aspects of his thought. It is in both his evolutionary theory and his social philosophy, and it affected his ideas about literature too. His introduction to *New Tales of Space and Time*, 'Why Science Fiction?', is perhaps the most extravagant of all the apologies for speculative fiction issued by its supporters. It represents science fiction (which, for Heard, includes British scientific romance as well as American science fiction) as an important new phase in the evolution of the novel, whose significance in the light of his own theory of social evolution is not to be underestimated. He claims that:

> Science Fiction signals the dawn of the psychological revolution that is already out-dating the economic. Also it indicates the re-emergence of man's integrated relationship with the whole universe. Take a single example from the most aloof of the sciences. The Renaissance demoted the stars from pointers of human destiny and as 'influences' on men's lives, to a play of irrelevant pin points that happened to amuse higher-mathematical astronomers. The new astronomy deals with such force-nodes as the radiation 'star' in Cygnus which may not be a star in any sense we have used the word – it can't be seen – but may be a focus whose radiation could affect our genes. It is with such a world as this, an inter-active universe, an environment in which ecology is revolutionising all the axioms of economics, that science fiction works with its parables and prophecies.[17]

Heard goes on to argue that science fiction itself has evolved through three phases, from a 'fancy-dress phase', through a phase of 'apocalyptic pessimism' to a new and contemporary phase which 'indicates the dawn of hope on a far vaster field of

311

reference' than has previously been available to the imagination . . . He elaborates this part of the argument as follows:

> We know from archaeological and dead-literature study that when a society confronts a crisis to which all its traditional reactions are inadequate, the most alive and on-the-spot of its minds write a fantastically compelling forecast of how the crisis is going to be resolved. The immediate Time of Troubles may seem to be becoming more acute. But these troubles are not symptoms of oncoming death. On the contrary they are the birth-pangs of a completely new order. The powers of Nature and the forces invisible are about to break through on to the stage of man's conflicts and another Aeon will so be ushered in.[18]

Whether this characterisation of the speculative fiction of the 1950s is apt must remain highly debatable, but it is certain that Heard could not have come to this conclusion had he had only the British tradition of scientific romance to refer to – or, for that matter, only the tradition of American science fiction. What he calls a 'third phase' is really a synthesis of the two traditions, in which the imaginative exuberance of American science fiction balances the frantic preoccupation with Frustration that became the hallmark of scientific romance in the period between the wars. In bearing witness to this synthesis – and participating modestly in its achievement – Heard joined Lewis in discovering new hope for social salvation, and in demonstrating that the end of the isolated tradition of scientific romance would be secured by its dissolution into the expanding genre of science fiction.

The Desolation of the Future

The explosion of the first atom bomb in 1945 did not cause any dramatic transformation of the images of the future contained in scientific romance. The arrival of some such awesomely destructive force had long been anticipated and accommodated within futuristic speculations. The advent of the new weapon did, however, serve to focus attention on its particular possibilities and to inspire some rather extreme new expressions of anxiety regarding the fragility of civilisation.

The Maniac's Dream (1946) by F. Horace Rose is proclaimed by its blurb to be 'the first novel about the Atomic Bomb', and was issued in a dust-jacket which simply shows a vast explosion generating a mushroom cloud. Rose had been a writer of oriental romances for some time, but had begun to tackle larger themes in *The Night of the World* (1944), whose visionary climax suggests that men have banished God from their affairs and voluntarily brought Hell to earth. *The Maniac's Dream* is similar in structure, beginning as a more or less realistic contemporary novel in which the issues of the day are straightforwardly discussed:

> The war with Japan was a detail, only an incident. So with Hiroshima and Nagasaki – what did *they* matter? – a flash, a roar, and those two great cities had vanished from the earth in a cloud of fire and smoke. The thousands that were not crushed to death in the hail of ruin that rained about them, were burned alive by the sheets of white-hot flame that licked them up, scorched, withered, and blasted, and cast down their blackened bodies in heaps, like piles of shrivelled leaves after an autumn storm. What did all that matter? It was all over and done in a flash. But the Atomic Bomb is not over. It is still here in the world, a silent, sleeping monster that will soon be awake again, – a fierce Angel of Destruction that has leaped out of Hell to deliver one frightful blow at the human race, and now only awaits opportunity to strike another and even more frightful blow.[19]

Later, the story elaborates this anxiety in the form of a vision credited to a vengeful lunatic who wants to use the new force to destroy the world. In the end, the threat is averted but we have nevertheless been treated to an extensive description of the obliteration of London and all the other cities of the world.

A more oblique, but in its way more effective, response to the revelation is to be found in H. de Vere Stacpoole's sentimental novel *The Story of My Village*, which takes the form of a set of memoirs extending over the greater part of the twentieth century. In 1945 the narrator is a newly married man, and as happy as a man can be – but his very happiness makes him all the more anxious about the future:

> It is this that makes me so fearful of the future, so afraid now of a renewal of world strife, of the new weapons that might be used and so speculative as to the probable ultimate results owing to the power of atomic energy.
> It came to me for the first time this morning (when the full news about Hiroshima came), and with a kind of shock, that this is really the mother energy of the universe we have tapped. The mother

energy carefully prepared, carefully hidden and wonderfully arranged, so that, seeping out slowly, it produces not only life but all the things we know that can feel life; all the things that make life desirable . . . and as this came to me I gave a sudden cry – as it might be the yelp of a dog suddenly hit with a stick – for I recognised, as through the light of a lightning flash, that we have not only released this mother creative force but used it not for creation but destruction!

Only the gods of evil, one might suppose, could have done that; and we are only mortals – or have we put on their robes and become, indeed, gods?[20]

In this story, as in Gerald Heard's benign disaster stories, men are saved from these godlike powers and responsibilities (for which they are not yet ready) by a great plague which leaves the great majority of men and one in two women blind. Under these circumstances city life cannot be sustained and all the world reverts to village life.

Another benign disaster is featured in George Borodin's *Spurious Sun* (1948), in which an atomic accident generates a Great Glow which threatens to sterilise the world, but forces the nations into co-operative action and the realisation that a New Era must begin to assure that such dangers can in future be kept at bay. The cost of mishandling such a political rationalisation was presented uncompromisingly in another novel published the same year: *Death of a World* by J. Jefferson Farjeon. A similar moral lesson is appended to Pelham Groom's interplanetary novel *The Purple Twilight*, also issued in 1948, in which travellers to Mars find Martian civilisation on the brink of extinction because of its mismanagement of atomic power. Like Horace Rose, Stacpoole, Borodin, Farjeon and Groom were all experienced writers of popular fiction, but none had been moved to tackle scientific romance until this time.

Stacpoole's suggestion that 'only the gods of evil' could reasonably be credited with inspiring the destructive use of atomic energy is echoed in the first and fiercest of the black comedies inspired by the bomb: *Ape and Essence* (1949) by Aldous Huxley. Huxley *had* written scientific romance before, and thus felt fully entitled to say 'I told you so' as bitterly and cruelly as he could. The main part of the story is a film script describing life in a future America devastated by atomic war. The survivors, struggling to cope with the obliteration of civilisation and the mutations induced by radiation in most of their children, have come to the conclusion that Belial is now in charge and that it is to him that their prayers must be addressed and their behaviour made responsible. Belial's Arch-Vicar explains how the cause of evil was so cunningly advanced:

> 'And remember this,' he adds: 'even without synthetic glanders, even without the atomic bomb, Belial could have achieved all His purposes. A little more slowly, perhaps, but just as surely, men would have destroyed themselves by destroying the world they lived in. They couldn't escape. He had them skewered on both His horns. If they managed to wriggle off the horn of total war, they would find themselves impaled on starvation. And if they were starving, they would be tempted to resort to war . . . From the very beginning of the industrial revolution He foresaw that men would be made so overwhelmingly bumptious by the miracles of their own technology that they would soon lose all sense of reality. And that's precisely what happened. These wretched slaves of wheels and ledgers began to congratulate themselves on being the Conquerors of Nature . . . In actual fact, of course, they had merely upset the equilibrium of Nature and were about to suffer the consequences. Just consider what they were up to during the century and a half before the Thing. Fouling the rivers, killing off the wild animals, destroying the forests, washing the topsoil into the sea, burning up an ocean of petroleum, squandering the minerals it had taken the whole of geological time to deposit. An orgy of criminal imbecility. And they called it Progress . . .'[21]

This widening of the scope of the debate, making the atom bomb merely a symptom of a more fundamental sickness, rapidly became commonplace. So too did the kind of surrealisation which Huxley found necessary in order to do justice to the extent of his outrage. Many writers abandoned realism in trying to find a more eloquent way to express their feelings. In Michael Harrison's novel *The Brain* (1953) the mushroom cloud resulting from an experimental atomic explosion forms itself into the shape of a gargantuan human brain, homologous in some mysterious way with the brain of the narrator. The brain is telepathic and immensely powerful, and as it continues to grow it offers the narrator the power and rewards of knowledge unlimited. In the end, though, he decides that he must put this temptation behind him because it is essentially diabolical. This novel contrasts sharply with Harrison's earlier scientific romance, *Higher Things* (1945), a charmingly ironic account of the tribulations of a man who discovers that he has the power to levitate himself.

There is also a surreal element in the fiction produced by Bertrand Russell in his eighties. His first collection of stories, *Satan in the Suburbs* (1953), contains only one scientific romance, 'The Infra-Redioscope', about hoaxers who use rumours of alien invasion to promote the sales of a useless machine and subsequently evoke the wrath of real aliens; but his second collection, *Nightmares of Eminent Persons* (1954), consists entirely of scientific romances and *contes philosophiques*. One of the 'Nightmares' is a sarcastic version of future war ('Dr Southport Vulpes's Nightmare: The Victory of Mind over Matter'), while the collection is filled out by two futuristic novellas, 'Zahatopolk' and 'Faith and Mountains', both of which are strongly critical of human gullibility in accepting and clinging to unproven creeds. Russell's subsequent exercises in fiction include the brief parable 'Planetary Effulgence' (1959), in which the inhabited planets of the solar system each fall victim in turn to nuclear wars. Some thirty-five years separate this story from *Icarus*, in which essay he had argued so eloquently that man could not be trusted to use the benefits of technical progress sensibly. Russell became one of the leading members of the Campaign for Nuclear Disarmament, and his advanced years did not prevent him from taking part in the early Aldermaston marches.

The explosion of the first atom bombs gave a considerable boost to the kind of cynicism regarding human uses of science which had been displayed in Russell's *Icarus*. Such cynicism is given particularly elaborate display in the works of Edward Hyams (1910–75), who very nearly warrants consideration as the last major writer of scientific romance, remaining peripheral only because the element of speculation in most of his imaginative novels is kept very carefully in check. Hyams's first venture in scientific romance was the future war story *Wings of the Morning* (1939), which looked forward to an imminent climactic war between socialism and Fascism but was very quickly overtaken by events in the real world. After the war he produced a group of three scientific romances, beginning with *Not in Our Stars* (1949), a realistic account of a biological experiment which accidentally reveals the existence of a fungus that has obvious potential as a weapon in biological warfare. The story offers a bitter account of the political response to the discovery. *The Astrologer* (1950) is a bolder but correspondingly less seriously inclined work, in which a new method of accurate prediction reveals that the world is heading for disaster because modern agricultural techniques are destroying the fertility of the soil. In order to avert this disaster a modern Lysistrata attempts to arrange a world wide sex strike. Hyams had considerable expertise in matters of agriculture and horticulture, and his anxiety about the dangers of widespread exhaustion of soils was real – with H.J. Massingham, he wrote a non-fiction book on the same topic, *Prophecy of Famine* (1953). Another scientific romance on the same theme is *Already Walks Tomorrow* (1938) by A.G. Street.

The third of Hyams's early scientific romances, *Sylvester* (1951; known as *998* in the USA), is another satire, in which an improbable device constructed as a joke by a junior naval officer is mistaken by enemy spies for a new weapon, and quickly acquires a reputation as a major deterrent in the Cold War arms race. At first it seems that the mistake will have beneficial consequences, but problems arise when the embarrassing secret threatens at last to leak out.

After publication of this work Hyams virtually abandoned speculative fiction for twenty years (following the pattern established by Beresford, Bell and Gloag), but returned to it late in life when his passionate support for socialist ideals again expressed itself in a series of near-future political fantasies, all of which are highly effective after their fashion: *The Final Agenda* (1973), *Prince Habib's Iceburg* (1974) and *Morrow's Ants* (1975).

As noted in an earlier chapter, there had been a trend before the war for political fantasies to become surrealised, as if it were only by means of caricature and grotesquerie that the nightmarish aspects of totalitarianism could be adequately represented. In many futuristic political fantasies produced in the post-war decade this element of caricature remains, but by a curious irony the absurd seems to have become much more realistic and believable. The dream-like quality of such novels as *Over the Mountain* and *The Green Isle of the Great Deep* is no longer to be found, and instead stories of the totalitarian future take on a new hard edge, accepting that with new gadgetry and the power of the mass media to help them, there will be no limit at all to the vicious oppressions which tyrants might heap upon their subjects. The key novel of this kind – which remains the most famous futuristic novel ever written – was George Orwell's *Nineteen Eighty-Four* (1949).

Whereas Huxley's *Brave New World* concentrated on the technologies of manipulation and social control, *Nineteen Eighty-Four* takes such things largely for granted, and concentrates instead on the motivation of ruling élites. In *Brave New World* oppression is secured by bribery; order and stability are bought with the currency of chemical pleasure. In *Nineteen Eighty-Four*, by contrast, oppression is much more direct and forceful, secured by fear, by propaganda and by violence. There is no Mustapha Mond here to defend his world with a moral ideology – O'Brien, the representative of the Inner Party who confronts the rebellious Winston Smith, offers neither defence nor apology, but simply observes that the power is there to be used, and that its exercise is its own justification. He offers us the most awful of all futuristic visions in a single telling phrase when he invites Smith to think of the future in terms of a boot stamping on a human face forever.

Brave New World alleged that the future might reduce people to the status of puppets, whose strings are insidious messages and biochemical flatteries. *Nineteen Eighty-Four* suggests that we may not need to become puppets (though it might be arranged if necessary) if our freedom of action can be efficiently circumscribed by all-seeing eyes and by a control of information so thorough that it erodes even the language that we think with.

The recent arrival of the year 1984 provoked a massive resurgence of popular and critical interest in *Nineteen Eighty-Four*, but much of that interest has inevitably focused on the novel as prophecy, and on comparisons of the real 1984 with the world of the book. This is mistaken, in that the book was not intended to offer a prophetic account of the year 1984, but the fact that such a discussion can still be carried on in all seriousness does testify to the awesome success of the book's break with previous tradition. *Nineteen Eighty-Four* was the first novel to present a nightmarish caricature future with the semblance of deadly earnest. It argued that what had previously been imaginable only in metaphorical terms, as part of an oblique rhetorical strategy, was now literally imaginable. Orwell demonstrated that the horizons of the imagination had shifted in an important way. Ideas which had previously been 'unthinkable' – and hence deployable only in satire and surealism – could now be made hypothetically convincing. Thirty-five years later those ideas are still hypothetically convincing; we find little difficulty in accepting that we might one day find ourselves living in a caricature world, and that there is no saving force to guarantee that we will never look up to see that boot coming down upon us again and again and again. It is not surprising, therefore, that we still treasure this particular text as one which brought to us a revelation of great importance, and did so in spectacular manner.

Nineteen Eighty-Four became the foundation stone of a new tradition in futuristic fiction. Dozens of works produced since its appearance have carried blurbs advertising their similarity to it. All modern dystopian fantasies invite comparison with it, because the character of modern dystopianism has been deeply affected by the revelation which it brought. Without Orwell's example, it might have taken some time for us to realise just how thinkable the unthinkable had become, and once *Nineteen Eighty-Four* had been written, there was a sense in which further dystopian visions could only be footnotes to its argument.

Most of the early political fantasies published in the wake of *Nineteen Eighty-Four* paled by comparison because they were noticeably less wholehearted. Either the caricature element that was in them was allowed to remain dream-like and 'unreal', as in *Bandersnatch* (1950) by T.E. Ryves or *The Sound of His Horn* (1951) by Sarban, or it was subdued in the service of a more down to earth realism, as in *One* (1954) by David Karp. It was really not until the 1960s that similar combinations of the earnest and grotesque became standard, as in such novels as *Facial Justice* (1960) by L.P. Hartley and *A Clockwork Orange* (1962) by Anthony Burgess. Some of the dystopias of the early 1950s are of some interest in their own right – particuarly, perhaps, *The Sound of His Horn*, which is an interesting 'alternate future' novel in which the Nazis won the Second World War and have reshaped European society in accordance with their curiously Romantic ideology – but none of them could possibly seem as *enlightening* as Orwell's. Those which extended the pre-war tradition by continuing to exploit the satirical and metaphorical potential of caricature – most obviously, *Love Among the Ruins* (1953) by Evelyn Waugh – seemed somehow to have gone astray. Such blatant sarcasm no longer seemed pertinent.

The imagery of *Nineteen Eighty-Four* is very much more complicated than the simple 'maniac's dream' of world destruction by atom bombs, but there is nevertheless a link between these alternative visions of future desolation. They might well be represented, after the fashion of Huxley's *Ape and Essence*, as the two horns of Belial, constituting a crucial dilemma. On the one hand, it was all too easy to believe that continued political wrangling and rivalry would lead in the end to nuclear Armageddon; on the other hand, it was also easy to believe that the suspension of political argument and the stifling of social conflict must take the form of rigid totalitarian control.

In the past, writers of scientific romance had been prepared to examine several ways of escaping this dilemma, especially the possibility of a kind of transcendence in which revolution and evolution occurred together, producing a New World for the New Men. Significantly, *Doppelgängers* – the last important novel to promote this magical synthesis – appeared shortly before *Nineteen Eighty-Four*. Images of transcendence by the evolution of superhumanity did not disappear – the science fiction of the 1950s, American as well as British, abounds in such imagery – but they were ripped out of the context in which they had first been evoked by Wells, Beresford and others. It was not, in the end, Stapledonian doubts which killed the myth, but Orwellian cynicism. The marriage between evolutionary theory and political theory, which writers like Wells, Beresford and Shiel tried in their various ways to secure, and which was watched over anxiously by so many of the other important writers of scientific romance, finally failed in the post-war years.

9
CONCLUSIONS

The Fusion of Scientific Romance and Science Fiction

AS WE HAVE seen in the previous chapter, the post-war decade saw the culmination of the trends laid down in the genre of scientific romance by the major writers of the 1930s. Although several of those writers survived into the 1960s, none added significantly to their achievements in scientific romance after 1954. By that time, it had ceased to make much sense to speak of a distinctive British tradition of speculative fiction that was still alive and continuing. It may seem odd to speak of the 'twilight of scientific romance' occurring in a period which saw a dramatic increase in the amount of speculative fiction being published in Britain, but the great bulk of this fiction contrasted sharply with the scientific romances of the thirties and forties. In theme, in style and in the manner of its marketing most of the speculative fiction published in Britain after 1950 was shaped in accordance with the rather different tradition of American science fiction.

Before the Second World War, as we have noted, there was already a small group of British writers who contributed to American pulp science fiction magazines. There was also a small community of British science fiction fans who were admirers of pulp science fiction. These science fiction enthusiasts even managed to run their own British pulp magazine, *Tales of Wonder*, for sixteen issues between 1937 and 1942. Science fiction, though, was insignificant in the British literary marketplace before 1945.

After 1945 the British popular fiction market changed very dramatically, principally because of the spectacular success of the paperback book. British paperback publishing on a large scale had begun in the thirties with the founding of Allen Lane's Penguin Books in 1935. Penguin determinedly maintained an image of literary respectability, offering cheap editions of rather upmarket 'middlebrow' novels. Lane did not involve himself with the more lurid versions of popular fiction, although he did make a concession in respect of the more genteel varieties of detective fiction. A combination of circumstances secured Penguin almost total domination of the paperback field for some ten years. The paper shortages which arrived with the war meant that Penguin thrived in competition with bulkier hardcover books, and it also made it more difficult for other paperback publishers to compete with them. Others did try, but Lane got the lion's share of the paper, and the lion's share of the market.

One corollary of Penguin's domination of the paperback market was that very little scientific romance found its way into this format. With such a vast range of accumulated middlebrow fiction to choose from, there was little incentive for Penguin to get involved with off-beat material. *The Hampdenshire Wonder* appeared as a Penguin in 1937 as part of the ordinary fiction line, and *The Invisible Man* was reprinted in the green-backed detective fiction series in 1938. *Last and First Men* completed a rather peculiar set in the same year by appearing as a blue-backed Pelican – part of a non-fiction series. Not until 1944, though, when Harold Nicolson's *Public Faces* appeared, was there another Penguin scientific romance. One or two scientific romances did appear from other publishers, including Neil Bell's *The Gas War of 1940* and Bernard Newman's *Armoured Doves*, but these were drops in the paperback ocean.

The early history of paperback publishing in Britain contrasted very sharply with the early history of paperback publishing in the USA. In Britain paperbacks were the 'descendants' of middlebrow hardcover books. In America, they competed with and eventually displaced the pulp magazines. Though the earliest American paperback publishers, including Pocket Books and the American Penguin, initially chose to publish middlebrow fiction and the more respectable kinds of detective fiction, leaving the bottom end of the market to the pulps, a different philosophy became evident when paper prices escalated after 1942. Publishers like Dell, Avon, Popular Library and Ace came, one by one, into the marketplace, and each one came a little closer to adopting the publishing philosophy of the pulps. Some of these new paperback publishers were, in fact, pulp publishers who were switching to the new format.

Like the British paperback publishers, the American paperback publishers played safe in selecting from the vast backlog of popular fiction the 'safest' material. Science fiction, though it had a secure corner of the popular fiction market, did not have wide enough appeal to make it attractive, and it was not until 1953 that Ace and Ballantine adopted the label and began issuing substantial sf lines. By that time, the situation in Britain had been dramatically transformed.

While the war lasted the more downmarket British paperback publishers enjoyed a precarious existence, but when it was over they enjoyed a spectacular boom. Companies established during and just after the war began issuing hundreds of titles, mostly novelettes and short novels rather than the full-length works still favoured by hardcover publishers and by Penguin. Many of these items featured rather lurid covers, invariably portraying women in various stages of undress, and were carefully aimed at the lowest stratum of the fiction-reading audience. These British publishers quickly identified some readily exploitable genres, achieving their greatest successes with gangster stories written in a curious mock-American style (inspired by the wartime bestseller *No Orchids for Miss Blandish* by James Hadley Chase) and slightly salacious stories of sexual immorality (mostly written under French-sounding pseudonyms). Once converted to the economic philosophy of genre publishing these publishers began to look for inspiration to the American pulps, and it was – ironically – in Britain rather than in America that paperback publishers first began to issue substantial science fiction lines.

The introduction of science fiction to British readers was seen by some paperback publishers as a problematic matter. Stephen Frances, director of the Gaywood Press, had scored a considerable success (and attained a certain notoriety) with gangster stories written in the first person under the name Hank Janson, and he elected to break it to his readers that he intended to diversify by appending a 'personal letter' from Hank – written in his own far from inimitable style – to one of his gangster novels:

> Maybe I'd better tell you how it's different. You see, this story should be described as Science Fiction and in Britain, whenever this

description is used, readers drop the book like it's red hot.

Now, this has always surprised me. Because the best selling fiction in the States is Science Fiction. Many writers are convinced the only future for writing is within the realms of Science Fiction. So why should the British readers rear back like a month old dead rat is being flourished under their noses whenever a bookseller offers them a Science Fiction book?[1]

In fact, the long apology for science fiction which followed this observation proved unnecessary, though Frances never established himself as a writer in the new genre even with the aid of the Hank Janson pseudonym. Curtis Warren Ltd took to the new genre most prolifically, issuing six titles in 1950, seventeen in 1951 and more than forty in 1952. They were preceded by Scion Books, who published *Operation Venus* by the British pulp sf writer John Russell Fearn in 1949, and then began issuing titles by the author in some quantity. Both Curtis Warren and Scion followed the practice of issuing their books under 'house pseudonyms' – a device which allowed the authors of gangster stories to sound as if they were American (usually Italian-American, in honour of mafia mythology) and writers of sexy scandal stories to sound as if they were French. Scion had odd ideas about what the names of science fiction writers should sound like, and poor Fearn was forced to become Vargo Statten, and eventually Volsted Gridban as well. The other British publisher who took up science fiction with enthusiasm was Hamilton, which issued four Fearn titles in 1950 before diversifying in 1951 to produce both the 'Panther' series of novels, including much science fiction, and the specialist series of 'Authentic Science Fiction Novels', which ultimately became a magazine. Several British writers who eventually became established under their own names as producers of good middlebrow science fiction, including Kenneth Bulmer, E.C. Tubb and John Brunner, began their careers by working for these publishers, but most of this fiction was unparalleled in its awfulness.

Under the influence of evangelically minded editors like John W. Campbell jr the American pulp sf writers had improved the quality of their product very markedly during the 1940s. Many of the writers working in the genre – especially those associated with Campbell's *Astounding Stories* (later *Astounding Science Fiction*, eventually transformed in the 1960s into *Analog Science*

Fact & Science Fiction) – were intelligent men with a good deal of scientific knowledge at their fingertips, who were perfectly prepared to be serious in trying to anticipate likely technological developments and their effects on society. Alongside them, however, were working writers who specialised in the production of gaudy costume dramas populated by gruesome monsters and fabulous machines. It was the latter group of writers who were mostly imitated by the British paperback writers, who plumbed depths of crudity and stupidity never attained before. Thus, the science fiction which emerged to take its place in the British fiction marketplace was quite unlike the science fiction which, in America, was just emerging from its pulp ghetto into the new respectability of hardcover anthologies and middlebrow digest magazines like *Galaxy* and *The Magazine of Fantasy & Science Fiction*.

The same period that saw the boom in British paperback science fiction also saw a boom in British editions of American science fiction pulps. There had been a British edition of *Astounding* for some years, though its appearance remained sporadic during the war, but between 1949 and 1954 half a dozen other US pulps were being reprinted in Britain. They eventually died – not long before the American originals – because they were out-competed by paperbacks and could not accommodate increasing paper prices. This influx of American material was also supplemented by hardcover publishers, who began to reprint many of the science fiction anthologies that were appearing in the USA. Grayson & Grayson began a science fiction line in 1951, Weidenfeld & Nicolson followed suit in 1952 and Sidgwick & Jackson secured the position of science fiction in the middlebrow fiction market when they began issuing a line of science fiction novels, and then founded the British Science Fiction Book Club in 1953.

The rapidity with which real and imitation American science fiction achieved domination of the British speculative fiction market can easily be seen by examining I.F. Clarke's bibliography of *The Tale of the Future*. For 1952, for instance, Clarke lists some 34 genre science fiction publications by native writers, all of which appeared as paperbacks (though some had hardcover editions too). He lists a further six paperbacks which consist of reprinted American science fiction, and seven hardcovers which are reprinted American material. This leaves only seven items produced by British writers for hardcover publication outside genre science fiction lines. When one bears in mind that the titles overlooked by Clarke would have trebled the number of items in the first category it can easily be appreciated that the fiction allied to the older tradition of scientific romance was simply swamped. There was still a certain amount of speculative fiction being published without the science fiction label, but by this time it was very difficult to avoid the identification of speculative fiction with science fiction – and to avoid all the prejudices that were associated with the label. From 1952 onwards virtually all British writers whose primary interest was in speculative fiction accepted as exemplars American science fiction novels, and virtually all of them found no alternative to selling their work in the science fiction marketplace.

As British genre science fiction developed from its crude beginnings it did acquire much of the sophistication of comtemporary American sf. The best of the British science fiction magazines, *New Worlds*, was edited throughout the 1950s by John Carnell, who encouraged the production of more ambitious material from his better writers – who included Brian Aldiss and J.G. Ballard – although he always bore in mind the tastes and demands of an audience that was predominantly young and which appreciated exciting story lines. With Carnell's aid, there emerged a group of British science fiction writers who kept British science fiction from becoming simply an imitation of American science fiction, and gave it a distinctive identity which managed to retain something of the tradition of scientific romance.

The most striking example of a writer who contrived to combine the traditions of British scientific romance and American science fiction is 'John Wyndham'. Wyndham was actually John Wyndham Parkes Lucas Beynon Harris, and as John Beynon Harris he had been one of the first British writers to sell material to the American science fiction pulps. He published some minor speculative novels in Britain in the 1930s under the name John Beynon, but his first major commercial success was achieved in 1951 with *The Day of the Triffids*, with which he began a new career under a new name. This was serialised in the 'slick' magazine *Collier's* before selling well as a book, and has since been filmed and produced as a television serial. The story begins with the great majority of the world's people being blinded, and it has certain ideative links with benign disaster stories like 'Eclipse' and *The Story of My Village*. Here, though, the benignity of the disaster is severely compromised, first by the author's cynical assumption that a Hobbesian war of all against all could easily follow the disintegration of social institutions, and second by the presence in the book's imaginary world of the ambulatory plants of the title, which quickly become homicidally dangerous in the post-catastrophe conditions. The book contrives, therefore, to be an exciting thriller full of suspenseful encounters, while also being interested in the psychology of disaster, and the possibility of rebuilding a saner social order. Wyndham followed up this novel with a whole series of similar books, mostly disaster stories, which clearly owe part of their inspiration to the ideas and literary strategies of pulp science fiction, and part to the peculiarly ambivalent disaster stories that emerged within the tradition of scientific romance. Significantly, Harris, as Wyndham, tried to shake off the burden of his past by insisting that his novels appeared in paperback (from Penguin) *without* the science fiction label. He did write for science fiction magazines in Britain and America – particularly for Carnell – but he made every effort to prevent his books being marketed as category fiction, preferring instead to cultivate an independent reputation. This he managed to do, and gathered a considerable following among readers who otherwise steered clear of labelled science fiction.

Another writer who followed a path very similar to Wyndham's was Christopher Samuel Youd, who signed his books John Christopher. He too first came to prominence with a distinctively British disaster story, *The Death of Grass* (1956), and he followed this up with several more novels in the same vein. Like Wyndham, he aimed his work at a rather wider audience than the community of science fiction aficionados, and eventually devoted himself almost exclusively to the production of imaginative fiction for teenagers. Like Harris, Youd had been a science fiction fan in the 1930s, but his fascination with the glamour and imaginative fecundity of pulp sf was clearly modified, when he began writing in the fifties, by interests and methods which were much more typical of British scientific romance.

Similar arguments can be extended in respect of the three most important British science fiction writers to emerge during the 1950s. In some cases the dual influences are clear. Arthur C.

Clarke, who was born in 1917 (fourteen years after Harris, but three before Youd), was already publishing in the American pulps before 1950, and though he later acquired a well-deserved reputation for expertise in scientific and technological matters – an expertise that allowed him to write much of the most realistic fiction about the exploration of the solar system – there is in much of his work a quasi-mystical streak which owes its inspiration to Olaf Stapledon. Although Clarke is much more of a materialist than Stapledon ever was, and steers clear of metaphysical speculations about the Spirit, it is clear that *Star Maker* did not impress him simply because of its scale. Clarke has always managed to combine the most earnest and hard-headed speculations about future hardware and its uses with a sense of the grandeur of the universe and the possible destiny of mankind which is essentially religious (though perhaps not consciously so, as Clarke tends to deny the proposition when it is put to him). Stapledonian elements can be seen clearly in early Clarke novels like *Against the Fall of Night* (magazine publication 1948; eventually revised as *The City and the Stars*, 1956) and *Childhood's End* (1953), and also in later works like *2001: A Space Odyssey* (film and book 1968) and its sequel *2010: Odyssey Two* (1982).

Brian W. Aldiss, who was born in 1925 and began publishing science fiction in the early fifties, was a voracious and omnivorous reader familiar with all the traditions of English literature, who probably brought to the writing of science fiction a more varied set of influences and inspirations than any other writer. In 1973 he published *Billion Year Spree*, perhaps the most important and most interesting of several histories of science fiction which endeavour to make a single story out of interwoven accounts of the development of British and American speculative fiction. Although this history ignores or pays only slight attention to many of the major writers of British scientific romance (Gloag, Beresford and Bell are not mentioned at all, Fowler Wright and Shiel only *en passant*) it demonstrates Aldiss's close acquaintance with and considerable sensitivity to the endeavours of H.G. Wells and Olaf Stapledon. Aldiss's later work includes books which, as well as being novels in their own right, are critical commentaries on the ideas contained in earlier classics of imaginative fiction: *Frankenstein Unbound* (1973) and *Moreau's Other Island* (1980). Earlier in his career he had made a particularly significant contribution to the British disaster story tradition, *Greybeard* (1965), and there are Sta-pledonian elements in his early collection *The Canopy of Time* (1959; known in the USA as *Galaxies Like Grains of Sand*) which would have been more pronounced had it not been for revisions imposed by the publishers. His brilliant far-future extravaganza *Hothouse* (1962) may also be more readily located in the tradition of *The Time Machine*, *The World Below* and *Last and First Men* than in the science fiction tradition.

J.G. Ballard, who began publishing short stories in John Carnell's magazines in the late 1950s, though he did not publish any books before 1960, was undoubtedly far less aware of British scientific romance than Aldiss, and was probably less familiar too with American science fiction. (Born in 1930, he was brought up in the Far East and spent several of his most important formative years in a Japanese internment camp.) Nevertheless, he became the heir to several of the preoccupations of scientific romance. His early novels were ambivalent disaster stories of a very striking nature, which can far more easily be related to *The Purple Cloud* and 'The Great Fog' (though it is entirely probable that Ballard had read neither story) than to any other works. He also became the chief exponent of surreal science fiction, and maintained a strong fascination with the psychological correlates of technological change. Ballard was eventually more successful in becoming a writer *sui generis* than John Wyndham or Brian Aldiss, and he is certainly very strikingly original, but in both his themes and his attitudes he does have literary ancestors in the field of scientific romance.

This argument could be further extended to take in writers who came to prominence in the 1960s, including Michael Moorcock, Christopher Priest and Richard Cowper, but there is no need to labour the point. Although there are several British science fiction writers who work solidly in the American tradition, and who exhibit only subcultural influences emanating from pulp sf, almost all the major writers have picked up trends and patterns which in the 1930s belonged to the writers of scientific romance, and have fused those trends and patterns with others more typical of the more sophisticated species of American science fiction. This has helped modern British science fiction to retain a marked distinctiveness that gives it a different flavour.

There is a sense in which the fusion of scientific romance and science fiction which occurred in Britain in the early 1950s helped to restore a balance that had been present in the best early scientific romance. It has already been suggested that an essential characteristic of scientific romance is its ability to be playful and serious at the same time, and it has also been observed that when American science fiction and British scientific romance grew apart at the time of the Great War this was because the former began to pay attention almost exclusively to the playful aspects while the latter concentrated much more intently on the serious aspects. H.G. Wells, in his early scientific romances, achieved a synthesis of the playful and the serious that has very rarely been matched, and those works have acquired paradigmatic status in both traditions. Since the Second World War American science fiction has undergone a process of evolution which has built in much of the seriousness that pulp science fiction so conspicuously lacked, while British writers have cultivated a new appreciation of the allure of the extraordinary and the aesthetics of speculation for speculation's sake.

From the American viewpoint it is fairly easy to see the evolution of science fiction as a process of 'maturation' from Wells-inspired pulp beginnings through a phase of pulp juvenility to fifties adolescence and then to seventies bestsellerdom. There has, though, always been something odd about this reconstructed 'history' as it appears in numerous books on the genre. The fact that Britain was flooded in the early fifties with American sf and imitations thereof – part of a more general process of cultural 'coca-colonisation' – should not be allowed to obscure the fact that there always had been speculative fiction in Britain, much of which was well-written, intelligent and interesting in the way that it reflected philosophical and social concerns of the day.

The fact that works of scientific romance always held a place in the middlebrow literary culture of Britain – even if they were never *quite* respectable – made it easier for British literary critics to take an interest in speculative fiction than it was for American critics. Thus, the earliest prestigious apologists for American science fiction were British – both C.S. Lewis and Kingsley Amis played important roles in helping sf to become more acceptable long before Americans like Leslie Fiedler deigned to notice that the genre had burst the confines of its lowbrow ghetto. It has also made it easier for British writers who have built a reputation as serious novelists to venture occasionally into speculative fiction. Futuristic works could still be published in Britain in the fifties and sixties without necessarily being tarred with the sf brush. Indeed, it is still possible for British writers to be loud in despising science fiction as a genre, after the fashion of Wells's preface to the *Scientific Romances*, while continuing to write speculative works themselves – an ambivalence which has produced such eccentric hybrid works as *The End of the World News* (1982), by Anthony Burgess, in which a science fiction story written in an embarrassed tone is interleaved with a biography of Freud and the script for a stage musical about Leon Trotsky's visit to America. No such obvious embarrassment, though, is evident in Burgess's earlier speculative novels, *A Clockwork Orange* (1962) and *The Wanting Seed* (1962). Nor does any significant measure of shame seem to have been involved in the production of a whole series of speculative works by established novelists, which extends from *Brave New World* and *Nineteen Eighty-Four* through several works already cited and such varied further examples as *Seven Days in New Crete* (1949) by Robert Graves, *The Old Men at the Zoo* (1961) by Angus Wilson, *Kings of Infinite Space* (1967) by Nigel Balchin, *Travels in Nihilon* (1971) by Alan Sillitoe, *Rule Britannia* (1972) by Daphne du Maurier, *The Alteration* (1976) by Kingsley Amis and *Gor Saga* (1981) by Maureen Duffy.

American 'mainstream' writers like Bernard Wolfe and Gore Vidal produced speculative fiction in the 1950s, but it was not until the seventies that ideas and themes previously central to speculative fiction began to spread very widely in American literature. In Britain, thanks to the tradition of scientific romance and its position in the cultural marketplace, there never was such a complete alienation of speculative material, and no such dramatic recovery has been necessary.

Scientific Romance: Ambitions and Achievements

Most writers of scientific romance who felt called upon to write introductions to their books, or look back over their careers, automatically went on the defensive. They worked from the assumption that the unspoken question facing them was why on earth they bothered to do it. They seem to have imagined this question being posed in a rather contemptuous way, as if

331

all literary men were likely to approach scientific romance in much the same frame of mind as Dr Johnson considering the preaching of a woman – not concerned with whether it is done well, but mildly astonished to find it done at all.

There are, of course, different styles of defensiveness. A writer of fantastic fiction can react to implied allegations of the worthlessness of his activity in several ways. Calculated philistinism, craven apology and reasoned argument in favour of overlooked merit are the three most popular strategies, but the contrasts between them serve only to make us forget that they all begin by surrendering the initiative and admitting that fantastic fiction does need an excuse for existing. It is surely a sad discovery to find H.G. Wells, in the preface to his collected scientific romances, offering embarrassed and sarcastic excuses for ever having written them, and promising (after the fashion of a flasher begging mercy from a magistrate) not to do it again now that he has seen the error of his ways.

The world, it seems, has for some time been hostile to the exercise of the imagination. Writers have found themselves having to defend such exercise even at the most elementary level – as, for instance, in Sir Philip Sidney's sixteenth-century *Defence of Poesy* and Shelley's nineteenth-century *Defence of Poetry* – and it is not surprising that in the face of such all-consuming accusation literary men have been keen to discriminate between precious and proper uses on the one hand and superfluous and silly uses on the other. It has always been taken for granted that some kind of special pleading is necessary if scientific romance is not to be dumped, *en masse*, in the latter category. This is because even the most eloquent apologists for the imagination have retained a strong sense of shame in respect of *some* fantastic indulgences. Mistrust of 'escapist fiction' and 'wish-fulfilment fantasies' has deep psychological roots – as, presumably, have the fantasies themselves.

Because of all this, it is not easy to write a convincing account of the 'ambitions and achievements' of scientific romance. It is necessary to assume that hearers of such a case will first want to be persuaded that the genre's ambitions were not completely silly and its achievements not entirely negligible. People who have actually chosen to read this book will probably be eager to resist such conclusions, but they will want reassurance that they can safely do so.

Conclusions

There is actually no shortage of apologies for speculative fiction that might be quoted here in order to provide such reassurance. Dozens of American academics and science fiction writers have written books about the history and criticism of speculative fiction, and they all begin with apologies of one kind or another. It seems more appropriate here, though, to quote one of the major writers of scientific romance, and a good account of the problem and its possible solution can be found in S. Fowler Wright's introduction to his 1949 collection *The Throne of Saturn*:

> One who is a friend, a man of no mean literary judgement, and who has been kind to some things which I have written, recently surprised me not merely by saying he could not read a phantasy of which I was the author, but that he could not understand anyone writing such books if capable of other and (inferentially) better work.
> Was this judgement sound?
> Every work of the imagination widens the frontiers of reality. It may have no objective reality, but precisely to that extent it adds to creation's sum. Men were; beyond that they built imaginations of things which were not. They may not have imagined facts; but it was a fact that they imagined things which had not been, and may never be.
> A foolish criticism of *Ivanhoe* (foolish alike whether correct or not) is that it represents a scene which has little historical basis. But it would be wiser to say that (being vivid as it is) the more it be a work of baseless imagination the more admirable it is.
> It is the contemporary habit to give first place to novels which portray men and events truly, observation rather than imagination being their inspiration. There is no need to depreciate such work, but they are only of the highest rank if it be better to crawl than to soar.
> To recognise this is not to assert that every fantastic tale is of high literary merit. It may be a sounder proposition that it is such in proportion to the verisimilitude which it attains. Beyond that, all serious works of imagination will contain a philosophy of life, and, the more they are without basis of mundane fact, the more clearly will that philosophy appear.
> For these and other reasons, having written works of imagination of many kinds, both in prose and verse, among which phantasy has not bulked prominently, I am disposed, without claiming any absolute value for such works, to place them relatively not last but first.[2]

It may seem an overstatement to say of works of imaginative fiction that they 'widen the frontiers of reality' and that they 'add to creation's sum', but such a case can be made. It is safer to begin, though, with the less controversial assertion that part of the work of the imagination is to widen the horizons of thought, and to help in the exploration of the possibilities of potential action. Human life, unlike the life of animals, is based in the power of the imagination, and our ability to calculate in imagination the possible consequences of our decisions. In this respect, the imagination plays a fundamental role in human nature, and the education of the imagination is not something to be taken lightly. If works of fiction can serve any function in this education, their utility is proven.

An argument along these lines will serve, perhaps, to justify the more serious side of scientific romance, which aspires to extrapolate present trends and issue warnings about future dangers. But this is clearly not enough, because so much of what is interesting in scientific romance is not concerned with careful extrapolation or with alarmism. We must remember also that imagination does other work for us in our everyday lives as well as helping to provide the basis for rational calculation.

Imagination provides us with the greater part of the substance of our actual mental life. We do not live by sensory information alone, and a great deal of our moment-by-moment experience is not much concerned with what our senses are telling us about the outside world. To a large extent we live inside a private world of thoughts, feelings and images, and much of our experience is of this private reality rather than the outer reality that surrounds us. We frequently absent ourselves from confrontation with our surroundings, and retreat into the inner realm of our own consciousness, where we attend primarily to the creations of our minds: memories; thoughts framed in words; images; fictions and fantasies.

This private world is no less real than the other, and this work of the imagination is no less fundamental than the other – nor is it any less vital to the business of being human. In order to serve this function, the imagination needs education, training and exercise just as it does to serve the other. People presumably differ in their natural endowment of imagination just as they differ in physique, but it is in serving private functions rather than in formulating rational calculations that these differences can be most fully expressed, just as differences in physique are more relevant to our sports and pastimes than to common utilitarian activities like walking and writing. As our hands may need to learn special skills in order to let us adopt particular roles in public life, so our imaginations may need particular stimulation in order to sustain particular modes of private experience.

It is because of this (though the argument is rarely spelled out) that certain kinds of imaginative fiction are stigmatised. It is assumed by those who disapprove of fantastic fiction (a) that there are certain kinds of private experience that are less worthy than others, being infantile, stupid and unhealthy; and (b) that fantastic fictions feed these unworthy modes of private experience. When disapproval of fantastic fiction manifests itself as a kind of imaginative allergy, expressed as loathing, one suspects that it stems from a sense of personal vulnerability and will be as difficult to overcome as any other phobia, but in so far as such disapproval can be opposed by reasoned argument it ought to yield to the criticism that assumption (a) is weak and assumption (b) even weaker.

To put the argument in a more concrete form, it is sometimes alleged that adults should have no interest in fairy tales because adults ought to be aware of the absurdity of believing in fairies. But this is ridiculous. It is not the case that an interest in stories about fairies requires or encourages a willingness to believe in fairies. It is an insult even to small children to suppose that an appreciation of fantastic imagery implies ignorance or uncertainty about the bounds of actual possibility. It is simply that, in children as in adults, pretence and belief are very closely related, but children are less inhibited about the range and display of their pretences. The sentimentalists who regret that as we grow up we increasingly reserve our powers of pretence for actual social interactions, and become very careful and conservative in our image building, are probably more clear sighted than those who conclude that children are stupid and gullible because they have a wide repertoire of pretences and use that repertoire so cleverly and so innocently.

We do not tell fairy stories in order that they shall be believed. The ability to appreciate fairy stories is not a failure of scepticism. Nor is it proof that in our private experience we are somehow limited and arrested in development if we can retain such an appreciation into adulthood. To argue thus is to mistake both the nature of private experience and its relation to fantastic fictions.

The fantastic motifs which can be built into fictions do not represent entities or events that we might expect to find in our sensory experience of the world, but this does not mean that they can bear no sensible relation to it. We can see this readily enough if we consider the functions of satire and caricature, where fantasisation is used to penetrate and explode the pretences of others rather than to support our own. Observation is not a passive process; to see is to interpret, and it is only by the exercise of imagination that we can test and revise our interpretations. In order to see at all we must go beyond mere appearances; in order to see more clearly we sometimes need to go further beyond. This is the sense in which we can sustain Fowler Wright's argument that every work of the imagination widens the frontiers of *reality*; the imagination cannot add new things to the world that is outside of us, but it can and does add to the ways in which we can construct and comprehend a 'reality' out of our sense data.

The second part of Fowler Wright's argument – that serious works of the imagination contain and display philosophies of life – should also be construed in the light of this fact. The philosophies of life that fantastic fictions contain are not 'morals' of the kind attached to Aesop's fables (though some scientific romances do have covert morals of this kind) but suggestions as to how we might discover and generate whole, coherent and meaningful 'worlds' from the jejune trickle of sensory data that leaks into our minds through our eyes and ears. The fantastic beings in fairy stories and scientific romances should not, therefore, be considered as catalogues of entities that we might look for in the outer world (such stories do not operate like a train-spotter's handbook) but as narrative devices whose function is to assist us in filling in what our senses cannot tell us: not what is *in* the world, but how the world *works*.

The ambitions of scientific romance, in this view, were to remake the world by remaking the way that its writers and readers organised their experience of it.

We have seen that scientific romance was syncretised as a genre in the decade of the 1890s. Most of its early contributors were born in the 1860s. Although the genre was not dissolved into the science fiction tradition until the 1950s, its last major

336

practitioners were born before the turn of the century. The writers of scientific romance, without any but very minor exceptions, were men who were born and grew up between the publication of Darwin's *Origin of Species* and the fighting of the Great War, in a period when ideas about human nature were undergoing very dramatic revision. It was not simply the arrival of new ideas that stimulated the imaginations of the writers of scientific romance, but the way that the new ideas challenged and overthrew older ideas which had suffered only minor modifications for centuries.

Most of the major writers of scientific romance were separated from their parents by acute ideological generation gaps. Many were sons of pious men who became freethinkers. Others found (or felt) themselves alienated from the world of their parents in different ways, and found themselves standing alone against the entire weight of past human folly. They all felt the need to try and figure out the world anew, because they were quite unable to accept the world that had been figured out for them. The shape and content of their scientific romances can be closely related in every case to the figuring out that they were doing, and in some instances scientific romance became (for a while) the chief imaginative medium in which that work was done.

Each of these writers was an individual, operating on his own. Each one found his own particular 'philosophy of life'. This is one of the things that makes it hard to classify scientific romance as a genre – it has no shared, unifying central dogma after the fashion of popular romantic fiction. Nevertheless, it *is* a genre and the philosophies which its practitioners developed do have many recurrent themes and motifs. This is not because they borrowed from one another (though they often did) but because they were in similar situations, drawing upon similar ideative resources. The political opinions and metaphysical ideas of the major writers were very various, but the horizons of possibility that they glimpsed through the lenses of contemporary scientific discoveries and theories were not.

The careers of individual writers, and the history of the genre as a whole, moved through two phases. The first was an exploratory phase where new notions were tried out for size and style; the second was a more utilitarian phase which brought writers into confrontation with what I have elected to call (following H.G. Wells) Frustration. This Frustration was a sense of history having gone wrong; a feeling that men, having discovered new opportunities, challenges and threats, were failing to cope. This loss of faith in people was very closely associated with loss of faith in God; the failure to cope was partly an insistence on clinging to shattered beliefs, partly a refusal to build new ones. The old God was clinging to His power over human imagination, when He should be making room for something else – a new God, or a new Man.

There is a strong vein of misanthropy in scientific romance: a misanthropy based in contempt and shame rather than hatred. There is a persistent call to account in which the brutishness of man is ruthlessly exposed and scathingly described. A frequent corollary of this exposure is the declaration that hope for the future (if there is any) must be tied to the transcendence of this brutishness, by education or evolution, or both. Utopian optimism was smashed by the realisation that a New World would need New Men to live in it, and that we were neither mentally equipped nor spiritually equipped to be New Men. Writers of scientific romance disagreed about what manner of men those new beings might be, and were ambivalent in their attitudes to them, but their very ambivalence intensified their preoccupation with the probable collapse of our civilisation and its possible transcendent renewal.

Although different writers produced different prospectuses for renewal, what was to be new about the New Men always had to do with the achievement of a new balance between reason and emotion. This new psychological balance was always to be reflected at the social level in a reordering of the relationship between Culture and Nature – with all that these words can imply. When they considered the possibility of such a restructuring of man's relationship with his environment writers were often pessimistic and always vague, but this was the point at issue across the whole spectrum of scientific romance. Many writers transposed the question into a discussion of an appropriate religiosity for future man. Some tried to redefine the relationship between man and God (some in the Voltairean sense of asking what kind of God men should now invent to replace the one that was worn out), others attempted to deflect religiosity away from God and into some other vein, but all were interested in the utilitarian aspects of faith. It could be argued, in fact, that what made this kind of speculative romance 'scientific' was as much its sociological approach to religion as its interest in the revelations of astronomy, the implications of evolutionary theory, and the possibilities of psychology.

It is not easy to estimate the achievements that can legitimately be credited to scientific romance in respect of these ambitions. It is not clear, in fact, what actually is to count as an achievement. If we were to assess scientific romance as a kind of propaganda, issuing horrific images of future war in the hope of preventing future war, then we would have some kind of test of its effectiveness, although it would still be difficult to answer the counterfactual question of what might have happened had no such images ever been produced. But if, as we have concluded, the relevance of scientific romance is much more to private experience than to manifest action, what criteria of success can we possibly apply? We can certainly argue that some of the writers managed to give eloquent expression to their own sense of philosophical crisis, and that some apparently managed to achieve a new and competent analysis of the human predicament with the aid of their speculative fictions. It probably would not be too hard to find readers in whom these expressions awoke some emotional resonance, and who borrowed from them in revising their own views of man's place in nature. But those readers would not be very numerous, because scientific romance was for most of its history a rather esoteric genre.

It is possible that we would be assessing 'achievements' too narrowly if we were simply to consider the effects of scientific romance on its writers and contemporary readers. In a literate culture fictions can stand outside time and speak across the generations; the achievements of scientific romance – potentially, at least – extend into the present day and into the future. The fact that the year 1984 has now come and gone has not rendered *Nineteen Eighty-Four* redundant, and the same is true of all the other works whose anticipations have been overtaken by events. Today's readers do not belong to the same generation as the writers of scientific romance, and do not experience the same ideological generation gap, but they are still in the business of building a coherent world-image out of what they see and know. A great many of the fundamental issues discussed in scientific romance remain pertinent, and will remain pertinent for the foreseeable future. In addition, we must remember that the history of scientific romance is part of the greater history of human thought. If we are to understand the past, then we must look at the products of the human imagination as well as the products of the human hand.

Scientific romance is one of the many reflections of the sense of crisis that developed in the early part of the twentieth century. It offers us one more path of insight into that crisis, adding one more dimension to the *verstehen* which we require in order fully to understand what that crisis was all about. A study of scientific romance ought to help us to understand what a discomfiting kind of enlightenment it is to lose religious faith and discover a future shaped by the myriad actions of men. If we undertake such a study as a part of the education of our own imaginations, then we may indeed find that there is something to be achieved.

NOTES AND REFERENCES

CHAPTER 1

1. Arthur H. Lawrence, 'The Romance of the Scientist', reprinted in *H.G. Wells: Interviews and Recollections* ed. J.R. Hammond, London: Macmillan, 1980. p.6
2. Patrick Parrinder, ed. *H.G. Wells: the Critical Heritage*, London, Routledge & Kegan Paul, 1972. p.63
3. *ibid.* p.75
4. *cf* 'Definitions of Science Fiction' in *The Encyclopedia of Science Fiction* ed. P. Nicholls, London: Granada, 1979. p.159
5. Darko Suvin, *Victorian Science Fiction in the UK: the Discourses of Knowledge and Power*, Boston: G.K. Hall, 1983. p.86
6. Bernard Bergonzi, *The Early H.G. Wells*, Manchester University Press, 1961. pp. 16–17
7. An account of this literary *'demi-monde'* can be found in *Fiction for the Working Man* by Louis James, London: Penguin, 1974
8. Suvin, *Victorian Science Fiction in the UK.* pp. 123–6
9. Patrick Parrinder and Robert M. Philmus, eds. *H.G. Wells's Literary Criticism*, Brighton: Harvester Press, 1980. p.219
10. Raymond Williams, *The Long Revolution*, London: Chatto & Windus, 1961. pp. 187–8

CHAPTER 2

1. Philip Babcock Gove, *The Imaginary Voyage in Prose Fiction*, New York: Columbia University Press, 1941. p.3
2. H.G. Wells, Preface to *The Scientific Romances of H.G. Wells*, London: Gollancz, 1933. p.vii
3. Robert H. Sherard, 'Jules Verne Re-visited', *T.P.'s Weekly*, 9 October 1903. p.589
4. For a more detailed account of *Across the Zodiac* see the article in *Survey of Science Fiction Literature* ed. Frank Magill, Englewood Cliffs, NJ: Salem Press, 1979. pp.11–15
5. Frank E. Manuel, 'Towards a Psychological History of Utopias' in *Utopias and Utopian Thought* ed. Frank E. Manuel, London: Souvenir Press, 1973. p.71
6. D.R. Oldroyd, *Darwinian Impacts: an Introduction to the Darwinian Revolution*, Milton Keynes: Open University Press, 1980. p.317
7. For a more elaborate account of Flammarion's work see the article on *Lumen* in Magill's *Survey of Science Fiction Literature* pp.1294–8. For a description of Rosny's work in this vein see J.P. Vernier, 'The Science Fiction of J.H. Rosny the Elder', *Science Fiction Studies* vol. 2 part 2 (July 1975). p.156
8. The full title of this book is *A Full and True Account of the Wonderful Mission of Earl Lavender, Which Lasted One Night and One Day: With a History of the Pursuit of Earl Lavender and Lord Brumm by Mrs Scamler and Maud Emblem*
9. Fred Polak, *The Image of the Future*, Amsterdam: Elsevier, 1973. pp.183–219
10. Ryszard Dubanski, 'The Last Man Theme in Modern Fantasy and Science Fiction', *Foundation* 16 (May 1979). pp.26–30
11. Polak, *The Image of the Future*, p.199
12. George C. Wallis, 'The Last Days of Earth', *Harmsworth's London Magazine* vol.6 (July 1901). pp.549–50
13. C.S. Lewis, 'On Science Fiction' in *Science Fiction* ed. Mark Rose, Englewood Cliffs, NJ: Prentice-Hall, 1976. p.109
14. For a fuller account of Marie Corelli's career and work see the essay in *Supernatural Fiction Writers* ed. Everett F. Bleiler, New York: Scribner's, 1985

CHAPTER 3

1. These and other biographical details in this chapter are taken from 'George Griffith – Warrior of If' by Sam Moskowitz in the Griffith collection *The Raid of 'Le Vengeur'*, London: Ferret Fantasy, 1974. pp.6–47
2. For the record, the major writers who were the sons of clergymen were Griffith, Shiel, Beresford, Hodgson and Heard. The more important minor writers whose fathers were clergymen were Grant Allen, Cutcliffe Hyne, Ranger Gull and Fred T. Jane. Fowler Wright's father was a lay preacher, and Gloag described his father as 'painfully religious'
3. Moskowitz, *The Raid of 'Le Vengeur'*, p.19
4. Robert M. Philmus and David Y. Hughes, *H.G. Wells: Early Writings in Science and Science Fiction*, Berkeley: University of California Press, 1975. pp.4–5
5. *ibid.* pp.105–47
6. *ibid.* pp.30–1
7. H.G. Wells, *The Time Machine* chapter 10
8. Hammond, ed. *H.G. Wells: Interviews and Recollections*, p.8
9. Philmus and Hughes, *H.G. Wells: Early Writings*, p.39
10. *ibid.* p.177
11. H.G. Wells, *The War of the Worlds*, chapter 4
12. H.G. Wells, *Anticipations of the Reaction of Mechanical and Scientific Progress Upon Human Life and Thought*, London: Chapman & Hall, 1901. p.2n
13. *ibid.* p.32n
14. *ibid.* p.99
15. Sherard, 'Jules Verne Re-visited'
16. H.G. Wells, 'The War that Will End War' in *H.G. Wells: Journalism and Prophecy 1893–1946* ed. W. Warren Wagar, Boston: Houghton-Mifflin, 1964. pp.79–82
17. Paul Spencer, 'Shiel versus Shiel' in *Shiel in Diverse Hands*, volume IV of *The Works of M.P. Shiel* ed. A. Reynolds Morse, Cleveland, Ohio: Reynolds Morse Foundation, 1979–83. pp.31–57. This multi-volume work includes a definitive bibliography of Shiel and much biographical information as well as reprinting the magazine versions of several Shiel serials and short stories
18. The revised edition of *The Lord of the Sea*, issued in 1929 by Gollancz, omits the introduction linking it to *The Purple*

Cloud and *The Last Miracle*, though the revised versions of both the other novels retain it. Many of Shiel's works were revised for this series of reissues, but the extent of the revisions varies considerably

19. Sam Moskowitz, *Explorers of the Infinite*, Cleveland: World Publishing Co., 1963. pp.146–8

20. Quoted by Spencer in 'Shiel versus Shiel', *Shiel in Diverse Hands*, p.37

21. M.P. Shiel, *The Purple Cloud*, Cleveland: World Publishing Co., 1946. p.202

22. M.P. Shiel, *The Last Miracle*, London: Gollancz, 1929. pp.274–5

23. P. Nicholls, ed. *The Encyclopedia of Science Fiction*, pp.134–6

24. William Hope Hodgson, *The House on the Borderland and Other Novels*, Sauk City, Wis.: Arkham House, 1946. p.108

25. Sam Moskowitz, 'William Hope Hodgson' in *Out of the Storm: Uncollected Fantasies by William Hope Hodgson*, West Kingston, RI: Grant, 1975. pp.9–117. The biographical information in this section is taken from this article, but most of it is ultimately derived from 'Some Facts in the Case of William Hope Hodgson' by R. Alain Everts, *Shadow* 19 & 20 (1973)

26. Hodgson, *The House on the Borderland and Other Novels*, p.637

27. Moskowitz, 'William Hope Hodgson', *Out of the Storm*, pp.95–6. H.P. Lovecraft, 'Supernatural Horror in Literature' in *Dagon and Other Macabre Tales*, Sauk City, Wis.: Arkham House, 1965. pp.396–7

28. J.D. Beresford, *H.G. Wells*, London: Nisbet, 1915. p.29

29. J.D. Beresford, *The Hampdenshire Wonder*, London: Sidgwick & Jackson, 1911. p.290

30. J.D. Beresford, *Nineteen Impressions*, London: Sidgwick & Jackson, 1918. pp.xiii–xiv

CHAPTER 4

1. I.F. Clarke, *Voices Prophesying War 1763–1984*, London: Oxford University Press, 1966. p.145

2. *ibid.* pp.144–5

3. Louis Tracy, *The Final War*, London: Pearson, 1896. pp.370–1

4. Erskine Childers, 'Preface to the 1913 Edition' in *Riddle of the Sands*, London: Smith Elder, 1913
5. M.A. Childers, 'Note' in *The Riddle of the Sands*, London: Sidgwick & Jackson, 1931. p.v
6. Robert Cromie, *A Plunge into Space*, 2nd ed., London: F. Warne & Co., 1891. p.182
7. Suvin, *Victorian Science Fiction in the UK*, p.60
8. A more detailed account of Hinton's career and ideas can be found in 'Life in the Fourth Dimension: C.H. Hinton and his Scientific Romances' by Rudy Rucker, *Foundation* 18 (January 1980) pp.12–18

CHAPTER 5

1. E.V. Odle, letter to S.B. McClean, quoted in *A Spectrum of Fantasy* by George Locke, London: Ferret Fantasy, 1980. p.168
2. Sam Moskowitz, *Under the Moons of Mars*, New York: Holt, Rinehart & Winston, 1970. pp.334–5
3. Olaf Stapledon, quoted in 'The Philosopher of Fantasy', an interview by Walter Gillings in *The British Scientifiction Fantasy Reveiw* vol.1 no.3 (June 1937). p.9
4. Julian Huxley, *Essays of a Biologist*, London: Chatto & Windus, 1923. p.viii
5. J.B.S. Haldane, *Daedalus; or, Science and the Future*, London: Kegan Paul, Trench & Trubner, 1924. pp.1–2
6. *ibid.* pp.2–3
7. *ibid.* p.3

CHAPTER 6

1. H.G. Wells, Preface to *The Scientific Romances of H.G. Wells.* p.x
2. *ibid.* p.x
3. H.G. Wells, *Experiment in Autobiography*, London: Gollancz, 1934. p.748
4. *ibid.* pp.748–9
5. H.G. Wells, *The Shape of Things to Come*, London: Hutchinson, 1933. p.428
6. *ibid.* p.431
7. H.G. Wells, *Mind at the End of its Tether*, London: Heinemann, 1945. p.17

8. J.D. Beresford, quoted in Millett, *Contemporary British Literature*, New York: Harcourt & Brace, 1940
9. J.D. Beresford, *A Common Enemy*, London: Hutchinson, 1942. p.208
10. S. Fowler Wright, *The World Below*, London: Collins, 1929. p.127
11. S. Fowler Wright, *Dawn*, London: Harrap, 1930. p.363
12. S. Fowler Wright, *The Throne of Saturn*, Sauk City, Wis.: Arkham House, 1949. p.166
13. S. Fowler Wright, *Power*, London: Jarrolds, 1933. p.25
14. The evidence proving that *Vengeance of Gwa* was written as a sequel to *Dream* is provided by Fowler Wright's diary for the period 1933–7, passages of which were read to me by Nigel Fowler Wright. The biographical details in this section were provided by various members of the Fowler Wright family, and a much more extensive account of Fowler Wright's career and work can be found in 'Against the New Gods: the Speculative Fiction of S. Fowler Wright', *Foundation* 29 (November 1983). pp.10–52
15. Sam Moskowitz, 'The Dark Plots of One Shiel' in *Shiel in Diverse Hands* ed. A. Reynolds Morse, p.66
16. Biographical information in this section is taken from Sam Moskowitz, 'Olaf Stapledon: the Man Behind the Works' in *Far Future Calling* by Olaf Stapledon, Philadelphia: Oswald Train, 1979. pp.15–70
17. W. Olaf Stapledon, *Last and First Men*, London: Methuen, 1930. pp.v–vi
18. *ibid.* p.4
19. Leslie A. Fiedler, *Olaf Stapledon: A Man Divided*, Oxford & New York: Oxford University Press, 1983. See especially pp.12–13, and also Fiedler's 'Introduction' to *Odd John*, London: Methuen, 1978. p.9
20. Olaf Stapledon, *Last Men in London*, London: Methuen, 1932. p.165
21. *ibid.* p.172
22. *ibid.* p.173
23. *ibid.* pp.220–1
24. Olaf Stapledon, *Star Maker*, London: Methuen, 1937. p.5
25. *ibid.* chapter VI, pp.115–22
26. *ibid.* p.296
27. *ibid.* p.309
28. *ibid.* p.333

29. Olaf Stapledon, *Sirius*, London: Secker & Warburg, 1944. p.29
30. *ibid.* see pp.118, 130 & 154–5
31. Neil Bell, *My Writing Life*, London: Alvin Redman, 1955. p.58
32. Neil Bell, *The Seventh Bowl*, London: Collins (2nd ed.), 1934. pp. 67–8
33. Neil Bell, *Precious Porcelain*, London: Collins (2nd ed.), 1938. p.352
34. Neil Bell, *Mixed Pickles*, London: Collins, 1935. p.125
35. John Gloag, letter dated 12 December 1979. All the information in this chapter relating to the career and opinions of Mr Gloag is taken from a series of letters which he wrote to me in 1979 and 1980. More extensive quotations from this correspondence, and a more elaborate account of Gloag's work can be found in 'The Future Between the Wars: the Speculative Fiction of John Gloag', *Foundation* 20 (October 1980). pp.47–64
36. John Gloag, *Artifex; or, The Future of Craftsmanship*, London: Kegan Paul, Trench & Trubner, 1926. p.11
37. John Gloag, *The New Pleasure*, London: Allen & Unwin, 1933. p.303
38. John Gloag, *Winter's Youth*, London: Allen & Unwin, 1934
39. John Gloag, *Manna*, London: Cassell, 1940. p.278
40. John Gloag, *99%*, London: Cassell, 1944. pp.166–7
41. John Gloag, *First One and Twenty*, London: Allen & Unwin, 1946. pp.vii–viii
42. John Gloag, letter dated 7 January 1980

CHAPTER 7

1. Edward Shanks, *People of the Ruins*, London: Collins, 1920. p.252
2. Winston Churchill, 'Shall We Commit Suicide?', *Nash's Pall Mall Magazine* September 1924, quoted in *Janus, or the Conquest of War* by William McDougall, London: Kegan Paul, Trench & Trubner, 1925. pp.23–4
3. *ibid.* p.25
4. Stanley Baldwin, speech in the House of Commons, 10 November 1932, quoted in *Invasion from the Air* by Frank McIlraith and Roy Connolly, London: Grayson, 1934. p.5
5. Muriel Jaeger, *The Question Mark*, London: Hogarth Press,

1926. pp.11–12

6. E.V. Odle, *The History of Alfred Rudd*, London: Collins, 1922. p.52

7. E.V. Odle, *The Clockwork Man*, London: Heinemann, 1923. p.110

8. Guy Dent, *Emperor of the If*, London: Heinemann, 1926. p.325

9. Claude Houghton, *This Was Ivor Trent*, London: Heinemann, 1935. pp.321–3

10. Andrew Marvell, *Minimum Man, or Time to be Gone*, London: Gollancz, 1938. p.284

CHAPTER 8

1. Olaf Stapledon, *The Flames*, London: Secker & Warburg, 1947. pp. 54–5

2. Olaf Stapledon, *A Man Divided*, London: Methuen, 1951. p.172

3. Neil Bell, *Alpha and Omega*, London: Hale, 1946. p.187

4. Neil Bell, *Life Comes to Seathorpe*, London: Eyre & Spottiswoode, 1946. pp.296–8

5. Eden Phillpotts, *Address Unknown*, London: Hutchinson, 1949. p.218

6. Eden Phillpotts, *From the Angle of 88*, London: Hutchinson, 1951. p.15

7. C.S. Lewis, *Perelandra*, New York: Macmillan, 1944. pp.91–2

8. Fiedler, *Olaf Stapledon: A Man Divided*. pp.130–1

9. C.S. Lewis, *That Hideous Strength*, New York: Macmillan, 1946. p.38

10. *ibid.* p.202

11. Gerald Heard, *The Emergence of Man*, London: Cape, 1931. p.295

12. *ibid.* p.299

13. H.F. Heard, *The Great Fog and Other Weird Tales*, New York: Vanguard, 1944. pp.48–9. (It should be noted that Heard's books usually appeared as by H.F. Heard in the USA and as by Gerald Heard in the UK)

14. Gerald Heard, *The Lost Cavern*, London: Cassell, 1949. p.80

15. Gerald Heard, *Doppelgängers*, London: Science Fiction Book Club, 1965. p.49

16. *ibid.* pp.213–27

17. H.F. Heard, 'Why Science Fiction?' in *New Tales of Space and Time* ed. Raymond J. Healy, London: Weidenfeld & Nicolson, 1952. pp.x–xi
18. *ibid.* pp.xii–xiii
19. F. Horace Rose, *The Maniac's Dream*, London: Duckworth, 1946. pp.10–11
20. H. de Vere Stacpoole, *The Story of My Village*, London: Hutchinson, 1947. pp.49–50
21. Aldous Huxley, *Ape and Essence*, London: Chatto & Windus, 1949. pp.92–3

CHAPTER 9

1. Hank Janson (Stephen Frances), *Corruption*, London: Gaywood Press, 1952. p.138
2. S. Fowler Wright, *The Throne of Saturn.* p.vii

SELECTED BIBLIOGRAPHY

Aldiss, Brian W. *Billion Year Spree: The History of Science Fiction*, London: Weidenfeld & Nicolson, 1973

Armytage, W.H.G. *Yesterday's Tomorrows: A Historical Survey of Future Societies*, London: Routledge & Kegan Paul, 1968

Bailey, J.O. *Pilgrims Through Space and Time: Trends and Patterns in Scientific and Utopian Fiction*, New York: Argus, 1947

Barron, Neil, ed. *Anatomy of Wonder: A Critical Guide to Science Fiction*, Second Edition, New York: R.R. Bowker, 1981

Bleiler, E.F. *The Checklist of Science-Fiction and Supernatural Fiction*, Glen Rock, NJ: Firebell, 1978

Bleiler, E.F., ed. *Science Fiction Writers: Critical Studies of the Major Authors from the Early Nineteenth Century to the Present Day*, New York: Scribner's, 1982

Clarke, I.F. *The Pattern of Expectation 1644–2001*, London: Cape, 1979

Clarke, I.F. *Tale of the Future from the Beginning to the Present Day*, Third Edition, London: The Library Association, 1978

Clarke, I.F. *Voices Prophesying War, 1763–1984*, London: Oxford University Press, 1966

Locke, George *A Spectrum of Fantasy*, London: Ferret Fantasy, 1980

Magill, Frank N., ed. *Survey of Science Fiction Literature*, Englewood Cliffs, NJ: Salem Press, 1979 (5 vols.)

Magill, Frank N., ed. *Survey of Modern Fantasy Literature*, Englewood Cliffs, NJ: Salem Press 1983 (5 vols.)

Morgan, Chris *The Shape of Futures Past*, Exeter: Webb & Bower, 1980

Moore, Patrick *Science and Fiction*, London: Harrap, 1957

Selected Bibliography

Moskowitz, Sam *Explorers of the Infinite: Shapers of Science Fiction*, Cleveland: World Publishing Co., 1963

Moskowitz, Sam, ed. *Science Fiction by Gaslight: A History and Anthology of Science Fiction in the Popular Magazines, 1891–1911*, Cleveland: World Publishing Co., 1968

Moskowitz, Sam *Strange Horizons: The Spectrum of Science Fiction*, New York: Scribner's, 1976

Nicholls, Peter, ed. *The Encyclopedia of Science Fiction*, London: Granada, 1979

Nicolson, Marjorie Hope *Voyages to the Moon*, New York: Macmillan, 1948

Parrinder, Patrick, ed. *Science Fiction: A Critical Guide*, London: Longman, 1979

Philmus, Robert M. *Into the Unknown: the Evolution of Science Fiction from Francis Godwin to H.G. Wells*, Berkeley: University of California Press, 1970

Polak, Fred *The Image of the Future*, Amsterdam: Elsevier, 1973

Rose, Mark, ed. *Science Fiction: A Collection of Critical Essays*, Englewood Cliffs, NJ: Prentice-Hall, 1976

Suvin, Darko *Victorian Science Fiction in the UK: the Discourses of Knowledge and of Power*, Boston: G.K. Hall, 1983

Tuck, Donald H. *The Encyclopedia of Science Fiction and Fantasy*, Chicago: Advent, vol. 1, 1974; vol. 2, 1978; vol. 3, 1982

INDEX

352